In the

Vanguard of Reform

In the

Vanguard of Reform

Russia's Enlightened Bureaucrats 1825–1861

W. Bruce Lincoln

DeKalb
Northern Illinois University Press

Publication of this book was assisted by a grant from
the Publications Program of the National Endowment
for the Humanities, an independent federal agency.

Library of Congress Cataloging in Publication Data

Lincoln, W. Bruce
    In the vanguard of reform.

    Bibliography: p.
    1. Soviet Union—Politics and government—
1825–1855.   2. Soviet Union—Politics and govern-
ment—1855–1881.   3. Bureaucracy—Soviet Union—
History—19th century.   4. Soviet Union—Economic
policy.   5. Soviet Union—Social policy.   I. Title.
JN6511.L55   947'.073   82–6509
ISBN 0-87580-084-X   AACR2
ISBN 0-87580-536-1 (pbk.)

To Bruce McCully and Bill Abbot, my first history teachers, and to Lee and Carol Congdon, two uncommon friends

Contents

List of Abbreviations

ANSSSR	Arkhiv Akademii Nauk S.S.S.R. (Leningrad)
CU/AREEHC	Columbia University. Archive of Russian and East European History and Culture (New York City)
GIALO	Gosudarstvennyi Istoricheskii Arkhiv Leningradskoi Oblasti. (Leningrad)
GIM	Gosudarstvennyi Istoricheskii Muzei. Otdel rukopisei (Moscow)
GPB	Gosudarstvennaia Publichnaia Biblioteka imeni M. E. Saltykova-Shchedrina. Otdel rukopisei (Leningrad)
IV	*Istoricheskii vestnik.* St. Petersburg, 1880–1914
LN	*Literaturnoe nasledstvo.* Moscow, 1931—
ORGBL	Gosudarstvennaia Biblioteka S.S.S.R. imeni V. I. Lenina. Otdel rukopisei (Moscow)
OZ	*Otechestvennye zapiski.* St. Petersburg, 1829–1884
PD	Institut Russkoi Literatury (Pushkinskii Dom) Akademii Nauk S.S.S.R. (Leningrad)
PRO	Public Records Office (London)
PSZ **sobranie 1-oe**	*Polnoe sobranie zakonov Rossiiskoi Imperii s 1849g.* Sobranie pervoe. 45 vols. St. Petersburg, 1830
PSZ **sobranie 2-oe**	*Polnoe sobranie zakonov Rossiiskoi Imperii.* Sobranie vtoroe. 55 vols. St. Petersburg, 1830–1882
RA	*Russkii arkhiv.* Moscow, 1863–1917
RBS	*Russkii biograficheskii slovar'.* 25 vols. St. Petersburg, 1896–1918.

Abbreviations

RS	*Russkaia starina.* St. Petersburg, 1870–1918
RV	*Russkii vestnik.* Moscow–St. Petersburg, 1856–1906
SIRIO	*Sbornik Imperatorskago Russkago Istoricheskago Obshchestva.* St. Petersburg–Iur'ev–Moscow, 1867–1916
TsGALI	Tsentral'nyi Gosudarstvennyi Arkhiv Literatury i Iskusstva S.S.S.R. (Moscow)
TsGAOR	Tsentral'nyi Gosudarstvennyi Arkhiv Oktiabr'skoi Revoliutsii (Moscow)
TsGIAL	Tsentral'nyi Gosudarstvennyi Istoricheskii Arkhiv S.S.S.R. (Leningrad)
VE	*Vestnik evropy.* St. Petersburg, 1866–1918
Velikaia reforma	A. K. Dzhivelegov, A. S. Melgunov, and V. I. Picheta, eds. *Velikaia reforma. Russkoe obshchestvo i krest'ianskii vopros v proshlom i nastoiashchem.* 6 vols. Moscow, 1911
ZhMGI	*Zhurnal Ministerstva Gosudarstvennykh Imushchestv.* St. Petersburg, 1841–1918
ZhMIu	*Zhurnal Ministerstva Iustitsii.* St. Petersburg, 1859–1868, 1894–1915
ZhMVD	*Zhurnal Ministerstva Vnutrennikh Del.* St. Petersburg, 1829–1861

Preface

The first decade of Alexander II's reign is known in Russian history as the Era of the Great Reforms, a time quite properly thought of by historians as the major era of social, economic, and institutional transformation in Russia between the reign of Peter the Great and the Revolution of 1905. Coming directly after the notoriously repressive last decade of the Nicholas era, the appearance of such a dramatic period of reform and transformation has led scholars to seek its causes in dramatic events. Surely some great, even cataclysmic, force must have driven Alexander II and his advisers to initiate what appeared to be such an astonishing change in policy. Historians, therefore, generally have focused upon two phenomena, one dramatic and, for Russian opinion, shocking; the other, less dramatic, but perhaps potentially more worrisome for mid-nineteenth-century Russian statesmen. The first of these was Russia's defeat in the Crimean War by a relatively small, ineptly commanded Allied expeditionary force. The second was the increasingly frequent serf revolts that the Empire experienced throughout the 1850s.

For such turn-of-the-century historians as Aleksandr Kornilov, the reason for the apparently dramatic change in the attitudes of Alexander II and his advisers after 1856 was to be found in the crisis of confidence brought on by the Crimean defeat itself. Russians were so shocked by the defeat, Kornilov insisted, that they demanded broad reforms, while Alexander II was so shaken that he was willing to heed their demands rather than punish the men who expressed them by arrest or exile as his iron-willed father would have done.[1] Soviet historians and, most recently, Iu. I. Gerasimova and others associated with M. V. Nechkina's symposium on the revolutionary situation in Russia during the early years of Alexander II's reign have argued that an even broader crisis, brought on by widespread serf revolts and the failings of the serf-based Russian economy, forced the Emperor and his counselors to initiate a broad reformist policy.[2] Only P. A. Zaionchkovskii, perhaps the greatest living Soviet specialist on nineteenth-century Russia, refrains from isolating one particular reason for the onset of the Great Reform era and sees it as the result of a variety of more complex factors.[3]

Western historians have tended to accept one or the other of these explanations, or they have combined the two in some way. As Terence Emmons wrote in the mid-1960s, "There are two overriding considerations to be perceived in the state's motivations for undertaking emancipation: concern for economic development, and a desire to ensure social and political stability. Both were directly related to the experience of Russia's defeat in the Crimean War."[4] On a somewhat differerent, though less well documented note, Alfred Rieber argued, also in the mid-1960s, that the Crimean defeat, coupled with its attendant fiscal crisis, convinced Alexander II that Russia required a modern military establishment patterned on the Prussian model and, because such an army had a large ready-reserve component, it could not be established until the Russian serfs were emancipated.[5] Finally, Daniel Field has explained that serfdom fell "by stages" as a consequence of the Imperial legislative process and that that process went forward because "nineteenth-century Russian serfdom lacked supporting ideological and political structures."[6] Field's work describes more accurately than earlier efforts by western scholars the process by which serfdom fell; yet it still does not explain fully why or how the reform process went forward so rapidly and effectively in the late 1850s and early 1860s.

All of these arguments, except for that set forth by Field, share the common assumption that the economic failings of serfdom, the problem of preserving political stability, and the need to restore Russia's tarnished military prestige were the major forces that impelled Alexander II's government to embark on a reformist path. Yet, while Alexander and his advisers obviously concluded that Russia's military establishment must be modernized and considered it essential to preserve the domestic peace that had been threatened by the widespread serf revolts of the 1850s, the broader issue of whether these factors actually impelled them to initiate the process of social, administrative, and economic transformation is much more complex. None of the ministers, nor even Alexander II himself, thought serf revolts dangerously threatening in 1856, and the Russian nobility were generally willing to take their chances with the ever-present threat of peasant violence, just as were plantation owners in the American antebellum South.[7] Likewise, the Crimean defeat posed no great threat to Russia's territorial integrity, and it raised no unusual concern about national security in the minds of Russia's policy-makers. Stated most simply, although the Crimean defeat and increased serf revolts may have made Alexander II and his advisers more aware of the need for reform, there is not much evidence to indicate that these factors made them feel any acute sense of urgency about embarking on a dramatic program of social and economic transformation.

Questions such as these cast doubt on the argument that a crisis of policy and a failure of Russia's servile economy impelled Alexander and his advisers along a previously uncharted reformist path. Equally important, the Great Reform legislation simply was too complex and required too much sophisticated knowledge about the Empire's economic, administrative, and judicial affairs to have been formulated in the short period of time between Alexander II's famous speech to the Moscow nobility in March 1856, and late 1862, when the bulk of the draft legislation was completed. To put the matter another way, one well might ask how the Russian bureaucracy, which contemporaries and historians have condemned as ponderous, inefficient, and corrupt, could have produced such a vast corpus of reform legislation in the space of about five years. After all, Catherine II and her advisers had devoted a full quarter-century to the much less complex task of restructuring Russia's administrative institutions and, in that time, had completed only the portion of the reform that dealt with provincial administration. Likewise, it had taken Alexander I and his counselors more than a decade to restructure Russia's central administration to coincide with that provincial apparatus Catherine had created. In the second quarter of the nineteenth century, Nicholas I and his "Chief of Staff for Peasant Affairs," Count Kiselev, had devoted nearly two decades to reforming the institutions and procedures with which they administered Russia's state peasants, and even so astute an administrator as the great Speranskii had needed nearly a decade to compile and codify Russia's laws. All of these were far less complex tasks, with significantly less far-reaching implications, than the Great Reform legislation of the 1860s.

Given this consistent record of glacially slow performance in dealing with comparatively less complex tasks of administrative reorganization and reform, how did the Russian bureaucracy draft, in the space of a mere half-decade, that vast body of Great Reform legislation that altered fundamentally the Empire's social, economic, and judicial order? The answer to this question cannot be found in Russia's Crimean defeat, nor can it be found in the crisis of her servile economy. It cannot be found in the personality of Alexander II, nor in the growing reformist sentiment expressed by educated Russians: Alexander II had neither the strength of character nor the powerful personality of his father; and the reformist sentiment that surged so dramatically to the fore among educated Russians on the eve of the Emancipation of 1861, emerged *after* Alexander's famous Moscow speech about the need to resolve the serf issue, not before it. Indeed, thinking Russians had greeted Alexander's accession with only modest expectations for change and the most minimal hopes for reform.[8] In 1855, no one in Russia, and Alexander II least of all, even remotely imagined that the Great Reforms would become an accomplished fact just more than a half-decade after the Crimean War ended.[9]

To answer more satisfactorily the questions about how the body of the Great Reform legislation was produced, and why it assumed the shape it did, we must look back to the era of Nicholas I and, especially, to its last decade, which historians generally have considered to be one of the most reactionary periods in Imperial Russia's history. Beginning in the late 1830s, an unusual group of young officials, whom I have identified in this study as enlightened bureaucrats, began to appear in St. Petersburg's chanceries. Such men held different attitudes about state service and reform than did most government officials. They rejected as useless those formalistic routines and rituals that had become so much a part of Russia's bureaucratic world by the 1840s[10] and demanded efficiency and innovation rather than time-honored custom in administration. Most of all, because they believed in a more aggressive sort of administration than did most bureaucrats, they quickly perceived that the information needed to formulate workable policies simply did not exist in Russia's central administrative offices. Therefore, one of their major activities during the 1840s became the collection of information about social, economic, and administrative conditions in Russia's provinces that was unlike any assembled by Russian officials before.

Increased quantities of more accurate data about Russian social and economic conditions were not in themselves sufficient to set the stage for the Great Reform legislation, although they were one of its prerequisites. Perhaps even more important, the enlightened bureaucrats' view of change had to evolve beyond that held by their mentors and superiors to one that perceived the need for a far broader and more fundamental transformation than even the most progressive Russian statesmen envisioned during the Nicholas era. Such a view, however, had to be firmly grounded in experience and not based mainly on theory, as was the case with the reform views held by most of the intelligentsia at the time. What that view was, how and why the enlightened bureaucrats developed it, how it came to exercise a decisive influence on the content of the Great Reform legislation, and how it was related to the unique institutional structure that emerged in the mid-nineteenth-century Russian state are some of the major questions that this volume will examine.

W. Bruce Lincoln
Sycamore, Illinois
New Year's Day, 1982

Acknowledgments

It would require a great deal more space than is available here to ac-knowledge the generosity and kindness of the many people who have in some way aided my efforts to write this book. Marc Raeff, Leopold Haimson, and Daniel Orlovsky have read and commented on several versions of this manuscript over the years, and their encouragement, combined with gentle urgings, have in large part been responsible for my seeing the task through to its end. Daniel Field, David Macey, and Richard Robbins read earlier versions of the manuscript, while Jacob Kipp and JoAnn Ruckman read parts of it at different times. All offered generous comments that helped to improve it, and whatever virtues it may have are in large part due to their collective wisdom.

In addition to these American scholars, Petr Andreevich Zaionch-kovskii deserves special mention. Not only has he offered me the benefit of generous scholarly counsel over many years, but he has served above and beyond the call of duty as my guide in learning about the many complex archival sources that related to the problems discussed in this book. Without his help, it would have been more than difficult to assemble the materials needed to begin to tell the story of Russia's enlightened bureaucrats.

During the past decade or so, I also have benefited greatly from discussions about the problems explored in this volume with many other scholars in the United States, the Soviet Union, and Poland. In this, Ludwik Bazylow, Helju Bennett, Valentina Chernukha, Lee Cong-don, Ralph Fisher, Brenda Meehan-Waters, Sidney Monas, Franciszka Ramotowska, Charles Timberlake, and Richard Wortman are at the top of what is, to my good fortune, a lengthy list. These and others too numerous to list have helped me to focus my explorations of the prob-lems related to the enlightened bureaucrats in Russia.

Here at Northern Illinois University I have had many sorts of sup-port over the years, for which I am indeed grateful. Carroll Moody, our department chairman during most of the years when I was working on this volume, has been generous in his efforts to juggle teaching sched-ules in order to give me the time I needed to write, and, on more than one occasion, he has shielded me from onerous committee duties when I needed to be free of such administrative entanglements. Since his arrival here several years ago, George Gutsche, my colleague in nine-teenth-century Russian literature, has been a source of wise counsel and good humor, both of which I have appreciated far more than may have been evident on some occasions. In recent years, I also have profited from the logistical and financial support that I have received from an unusual group of senior administrators, all of them accomplished scholars in their own right, who have assembled here to direct the course of a university that has been in the throes of transition. Among them, I particularly want to thank William Monat, James Norris, Jon Miller, John LaTourette, and Dean Jaros, all of whom have supported my work in important ways on more than one occasion. Finally, but certainly not least, I owe much more than ritualistic thanks to Mary Livingston, director of Northern Illinois University Press. I am grateful indeed for her helpful efficiency in getting this volume into print.

My wife Patti deserves her own special paragraph of thanks in any acknowledgment of the help I have received in writing this book. Her good humor and good sense, not to mention her willingness to put up with my quirks and foibles, have helped more than I can express here.

Institutions, too, have been generous in supporting the research that went into this book, and my debt to them is very great. Grants from the International Research and Exchanges Board and the Fulbright-Hays Faculty Research Abroad Program supported my research in the archives of Leningrad and Moscow on several visits to the Soviet Union during which the Academy of Sciences of the U.S.S.R. and the Institutes of History at Moscow and Leningrad State Universities served as generous and helpful hosts. Likewise, the Historical Institute at the University of Warsaw outdid itself in making me welcome during a term as a Fulbright-Hays scholar in Poland. The Russian Institute at Columbia University supported my early efforts to write this book, and the Russian and East European Center at the University of Illinois has been particularly generous in making its resources available to me over the past decade. A variety of grants and other sorts of support from the American Council of Learned Societies, the American Philosophical Society, and the Northern Illinois University Graduate School Fund have rounded out the generous support I have received over the years.

Even the best efforts of family, colleagues, friends, and generous research organizations cannot help a scholar in his work unless libraries and archives make their resources available to him. In this respect, I have been more than fortunate. Serafima Grigorev'na Sakharova at the Central State Historical Archive in Leningrad has placed her awesome knowledge of nineteenth-century archival materials at my disposal over the years, and my debt to her is very great indeed. In the Soviet Union, many other archivists and librarians at the Central State Historical Library, the Lenin Library (and its manuscript section), the Archive of the October Revolution, the Saltykov-Shchedrin Public Library (and its manuscript section), the Archive of the Academy of Sciences, the State

Acknowledgments

Historical Archive of Leningrad Region, the State Historical Museum, Pushkinskii Dom, the Archive of the All-Union Geographical Society, and the Central State Archive of Literature and Art have been generous in their help. They, and their counterparts at the Central Archive of Ancient Acts and the University Library in Warsaw, the British Museum, the Public Record Office, the Archive of Russian and East European History and Culture at Columbia University, the Regenstein Library at the University of Chicago, and the Founders Memorial Library at Northern Illinois University, must remain the unsung heroes in the lengthy tale of the research that went into this book.

As helpful as these many people have been, I must acknowledge yet a further debt to Rebecca Atack, Marianna Tax Choldin, Laurence Miller, Frankie Mosborg, and June Pachuta at the University of Illinois Library for their efforts on my behalf and for the dedication and good humor with which they always met my sometimes outrageous requests for assistance. To them, and to many others in the United States, England, Poland, and the Soviet Union, I owe a special debt that formal thanks such as these cannot begin to repay.

Note on Transliteration

With a few exceptions, the transliteration that I have used in this book follows the Library of Congress system. I have transliterated most names of foreign origin (including Baltic German) directly, without converting them to their national counterparts. The only exceptions to this rule have been the names of foreigners who lived for a time in Russia but did not become Russian citizens. According to the usual practice, all dates are given according to the Julian calendar which, in the nineteenth century, was twelve days behind the Gregorian calendar used in the West.

In the

Vanguard of Reform

ChAPTER I

Russia's Bureaucratic
World, 1825-1855

"Bureaucratic formalities have reached the point of absurdity."

Count Perovskii

Some months after the death of Nicholas I, a desperate and bitter Russian official complained that "the most distinctive features [of our state administration] consist of a universal lack of truth, the government's distrust of its own instruments, and its contempt for all others." The author of this indictment was P. A. Valuev, Governor of the Baltic province of Courland and soon to become one of Imperial Russia's most effective Ministers of Internal Affairs. Valuev saw the extreme centralization of the Russian bureaucracy and the increasingly mechanistic nature of its administrative processes as two further obstacles that the civil service posed to effective government in Russia. Form, not content, had become his colleagues' chief concern. "All government agencies," he lamented, "are more occupied with each other nowadays than with the substance of those matters for which they are responsible."[1]

Russians long had cursed their civil officials' unyielding devotion to rigid procedures, and Valuev's caustic remarks were unusual only in that they came from the pen of a man who stood near the apex of the Imperial establishment and were circulated widely among the nobility and intelligentsia of St. Petersburg. Still, devotion to the bureaucratic ideals of form and procedure are common in any administration, and the Russian bureaucracy was not dramatically different in that respect from a number of others. For Russians, their officials' unfortunate dedication to these universal bureaucratic traits was made worse during the ͨⁿ⁻

1

tury before Nicholas I ascended the throne because so many of those who labored in the Tsar's service were poorly educated and understood only imperfectly the problems that confronted them. As we can best determine, less than one out of every five Russian civil servants in 1755 had any formal schooling, and the home educations that many of the remainder received from haphazardly trained tutors often were very poor indeed. By the middle of the eighteenth century, a full forty percent of the men who headed St. Petersburg's central administrative colleges still had no formal education, and only four of their twelve deputies ever had been to school. By comparison with their European counterparts, the educational achievements of the Russians were little short of wretched, but the sad truth was that Russia's rulers could expect little better from even their senior officials because the number of institutions able to provide education beyond the elementary level literally could be counted on the fingers of two hands. Russia's first university was founded only in 1755, and its graduates did not begin to reach the higher echelons of the civil service in noticeable numbers until after the turn of the century.[2]

While the bureaucracy remained relatively small, and the problems facing it reasonably uncomplex, Russia's rulers could rely on special civil and military agents to carry their orders into the provinces and bypass many of the obstacles that a poorly educated, uncompromising, and venal bureaucracy posed to the administration of such far-flung domains as theirs. The use of civic and military agents was a time-honored practice, used ever since Muscovite times, and it continued to be reasonably effective in the hands of officials who still were guided by Muscovite administrative traditions and precedents.[3] Above all, it enabled them to circumvent an otherwise deadly administrative dilemma in which, as Professors Pintner and Rowney recently concluded, "the most talented and best-trained" officials had to rely on "the least educated and least ambitious to execute their policies throughout the realm."[4]

The origins of this dilemma lay in the reforms of Peter the Great. Peter had imposed different imperatives upon his central administration than had his seventeenth-century predecessors, and he had endeavored to alter the structure and organization of the administration to meet his new demands more predictably and efficiently. He therefore had established a more rational institutional structure for Russia's administration by creating the Ruling Senate in 1711 and by founding a series of collegial executive institutions (*kollegii*) between 1718 and 1720. Headed by a board of between ten and thirteen tsarist appointees, each administrative college became responsible for a particular functional area of Russia's government. Its decisions were to be reached collectively, and its members were to take collective responsibility for them.[5] According to the theories of the seventeenth-century German cameralists from which such collegial administrative principles were derived, this form of government made it possible, in the words of one scholar, for "an absolute ruler who wished to increase his revenue and support a standing army . . . [to] impart a measure of rational organization to a political order that rested on a variety of disparate traditional estates."[6] In theory, it also made it possible to diminish challenges to an absolute ruler's authority. "Simple people are prone to mistake an individual . . . as equal to or above the Tsar," wrote Feofan Prokopovich, Peter's leading churchman and political theorist. "They will not be so led astray by an impersonal, collegial body."[7]

Although Peter could establish a new institutional structure for his newly proclaimed Empire, he could not create a new administrative tradition to guide the manner in which officials served him and his government on a daily basis.[8] Peter's civil officials found it all but impossible to comprehend their Emperor's demands, and they therefore sought refuge in the administrative procedures with which they were comfortable and familiar. Especially because senior officials often had limited administrative experience and were not infrequently incompetent, illiterate, or both,[9] the conduct of official matters usually fell to those lesser officials and clerks who served in their personal chanceries, and these often had direct ties with the seventeenth-century Muscovite administration.[10] As the pre-revolutionary historian A. N. Filippov very properly pointed out, such men "were hardly able to introduce a new spirit into the administration and, especially after Peter the Great, they almost completely failed to create that independent administrative body free from arbitrariness about which Peter and his closest associates had dreamed."[11]

Whatever innovations in the spirit and purpose of administration Peter had endeavored to introduce into Russia's institutions of central government faded very soon after his death.[12] Between 1725 and 1762, and even during the early parts of Catherine II's reign, executive functions in Russia's central administration became the province of Imperial favorites. On those occasions when such men exercised their power collectively, they did so through special supreme bodies that stood outside the institutional framework of Russia's central administration, not through Peter's new executive institutions. Only in the mid-1770s and 1780s did Catherine endeavor to re-establish some form and order in Russia's administration when she realized that her Empire's polyglot institutions and traditions could not respond effectively to the changed conditions in Russia. The most dramatic statement of that fact came from the Pugachev Revolt, which burst out of control in 1773–1774, largely because hopelessly tangled lines of authority and slow-moving bureaucratic communication prevented local authorities from crushing it before it got out of hand.

Catherine knew only too well that as a recognized European Power, her Empire could not tolerate such social and economic dislocations as those that stemmed from Pugachev's Revolt. Clearly, civil peace must be preserved, taxes collected, recruits assembled, and iron ore mined, smelted, and forged into weapons to equip Russia's immense standing army if she were to continue the foreign commitments that her status as a Great Power imposed upon her. Such functions required more efficient institutions and more effective administrative precepts than those that had guided Muscovite and Petrine civil servants. Likewise, as senior Russian officials became acquainted with modern Prussian and French bureaucratic practice and, as at least a handful of them were schooled in the principles of the French Enlightenment and the corresponding *Aufklärung* in Germany, they understood that the pre-modern military and fiscal concerns of Muscovite Tsars conformed poorly to the image of a Great Power that their sovereigns hoped to project. To be sure, Russia's military needs continued greater than ever, but, as a Great Power, she also must exhibit some proper concern for her citizens' welfare.[13] To do so, fifty far-flung provinces, spread over a sixth of the globe's surface, had to be tied effectively to a capital that stood geographically remote from most of the Empire.

To meet these more complex demands, Catherine issued her Statute of November 1, 1775, which eliminated the last vestiges of Muscovite forms in Russia's administration. Perhaps most significant of all, she separated the military from Russia's civil administration for all time, so that never again would the army be used to enforce the Sovereign's decrees and collect revenues, as it had under Peter the Great and his early successors. Catherine placed those tasks into the hands of a systematically organized corps of civil officials who extended the bureaucracy that Peter had established only in St. Petersburg and Moscow into Russia's provincial and district capitals.[14] Yet this achievement also had its negative side because the Empress created her new provincial administration only at the cost of Peter's central government. Catherine's new provincial and district agencies usurped many of the central administration's functions, and, for all practical purposes, all but three of Peter's administrative colleges had ceased to function by the end of the century. As the nineteenth century opened, Russia faced a new institutional crisis of staggering dimensions.[15] Just at the moment when Napoleon was beginning to employ France's more effective bureaucracy to marshal her national resources on an unprecedented scale, Russia found herself without a viable central administration.

Thus, perhaps the most pressing problem to confront Alexander I when he ascended the throne in 1801 was the urgent need to reconstruct the partially defunct central administration which his grandmother and father had bequeathed. During the first decade of the new century, the young Emperor and his advisers erected the framework for new ministerial institutions that had the potential for governing Russia more effectively. At least in theory, Russia's central administration became concerned with law and legality, exercised increased monocratic authority over subordinate officials and institutions, and saw as its purpose a more intimate and pervasive involvement in the daily lives of the Emperor's subjects.[16] The new ministerial institutions that were to express these broader new concerns were created by the Manifesto of September 8, 1802, which at first did little more than regroup Peter the Great's administrative colleges under the direction of individual ministers rather than resurrect them under the headship of Petrine collegial boards. It was a modest beginning, but from it evolved an administrative apparatus that eventually grew powerful enough to erode the unlimited and undivided power of the autocracy itself.

If Alexander's newly appointed ministers were to wield monocratic authority effectively, they needed at their command officials who could function as true Imperial administrators rather than as defenders of that pre-modern tradition that conditioned the attitudes of most Russian civil servants at the time. As early as 1802, Alexander's brilliant adviser, the great bureaucratic reformer Mikhail Speranskii, insisted that officials be properly educated, not merely trained on the job, and that allegiance to the interests of the state must precede class loyalty in their official duties.[17] Perhaps more obvious than anything else, the administrative difficulties posed by the vast national mobilization of men and resources that Alexander ordered in 1806 showed the validity of Speranskii's argument. Clearly, if Catherine's earlier effort to transfer from the army to the civil service the critical duties of collecting revenue and enforcing the sovereign's will in the provinces was to succeed, if the state was to serve its citizens' welfare, and if these functions were to be coordinated at the center of the government by Alexander's newly appointed ministers, it was essential to have better-educated officials who understood Russia's broader needs and interests.

A search for such officials, and the means to ensure a regular and continuing flow of them into the bureaucracy, occupied progressive Russian statesmen for the next half-century, and their failure to solve that problem became a major element in the Empire's increasing backwardness as mid-century approached. Officials who did not comprehend the broader issues facing Russia, or who defined them primarily in terms of narrow aristocratic self-interest, could not serve as effective instruments for confronting those complex policy issues that centered on Russia's changing economic and social life, even in the limited manner advocated by Nicholas I and some of his closest counselors. Like their eighteenth-century predecessors, such officials hastily withdrew behind that screen of excessive formalism which, for so long, had offered refuge for men who were unwilling, unable, or unprepared to confront those new and complex questions of administration and policy posed by a world in which the tempo of change accelerated at an ever-increasing pace. Inevitably, such an adoration of bureaucratic formalities fed upon itself to generate yet more of the same. As Russia reached mid-century, Minister of Internal Affairs Perovskii had good reason to lament that "it is impossible not to recognize that bureaucratic formalities have reached the point of absurdity."[18] In the words of one of his junior colleagues, these years, the era of Nicholas I, marked "the heyday of formalism."[19]

"The Heyday of Formalism"

Like all bureaucracies, that which functioned in Russia during the second quarter of the nineteenth century was slow, inefficient, and flawed in many ways. Nonetheless, and again like other bureaucracies, it somehow muddled through, and the one indisputable fact was that the Russian Empire continued to function. But there were fundamental differences between the bureaucracies of Russia and Europe. Most particularly, the bureaucratic systems in the West did not act to impede national development when European nations began to enter the Industrial Age. If Russia was to meet the challenge posed by the rapidly industrializing West, she, in turn, had to find some way to achieve greater administrative efficiency and instill into her middle- and upper-level officials a measure of support for change. Russia's bureaucrats had to become responsive to the needs of the nation they served, and some means had to be found to enable those few who were well informed about complex social and economic issues to gain input into the tsarist policy-making process.

Yet the very nature of autocracy worked against the development of impersonal policy-making instruments such as had evolved in the bureaucracies of western Europe. Although Paul I's Fundamental Laws decreed that "the Russian Empire is administered on the bases of absolute laws, regulations, and statutes," they also decreed that all laws "originate with the Autocratic Power." The Emperor was "an Autocratic and Absolute Monarch [and] submission to his supreme authority must

6

come not from fear alone but as a matter of conscience."[20] Coupled with these notions of their absolute power, the preservation of the Romanov dynasty became a fundamental mission of nineteenth-century Emperors, and that dynastic mission stood in opposition to the ideal of a state administered by impersonal institutions "on the bases of absolute laws, regulations, and statutes."[21] The autocrat remained the ultimate source of justice, law, mercy, and many types of privilege, and as Russia entered the post-Napoleonic era, the Emperor, not his ministers, formulated policy. As a result, just when the new social and economic groups that comprised the middle class were eroding the power of absolutism in the West, it was strengthened in Russia.

The obvious dichotomy between impersonal institutions and the Autocrat's personal power had, in fact, been expressed in the Manifesto of September 1802, which replaced Peter the Great's administrative colleges with ministries, for its authors clearly viewed the ministers as the Emperor's personal agents entrusted with certain commissions (*poruchenii*) or administrative responsibilities.[22] The more militaristic order instituted by Nicholas I intensified that view, for he regarded himself as Russia's "commander" and his ministers as his adjutants in a much stronger sense than had his elder brother.[23] He stated that view most dramatically when he designated Minister of State Domains P. D. Kiselev as his "Chief of Staff for Peasant Affairs,"[24] but it applied to all who served him in ministerial capacities. Such minister-adjutants could undertake specific commissions and perform routine tasks, but, just as a military commander insists on holding responsibility for command decisions in his hands, so Nicholas preserved control over each and every policy-making decision in Russia's central administration. Because he insisted on imposing a military command structure upon Russia's central administration, Nicholas thus preferred men who shared his view that "all human life is nothing more than service"[25] to those known for their expert knowledge and technical expertise, especially because such talents tended to be found in men who also had a taste for independent thought.

Nicholas was further encouraged to prefer the service of men over institutions by his association with the historian and conservative ideologist N. M. Karamzin, who was perhaps his closest adviser during the first weeks of his reign. Many of the historian's political views coincided so closely with the young Emperor's own that it appears Nicholas even wanted to appoint Karamzin, a recognized foe of Alexander's new ministerial institutions, to a ministerial post.[26] Karamzin had exhorted Alexander to pay "more attention to men than to forms," to remember that "one of the worst political evils of our time is the absence of fear" and that "skill in choosing and handling men is foremost among the skills that a Russian sovereign must possess."[27] Such sentiments appealed to Nicholas, who had heard similar injunctions from his mother and his tutors throughout his youth.[28] On occasion his elder brother had expressed a preference for administration by institutions, but Nicholas always placed his confidence in men, even as Alexander's ministries continued to develop as the key administrative institutions in Russia.

As might be expected in an autocratic state, it took only a short time before Nicholas's assumption that ministers of state were mere adjutants extended downward throughout the Russian bureaucracy to the relations between senior officials and their subordinates. During the second quarter of the nineteenth century, Russia's central administration saw a dramatic increase in the number of agents of special commissions (*chinovniki osobykh poruchenii*) under the direct control of ministers or their subordinate department heads. According to the "temporary" Tables of Organization (*shtaty*) of the Ministry of Internal Affairs issued in December 1834, there were only twenty such agents in the entire ministry.[29] A mere decade later, ten were assigned to Nikolai Miliutin's Provisional Section for the Reorganization of Municipal Government and Economy in the Ministry's Economic Department alone.[30] Such agents did not serve as mere bureaucratic adjuncts, nor were their positions sinecures for well-born lords who wished to be in service but not to serve. They comprised a vital part of Russia's ministerial administration because they acted as direct extensions of their superiors' authority, and many of those who emerged as enlightened bureaucrats in the 1850s served in such capacities at some point in their careers. Indeed, service as agents of special commissions became an important factor in helping such men to achieve the visibility they needed to rise to higher positions in the bureaucracy.[31]

Nicholas knew that the bureaucratic instruments he had inherited posed serious obstacles to the implementation of policy in his far-flung domains. Yet his efforts to improve them were neither bold nor broadly conceived. His first inclination was to make the bureaucracy more responsive to his will by relying upon minister-adjutants chosen from his circle of closest friends. Very quickly he increased their numbers by establishing the Third Section of His Majesty's Own Chancery, an entire corps of adjutants established to serve as extensions of his autocratic *persona* throughout Russia. Although their numbers increased, all of Nicholas's adjutants found their spheres of activity severely circumscribed by their Emperor's narrow perception of the bureaucracy's flaws and his limited understanding about how such might be remedied. Perhaps Speranskii stated this view most clearly when he endeavored to define the responsibilities of a special committee that Nicholas had established on December 6, 1826. The Committee of December 6th was to examine Russia's administration and comment on the social and political problems it faced, but Speranskii insisted that its task could not be "the full alteration of the existing order of government, but only its refinement by means of a few particular changes and additions."[32] Nicholas never questioned the functions of Russia's ministries and administrative departments. He merely insisted on further regulation and pressed for more precise information about how his Empire's administration functioned under the adjutants he had put into key positions. Therefore, it was no accident that Russia's government agencies kept better statistical data during the reign of Nicholas I than they did during the 1860s and 1870s. That was the only way in which they could respond to the Emperor's efforts to define more precisely their tasks and relationships to each other.[33]

Nicholas's misplaced confidence that properly chosen adjutants could implement his will throughout his domains was probably best reflected in Mikhail Pogodin's joyous reassurances to Russia's reading public that "one educated, zealous, active superior—and the entire department entrusted to him is . . . aiding other departments by its example, organization and training of officials. One governor with such qualities—and one fiftieth part of Russia is prospering."[34] Nicholas endeavored to find just such men for top posts in his government, and he encouraged them to recruit others to serve under them. But, he emphasized the virtues of zealous service at the expense of education and thoughtful planning, with the result that Russia's central bureaucracy dissipated its resources by a show of frenzied activity that served no worthwhile purpose and produced few results. It became more important to appear busy than to become seriously concerned about vital issues of state policy. "Always say that you are occupied, but do not explain the nature of your work," wrote one senior official in a satirical commentary about bureaucratic life. "Let people think your work is part of a secret inquiry. That way, people will think that you are involved with important state affairs."[35]

Emphasis on zealous service and the quantity of reports and communications that each department generated encouraged the production of documents (the process known in Russian as *deloproizvodstvo*) to flourish unrestrained by any limitations of common sense. The quantity of reports written, and the number of official cases processed, became measures of each agency's achievement and figured prominently in its annual report.[36] As Minister of Internal Affairs Lev Perovskii so aptly put it, Russia's civil servants had become mere "record-keepers,"[37] who engaged in what one frustrated young official called "a lot of arguments and passing official papers from hand to hand."[38] The question of mak-

ing policy slipped further out of focus as harassed senior officials struggled to deal with the flood of petty administrative tasks they faced every
day. Each year, frantic provincial governors confronted an appalling
mountain of more than 100,000 documents that required their signa-
tures,[39] and senior statesmen in St. Petersburg were no less pressed.
Once established, this ubiquitous routine of wasting statesmen's time
on administrative detail persevered. Writing in the 1870s, Russia's then-
retired Minister of Public Instruction A. V. Golovnin complained that
petty bureaucratic tasks still prevented statesmen from giving their best
attention to the serious business of government:

> From conversations with our present-day statesmen [Golovnin
> wrote], it is evident that, because of the vast quantity of matters
> of secondary importance ... [and because of] their Court and
> social obligations, they have absolutely no opportunity ... to re-
> flect upon things, and to gain some perspective upon the general
> state of affairs, the general course of legislation, and the nature of
> our administrative activities in general.[40]

Perpetuation of the bureaucratic process, not the serious tasks of
policy-making and creative administration, thus consumed the time of
Russia's statesmen and sapped their energies. Much was talked about,
but little was accomplished. "We go one step forward and take two
steps backward, and we shall not get very far in this manner," wrote one
amazed newcomer to the St. Petersburg bureaucracy at mid-century.
"Today, we say: 'Excellent!' 'Let's do this!' But tomorrow, we shall say,
'Yes, this is fine to be sure ... but it can wait.' And then we shall turn
to a new matter altogether."[41] The Emperor and his closest advisers
might believe that men, not institutions, could produce the most effective administration, but men overwhelmed by regulations and trivial
daily tasks simply could never get the forest into focus because they
were obliged to spend all their time pruning and cultivating each tree.
That problem was made even worse because there were so few officials
who were well enough educated to even comprehend the forest's dimensions. As had been the case since the days of Peter the Great, the
issue of education continued to assume critical importance.

Although the demand for better educated, better trained civil officials never was satisfied during the first half of the nineteenth century,
at least some statesmen tried to find ways to meet it. Soon after it was
established in 1802, Alexander I's new Ministry of Public Instruction
prepared grandiose plans for increasing the number of district schools,
provincial *gimnazii,* and universities in Russia. Even though the entire
scheme never was realized, the first two decades of the century saw

universities established at Vilna, Dorpat, Kharkov, Kazan, and St. Petersburg.[42] Perhaps most significant of all, in 1811, Alexander founded a lyceum at Tsarskoe Selo for the avowed purpose of "educating those youths especially destined for important spheres of state service."[43] The Lyceum was to provide an elite education for aristocratic youths who planned careers in Russia's service, and its graduates were promised the same service grades as young men who completed the course at the university. At Speranskii's urging, Alexander insisted that the Lyceum develop a progressive curriculum to educate students in those areas needed by nineteenth-century administrators.[44]

Alexander I, Speranskii, and those statesmen who supported their efforts to develop Russia's educational facilities first had to convince the sons of nobles to abandon casual study with tutors and submit to the rigidity of a formal curriculum at the Empire's new schools and universities. With the Emperor's personal sponsorship, and its elite student body, the Tsarskoe Selo Lyceum attracted, from the very beginning, its full complement of talented students, but the new *gimnazii* and universities remained only partly filled, despite an ominous paragraph in the Decree on the Establishment of Schools (January 29, 1803) which warned that after five years, "no one who has failed to graduate from a public or private secondary school will be admitted to the civil service in posts requiring juridical or other specialized knowledge."[45]

Although at first there was some room to argue about which posts in the civil service required "other specialized knowledge" and which did not, the Emperor removed all cause for doubt in 1809 when, in consultation with his closest advisers, he made good on the warning he had issued in 1803. After noting that most schools were still short of students and that Russia's civil administration required far more educated officials than were graduating from the Empire's schools, Alexander decreed on August 6th that no official could be promoted to the rank of *kollezhskii asessor* (grade eight, which conferred lifetime nobility) unless he had graduated from a university or an elite school, such as the Tsarskoe Selo Lyceum, or passed an examination judged to measure university level education. For officials who already held grades eight through six, their path toward the coveted rank of *statskii sovetnik* (grade five, which conferred hereditary nobility) was barred unless they met the same requirements.[46]

This decree engendered bitterness among a substantial number of Russian bureaucrats. Nikolai Karamzin, the Empire's official historian and self-appointed spokesman for the nobility, complained that:

> In Russia, the official presiding in the Civil Court must know Homer and Theocritus, the Senate Secretary—the properties of

11

oxygen and all the gasses, the Deputy Governor—Pythagorean geometry, the superintendent of a lunatic asylum—Roman law, or else they will end their days as Collegiate and Titular counsellors [the ranks immediately below those of *statskii sovetnik* and *kollezhskii asessor* in the Table of Ranks]. Neither forty years of state service, nor important accomplishments exempt one from the obligation of having to learn things which are entirely alien and useless for Russians.[47]

Of course, the law was not always applied stringently, and, in 1834, it was changed so that an official's lack of higher education merely slowed his rise but did not halt it.[48] Nevertheless, even before Nicholas I ascended the throne in 1825, it had become clear that the Russian Emperor required better educated officals than were generally available to staff the middle levels of his civil service.

A shortage of officials sufficiently well educated to confront increasingly complex social, economic, and technological issues was only one of the serious problems that plagued Russia's administration in the post-Napoleonic era. More generally, and setting aside the issue of the provincial bureaucracy's many faults, which cannot concern us here, Nicholas I and his senior advisers simply did not have at their disposal a corps of officials who could supply them with accurate information about the social, economic, or political conditions in the Empire at any given time. Although the bureaucracy had achieved a minimal level of semi-literacy, it had not yet become the sort of instrument that Nicholas and his confidants required to resolve the problems that Russia faced in the 1830s and 1840s.

During the first half of the nineteenth century, and especially as its mid-point neared, the Russian bureaucracy grew from a relatively compact corps of noble officials assisted by a few near-proletarian scribes into a more ponderous administrative body that was even less responsive to the autocrat's will than its eighteenth-century predecessor had been. In terms of raw numbers, personnel in the Table of Ranks increased from approximately 16,000 in 1796 to 75,201 in 1850, while the Empire's population increased from approximately 36 to 69 million.[49] Thus, in the space of fifty years, the number of civil officials burgeoned by an astounding 470 percent while the population they served did not quite double. Although it has been argued that the tsarist administration employed only a quarter as many civil servants in proportion to Russia's inhabitants as did its counterparts in France and England,[50] the fact remains that a third of the Empire's population never saw a government official from one decade to the next. Throughout the first half of the nineteenth century, the Empire's serf-owners or their bailiffs collected taxes, assembled recruits, and administered justice to the 22 million men and women who tilled their estates. Only Russia's nobles and townsfolk dealt with state officials in the manner of English and French citizens, and state peasants (the largest single group in the Empire) encountered them far less frequently.

The economic disruption and social dislocation caused by the Napoleonic wars, coupled with Alexander I's neglect of domestic affairs during the last decade of his reign, meant that much of the rapid growth in Russia's bureaucracy occurred during the reign of Nicholas I. Yet the significant influx of new officials into the civil service did not mean that increased numbers of men and women came to know the relative comfort and prestige enjoyed by numbers of Catherinian civil servants a half-century before. Throughout the first half of the nineteenth century, tsarist statesmen treated the rank and file in Russia's army of civil servants as a sort of clerical proletariat whose ranks were swollen further by thousands of chancery copyists who had not yet reached even the lowest grade in the Table of Ranks. The numbers of these so-called *kantseliarskie sluzhiteli* increased from 26,377 in 1850 (the first year for which figures are available) to 32,073 in 1857, although their ratio to the civil servants holding grades in the Table of Ranks generally remained quite constant.[51] Clearly, such men were at the bottom of the civil service pyramid, and it was rare for one of them to rise very far into the Table of Ranks. In fact, Valuev was one of a mere handful of civil servants to rise to high office in nineteenth-century Russia after entering the bureaucracy as a humble *kantseliarskii sluzhitel'*.

In 1845, a decade before he penned his well-known indictment of Russia's civil administration, Valuev confided his thoughts about the aspirations of middle-level civil servants to a memorandum that he addressed to Minister of Internal Affairs L. A. Perovskii. By that time he already had become a *kollezhskii asessor* and had enjoyed for more than three years the privileges of lifetime nobility that his rank conferred. Perovskii had just attached him to General E. A. Golovin, Governor-General of Riga, as an official of special commissions on an assignment that earned him three extraordinarily rapid promotions so that by January 1850, more than nine months before his thirty-fourth birthday, Valuev had won hereditary noble status.[52] "Everyone knows that the lower official grades are only a Purgatory through which runs the measured highway to the paradise of delights [i.e. the rank of *statskii sovetnik*] for those who are ambitious,"[53] Valuev wrote from this vantage point as a highly successful civil servant. His comment summarized the goal of every ambitious junior official in the Empire. The more serious question was how many such men had a reasonable hope of realizing that aspiration.

No one would dispute that promotion to the rank that carried with it hereditary noble status was ardently sought by junior civil servants in Russia, but its attainment usually was an arduous undertaking. The Civil Service Statute of May 1834 divided officials into three categories *(razriady)* based on their level of formal education, and each category had a different schedule of promotions for time served in grade *(za vyslugu let)*.[54] It took an official in the first category twenty-four years to rise from the rank of *kollezhskii registrator* (grade fourteen) to that of *statskii sovetnik* (grade five) by means of promotions for time served in grade, while it required thirty years for officials in the second category, and thirty-seven years for those in the third. These promotion schedules were lengthened for officials who were not of noble birth, so that it required twenty-six, thirty-six, and forty-two years for first, second, and third category plebian officials to reach the rank of *statskii sovetnik* if all their promotions were for time served in grade and came on time.[55]

Even though officials were eligible for time-in-grade promotions after a specified number of years, that did not guarantee that promotions would come on schedule. At mid-century, the portion of officials in the Table of Ranks who received promotions each year ranged between only six and ten percent, although most promotions below the rank of *statskii sovetnik* required no more than four years of service in grade. Because considerably more civil servants were eligible for time-in-grade promotions than the number who received them, there was no certainty that an official could, in fact, reach the coveted rank of *statskii sovetnik* before middle age or, even, before retirement, though it was theoretically possible to do so according to Russia's civil service statutes.

This arduous promotion schedule could be shortened if an ambitious official could win promotions for merit *(za otlichie)* rather than wait to be advanced for time served in grade. In that way, an official in the first category could reach grade five from grade fourteen in the space of fifteen, not twenty-four, years, while his counterparts in the second category could do so in twenty-two, and those in the third in twenty-six years. For civil servants with elite or university educations, who often entered the bureaucracy at grades nine or ten, it became possible to reach hereditary noble status in as little as nine years, or before they reached the age of thirty.[56] To be eligible for such promotions, they needed to accomplish "some particular achievement on behalf of the service in administrative affairs, or demonstrate particular merit and achievement as an official."[57] One might expect that in a country where the Emperor preferred senior officials who were "not so much wise as service-oriented,"[58] and where he valued service longevity in making high-level appointments,[59] promotions for merit would have been relatively rare, but they came frequently enough, in fact, to encourage

14

ambitious young men to strive for them. Between 1847 and 1857 (the only decade during the first half of the nineteenth century for which we have information), the percentage of promotions for merit ranged between six and eighteen percent of the total. Certainly that was sufficient to give some encouragement to that minority of truly ambitious young men who entered the Table of Ranks at its lower levels, and a number of prominent statesmen of the 1860s and 1870s built their careers in just such a fashion.[60]

Of course advancement in the Russian bureaucracy was a considerably more complex matter than such raw statistical data indicate, and promotions for merit did not hinge only upon "some particular achievement in administrative affairs on behalf of the service" or "particular merit and achievement as an official." It was so well known to nineteenth-century Russians, for example, that an ambitious official could advance rapidly if he won the patronage of a high-ranking statesman that this became a recurring theme in the letters, diaries, even the *belles lettres,* of the period. "By the fortunate chance of drawing attention to oneself by a clever trick or by successful flattery, the careers of many [officials] in Russia are advanced," wrote one young army officer who had just come to St. Petersburg in the mid-1840s.[61] S. I. Zarudnyi, later to play an important part in drafting the Judicial Reform Statute of 1864, put the matter even more bluntly in a satirical essay when he concluded that, "if you have patronage, you will be considered a genius, able to undertake any task, and you will advance rapidly. But, if you do not have patronage, then you will be considered an utter fool, fit for nothing, and knowing nothing."[62]

Data for the mid-century make it clear that promotions for merit came far more frequently in certain agencies and that ambitious young civil servants obviously had better opportunities to advance their careers in some ministries than in others. At the top of the scale stood a group of elite ministries and central directorates where advancements for merit accounted for between thirty-five and one hundred percent of all promotions granted. These included (in descending order) the State Secretariat for the Affairs of the Grand Duchy of Finland (100%), the Chancery of the Committee of Ministers (51.5%), the Commission on Petitions (48.6%), the State Chancery (48.14%), His Majesty's Own Chancery (41.7%), the Ministry of Foreign Affairs (40.1%), and the State Secretariat for Polish Affairs (35.7%). Men who served in these agencies clearly comprised a privileged group, and their careers usually advanced rapidly, according to an elite pattern.

Below those elite agencies in which positions were obtained particularly as a consequence of birth or high influence stood a second group of ministries and directorates where merit promotions accounted for between twelve and seventeen percent of the total. These were the Ministry of State Domains (16.8%), the Office of the State Comptroller (14.7%), the Ministry of Internal Affairs (14.2%), and the Ministry of Justice (12.4%). Actually, the percentage of merit promotions for officials serving in the central offices of the Ministries of Internal Affairs, Justice, and State Domains must have been considerably greater than these raw data indicate because a very large portion of these agencies' personnel served in the provinces, where chances for merit promotions were very limited. Indeed, according to the annual reports of the *Inspektorskii Departament,* only 4.3% of the officials in the Ministry of Internal Affairs, 14.9% of the officials in the Ministry of Justice, and 22.5% of the officials in the Ministry of State Domains served in St. Petersburg, and it was they who received most of the promotions for merit.[63]

In Russia's remaining ministries, the portion of merit promotions was below ten percent. Clearly, these were not the agencies in which an energetic and ambitious young official would choose to serve, for in these, merit seems to have been rewarded only in rare instances.[64] Most important for our purposes, that fact seems to have led those young, ambitious officials who emerged as Russia's enlightened bureaucrats at mid-century to seek positions in the Ministries of Internal Affairs, State Domains, and Justice. Those who were less aggressive or less competent were content to allow their careers to advance more slowly by promotions for time served in grade in such agencies as the Ministry of Public Instruction, the Postal Department, and the Directorate of Roads and Public Buildings. Probably it is not mere coincidence that no cadres of enlightened bureaucrats emerged from those ministries in which seniority played the central role in career advancement.

In whatever ministry they were employed, and wherever they served in the Russian Empire, ambitious civil servants aspired to serve in the chanceries of the capital and, once they obtained a position, to remain there at all costs. St. Petersburg was the Empire's cultural center, and Russians served there to be near the heart of its cultural life as well as to be close to the glittering and opulent world of the Imperial family, prominent statesmen, and famous courtiers. The great brick and stone buildings of Peter's northern capital, their tall glass windows staring out upon wide avenues and canals, the city's cleanliness in comparison to other Russian urban centers, the rich array of goods in its shops, the elegant equipages that rolled along its boulevards, and, perhaps most of all, the chance of encountering some great lord, statesman, or even the Emperor in the street made St. Petersburg a fascinating place for newly arrived provincials.[65]

Besides these tangible attractions, Russia's capital exerted an almost magnetic pull upon men born and educated in the provinces, as M. E. Saltykov-Shchedrin, himself a civil servant of some considerable experience in St. Petersburg, later explained in his *Diary of a Provincial in St. Petersburg*:

> We provincials [he wrote] somehow turn our steps toward Petersburg instinctively. We may sit at home for days and months on end—and suddenly, we begin to move. . . . A person will be sitting around and suddenly, as if a light had dawned, he begins to pack his things. "You're going to Petersburg?"—"To Petersburg!" he replies. And that says all that needs to be said. It is as if Petersburg, all by itself, with its name, its streets, its fog, rain, and snow, could resolve something or shed some new light on something.[66]

Some years after he had come to the capital to serve in the Ministry of Internal Affairs' chancery, A. I. Artem'ev, a young statistician from Kazan, thought in similar terms when he confided to his diary that "I still do not understand very clearly why I came to St. Petersburg, for I had not one single acquaintance among the city's half-million inhabitants . . . and absolutely no patron whatsoever."[67] Again, it was the dream that radiated from Russia's great capital, the city so unlike any other in the Empire, that drew Artem'ev and the people Saltykov-Shchedrin described to it. Like most provincial Russians, they expected something new, different, and somehow better to happen in their lives once they reached it. At first, they were caught up in its magical aura, in that illusion which the novelist Nikolai Gogol, himself a provincial who had come to the capital, characterized so vividly in his early stories. "O, do not trust the Nevskii Prospekt!" he warned the readers of his tale that bore the great avenue's name. "Everything's an illusion. Everything's a dream. Everything's not what it seems!"[68]

For young civil servants who sought to make their way in St. Petersburg, the most illusory phantom of all was success itself. Artem'ev's retrospective wonderment at his youthful audacity in coming to the capital when he had no patron is especially understandable because patronage was doubly important to the success of any young man's career in St. Petersburg. So important was a patron's support that young Ivan Roskovshenko, who came to St. Petersburg from Kiev in 1831, went immediately to buy cloth for a new suit so that he would make the proper impression on those who might start him on his way. "I cannot yet appear before any of my future patrons," he lamented to a friend as he searched frantically for a way to earn enough to pay the tailor and collect his new clothes.[69]

Most would-be civil servants did not share Roskovshenko's good fortune to have the names of several senior officials to call on. Most had no patron and knew no influential men. Some carried deep within an inner pocket a precious slip of paper that bore the name of some third-hand acquaintance—a friend of a friend of a distant relative, perhaps—who, they hoped, might offer guidance or, perhaps, even a much-needed introduction. Failure was common. Many never found a position because even graduation from an elite school did not guarantee them a place in the bureaucracy. Graduation only conferred upon them the privilege of entering the civil service at a certain rank when, or if, they found a vacancy. Sometimes, fortuitous accident aided their search, as in the case of young Konstantin Veselovskii, who graduated first in his class at the Lyceum at Tsarskoe Selo and later became a noted member of the Imperial Academy of Sciences.

> One fine day in the fall of 1838 [Veselovskii recalled many years later], I found myself in the streets of St. Petersburg, all alone as if in a forest. I had no patrons and no useful acquaintances; there was not even anyone to offer advice. My entire circle of acquaint-ances was limited to my comrades from the Lyceum, who were just as inexperienced in practical matters as was I. . . . Knowing from gossip just how difficult it was to find a position without a patron's support . . . I decided that I stood a better chance in the . . . only recently established Ministry of State Domains, in which the right of occupying vacant positions could not as yet have been established by seniority.[70]

That a winner of the first-place gold medal in the Lyceum's final examinations should find himself in such a position after he had gradu-ated from the school whose avowed purpose was to train future Russian statesmen was one of countless absurd situations that plagued the Rus-sian bureaucracy in those years. Even more absurd, when they found a position, such talented young men needed a patron to raise them above the anonymous mass of low-ranking officials that filled St. Pe-tersburg's chanceries. There is no way to determine even approximately how much talent was lost to the Russian government because men of ability failed to find positions or did not win the attention of some senior official. Certainly, the loss may have been considerable, and it was openly regretted by at least one of the progressive statesmen who served Alexander II during the Great Reform Era.[71]

Added to the difficulties of finding positions and patrons, the exorbitant cost of living in St. Petersburg was the most ubiquitous problem that civil servants faced. During the 1830s and 1840s, the most modest lodgings cost from ten to fifteen silver rubles a month, so that even if several shared a small flat, the cost to each still was high.[72] Food consumed an equally large portion of the young officials' meager salaries because lodgings which rented for under twenty rubles a month usually had no kitchens. Many young officials took their meals in inexpensive eating houses *(kukhmisterskie)*, but the cost of approximately seven silver rubles a month was so high that three junior civil servants often pooled their resources to purchase two monthly meal tickets and then shared the meals. Those who could not afford even that sum took their meals with private families whose poverty made them willing to share their humble fare with strangers in return for the few kopeks they received for meals that were neither nourishing nor palatable.[73]

Throughout the Nicholas era, tsarist statesmen treated the rank and file civil officials who staffed Russia's government offices as a sort of clerical proletariat who were not expected to live comfortably or even decently. To understand better the burden that St. Petersburg's high cost of living placed on this growing army of impoverished civil servants, we should look for a moment at the salaries they received. According to the surprisingly accurate records maintained by the *Inspektorskii Departament,* which functioned as a sort of oversight bureau for the civil service during the last decade of Nicholas's reign, almost ninety percent of Russia's officials received salaries that were too low to provide even a modest standard of living. In 1847, the average monthly salary earned by St. Petersburg civil servants (including food and housing allowances for which many lesser officials did not qualify) was 67.8 rubles. Such a sum hardly seems generous, but it becomes significantly lower when we take into account that such calculations are inflated by the unusually high average monthly salaries (ranging from 120 to 238 rubles) that were paid to officials in His Majesty's Own Chancery, the State Chancery, and the State Secretariats for Polish and Finnish Affairs. Average monthly salaries and allowances in most ministries were well below 67 rubles, and, in the Ministry of Justice, it stood at the truly miserly level of 37 rubles 10 kopeks, a figure that actually declined during the next decade.[74] Lesser officials received well below the average, since it was a fact of life in the Russian bureaucracy that senior statesmen received princely salaries ranging up to as much as 16,000 rubles a year.[75]

Complaints confided to diaries, letters, and memoirs confirm the gloomy picture of penury presented by these impersonal statistics, and it seems that it was not at all unusual for a junior civil servant to earn a monthly salary of less than twenty silver rubles.[76] Of course, poor salaries for young men who were learning a trade or business were the rule in western Europe and the United States at the same time, but it was a premium that many were willing to pay in return for the chance at greater rewards later on. In Russia, young officials could not consider their low salaries as mere poorly paid short-term apprenticeships because many years often passed before their ranks and salaries allowed them even a passable standard of living. The question of wages and prices in St. Petersburg at this time still remains largely unexplored, but the limited evidence suggests that it was not until an official reached the position of *stolonachal'nik* (chief of an office section) that he even had a modest hope of living in moderate comfort.[77] Yet it was more a hope than a certainty, for even a *stolonachal'nik* could not live comfortably on his regular monthly salary of approximately 60 rubles plus food and housing allowances, and it was necessary for him to come close to doubling that income to be assured of a comfortable standard of living.[78]

Officials' pressing need to supplement their salaries made corruption and bribe-taking a certainty. Of course, it is now no secret that many Russian officials thought it no sin to accept bribes as a means to raise their salaries. But it is important to remember that bribes supplemented the salaries mainly of officials whose incomes already were well above the subsistence level, not those for whom even a few additional rubles could have made a critical difference in their way of life, because low-level bureaucrats could provide very little in the way of services. Those who had limited access to bribes, or were perhaps too honest to accept them, had to augment their meager incomes in other ways. Writing for literary, scholarly, and technical journals was a source of income that sustained a number of the progressive young men whose careers, ideas, and political methods we shall examine at greater length in subsequent chapters. It was no accident that the Ministries of State Domains, Public Instruction, and Internal Affairs began to publish official journals during the Nicholas era or that during the 1840s senior officials used these journals as a means to supplement the salaries of talented young bureaucrats who served in their departments. Several of the men who stood in the ranks of the enlightened bureaucrats or were closely associated with them in the 1850s and 1860s used their editorship of these journals as a means for developing effective networks of influence within the central bureaucracy during the 1830s and 1840s.[79]

Drab, poor, and lonely though their lives were, the majority of St. Petersburg's clerkish legions were convinced that their daily labors were worthwhile and important. "I believed so absolutely in the usefulness of such office work," one official recalled, "that each new document we produced seemed to me to be a new current of benevolence flowing from

Caricature of a government office, from A. Agin's illustrations of Gogol's Dead Souls

[our office near] Chernyshev Bridge into the vastness of Russia."[80] If such sentiments had expressed a conviction that civil servants were capable of exercising a positive influence on Russian life, they would have been commendable. To Russia's misfortune, they articulated only a groundless faith in the efficacy of bureaucratic measures, and a belief that form and routine in themselves could achieve positive ends. At best it was a misplaced hope; at worst, it perpetuated the myth of Russia's benevolent bureaucracy. "Just look at the annual reports [prepared by each ministry and directorate]," Valuev exclaimed in disgust. "Everywhere, everything possible has been done. Everywhere success has been achieved. Everywhere the prescribed order is being established, if not immediately, then at least gradually.... On the surface it all seems splendid, but it is rotting away underneath." It all was part of an attempt, Valuev concluded, to "perpetuate the official lie" that the bureaucracy was working energetically to achieve real and positive benefits for the nation.[81]

Contrary to so many bureaucrats' image of themselves, it probably would not be an overstatement to say that the official who spent a portion of his day working on a matter of some real significance was the exception rather than the rule. At all levels of the central government, civil servants dedicated countless hours to trivial forms and regulations. Even in the State Council, very minor issues—for example, irregularities in the records of a provincial court or the release from service of a minor bureaucrat who had falsified his residence permit—absorbed the attention of high officials who should have thought about far more important matters.[82] Outside the State Council, a single example can illustrate how absurdly time-consuming even the most routine procedures had become during the Nicholas era if we remember that whenever a nobleman put a piece of land up for sale, the bureaucracy at the central and local levels produced at least 1,351 separate documents.[83]

Of course paperwork did not increase in the Russian bureaucracy only because officials hoped to create work with which to occupy their time, although that was a factor. As Minister of Internal Affairs L. A. Perovskii pointed out in one of his reports, a number of regulations and procedures had been implemented during the previous quarter-century in an effort to reduce bureaucrats' despotic treatment of the people they were supposed to serve.[84] This effort had gone too far, Perovskii hastened to add, and the entire administrative process had become burdened by "difficulties resulting from the never-ending increase of official files and papers."[85] By mid-century, files of official papers were piling up in St. Petersburg's chanceries at such a rate that agencies had to establish procedures for destroying them in order to make room for the new ones their officials were producing. "Here in Russia, the most simple and inconsequential matter, which is dealt with by the stroke of a pen elsewhere, generates a whole series of official papers: inquiries, communications, and applications," the noted economist L. V. Tengoborskii wrote in a secret memorandum. "Records and letters seem to reproduce themselves, one might say, in geometrical proportions."[86]

This paper avalanche caused many officials to see administration in terms of producing documents rather than solving important problems.

Most of all, these officials developed mechanistic responses to the situations they confronted, as Mikhail Veselovskii, a young civil servant who found a position in the Petersburg office of the Ministry of Internal Affairs after serving for a number of years in the provinces, later recalled.

> The administrative machine functioned with irreproachable harmony and elegance of detail [he wrote]. Officials believed in the usefulness of their work and loved it for itself alone. It was enough simply to look at the Director of the Department of General Affairs, A. A. Gvodzev, to gain some insight into the quintessence of St. Petersburg's elegant and majestic official world. When he, elegant, freshly shaven, and perfumed, entered the reception chamber . . . and approached those subordinates and petitioners who awaited him, it was impossible to tear one's eyes away from the elastic, undulating movements of his body. Depending on to whom he was speaking, he resembled either the awe-inspiring countenance of Jupiter or the fawning figure of an enchantress seeking to curry favor.[87]

In this world of petitions, applications, inquiries, and reports, the production of documents became an important criterion by which civil servants measured their importance against their rivals. To make certain that senior officials would call on them to prepare important documents, ambitious chancery scribes and junior officials labored to make their handwriting elegant, embellished reports with eye-catching designs, and even on occasion added charts hand-tinted with watercolors.[88] Even the shade of ink was important, and superiors often ordered scribes whose ink was too faint, or who failed to space the lines of the text with absolute precision, to copy documents again and again.[89]

Extreme emphasis upon form over content thus seriously hindered the business of administration in the Russian Empire. Even though he had a hand in creating the problem,[90] Minister of Internal Affairs Perovskii was very candid in pointing out that forms and regulations were beginning to paralyze the bureaucracy. "Endless correspondence absorbs all the attention and energy of men who are supposed to execute policy, and, instead of true supervision and administration, we have, for the most part, only record-keeping and accounting for documents," he reported to the Emperor in 1851.[91] Yet overriding concern with unimportant matters was only part of a larger problem that was made much worse by the central offices' frequent "urgent" requests for information from other agencies. St. Petersburg officials often labeled requests for information as urgent because anything sent through normal channels moved with such glacial slowness that, according to at least one account, even the Emperor had to wait for four or five months for offices in the capital to reply to some of his routine requests.[92] Because each agency had its own prescribed form in which replies to "urgent" requests had to be submitted, each had to be dealt with separately, even though there was a great amount of duplication. Perovskii was amazed to find that his own ministry dealt with more than 165,000 "urgent" requests every year and was even more appalled to learn that a very substantial number were for nothing more than information needed to bring officials' personal service records up to date.[93] Because civil servants had to set all else aside to deal with such "urgent" requests, Perovskii found that questions of real substance and importance sometimes were set aside for years while officials labored to keep abreast of the endless routine matters that flooded into their offices.[94] Even the most diligent efforts to stem this tide seemed doomed. One recent study estimates that as many as 3,300,000 requests and decrees still awaited action in the early 1840s.[95]

Not only was the St. Petersburg bureaucracy slow to respond to requests for information, and even slower to implement new administrative policies, but the accuracy of its reports was marred because officials often reported only what they thought their superiors wanted to hear. Particularly after 1850, when senior bureaucrats received absolute and arbitrary power to remove subordinates from office, lower-ranking civil servants lived in fear of arousing their displeasure and tempered their memoranda accordingly.[96] A. I. Artem'ev admitted as much in 1855, but he confided his frustrations only to the pages of a diary where they remained hidden for more than a century. "If only one line of my lengthy report [about the Old Believers] could be thought of as fully satisfying, deserving of consideration, and persuasive, I would be content," he lamented. "But there are so many misgivings and doubts," he continued. "In all good conscience, I ought not to be silent ... but they [his superiors] can wipe me from the face of the earth. And thus," he confessed, "from necessity, one remains silent."[97] Artem'ev wrote about an area of Russian experience that was sensitive in both political and religious terms, and he obviously felt the need for caution. Yet his fear of reporting accurately the facts that contradicted what his superiors wanted to hear seems to have been the rule, not the exception. Even a decade later, A. V. Golovnin remarked on similar problems at the ministerial level and noted that no one wanted to report bad news to the Emperor for fear of losing his position.[98]

Underpaid, poorly educated officials who were overwhelmed by the endless petty routines that Russia's formalistic bureaucratic system imposed upon them made long-term administration difficult and the chances for effective transformation remote. Yet the myriad and complex problems Russia faced during the Nicholas era needed to be confronted and solutions considered, at least in terms of renovating the existing order, if not its full-fledged reform. There is no need to list here the economic, social, and political difficulties that Russia faced at the time, for these now are well known and often commented upon.[99] But to Russians living during the Nicholas era, the gravity of the problems was far less obvious and the apparent solutions not very complex. Daniel Orlovsky pointed out recently that during the 1860s and 1870s, bureaucratic reformers in the Ministry of Internal Affairs found it "easier to co-opt social groups or institutions into the bureaucratic system they understood best than to identify and eliminate deeper causes of problems."[100] For the senior statesmen who served Nicholas I, the issues at first seemed even less complex, and the problems seemed to have no deeper causes. Convinced as they were that politics lay fully within the realm of administration, and that all political action therefore must be confined within the chanceries of St. Petersburg, these statesmen saw renovation in terms of careful administrative adjustment. In their view, the political instruments of autocracy were well conceived and structurally sound. All that was needed, they thought, was to adjust the machinery of government so that everywhere it would function with that "irreproachable harmony and elegance of detail" that so entranced young Mikhail Veselovskii when he first witnessed the workings of Gvozdev's Department of General Affairs at mid-century. For senior officials of the 1830s and 1840s, the dilemmas Russia faced could best be resolved by adjusting bureaucratic instruments of authority so that they could serve all the functions that their creators had entrusted to them at the beginning of the century.

Adjusting Bureaucratic Instruments of Authority

Not long after Paul I's assassination in 1801, Alexander I's close friend and frequent confidant Count Pavel Stroganov insisted that the superior sensibility and understanding of the Emperor's most intimate advisers should "stand in the same relationship to our body politic as does the art of a physician to the healing of illness."[101] Among Alexander's Young Friends, who formed the so-called "Unofficial Committee" at the beginning of his reign and endeavored to realize Stroganov's vision as Imperial advisers, efforts at administrative reorganization and reform were a response to the political pressures they confronted in the decade after the French Revolution, to the psychological and intellectual crisis that accompanied their rise to power, and to the administrative and institutional dilemmas the Russian state had faced during the last quarter of the eighteenth century. These pressures were intensified by the manner in which they had encountered the ideas of the Enlightenment on the eve of the French Revolution. Close family ties had been absent from their childhood and adolescent experiences, and they had turned to the writings of the late Enlightenment and early sentimentalism in the absence of any traditional environment from which to draw their beliefs and values.[102] From these works they drew their ideals about life, service, and reform. They therefore came to maturity in a European cultural and intellectual world that combined those very elements of middle-class thought and aristocratic life that the French Revolution had so recently proved incompatible.

The views held by Alexander and his Young Friends embodied both authoritarian and libertarian elements, and the authoritarian strand was quickly strengthened at the expense of the libertarian one. Perhaps most important, Paul I's dynastic legislation had proclaimed self-preservation to be a major mission of autocracy, and that set the course which Alexander and his Young Friends chose to follow.[103] Their choice of the authoritarian elements of Enlightenment thought led them to defend autocratic power rather than impose upon it those limits advocated by the teachings of such mentors as the Tsar's famous Swiss tutor LaHarpe, and, in the ministerial reform of 1802, they therefore endeavored to allocate administrative functions to various ministries in a more rational manner without infringing upon the autocrat's power.[104] In contrast to their predecessors in Peter the Great's administrative colleges, ministers were endowed with increased monocratic authority, but it could be exercised only in the realm of administration that lay beyond that encompassed by the Emperor's personal purview.

Alexander and his Young Friends thus combined the monocratic principle and the institutional precepts established by Paul I with their interpretation of Enlightenment thought to produce more rational allocations of administrative function which, although they vested ministers with greater monocratic authority, did not threaten the power and pre-eminence of the autocrat.[105] The nature and character of this achievement often have been obscured by undue emphasis on the "constitutionalism" of Alexander and his Young Friends and, especially, by historians' efforts to define that phenomenon in western liberal terms. Certainly Alexander and his associates used the term "constitution" in their writings and discussions about state affairs, but, as Marc Raeff has shown in his thoughtful and convincing analysis of the problem, the term held a very different meaning for them than it did for their western contemporaries. Alexander and his Young Friends therefore spoke and wrote in western terms, but, like Catherine II before them, they gave these terms meaning in the context of Russian, not European, experience. For them, the division of powers, a sacred element in the English and American constitutions, meant division of functions for the purpose of achieving an efficient state administration. The ideal to be achieved was a finely tuned machinery of administration that would govern the Russian Empire in an efficient and orderly fashion on the basis of precise regulations and laws.[106] To attain that goal, they agreed that the unlimited and undivided power of the autocrat must be preserved. In the established Russian political and administrative tradition, ministers, therefore, were to serve as the Emperor's personal agents, endowed with his personal commission *(poruchenie)* to assume specific responsibilities.

As they emerged in the early years of Alexander's reign, Russia's central administrative institutions thus were conceived to serve as extensions of the ruler's personal will. Stroganov insisted that it must be the Tsar's benevolent activity, "limited only by the principles of natural justice and universal morality" and extended throughout the state administration by his agents, Russia's ministers, that could ensure efficiency in directing the Empire's domestic affairs.[107] Yet the area of responsibility for which each minister was personally responsible was too broad to be controlled by his personal supervision. If the Emperor was to achieve his constitutional aim of creating a finely tuned administrative apparatus free from bureaucratic tyranny, it was necessary to establish procedures that would control the behavior of officials and guarantee that they functioned as he and his ministers wished. Ideally, this meant depersonalizing the Empire's central bureaucratic instruments to emphasize administration by institutions governed by regulations rather than by officials functioning under the Emperor's traditional personal commission. This effort was primarily the work of one of nineteenth-century Russia's greatest statesmen, M. M. Speranskii, who set out to redefine Russia's new ministerial system toward the end of Alexander's first decade on the throne.

Mikhail Mikhailovich Speranskii, son of a village priest, was born on January 1, 1772, and educated at the Aleksandro-Nevskii Seminary in St. Petersburg. He was appointed to the Seminary's faculty in 1792, but left it four years later to become the personal secretary of Prince A. B. Kurakin, the man whom Paul I appointed to the powerful position of *General-Prokuror* soon after his accession. As Kurakin's secretary, Speranskii gained administrative training at the highest levels of Russia's government, and he broadened his experience in the early nineteenth century as an assistant to D. P. Troshchinskii in the Senate, and then as a member of the staff of V. P. Kochubei, one of the Young Friends, who become Russia's first Minister of Internal Affairs. In mid-1803, Speranskii assisted Kochubei in drafting a full-scale

Nicholas I

M. M. Speranskii

structural organization of the new ministry along monocratic lines, and that served as the model for his proposals to reform the entire ministerial system less than a decade later.[108] Speranskii and Kochubei argued that a hierarchical organization of authority and responsibility was essential to the proper functioning of Russia's central administrative apparatus and regarded its absence as the most critical weakness in Russia's new central administration because it left the minister responsible for deciding even the most trivial questions. A rationally arranged chain of administrative authority throughout the ministry's structure, where each level in the hierarchy would have its own area of activity "to direct and be answerable for," could remedy that defect, they insisted, because lesser issues could be resolved in the course of their ascent upward through the administrative chain of command.[109]

Speranskii's opportunity to redefine the structure of Russia's central administration came after he became Alexander's leading adviser on questions of domestic reform and administration, and his General Statute on Ministries, published on June 23, 1811, served as the constitutional basis for Russia's central administration until January 1906. As such, it introduced into the Empire's ministerial system those hierarchical principles he considered so essential to the proper functioning of bureaucracy, but, although he sought to establish that division of function and delegation of authority characteristic of a modern bureaucratic structure, he subordinated Russia's new ministers to the autocrat so that they could function only as agents empowered to act by virtue of his personal commission. "Ministries represent the institutions by means of which the Supreme Executive Power acts upon all parts of the administration," the statute decreed. "All ministers are directly subordinate to the Supreme Power in all their activities," and "the essence of the power entrusted to ministers belongs exclusively to the executive catetory. Absolutely no law, statute, or any changes of those in existence," the new statute continued, "can be instituted by the authority of a minister. . . . The relationship of ministers to the Legislative Power consists in the fact that they can make recommendations about the need for a new law or statute or recommend changes in existing ones."[110]

This complete subordination of ministers to the autocrat, although fully in keeping with Russia's administrative and political tradition, carried within it the seeds of some of the most serious difficulties that the Empire's administration encountered during the next century. Most important, the principle of complete subordination to higher authority was extended further down in the bureaucracy, and during the reign of Nicholas I, this produced an exorbitant degree of formalism that seriously impeded effective administration, even though this sort of bureaucratic paralysis had not been Speranskii's intention. He had, in fact, championed a rational allocation of function and responsibility precisely to avoid such problems, but the basis for excessive formalism remained in his 1811 General Statute, not only because ministers were subjected to the authority of the autocrat but because Speranskii proposed no effective measures to overcome the tradition of complete subordination to higher authority within the ministries themselves. As the Statute specified, "the separation of various areas of administration within the ministries does not constitute the division of administration itself, for this, by its very nature, must always remain monocratic."[111] Within the context of Russian administrative tradition and practice, this meant that the authority of ministers over subordinate agencies became a reflection of that same power that the autocrat exercised over his ministers themselves, and, in the context of Russian administrative tradition, this power was by nature capricious and arbitrary. This became far more apparent during the Nicholaean era when, as a result of the Emperor's efforts to impose military characteristics upon his civil servants, the nature of such power became even more personalized. Speranskii's notion of administrative institutions governed by impersonal regulations thus rapidly gave way to administration predicated on caprice, and in further efforts to adjust Russia's instruments of authority to function more efficiently and effectively, Nicholas and his senior advisers personalized the nature of power even further. Continual surveillance was the means that Nicholas used to ascertain the state of his "command," and his ministers, many of them military men themselves, followed his example.

In contrast to Alexander's Young Friends, the minister-adjutants who served Nicholas I held a far more modest view of their role in policy-making and administration. Their perceptions of what their best efforts might reasonably achieve were more limited, and they saw themselves not as Stroganov's master physicians summoned to cure their nation's ills but as technicians called upon to adjust bureaucratic instruments that were fundamentally sound. Nevertheless, they expected to improve the ability of those instruments to respond to their nation's needs as they perceived them, and they set out to recruit better-educated and more talented young officials to staff their ministries. At the same time, they set out to refine the workings of their agencies with a confidence born of the belief that more precise regulation and supervision could make the bureaucracy as a whole operate more efficiently. "Each agency had to direct its attention to refining the manner in which it functioned," one eyewitness wrote. "Beginning in the 1830s, every department concentrated upon improvements . . . in the details of its internal administrative apparatus."[112]

Three of Nicholas's leading ministers were especially important in supporting that unique combination of talented officials dedicated to the ideal of effective administration from which Russia's enlightened bureaucracy emerged at mid-century. Minister of State Domains Count P. D. Kiselev, Minister of Internal Affairs Count L. A. Perovskii, and Minister of Justice Count V. N. Panin all served as living testimony to their Emperor's principles as they labored to reshape their agencies to reflect their shared creed of service, duty, and devotion to their Emperor. These men saw a beneficient paternalism in Minister of Public Instruction Uvarov's famous precepts of Orthodoxy, Autocracy, and Nationality, and they were convinced that, if properly applied, these would produce the best form of administration for the Empire. In sharp contrast to Russia's emerging radical intelligentsia, these statesmen confidently accepted the assumptions that underlay the Nicholas system and saw it as their main task to make their Emperor's vision of a service-state a reality. Although they all dedicated their lives to the Tsar's service, none remained constant to his principles for a longer time than did Pavel Dmitrievich Kiselev, whose career as a cavalry general, Imperial aide-de-camp, Minister of State Domains, and ambassador to France spanned more than a half-century. A dashing cavalry officer, Kiselev became an astute statesman and a courtly diplomat who possessed the rare ability to win the affection of men and command their best efforts on behalf of his Imperial masters.[113] "He is the favorite, most fashionable [salon] guest among all our great lords and, when he is in a good frame of mind, he is without doubt the most charming," remarked one courtier in the mid-1830s.[114]

As the eldest son of one of Moscow's most prominent noble families, Kiselev was groomed from early childhood for a career in Russia's service. Like most of his peers, he studied at home with a French tutor, and his mother, an Urusov princess, broadened his education by inviting some of Moscow's most talented writers and poets into her home. Among the intellectual and cultural elite who assembled at the Kiselev townhouse on Moscow's elegant Tverskaia were Karamzin and Ivan Dmitriev, as well as the young poets Aleksandr Turgenev and Prince P. A. Viazemskii, who became Kiselev's friends and shared with him their adolescent, sentimentalist dreams.[115] For most of them, such ideals made it possible as adults to accept the faults of the real world and divorce their feelings, thoughts, and inner spiritual lives from their duties as Russian officials. As we shall see further on, this became especially important in the experience of Count Panin, but, for Kiselev, sentimentalism was tempered by other influences which led him to view the process of change in more aggressive terms from the moment he chose to join the army rather than the foreign or civil service as had several of his closest friends.

Kiselev entered Russia's army as a cadet in January 1805 to serve on the staff of Quartermaster General Prince D. P. Volkonskii in St. Petersburg.[116] Soon he transferred to the Chevalier Guards and became part of an elite group of young noblemen who rose to high positions during the reign of Nicholas I. Most prominent were captain A. I. Chernyshev, later Minister of War (1827–1852), and staff captain V. V. Levashov, future president of the State Council's Department of State Economy (1839–1848) and president of the Committee of Ministers (1847–1848). They fought as comrades against Napoleon in 1807, and the shared dangers bound them for the rest of their lives. During the short years of peace that followed the Treaty of Tilsit, Prince A. S. Menshikov and A. F. Orlov joined their company. Together they prospered until they came to share places in the inner circles of the Tsar's advisers two decades later.[117] Kiselev thus quickly laid the foundations for a brilliant career; then, during Napoleon's invasion of 1812, he won the recognition that inspired Alexander I to name him an aide-de-camp and a general before he reached thirty.

Kiselev's first practical experience as a reformer came during the last decade of Alexander's reign when he transformed Russia's crumbling Second Army into a disciplined military force capable of defending the Empire's southern frontier, and this indicated the direction his views would take during the next quarter-century. Simplified administrative functions and centralized instruments of authority, he insisted, were the keys to his success.[118] At the same time, his readings of Chateaubriand, Benjamin Constant, Jeremy Bentham, and Adam Smith reinforced his caution in approaching social and economic renovation.[119] Beginning with a memorandum about serfdom in 1816, he urged Russia to begin a program of gradual social and economic change to prevent revolutionary upheavals from forcing such a course upon her.[120]

Although Kiselev's reform of the Second Army was a notable achievement for a young general, Nicholas imposed far more complex burdens upon him when he named him Plenipotentiary President of the Divans of Moldavia and Wallachia in the fall of 1829.[121] As Plenipotentiary President, Kiselev's task was the administrative, political, and economic renovation of a region plagued by corrupt police and oppressive lords whose serfs bore a yoke unequalled anywhere in Europe.[122] The difficulties proved too great and Kiselev's experience too limited, for he moved too quickly and on the basis of too little accurate information. In large measure, he failed, but his attempt convinced him that hard data and an expert understanding of the problems to be resolved were the most important prerequisites for effective administration and successful reform.[123] This conviction lay at the center of his views throughout his years as Russia's first Minister of State Domains. Again and again, he impressed this upon his subordinates, with important consequences for the future course of their efforts at social and economic renovation in Russia. From Kiselev's early insistence that policy decisions be based on accurate data evolved a broader movement in the Ministries of State Domains and Internal Affairs to expand the quantity of statistical information available to Russian statesmen.

Although Kiselev's efforts to lessen the burdens borne by the serfs in Wallachia and Moldavia were far from successful, they brought him to the Emperor's attention as a young statesman whose views on peasant reform might apply in Russia itself. "The thing most necessary of all for our Motherland," Kiselev insisted, "is the publication of an organic law which can equitably and precisely define the rights and obligations of serf-owning lords and tillers of the soil. All sensitive people recognize that it is necessary to provide institutions and guarantees for these millions of people before they get the idea of demanding them themselves."[124] Nicholas soon gave him an opportunity to test these precepts. "You will be my Chief of Staff for Peasant Affairs," he told him on February 17, 1836, when he named him head of the newly created Fifth Section of His Majesty's Own Chancery.[125]

The Emperor's decision to create the Fifth Section and to appoint Kiselev his Chief of Staff for Peasant Affairs stemmed from the failure of several secret committees to recommend ways for improving the conditions under which Russia's peasants lived.[126] Having failed to resolve this broader issue, Nicholas turned to improve the economic position of peasants living on state lands—the so-called *gosudarstvennye krest'iane*—in an effort to set an example that the nobility might be induced to follow.[127] As Chief of the Fifth Section and, after December 1837, as Minister of State Domains,[128] Kiselev tried to define the obligations between the *gosudarstvennye krest'iane* and the Imperial treasury in law rather than custom. At the same time, he set out to establish an efficient administration to deal with their affairs. Unlike his Imperial master, Kiselev shared Speranskii's opinion that rationally designed institutions held the key to effective administration, and he was certain that proper adjustments in bureaucratic instruments of authority would, by definition, better the economic position of Russia's state peasant communities.[129]

Kiselev insisted that change and reform could be initiated only at the center of the Imperial administration because "in Russia, nothing can be undertaken or completed without the leadership of the government."[130] Yet he was convinced that it was first necessary to assess economic and social conditions among the state peasants and judge the effectiveness of the state's administrative instruments if his ministry were to draft workable legislation. Therefore, he journeyed into the provinces to study these questions himself and, as a consequence of his on-the-scene investigations, urged a complete reversal in the state's attitude toward the peasant commune. Earlier in the century, Speranskii, Minister of Finance Kankrin, and several other prominent statesmen had urged the abolition of this fundamental unit of peasant society and administration in the Empire.[131] Kiselev now argued that the commune must be preserved as an instrument for strengthening state administration and control in the countryside if the government hoped to halt social and economic decay among its peasants.[132]

Initial investigations led Kiselev to a number of important conclusions but also convinced him that similar studies were needed for all provinces before an effective renovation of state peasant affairs could be undertaken. Between 1836 and 1840, he sent his "adjutants" (in this case agents of special commissions) into forty-seven Russian provinces, and, throughout his tenure, he commissioned further studies so that the central administration could respond more effectively to local conditions.[133] To undertake this task, and to establish the proper institutional base in St. Petersburg, he had to staff an entire new ministry with officials who were capable of initiative and the sort of independent judgment that usually was not found among Russian bureaucrats. Kiselev needed well-educated officials who had not yet become mired in the procedures and traditions of Russia's central administration, and he attempted to entice them from other agencies with promises of promotions, higher salaries, and opportunities to participate in policy-making decisions, even though such were, of necessity, limited to administrative issues. At the same time, he recruited new graduates from Russia's elite schools and universities.[134] He thus became the first of Nicholas's ministers to assemble those cadres whose ranks yielded up an enlightened bureaucracy at mid-century.

Kiselev's example soon was emulated by the man whom Nicholas appointed as Minister of Internal Affairs in September 1841. Lev Alekseevich Perovskii was born the son of Count A. K. Razumovskii's mistress on September 9, 1792. Like his half-brothers Nikolai and Vladimir, he was reared at the home of an aunt where he received a first-rate education from Razumovskii's chosen tutors, because the Count was determined to see his offspring well placed in Russia's service despite the circumstances of their birth.[135] Before his appointment as Russia's second Minister of Public Instruction in 1810, Count Razumovskii served as Rector of Moscow University, and it was while he held that post that Lev Alekseevich studied there. He too was touched by the sentimentalist currents so cherished by educated Moscow society, but, like Kiselev, he followed a military career while such Moscow friends as Dmitrii Bludov and S. S. Uvarov chose to serve in the elite Moscow Archive of the College of Foreign Affairs, where they could pursue their literary interests more readily. During Napoleon's invasion, Perovskii fought at Borodino, Malo-Iaroslavets, Lützen, and Leipzig. As a captain on the Guards General Staff in early 1815, he was wounded during the Hundred Days' campaign, recovered, and returned to Russia to become Chief Quartermaster of the Moscow Guards Division. He was one of the founders of the Union of Welfare in 1818, but resigned when its members chose revolution over reform in 1821.

Perovskii exchanged his military career for one in the Court and civil service when he exchanged his colonel's rank for that of a *statskii sovetnik* in the College of Foreign Affairs late in 1823. Some three years later, he transferred to the Department of Crown Lands of the Ministry of the Imperial Court, served as its vice-president until late 1840, as Deputy Minister of Crown Lands until 1852, and as Minister of Crown Lands until his death in 1856. During most of his tenure as Deputy Minister of Crown Lands, he also served as one of the most able Ministers of Internal Affairs to appear during the first half of the nineteenth century.[136]

The Department of Crown Lands administered the personal estates of the Imperial family, which held just under 600,000 male peasants at the time of Perovskii's transfer.[137] Because the income from these estates was designated for the private use of the Imperial family, their administration was a matter of direct personal concern to the Emperor, and that gave Perovskii an unparalleled opportunity to display his abilities as an administrator before Nicholas I himself. He launched a series

L. A. Perovskii   *P. D. Kiselev*

of reforms that more than doubled the direct income from Crown Lands in the quarter-century between 1820 and 1845 and, as a result, quickly established his reputation as a brilliant administrator.[138] His most important and innovative effort came in 1829, when he shifted the Department's basis of taxation from a levy on all male peasants (as had been applied to all privately owned serfs, state peasants, and Crown peasants since the reign of Peter the Great) to a system of rent dues based on the quality of the land they tilled. Perovskii's reform not only impressed Nicholas, but it became a model for the broadly reformed tax collection program that Kiselev and his subordinates implemented in the 1840s.[139]

Although a large responsibility (the Department of Crown Lands administered about five times as much land and peasants as did Russia's greatest serf-owners, the Sheremet'evs), Perovskii's department dealt with only about ten percent as much land and peasants as did Kiselev's new Ministry of State Domains in 1840.[140] Accustomed to smaller, more manageable administrative units, Perovskii suddenly confronted the vast operation of Russia's largest and most complex ministry when Nicholas appointed him Minister of Internal Affairs in 1841. From the first, he was appalled by the manner in which trivial duties sapped the energies of Russia's senior officials in capital and province alike. "The mechanical work of correspondence alone," he wrote in 1843, "surpasses the physical capabilities of the central offices of the provincial administration . . . and formalism devours the true essence of any administrative question." In his view, "all official correspondence ought to be merely the result of [a governor's] activity, not the main focus of it."[141] Yet he could do little to stem the tide. During his first year in office, the Ministry of Internal Affairs received and sent out a total of 22,326,842 separate documents; less than a decade later that figure had increased by more than forty percent, to 31,103,676.[142]

If he suffered defeat in his campaign against wasteful paperwork and useless formalities, Perovskii had more success in improving the manner in which his ministry functioned. First, he created a special chancellery to take on the flood of routine paperwork, and he soon extended that instrument to the offices of provincial governors and to all other central departments in his ministry. Assistant governors and deputy directors, he hoped, could free department directors and provincial governors from the pressures of routine administration so that they could become more directly involved in making policy. Together, he hoped that these officials could serve as a power base from which administrative reforms could be generated.[143]

Like the Emperor, Perovskii used his special chancellery as an extension of his administrative *persona* and therefore appointed to it men who held his closest confidence. Most important was the philologist V. I. Dal', his assistant in the Department of Crown Lands, whom he brought to the Ministry of Internal Affairs to head his special chancellery. Perovskii spoke of Dal' as his right hand and entrusted to him many tasks that Imperial ministers customarily reserved for their personal attention.[144] In doing so, he delegated responsibility more boldly than did most of his ministerial colleagues, and he extended the principles involved in that appointment much further downward in his ministry than they dared. Like Kiselev, he recruited well-educated young officials and drew them from a much wider variety of sources, including political exiles, recent graduates from elite schools and universities, university professors themselves, and men of established literary reputations.[145] Once they proved themselves, Perovskii gave these young men rare responsibilities for formulating policy and legislation, even though some of them were not yet out of their twenties. Under his tutelage, a number of prominent reformers of the 1860s gained their first practical experience with Russia's autocratic legislative process.

Like their Emperor, Kiselev and Perovskii continued to reserve all "command decisions" to themselves during the late 1830s and 1840s, but they used their ministries' departments to generate administrative policy in a manner unknown in Russia's bureaucracy at the time. In doing so, they established an institutional base that proved capable of broader effort at renovation some two decades later. Yet if the Russian bureaucracy was to find any significant success at the level of policy implementation, it needed far greater efficiency than it enjoyed during the first quarter of the nineteenth century. Count V. N. Panin, who became Russia's Minister of Justice in 1840, stressed "firm precision" in administration, even more than did Kiselev or Perovskii. He demanded subordination rather than encouraging independence, but his effort to make the Ministry of Justice function as a precise, efficient administrative instrument became an important factor in developing those administrative cadres from which Russia's enlightened bureaucracy emerged.[146]

Born in Moscow on March 28, 1801, Count Viktor Nikitich Panin came from a family whose stubborn arrogance had brought them disfavor, disgrace, and exile during the latter years of the eighteenth century, and he was acutely conscious that his ancestors' independent views had gotten them into trouble. As one scholar noted recently, Panin "went through life burdened by the sense that he had inherited a disgrace ordained for disobedience."[147] As a result, subordination to authority became the central element in his code of behavior. Panin obeyed his father, his teachers, and his superiors. Most of all, he obeyed his master, the Emperor. While the loyalty of Kiselev and Perovskii to their Emperor stemmed from their convictions as senior army officers, Panin's was born of the equally firm obedience of a Prussian Junker for, although Russian by birth, he became Prussian in manner and belief. "Because of my oath of allegiance," he once told Grand Duke Konstantin Nikolaevich, "I consider myself bound first of all to learn the views of my Emperor. If the Emperor has a view different from mine, then I consider it my duty to abandon my convictions immediately and even to act against them with the same, or even greater, energy than if I were acting according to my own opinions." Such subservience, combined with a love of order, precision, and regulation, recommended Panin highly to Nicholas I and to his son, who once remarked that Count Panin "has absolutely no convictions of his own, and his only concern is to please me."[148] Before his thirty-ninth birthday, Nicholas named this strange but intensely loyal man Russia's Minister of Justice.[149]

Panin's personality was as unpleasant as his career was brilliant. He was dry, cold, and unbending in his relations with equals. While Kiselev remained the dashing cavalryman, brilliant in high society, and Perovskii an elegant, well-educated lord, Panin was something of a recluse. His tall, ungainly frame misshapen by a pronounced stoop, he shunned polite society and conversation with others. It was reported that he kept parrots in his apartments and that he would converse with them because, when they replied, "they did not violate the rules of seniority."[150] It also was said that he had read Russia's entire *Digest of the Laws,* and that he had learned great chunks of it by heart. He obeyed his Emperor unquestioningly; he expected total subservience from his subordinates. Nikolai Semenov, who served under him for many years, remembered that "he considered the will of the sovereign to be sacred, and he thought the form of unlimited monarchical government to be the best of all possible systems. He fulfilled Imperial commands to the letter, without question, and demanded a similar obedience to his orders from his subordinates."[151] As Minister of Justice, Panin became "a real satrap, malevolent, fault-finding, merciless, and cold."[152]

If Panin seemed devoid of personal warmth, his devotion to duty, to the service, and to his Emperor had a positive effect upon the personnel of his ministry nonetheless. His belief in the law, as set forth in the *Digest of the Laws,* his adoration of firm precision, and his insistence that official matters be dealt with quickly and accurately were qualities rarely found in Russia's central administration. Even more than Kiselev and Perovskii, he insisted that the bureaucracy must function with the precision that he and his Imperial master so adored. As did the directors of the Ministries of State Domains and Internal Affairs, he required officials who were educated and diligent, for, as he once said, "an uneducated official, with only experience to his credit, [cannot] be truly useful."[153] Aside from the Imperial School of Jurisprudence, which graduated its first class of elite officials just as he became Minister, Panin recruited university graduates because he thought them "distinguished in service affairs by their well-founded knowledge," and he brought a significant number of them into his ministry.[154] As one of his subordinates later recalled, many of these men eventually found the rigid formalism of his regime "difficult and even intolerable for a person wishing to be independent to some degree," and a number fled to other agencies during the 1850s and early 1860s.[155] But this flight did not occur before some of Panin's recruits had formed a cadre that created the institutional base for reform work within the Ministry of Justice. S. I. Zarudnyi's so-called "school" in the Ministry's Consultation and the Moscow Departments of the Senate were especially important in that regard.[156] There, such eminent figures as Zarudnyi, K. P. Pobedonostsev, and D. A. Rovinskii, who played a major role in drafting the Judicial Reform Statutes of 1864, assembled during the last decade of Nicholas I's reign. Although they rejected Panin's rigidity and formalism, these younger men preserved his emphasis on precision, accountability, and loyalty to the Emperor. Under his tutelage, they developed an expertise in the law and an awareness of its shortcomings that was unequalled in Russia's administration.

Men such as Kiselev, Perovskii, and Panin belonged to the first generation of statesmen who began their careers in Russia's ministerial administration. Unlike such great Catherinian lords as Gavrila Derzhavin and Dmitrii Troshchinskii, they had not participated in its creation in the provinces, nor had they, like Alexander I's Young Friends and Speranskii, played a role in its establishment in St. Petersburg. Beginning their careers just as Russia's ministerial administration developed its institutional base, they were acutely aware of those limitations and shortcomings that emerged during its first years of testing. Because they considered the instruments of Russia's ministerial administration imperfect, Perovskii and Kiselev adjusted those agencies that lay within their ministries to improve their overall functioning; by contrast, Panin adjusted only the procedures by which various departments within the Ministry of Justice functioned.

Although Kiselev and Perovskii differed from Panin about the nature and scope of adjustments required to make Russia's ministerial administration function properly, they were more closely in agreement about the sort of personnel they required. As the sons and grandsons of men who had served the autocrat personally in the highest levels of government, they had been raised on the Karamzinian maxim that "a wise government finds the means to encourage the good tendencies in public officials and to restrain the inclination toward evil," and that "the minister [should] answer ... for the choice of leading officials."[157] Equally important, they understood that the more complex problems that Russia's ministerial administration faced required officials who were better educated. Finally, they knew that bribery, corruption, and incompetence among lower-ranking officials must be eliminated if Russia's ministerial administration were to function properly.[158]

Certain that better-educated, better-trained, and more honest officials would produce better administration, Kiselev, Perovskii, and Panin recruited them from among the graduates of Russia's elite schools and universities. Yet the young men they brought into their ministries came from different backgrounds, shared different experiences, and held different views about administration and change than they. While their mentors in the service remained convinced that the precepts of the Nicholas system, when properly applied, would produce the best form of administration for Russia, such young officials as Andrei Zablotskii-Desiatovskii, Nikolai Miliutin, Sergei Zarudnyi, and a number of their friends and close associates, came to understand that broader changes were needed. Procedural and institutional adjustments, they realized, could not resolve the problems that faced Russia and the Imperial administration. Some effective means had to be found to change policy and, once changed, to implement it effectively. Neither could be achieved under the regimes of such statesmen as Perovskii, Kiselev, or Panin, whose efforts to make their ministries more "efficient" produced the "heyday of formalism." Mere adjustment in the bureaucratic instruments of authority was not enough to embark upon the program of conservative renovation that Russia required, but the next step was by no means clear.[159] A search for the means to go beyond the limitations posed by these elder statesmen's views occupied progressive young Russian officials throughout the 1840s and well into the 1850s.

Chapter 2

New Men and New Aspirations

"Their ideal was the introduction of justice into all spheres of life. . . . Along the way to attaining this ideal they had two guideposts: hard work and a sense of duty."
A. P. Zablotskii-Desiatovskii

The young officials whom Kiselev, Perovskii, and Panin recruited into the lower echelons of their ministries came from impoverished noble families with traditions of service to Russia. Their fathers, who frequently had started their careers in the lower ranks, had reached the middle levels of Russia's army or bureaucracy; and, from the moment the sons grew beyond infancy, they were encouraged to follow in their fathers' footsteps. At considerable expense and personal sacrifice, these men employed tutors to give their sons an elementary education. As soon as they were old enough, they were enrolled in elite schools where the ideals of service to the state formed an integral part of their adolescent experience. At such institutions as the Lyceum at Tsarskoe Selo, the Boarding Schools for Sons of the Nobility at Moscow and St. Petersburg Universities, and then at the universities themselves, they were conditioned to think of themselves as part of an elite, especially because they were distinguished by impressive educations in a milieu where such were uncommon.[1] These young men graduated from school intent upon serving Tsar and country and anxious to build successful careers for themselves in the process.

Young men who nourished ambitions to better their social and economic status through successful careers in the civil service automatically turned their steps toward St. Petersburg, only to encounter those many frustrations that lay in wait for all but those with close ties to the

Imperial Court. Victims of a painful metamorphosis, these young men were transformed from members of an elite into the rank and file of a shabby clerical army to which the most inconsequential and demeaning tasks were assigned. Like Aleksandr Aduev, Goncharov's university graduate who entered the bureaucracy expecting to deal with important affairs of state but found himself assigned to menial clerical duties instead, these young men at first felt trapped by a system that gave little immediate recognition to their talent and education. Regarded as nameless cogs in the endlessly interlocking wheels of the machinery of Russian officialdom, they earned salaries that barely enabled them to subsist in the midst of St. Petersburg's luxury and opulence.[2]

These years of material deprivation and psychological degradation were critical to the making of successful careers, for it was at this time that young men had to find a means to rise above that faceless mass of petty officials among whom they had been cast. They had to succeed or be condemned to lives of drudgery, misery and, in their own terms, failure. Aside from family connections, which most did not have, one of the most effective ways to gain attention in the bureaucracy was to become an expert in some field. In the Ministries of Internal Affairs and State Domains especially, Perovskii and Kiselev sought out men from all over Russia who could provide those accurate data about local conditions which they thought essential to the role they envisioned for their ministries, and a young official who could assemble such information, sift it efficiently, and present it in the form of a comprehensive and comprehensible report, stood a good chance to begin a successful career under their tutelage.

The process of becoming such a specialist involved more than theoretical study, however. The information recorded in provincial offices usually was grossly inadequate for even the most crude statistical work, and suspicious local officials often were uncooperative. Therefore, it was necessary for an ambitious young man to visit the area in question in order to compile the necessary statistical information from personal study and observation, and this often unpalatable task posed one of the major dilemmas in the lives of young bureaucrats who aspired to higher positions.[3] On the one hand, chances for visibility and promotion were greater in the capital; on the other, to obtain the expert status that could be an important factor in gaining the attention of his superiors, an official might have to spend months or even years in the provinces. An ambitious young official thus had to spend sufficient time in the provinces to gain the expertise needed to win attention yet not spend so much time away from the capital that his superiors lost sight of him.[4] The effort to strike a balance between service in the St. Petersburg bureaucracy and visits to the provinces was characteristic of nearly all the men whom we shall discuss in this chapter. All received assignments as agents of special commissions in the provinces during the first decade of their careers, and some spent nearly all of the 1840s away from St. Petersburg. Not all properly balanced service in the provinces against service in the capital, with the result that they sometimes rose to responsible positions within their respective ministries but never achieved influence as policy-makers. When it came time to draft the Great Reforms, these men did not play a visible, public part.[5]

Elite education, good fortune, devotion to ministerial affairs, and a willingness to forsake temporarily the comparative comforts of the capital for a more difficult life in the provinces served to advance the fortunes of a number of young officials who rose to responsible positions under Kiselev, Perovskii, and Panin in a manner that generally was uncharacteristic of the careers of most civil servants. They rose quickly, often earning the rank of *statskii sovetnik* in twelve to fifteen years, so that they reached senior rank before they became so steeped in the bureaucracy's formalistic tradition that they could not envision different approaches to the more complex problems Russia faced at mid-century. For these men, the period between the late 1830s and early 1840s was a time of study and personal development. They examined Russian conditions, re-cast their views about the types of reforms needed to improve the quality of life in the Empire, and developed a new vision of the bureaucratic instruments Russia required. They soon became a living body of collective knowledge about Russian provincial life that was unequalled in the Imperial administration.

Andrei Zablotskii-Desiatovskii and Russia's State Peasants

Perhaps no issue of the 1840s commanded the attention of educated Russians more urgently than did serfdom. Few senior officials or great serf-owners believed that it could continue for long without major transformations. "The question of the abolition of serfdom astonishes no one now," wrote one official in 1841,[6] and, just a few years later, Perovskii told Nicholas that "time and new [economic] relationships have completely altered the view of the educated *pomeshchiki* toward serfdom. . . . The *pomeshchiki* are themselves beginning to understand that the serfs are a burden to them and that it would be desirable to alter these mutually disadvantageous relationships."[7] Statesmen, bureaucrats, and the educated public therefore had to ask how the dilemmas posed by serfdom might be resolved, in what manner the relationship between master and serf ought to be changed and, the most fearsome question of all: when should substantive alterations in the serf order be undertaken? These were cursed questions indeed, and they plagued Russians throughout the Nicholaean era.

Because the economic well-being of the Empire's privileged elite class—the nobility—was involved in any effort to alter serfdom, it became more difficult to agree on the means for resolving these questions. For Russian noblemen who had suffered the elemental force of peasant wrath from time to time and for state authorities who valued the preservation of order above all else, the fear that an emancipation might usher in an era of peasant violence posed very real dilemmas. "The educated *pomeshchiki,*" Perovskii warned Nicholas, "fear the consequences of freedom [for the serfs], knowing the unbridled nature of the masses."[8] Throughout the second quarter of the century, statesmen made little progress toward resolving these dilemmas but continued to hope that the passage of time somehow would render them less complex. "Questions which now seem vexing will doubtless be untangled through experience,"[9] Nicholas once remarked. He evidently hoped that Kiselev's work with the state peasants could become one of the major sources of such experience. By concentrating on them, he thought that the government might set an example that perhaps could induce the nobility to limit serfdom on their estates.[10]

Few officials became so deeply involved in the study of life among the state peasants during the 1840s as did Andrei Parfenovich Zablotskii-Desiatovskii, chief of the Statistical Section of the Department of Rural Economy in Kislev's Ministry of State Domains. Born in Chernigov province, Zablotskii was a member of an impoverished, but ancient, noble family. He grew up in the Ukrainian countryside, where his father managed the estates of a rich lord, studied at the local *gimnaziia* at Novgorod-Seversk, and lived in close daily contact with serfs throughout his childhood. We know little else about Zablotskii's early life, nor do we know the impressions that his broad experience with serf life made upon him. As a well-educated, but serf-less, landowner, his father must have realized that education was the only key that might unlock for his son the door to success in the state service, and, almost certainly, he encouraged him to study at the University of Moscow, where Zablotskii graduated with a gold medal in 1827, and received an advanced degree in 1832.[11]

The primitive state of statistical studies in Russia's central administration was a problem Zablotskii encountered almost from the moment he entered the Ministry of Internal Affairs in 1832. Western European states long since had incorporated statistical agencies into their bureaucratic structures, but the first in Russia was established in the Ministry of Internal Affairs at Speranskii's urging only in 1802. Transferred to the short-lived Ministry of Police a decade later, this organization did little more than compile the crude data that provincial governors submitted about population movements. At about the same time, the Ministry of Finance began to collect information about state peasants, the output of state mines, foreign and domestic trade, and tax collections. But it had no separate agency for this purpose and did not compile its data on a regular or comprehensive basis.[12] It was not until 1835 that the Ministry of Internal Affairs, the central agency in the Empire most broadly concerned with domestic policy, incorporated a regular statistical office into its structure. Konstantin Arsen'ev, tutor to Grand Duke Aleksandr Nikolaevich in history and statistics, became its first director. Despite Zablotskii's very junior status, Arsen'ev chose him as secretary of this new agency and supported his promotion to the rank of *kollezhskii asessor* at the age of twenty-seven.[13]

Under Arsen'ev's tutelage Zablotskii's early career bore every mark of success, but he transferred to Kiselev's Fifth Section in early 1837 nonetheless. We do not know for certain why he chose to stake his future on the chance of advancement in a new and untried state agency, but a number of factors may have influenced his decision. Most obviously, the newly organized Fifth Section offered broader opportunities for promotion and was less controlled by those formal routines and procedures that he and men like him so despised.[14] The Fifth Section offered him a chance to organize a small agency according to his own precepts, and that attraction may have been heightened by Kiselev himself, who had already recruited V. I. Karneev, Director of the Ministry of Internal Affairs' Economic Department. Karneev may in turn have urged Zablotskii, as a young official of recognized promise in his agency, to follow him.[15]

Zablotskii's transfer to the Fifth Section placed him on one of the most unusual bureaucratic staffs in Russia, its talent equalled perhaps only by the group of unusually well-educated young officials Speranskii had assembled in the Second Section during the 1820s to codify Russia's laws.[16] The majority of Speranskii's jurists came from wealthy aristocratic backgrounds and therefore shared what one scholar has called a "new nonchalance, a sophisticated and detached acceptance of the frailties of the system."[17] Most of them never experienced the vicissitudes of life in the lower depths of the bureaucracy and, because of their high birth, remained relatively isolated from the reality of Russian provincial life. Such men never could share Zablotskii's deep concern about the gap between senior state officials and the problems for which they were responsible, while he never could share their blasé self-confidence that even without careful study, a statesman's superior intellect could transcend that administrative abyss and formulate workable solutions to economic and administrative crises. "Governmental activity," Zablot-skii insisted, "ought to be based not upon theoretical understanding, but on the study of subjects in real life."[18] No longer should the Russian Empire be governed "simply upon the basis of practical knowledge about administrative affairs [deloproizvodstvo], with no specialized study of the problems that were dealt with."[19]

In Kiselev's new Ministry of Internal Affairs, Karneev's Third Department was the first agency in St. Petersburg to recruit men almost solely on the basis of educational qualifications. The result was impressive. Like Zablotskii, a future member of the Editing Commissions of 1859–1860, Ivan Arapetov, had just graduated from Moscow University when he entered the Third Department as a translator.[20] A. K. Girs, who played a major role in the urban studies that Nikolai Miliutin's Municipal Section produced between 1842 and 1856, had graduated from the Lyceum at Tsarskoe Selo with a silver medal only three years before, was dissatisfied with his position in the Ministry of Justice, and entered the Third Department as a deputy chief of an office section.[21] K. K. Grot, like Girs a recent graduate from the Lyceum, also transferred to the Ministry of State Domains in 1838 for much the same reasons. Grot later became Governor of Samara province.[22] V. A. Insarskii, later a close associate of Prince A. I. Bariatinskii in the Caucasus, became chief of an office section under Karneev,[23] as did A. F. Shtakel'berg, a St. Petersburg University graduate who later studied urban economy and administration in the Baltic provinces.[24] Konstantin Veselovskii, a member of the Imperial Russian Academy of Sciences at the age of thirty-seven and one of Russia's most noted statisticians, also found his first service post in Zablotskii's statistical bureau in the Third Department, and he summoned younger graduates from his *alma mater* at Tsarskoe Selo to join him there.[25] As a result, an agency that had been unusual for the high level of its officials' education from the beginning became even more so.

Most of these young men shared a common aristocratic background, although few were rich. For them, state service offered the best means to win status, privilege, and power and to rise above their middling noble origins. To the degree that such is possible in a bureaucracy, they possessed a rare measure of self-confidence and that led them to forsake the security of time-in-grade promotions in other state agencies for the prospect of more rapid promotions based on merit. They were thus distinguished from most bureaucrats by their willingness to let ability, rather than longevity, determine the course of their careers. They were so confident of their ability that, a few years later, they transferred *en masse* into Miliutin's new Municipal Section, at the cost of their seniority, to take advantage of the opportunities it offered to develop new specialties in assembling and analyzing urban statistics.

Zablotskii and his colleagues thought that decisions should be made not according to "general rules of bureaucracy, but on the bases of knowledge and enlightenment."[26] Zablotskii himself characterized this new attitude even more forcefully. In describing his colleagues, he once wrote:

> Their ideal was the introduction of justice into all spheres of life. . . . No one preached about this ideal. As naturalists say, it was conceived among them spontaneously. Along the path to attaining this ideal, they had two guide-posts: hard work and a sense of duty. In hard work, they saw not only the means without which it is impossible to improve one's position in society legitimately, but also a necessary requirement for the full enjoyment of life. In the fulfillment of their duty, they saw a basic law of morality.[27]

The men who entered the Third Department of the Ministry of State Domains in the mid- to late 1830s thus were officials of a new breed: talented, well-educated, willing to let ability stand as a measure of their worth and, because of their relatively impoverished backgrounds, anxious to make their mark in the state service. Under Zablotskii's leadership they found an opportunity to test their talents during the late 1830s and 1840s.

Zablotskii and his associates first had to examine earlier proposals for improving the administration of the state peasants' domains and then codify the legislative materials that related to them. Then, as a preliminary step to preparing new plans for administrative reform, they compiled the scattered data available about state peasants. To an important extent basing their actions upon Speranskii's example, they expressed a deep faith in the value of such preparatory work. In an administration where few statesmen ever overcame bureaucratic inertia sufficiently to produce large-scale administrative reforms, the success of Speranskii's efforts loomed large. Speranskii first had reorganized the administration of Russia's vast Siberian domains and had followed that achievement by completing within a decade that task of codification that had defied the best efforts of Russian administrators and jurists since Peter the Great. During the 1830s (Zablotskii wrote some years later), "the works of a statesman who combined a rare mind with practical ability—Count Speranskii—began to influence our administration."[28] Speranskii's achievement and personal example thus had a great impact on the administrative reform processes of the 1830s. "In addition to being of immediate use in daily administration, the *Digest of the Laws* had other very important influences," Zablotskii remembered. "Setting forth in their totality the existing laws on each area of administration, the *Digest* revealed . . . all their shortcomings, their insufficiencies, and contradictions, which, until that time, had gone unnoticed."[29] Speranskii's successful compilation of the laws thus instilled in Zablotskii and his friends a deep faith in the virtue of codifying materials before undertaking any administrative venture. Speranskii's application of codification techniques to Russia's laws soon raised the process itself to a level of truth in which Imperial statesmen believed until the twentieth century.

Because Zablotskii played no role in the actual preparation of the eight laws that the Ministry of State Domains drafted under Kiselev's guidance between 1837 and 1840 to improve the state's administration of its peasants, their substance need not concern us here.[30] Those laws dealt exclusively with administrative issues because Kiselev saw effective administration as the key to improving life among the state peasants. "The main thing [is to work out] effective administrative measures," he once wrote.[31] More important for our purposes here, Kiselev ordered detailed investigations of the manner in which the state peasants lived, and Zablotskii played an important part in these throughout the late 1830s and 1840s. His first official assignment to study local peasant life came in early 1837, even before his formal appointment to the Fifth Section. Under the direction of the famous academician Petr Keppen, a statistician even more renowned than Arsen'ev during the 1830s, Zablotskii and Nikolai Miliutin, a young official from the Economic Department in the Ministry of Internal Affairs, studied life in Southern Russia's state peasant villages during the spring and summer.[32] Both Zablotskii and Miliutin received valuable statistical training from Keppen, and they began a friendship that lasted throughout their lives.

The pattern of Zablotskii's and Miliutin's assignments diverged sharply during the decade after they served with Keppen in Southern Russia. Miliutin soon became deeply involved in the legislative process itself, and his work confined him to St. Petersburg's chanceries, while Zablotskii continued to learn more about rural life as he pursued official assignments from the Baltic to the Caucasus. Zablotskii's isolation from the legislative process endowed him with an unusually broad view of Russian peasant life, from which he concluded that the problems he witnessed in Russia's countryside stemmed from the institution of serfdom. Zablotskii expressed a deep sense of moral outrage at the injustice of the serf system, for he believed in the law and saw in its statutes the way to progress. "The first condition by which . . . the success of all administration is guaranteed is the understanding of lawfulness," he once remarked.[33] Yet he found little that resembled legality or lawfulness in the relationships between master and serf. "Not being able to possess property, the serf cannot defend his rights in the courts," he pointed out in 1841. "What a strange state of affairs," he concluded. "Half of the state's inhabitants, according to the law, are excluded from any protection of the law."[34]

If serfdom contradicted Zablotskii's ideal of a society based on law, he also indicted the system on economic and moral grounds. Because it offered no incentive for the serf to produce anything beyond the bare minimum, Russia's agricultural and industrial output could not be expanded through increased productivity.[35] This did not mean that individual serf-owners could not increase their incomes, Zablotskii argued, but that could only be accomplished if the *pomeshchiki* took more and left their peasants with less.[36] Thus, serfdom was one man's direct exploitation of many in a relationship ruled by the highest degree of caprice. There were few legal restraints upon a nobleman's dealings with his peasants, and, in Zablotskii's opinion, that had led to a profound erosion of peasant morality. "The poverty of the majority of the nobles' peasants and the frequent changes in their fortunes," he wrote in a memorandum to Kiselev, "have given birth to an important vice among them—the loss of shame." In turn, this led peasants to prefer begging to honest work.[37] The hopelessness of such a life, Zablotskii reported, turned peasants into drunkards, and *pomeshchiki* even encouraged that vice by producing spirits on their estates and selling them to their serfs.[38]

From his observations about peasant life in the late 1830s and early 1840s, Zablotskii concluded that Kiselev's efforts to refine the state's instruments of administration and authority could not improve Russia's rural economy. In his view, none of the major impediments to bringing greater prosperity to Russia's state peasants could be resolved by administrative *fiat*. The first of these obstacles stemmed from the quality of the statistical data that central government offices received from provincial officials. "Whoever has looked over any of the materials compiled by lower-level administrative agencies," Zablotskii complained, "knows how tangled and inaccurate they are. The consequences of this are evident in those legislative proposals which are based upon such incomplete data."[39] The only solution was to send into the provinces trusted officials who were capable of obtaining the sorts of data which central agencies required. First as chief of the Statistical Section of the Third Department, then as a member of his ministry's scientific council, and, finally, as head of the Third Department itself (by then re-named the Department of Rural Economy), Zablotskii developed a body of accurate information about state peasant life in the Ministry of State Domains so that legislative proposals could take conditions in the countryside more accurately into account.

Zablotskii's efforts to assemble accurate information about provincial life aided his attempts to break down the peasants' ignorance about modern agriculture which, in his view, was the second major obstacle to increasing rural prosperity in Russia. During the early 1840s, he enlisted the help of Prince V. F. Odoevskii, a colleague in the Ministry of State Domains and a close personal friend, to publish a series of booklets which bore the title *Sel'skoe chtenie*. The impetus for the project grew out of the Third Department's efforts to prepare a "catechism on the most important principles for successful agriculture" that would instruct state peasants about how to farm more effectively.[40] Though admirable in conception, the task fell upon a number of overworked officials who kept setting it aside as more pressing (though usually less important) administrative matters demanded their attention. Convinced by late 1842 that the catechism would be a long time in coming (in fact, it still was in preparation at the end of Nicholas's reign), Zablotskii decided to pursue another course.[41] His official inquires about conditions in state peasant villages, as well as the secret studies about serf life that Kiselev had commissioned him to undertake, convinced him that the spiritual and moral degeneration of Russia's rural population had become so serious that direct action could not wait.

Four *Sel'skoe chtenie* booklets appeared between 1843 and 1848, as Zablotskii and Odoevskii enlisted the services of such writers as Vladimir Dal' and Count V. A. Sollogub. Their writings combined a variety of moral aphorisms with injunctions about the virtue of sobriety and simply stated agricultural advice to peasant readers. "If you want a good harvest, choose the type of soil best suited to the seed you intend to plant," they explained. "Choose the very best seed. If you sow poor seed, you might as well sow sand. Your labor and time will be wasted." Such advice was combined with folksy tales about "How the Peasant Spiridon Taught the Peasant Ivan Not to Drink Vodka and What Happened as a Result" and "An Accounting of How Much Money Can Be Saved by Not Drinking Vodka," as Zablotskii set out to curb peasant alcoholism.[42] The impact of his efforts is impossible to measure, of course. But it is certain that Zablotskii found an audience for his preachings. Each of the *Sel'skoe chtenie* booklets went through several printings totaling well over 30,000 copies before 1848, at which time Russia's senior statesmen, with the example of the Galician peasant revolts of 1846 still fresh in their minds, grew fearful for the security of the Empire's rural areas and stopped him from publishing further issues.[43]

By the mid-1840s, Zablotskii had concluded that administrative regulations could not restructure social and economic relationships in Russia and that the state must in fact alter the attitudes of Russia's rural dwellers if it wished to improve the quality of provincial life. During the late 1840s and early 1850s, Zablotskii expanded his ministry's efforts to establish agricultural schools and model farms, but he did not abandon his efforts to influence serf life more directly. For the moment, he altered his focus and turned to the serf-owners themselves in order to acquaint them with technological and agronomical innovations. For that purpose, he sponsored regional agricultural exhibitions and encouraged the development of new agricultural societies. For the mass of petty serf-owners—that 80 percent of the nobility who owned a mere 20 percent of the serfs—his efforts at enlightenment evolved directly from *Sel'skoe chtenie*. Therefore, in the late 1840s, Zablotskii published a series of "Agricultural Aphorisms" in the progressive journal *Otechestvennye zapiski*, which presented Russia's squires with agricultural principles only slightly more sophisticated than those he had prepared for their peasants a few years earlier.[44]

Although Zablotskii continued to learn about rural life and the problems that Russia's peasant millions faced during the 1840s, the nature of his administrative duties continued to shield him from the complex autocratic legislative process upon which the success of any gradual transformation of rural Russia depended. That task became a central focus of the efforts of his close friend Nikolai Miliutin, who became deeply involved in legislative work in St. Petersburg while Zablotskii studied Russia's countryside.

Nikolai Miliutin and the Autocratic Legislative Process

At the beginning of the nineteenth century, Alexander I, his Young Friends, and Speranskii had tried with limited success to create a state administration in which the precepts of autocracy were combined with the rule of law. They hoped to achieve their goal through the instruments of Russia's new ministerial government, which delegated executive authority to the Empire's ministers but left legislative power exclusively in the hands of the autocrat. Yet, if Russia's laws denied legislative power to her chief ministers, they did not exclude them from the legislative process, for their ministers were empowered to make "recommendations about the need for a new law, or statute, or recommend changes in existing ones."[45] During the Nicholaean era, Imperial ministers used their authority to recommend increasingly complex legislation, and this had the practical consequence of bestowing considerable legislative power upon them. Well before the middle of the century, ministerial legislative "recommendations" evolved into lengthy and precisely worded documents drafted according to the format of statutes issued by the Ruling Senate. As a result, the autocratic legislative process was expanded to include a series of negotiations among the Emperor, the State Council, and Russia's ministers and their subordinate executive organs.

One of the most complex areas of bureaucratic activity in which a young official could gain expert status during the 1830s and 1840s was the functioning of this legislative process. To do so was especially difficult, not only because opportunities to engage in planning reform were very limited but because it was rare indeed for a young official even to encounter the devious processes that senior officials employed to resist or permit change. Nikolai Miliutin, who entered the Ministry of Internal Affairs in November 1835, thus remains an unusual example of an ambitious young official who used to good advantage a rare opportunity to guide reform legislation through Russia's central bureaucracy. Miliutin's unique experience in the 1840s became especially valuable to him and a number of his colleagues when they began to draft Russia's Great Reform legislation after the Crimean War.

Nikolai Alekseevich Miliutin's family had risen to prominence in the 1750s and was numbered among Moscow's richest nobles when Alexander I ascended the throne in 1801.[46] Extravagance and mismanagement dissipated the family fortune quickly, and when Miliutin was born on June 6, 1818, their standard of living had diminished to a mere shadow of its former brilliance. Because his parents no longer could afford to live in Moscow, Miliutin spent the first decade of his life at Titovo amidst the decaying elegance of what only a half-century before had been a flourishing noble demense in Kaluga province with more than 1,000 serfs and seventy mills producing velvets and damasks.[47]

Although nature had endowed Miliutin's father with few entrepreneurial skills, he was well educated by early nineteenth-century standards and knew that his sons' best chance for success in life lay in the state service. Thanks to the influence of Kiselev, his wife's eldest brother, he enrolled his three eldest sons in the Boarding School for Sons of the Nobility at Moscow University, where much of the teaching was done by prominent scholars from the university's own faculty.[48] Touched by that romanticism that consumed sensitive Russian noble youths in the 1820s and early 1830s, Miliutin remained a supreme dilettante during his six years at the Boarding School. Often plagued by "melancholic and agitated states of mind," he extolled the virtues of sensitivity and lived out a variety of adolescent fantasies about careers for which he was unprepared and unsuited.[49]

Miliutin's fantasy world was partly an effort to escape a painful awareness that he, his brothers, and his parents all were abjectly dependent on the Kiselevs.[50] He found such dependence a bitter pill, and one

might speculate that it colored many of his attitudes during his adolescent years. Once in Russia's civil service, he clearly displayed a brilliant
mind and a rare ability to grasp the essence of complex affairs of state.
Yet during those years when each day in the classroom reminded him
of his dependence on Kiselev's patronage, Miliutin exhibited scarcely a
glimmer of these talents. Kiselev had opposed his sister's marriage to
Miliutin's father, whom he considered too close to middle age, too inept,
and too far beneath her social status, and Kiselev never forgave him
for taking his cherished sister away from the luxurious family nest
to the spartan surroundings of the Miliutin provincial estate.[51] The
"charity" he doled out never could be mistaken for kindness or generosity. Miliutin knew whence came his chance for the elite education
that offered him a chance at a successful career, and his reaction
appears to have been stubborn, almost self-destructive, rejection. Ten-
sions between uncle and nephew continued for several decades,
until Miliutin could approach Kiselev on a more equal footing. Not
until the early 1860s did nephew and uncle begin to enjoy a warm
relationship.[52]

Among other things, Miliutin's adolescent fantasies centered upon
a life devoted to literature. His efforts to realize that dream revealed his
meager literary talent, for his endeavors went no further than shallow
imitations of Byron and Aleksandr Bestuzhev-Marlinskii.[53] Miliutin's
emotional commitment to romanticism in the 1830s differed sharply
from the more deeply rooted variety that was central to the intellectual
experiences of the fervent Moscow youths of his generation. For such
young men as Nikolai Ogarev, Aleksandr Herzen, Nikolai Stankevich
—even the supreme realist Vissarion Belinskii—romanticism exalted
their spirits and gave them that sense of common purpose which enabled them to stand together even against the authority of the autocrat. Briefly, Miliutin, too, was critical of the existing order, but in a
more shallow and self-interested vein. To be sure, he found life in the
lower ranks of St. Petersburg's clerical army dreary, and he proclaimed
bitterly to all who would listen that chancery work was an *"existence
manquée,"*[54] a bottomless sea of bureaucratic mud that sucked at his
well-worn boots and threatened to draw him into its lower depths.
But, in sharp contrast to Russia's alienated intelligentsia of the 1830s,
Miliutin soon carved out an emotionally satisfying life within the confines of that very bureaucracy they so despised. In patronage-conscious
St. Petersburg, where, as one observer noted, success usually came
through deceit and "by the fortunate chance of drawing attention to
oneself by a clever trick or by successful flattery,"[55] he found that
recognition he had craved ever since he first entered the Boarding
School.

Such did not come immediately, but at least a small recognition of his ability came in 1837, when a group of talented young officials and scholars invited him to compile data about trade, guilds, and small industries in Russia's cities and ports for *A Library of Commercial Knowledge.* Most prominent among the contributors were Zablotskii, his mentor Arsen'ev, and the statistician G. P. Nebolsin, who thought that before Russia could embark upon the path to progress, her officials must assemble accurate information about the economic and social conditions within her borders. More important, perhaps, this undertaking assured Miliutin that worthwhile tasks could be found in Russia's bureaucratic world and thus introduced him to that study of urban problems which consumed much of his attention for the next two decades.[56] Within the inner reaches of the Ministry of Internal Affairs' Economic Department, he no longer was dependent on Kiselev's charity, and he began to gain that measure of self-esteem needed for success.

Miliutin's work on *A Library of Commercial Knowledge* did not immediately free him from the lower depths of St. Petersburg's clerical world. Most probably because he had been so dependent on Kiselev's charity during his adolescent years, he found repugnant that sort of patronage needed to advance a career in Russia's capital. Eventually, powerful men aided his career, but he remained unable to bring himself to curry their favor.[57] Rejecting flattery as a means of making his way, he set out to command his superiors' attention as an efficient civil servant. That at first proved difficult because the Minister of Internal Affairs at the time was Count D. N. Bludov, an official whom one courtier characterized as a nonentity in the ranks of Russia's statesmen.[58] Such a remark may have been more uncharitable than was warranted, but it was true that Bludov suffered from an uncritical faith in the merits of Russia's ministerial administration, and he tolerated ineptness, even incompetence, among his subordinates.[59] Courtly, urbane, extremely well-educated, and possessor of considerable literary talent, he was not a man to urge a better understanding of conditions in an Empire he thought already well governed. Bludov was not the kind of statesman upon whom a young man of Miliutin's type would make an impression, and Miliutin found few opportunities for advancement under Bludov's stewardship. The years from 1835 to 1839 became for Miliutin a time of preparation and training in the language and practice of bureaucracy which Bludov himself once described as "habit, love of precision, and subordination."[60]

A change of ministers in 1839 provided Miliutin with new opportunities for advancement. Count A. G. Stroganov, and the energetic and forceful Perovskii who followed him as Minister of Internal Affairs, preferred a different breed of official than had Bludov. Miliutin's carefully balanced criticism of his ministry's famine relief programs in the region between St. Petersburg and Moscow first brought him to Stroganov's attention and, when the Count left his post in late 1841, he recommended Miliutin to Perovskii as a young man with unusual administrative gifts. A brief acquaintance convinced Perovskii that Stroganov had been correct; just over a year later, he entrusted Miliutin with an important new agency.[61] At age twenty-four, Miliutin thus took on the headship of the Economic Department's Provisional Section for the Reorganization of Municipal Government and Economy and was assigned to examine the economic and administrative structures in the Empire as a first step to preparing plans for renovating Russia's nearly defunct system of municipal government.[62] This work drew him directly into the autocratic legislative process. For the next several years he carried on a complex series of legislative negotiations with Perovskii and the State Council which produced the Statute on the Reform of St. Petersburg's Municipal Administration in 1846.

Had they remained faithful to Russia's bureaucratic traditions, Miliutin and his Provisional Section might have drafted nothing but proposals for minor adjustments in Russia's administrative apparatus. Yet despite his youth and inexperience, or, perhaps, because of them, Miliutin eventually produced a broad study of urban social and economic conditions in Russia and used the Provisional Section as a base from which to develop more important reform proposals.[63] To succeed, he needed investigators able to break with the formalism of Russia's administrative tradition and think in broader terms than were common in the St. Petersburg bureaucracy. Such men must be willing to ask questions that most bureaucrats feared to ask and to report corruption and incompetence without regard for the reputations of senior provincial officials. They had to possess the tenacity to ferret out evidence about such failings when local authorities proved uncooperative, and they had to be willing to remain away from the capital long enough to succeed. It required more than a decade to complete the ambitious task Miliutin had begun, but it provided him and his associates with a broader understanding of Russia's administrative processes. Even more important, it enabled him to assemble a cadre of talented officials within his agency to rival those whom Kiselev, Karneev, and Zablotskii had recruited into the Ministry of State Domains a few years before.

Although he criticized formalism and incompetence, Miliutin's efforts to deal with the administrative problems uncovered by his subordinates proved that he had not yet formulated broader solutions to the growing crisis in Russia's administration. He held a broad commission to draft a reform of Russia's municipal government institutions. Yet he shied away from doing so and allowed his preliminary studies in late

1842 and early 1843 to convince him that urban life was too varied and complex to fit any general administrative rules. Like his mentor Perovskii, he at first thought only of adjusting Russia's administrative apparatus to achieve the ideal of a well-ordered, finely tuned executive machine and narrowed his reform goals as a result.[64] At first determined to streamline the administration, not transform it, Miliutin could not formulate new and effective solutions to the problems that confronted him in Russia's cities, and he could not yet envision changes in the very concept of administration itself.[65] Anxious to postpone concrete attempts to transform provincial administration, Miliutin turned his attention to St. Petersburg, although he continued to send agents of special commissions into the provinces.

Beginning in the fall of 1843, Miliutin's efforts to draft a new municipal statute for St. Petersburg demonstrated the traditional limitations in his views about administration and government at that point as well as some modest innovations. Not satisfied with data obtained through usual sources, he consulted directly with elected city officials to learn how St. Petersburg's administrative agencies might be made more effective.[66] Sharing Zablotskii's faith in codification, he and his staff assembled all the materials available in central government offices about St. Petersburg, studied them, and prepared a thorough critique of earlier efforts to reform the city's government. By the end of 1843, he had assembled overwhelming evidence that the city's administration was a morass of incompetence, tangled lines of authority, and deeply rooted corruption. Such discoveries were hardly new, nor were his solutions.[67] He proposed to instill a sense of civic responsibility in elected city officials, an obviously difficult task when they were surrounded by an army of corrupt civil servants.[68] Then he defined more precisely the responsibilities of elected officials, broadened the base of class representation in St. Petersburg's central administration, and clarified administrative lines of authority.[69]

The provisions of Miliutin's reform proposals that Perovskii laid before the State Council in June 1844 have been discussed elsewhere and need not be reiterated here.[70] Like his conclusions about the renovation of city government in Russia, they remained quite traditional except on the question of taxation, where he opposed class privilege and championed state interest. During the 1820s and 1830s, the value of real estate in Russia's capital had soared. When he found that it was not reflected in the city's tax assessments, Miliutin hastened in mid-1843 to institute St. Petersburg's first property reassessment in more than two decades. As he uncovered cases of outright tax evasion among the city's aristocratic dwellers, he more than doubled their tax bills.[71] In reply, St. Petersburg's great lords immediately branded him an enemy of the aristocracy, and he bore that scar for the rest of his public life.[72] His challenge to noble class privilege became the main source of dispute between the Ministry of Internal Affairs and the State Council when it discussed his proposals for a new municipal statute late in 1844.

If Miliutin's reassessment of the properties of St. Petersburg's noblemen earned him their enmity, his plans for administrative reform drew the wrath of the city's merchant community when he sought their comments before submitting his proposals to the State Council. Such consultation with public opinion outside the bureaucracy had not been attempted since Catherine II's much-heralded Legislative Commission had failed in 1767. Yet far from acclaiming his efforts to encourage debate about important reform issues in their city, St. Petersburg's merchants rejected any attempt to regularize its administration, on the grounds that it violated traditional practice. Miliutin's proposals, they insisted, stood against the principles of autocracy and the "spirit of the Russian people," and even violated the fundamental laws of the Russian Empire.[73]

Although Miliutin's efforts to consult public opinion departed from autocratic legislative tradition, the merchants' opposition ensured its failure. Their rejection led him to conclude that only competent and far-seeing officials, backed by the authority of Russia's autocrat, could neutralize class opposition to change. Miliutin still carried that view to his work on the Great Reforms some fifteen years later. Rather than seek support among those segments of the nobility who were sympathetic to emancipation, he insisted that aristocratic participation in the Editing Commissions' work be minimized because he thought it unreasonable to expect those with a material stake in the old order to support its reform.[74]

Russia's senior statesmen shared Miliutin's desire to make St. Petersburg's administration more effective at the State Council hearings in October 1844, and they readily approved his plans to clarify administrative lines of authority and induce better elected officials to serve the city.[75] They opposed his efforts to establish any effective all-class decision-making bodies, insisted that the nobility have a decisive voice in the capital's affairs, and attempted to exclude some 3,000 of the city's smaller property holders from effective participation in its government.[76] It was a tribute to Miliutin's budding skill in guiding draft legislation through the higher reaches of the ministerial administration that he was able to strike a compromise with the Empire's senior statesmen on these issues.[77] The new St. Petersburg Municipal Statute gave representation to all classes on the General City Council, the capital's chief administrative policy-making body. In return, Miliutin had to watch the city's Administrative Council, the body that controlled tax levies and property assessments, become weighted heavily in favor of its noble residents.[78]

As it emerged from the State Council on February 13, 1846, the St. Petersburg Municipal Statute represented a compromise that served as a prototype for the municipal reform statute of 1870. Miliutin's achievement also had a broader significance because he had begun to use his Provisional Section as a testing ground for those young officials whose integrity, intelligence, and efficiency drew them to his attention. Miliutin's agency became another nucleus in the bureaucracy from which cadres of enlightened bureaucrats emerged to play a major role in planning the Great Reforms. Perhaps equally important, Miliutin's Municipal Statute provided him with rare experience in the autocratic legislative process. Of all those enlightened bureaucrats who drafted the Great Reforms, he was the only one with practical training in preparing reform legislation and guiding it through the upper reaches of the Russian administration. While others among his friends and colleagues boasted broader knowledge about local needs and conditions only Miliutin actually had taken a serious part in the legislative process that was so important for drafting and implementing change in Russia.

The conclusions that Miliutin drew from his experience in the 1840s embodied many of the positive and negative features of the enlightened bureaucrats' attitudes toward some of the most critical questions of the Great Reform era. To what extent should public opinion be consulted about reform legislation? What interaction should there be between officials, the autocrat, and Russia's privileged elite in the reform process? What motives should guide the state in fostering social transformation in Russia? The enlightened bureaucrats' responses to these vital questions had much of their genesis in Miliutin's experiences with the autocratic legislative process in the mid-1840s, although there were other factors that also influenced their views. Perhaps the most important among them was respect for the law. These men insisted that the law must control the exercise of power, and that power, capriciously applied, was one of the greatest blemishes upon the face of Russia at mid-century. Even though their opportunities were limited, they began to study Russia's laws, catalogue their faults, and plan ways to replace arbitrary authority with a rule of law during the latter half of Nicholas I's reign. Sergei Ivanovich Zarudnyi, a young man whom Panin thought the model state official, led the way in that endeavor.

Sergei Zarudnyi and Russia's Laws

In the Russia of Nicholas I, the absolute power of the Emperor reflected downward through all levels of society. If the Emperor's will, in theory, governed the acts of those below him, the same applied for those chief adjutants—his ministers—who spoke in his name. Such arbitrariness was even more deeply ingrained in the fabric of Russian society because noblemen possessed absolute authority over their serfs and brought that cast of mind into the bureaucracy. This was especially true of Russia's courts, where those who administered justice and the law usually were of noble background and were accustomed to exercising their unfettered will from birth. True justice, therefore, had become relatively rare by the 1830s and 1840s. Remarked one observer, "Russia ... resembled a lake, in the depths of which great fish devoured the smaller ones, while near the surface everything was calm and glistened smoothly, like a mirror."[79] Of course Russian statesmen knew what went on in the depths of the lake, but, because the autocrat's jealousy about his prerogatives was nowhere more evident than in the dispensation of the law, they thought in terms of adjustments, not broader reforms.

If the law originated with the person of the ruler, then any effort to interpret it implied an undercutting of the autocrat's authority. For that reason, Russian rulers were particularly insistent that judges and other legal officials should administer the law, never interpret it. Especially after Speranskii made the law available in digest form, judicial officials were expected to apply it in the same manner as other civil servants applied other sorts of regulations. This was merely an instance of that more general phenomenon in which, as the French scholar Michel Crozier has shown, decisions must be made at the locus of power in any bureaucratic structure and, the more extreme its centralization, the higher the point in the hierarchy where decisions must be made.[80] If autocrats were to remain the only source of law, then they must preserve all power to make law in their hands alone. "Only the lawgiver, as the figure representing in her person all of society and holding all powers in her hands, has the right to make laws," Catherine II had written in her *Nakaz*. "There is nothing more dangerous," she warned, "than the general dictum that one must take into account the spirit of the law and not hold strictly to its letter."[81]

Because those who dispensed justice in Russia were to be no more than administrators of laws handed down by an absolute sovereign, they became abject agents who implemented, with mechanical precision, what they assumed was the Emperor's will, and gave little or no thought at all to true justice. One of Zarudnyi's contemporaries described an extreme instance of this way of thinking in his reminiscences about the Nicholas era:

A gendarme [regarded by the Emperor as a direct extension of his own person] appeared in the chamber [of justice] and urgently demanded the execution of the instructions which he presented. The President [of the Chamber of Justice] immediately fell to thinking: "What was to be done?" After this, he ordered all the cases to be brought from the chancellery. Then he took one case, and raising it to his eyes, or, perhaps more accurately, to his nose, he declared: "Sustain the decision of the court," and laid [the papers relating to] this case to his right. Then he took another case and, repeating the process, declared: "Overturn the decision of the court." Then, with these motions, he rapidly began placing cases to the left and to the right, calling out: "Sustain! Overturn!" and so forth. When this was finished, the gendarme departed with the reports and all the cases in the Chamber of Justice had been decided.[82]

Even though justice itself had been poorly served, the will of the Emperor was fulfilled to the letter.

By the 1840s, the dispensation of justice in Russia had been reduced to a series of formulae which, ideally, could and should be applied without question, as Count Panin continued to insist that interpreting the law was irrelevant, even dangerous. Interpretive law texts were nonexistent, and the textbook of Russian law remained the *Digest of the Laws* itself. Not until 1845 did Professor D. I. Meier offer Russia's first university course on Russian civil law at the University of Kazan.[83] To study the law in Russia during the reign of Nicholas I meant to learn the *Digest of the Laws* and to apply its prescriptions just as any other set of administrative regulations might be applied. Russians who studied the theory of law studied it only in the abstract and only as it applied to legal systems in other countries.

To study Russian law itself—to begin to understand it and to learn its conflicts and inconsistencies—it was necessary to go to the source of its dispensation. This was the Consultation in the Ministry of Justice, where legal decisions were reviewed as part of a process by which that ministry prepared recommendations about disputed cases that had been brought before the Ruling Senate. Yet it was a difficult task to study the laws in the restricted environment of the Consultation because most who served there saw little difference between themselves as bureaucrats administering the law and officials in other ministries administering other affairs of state. No less than any other agency, the Ministry of Justice was staffed by *chinovniki* whose main concern was to move papers from one office to another.[84]

Sergei Zarudnyi's outlook differed sharply from his colleagues in the Ministry of Justice, and he became one of the first to study Russian laws at their source. Like Zablotskii and Miliutin, Zarudnyi came from impoverished noble roots and, again like them, he grew up in the country in intimate contact with serf life.[85] Although poor, his elders were well acquainted with the ideas of the Enlightenment, and books were his father's greatest passion. From his parents, Zarudnyi learned French, Italian, German, and English, and spoke the first two languages fluently before he left home.[86] The eighteenth-century Zarudynis had carved out respectable careers in the Imperial Guards, and Sergei diverged from that tradition only slightly when he chose to enter the Naval Cadet Corps. A simple error on his birth certificate ended his dreams of a naval career and left him with no means to continue his education. Crushed by such poverty that he could not even afford tutors to help him prepare for entrance examinations, he went to the southwestern university city of Kharkov, where he had to make his own way at the age of fourteen.[87] He seemed determined to seize hold of destiny in order to rise above his poverty. "Life is in opposition to the dictates of fate," he wrote.[88]

Although he earned a degree in mathematics at the University of Kharkov,[89] Zarudnyi never abandoned his childhood passion for literature. Like Miliutin, he fell under the spell of German romanticism, and that sustained him in his poverty. Prompted to search for a deeper meaning in life, he found it in struggle—in struggle against the dictates of fate, in struggle against passions, the external forces. "External forces —they are my enemy," he confided to his diary. "I want to think, but external forces do not permit me." To triumph over external forces meant to conquer passions, and Zarudnyi sought this "high moment of our life" in science and abstract thought.[90] In 1842, he applied unsuccessfully for a position at Russia's new Pulkovo Observatory, and so, in a desperate attempt to support himself, he turned to the civil service.[91] The brother of a distant relative was director of the Ministry of Justice's Department and grudgingly gave him a position. On November 27, 1842, Zarudnyi became a *kollezhskii sekretar'* in the Ministry of Justice.[92]

Zarudnyi entered Russia's Ministry of Justice under the regime of Panin, whom one historian has called the "most gloomy and callous representative of the old bureaucratic system,"[93] but who, like Kiselev and Perovskii, prized education in his subordinates. However, Panin made no effort to spare educated young men the frustration of inconsequential chancery tasks and, in fact, used it to test their mettle. Like Miliutin and Zablotskii, Zarudnyi found his first years in St. Petersburg devoted to those deadening bureaucratic routines that contemporary sources cursed as "a kind of clerkish rot and ignorance."[94] Zarudnyi proved himself capable and, in less than six months, became the senior assistant to the Office Section Chief in his department.[95] From that position he was able to turn the system to his advantage, as his scholarly abilities and analytic mind earned him that expert status that was so

N. A. Miliutin   *Sergei Zarudnyi*

important for liberating talented young men from the lower depths of the bureaucratic hierarchy.

As Head of the Second Section of His Majesty's Own Chancery, Count Dmitrii Bludov decided, in 1843, to investigate how the processes of Russia's civil law worked in practice and requested Count Panin to assemble comments from a number of judicial officials throughout the Empire for that purpose.[96] As the reports came into the Ministry of Justice's central offices, Zarudnyi was assigned to read and excerpt them before sending them on to the Second Section. It was a menial duty that Zarudnyi himself later described as one which "resembled most closely that of a postman."[97] Nonetheless, he made much of what seemed to others, from their formalistic, rank-conscious perspective, an inconsequential task, and he became an expert on the deficiencies in Russia's civil law code. "I had absolutely no knowledge whatsoever about the laws in general, or about our laws in particular," he later confessed in describing his first years in the Ministry of Justice. "After [studying] these imperfections in the laws, I went on to study the laws themselves," he continued. "The more imperfections I found in our laws, the more I enjoyed studying them. This was my school."[98] And there probably was no better school in which to study Russia's laws at the time. Even students at the Imperial School of Jurisprudence were trained only to administer the law efficiently, in keeping with the Emperor's view that the autocrat alone could make or interpret it. Zarudnyi's new expertise was much broader than such students of jurisprudence possessed.

In January 1847, Zarudnyi became an Office Section Chief in his Ministry's civil section to replace M. Kh. Reitern, a young official who soon rose, under the patronage of Grand Duke Konstantin Nikolaevich, to became Minister of Finance in the 1860s.[99] Zarudnyi's new duties placed him under the direct supervision of Mark Liuboshchinskii, the Department's Director. Also from impoverished aristocratic roots, Liuboshchinskii had entered the civil service some four years before Zarudnyi, after graduating from St. Petersburg University with a degree in law.[100] A friend of Miliutin, Zablotskii, and Reitern, Liuboshchinskii brought Zarudnyi into the company of well-educated, progressive young officials who were just beginning to seek alternatives to the administrative adjustments their superiors espoused. As men who respected the law and, in Zablotskii's words, "sought to introduce justice into all spheres of Russian life,"[101] they must have found Zarudnyi, with his passion for searching out contradictions and other failings in Russia's civil laws, a stimulating addition to their circle. By this time, Zarudnyi's deep interest in the law had grown far beyond any narrow concern about its unquestioning application.[102] That summer, he went abroad to be treated for an eye malady and tried to confirm his idealized view of Western law by what he later called "the realization of my democratic ideals." In Paris, he expected to find "those masses among whom the understanding of true law overcomes greed, where freedom defends itself with publicity, [and] where the aspiration for truth receives its fullest expression."[103] He haunted the city's law courts, was entranced by the orations of Jules Favre and Berryer, and became convinced that *glasnost'* (publicity), in legal proceedings, constituted one of the most fundamental guarantees that justice would prevail.[104] Not until the 1860s did he question his faith and realize that publicity in legal proceedings could not, by itself, assure the triumph of justice.

When Zarudnyi returned to take up his new duties in his Ministry's Department that fall, his ability to prepare clear and precise legal reports quickly endeared him to Panin, who once reportedly exclaimed: "If, just once in my life, I could present a report, or write a proposal, in the manner of Zarudnyi, then I should think that my life had not been lived in vain."[105] Zarudnyi thus assured himself of influence in Panin's ministry by excelling in those very routines he despised. While a number of his friends were critical of the bureaucracy's excessive formalism, none penned a more caustic critique than he about those tasks that Panin's regime obliged him to pursue with such apparent dedication. His criticism was not published until more than a decade after his death, when his son arranged for its publication in the historical journal *Russkaia starina.* Yet it almost certainly circulated in manuscript among his closest friends during the late 1840s and early 1850s, and it may well have been the subject of those private discussions at Miliutin's lodgings that Prince D. A. Obolenskii described in his memoirs as ones in which "the service milieu and senior statesmen were subjected to bitter and derisive criticism."[106]

Zarudnyi formulated his criticism of the bureaucracy in terms of a brilliantly satirical "letter from an experienced bureaucrat of the 'forties to a junior colleague just entering the service,"[107] in which he set forth a series of rules to guide young officials toward success. "Begin with the ABCs,"[108] he counseled, in terms clearly reminiscent of Bludov's advice to his son in 1838 to study the "alphabet of service."[109] Bludov had defined such an alphabet as embodying "habit, love for precision, and subordination."[110] For Zarudnyi, it represented that intense degradation to which a junior official must subject himself if he hoped to succeed in Russia's service. "Learn by heart such expressions as 'Your Excellency,'" he urged his fictitious junior colleague. "Begin and end your comments with this phrase when you address your kind and generous superior."[111] But Zarudnyi offered more than a criticism of the self-degradation demanded from junior bureaucrats, and he criticized the entire civil service for its rigidity, favoritism, and incompetence:

> Do not depend so much upon your talents as upon patronage [*protektsiia*]. In spite of all your abilities, seek to shelter yourself under the wing of a successful patron. If you have *protektsiia*, then you will be considered a genius, able to undertake any task, and you will advance rapidly. But if you do not have *protektsiia*, then you will be considered an utter fool, fit for nothing, and knowing nothing, and you will never prosper in the service....

> If you are diligent, but do not complain that you have a thousand and one things to tend to, then you will never rise in the opinion [of your superiors]. Complain that you are absolutely snowed under with work and that, while others are doing nothing, you must work day and night. Always take home a portfolio bulging with papers and, although you may be working on something else at home, say that you are working on department affairs.

> Try to pile all departmental cases upon others and, at the same time, complain that they are dumping all the work on you ... so that you will be regarded as an able, experienced, and hard-working civil servant.... The first question you should ask yourself when you are assigned a case to work on ought to be: "How can I get out of doing it?"

> Never stand on the side of truth when stronger forces, standing on the side of falsehood (but taking refuge in legal forms) are arrayed against you.... Never pay anywhere near as much attention to the substance of cases as to the people involved in them.... Never speak precisely on the basis of a particular law, but speak vaguely about legal bases.[112]

Such was Zarudnyi's perception of the central bureauracy in general and the Ministry of Justice in particular. His bitterness was easily the most intense of any expressed by his friends and like-minded associates, for Zablotskii, Miliutin, and those young men who worked with them during the 1840s at least had the comfort of serving under superiors who favored modest adjustments in the broader framework of the Nicholas system. Zarudnyi and his colleagues in the Ministry of Justice labored beneath the heavy hand of a minister who raised that very bureaucratic formalism they so despised to the highest level of virtue in order to enhance his personal authority.

Despite his inner feelings, Zarudnyi used Panin's favor to rise to positions of greater influence in the Ministry of Justice. In late October 1849, he became senior juridical consultant in the Ministry's Consultation, where senior officials frequently consulted him about difficult legal questions.[113] Panin reportedly called him "a master of [his] craft"[114] and placed considerable faith in his judgment, even though Zarudnyi was far more innovative than Panin's ideal of a legal specialist "trained to follow the law and orders."[115] Indeed, Zarudnyi used his new position to assemble young men of outstanding talent and education and to train them in the law in a way that universities and the Imperial School of Jurisprudence could not. "Zarudnyi managed to organize within the Consultation an entire school in which he tested the skills of the most talented young jurists," recalled Dmitrii Shubin-Pozdeev, one of the young men who served under him at that time.[116] Zarudnyi thus used the Ministry of Justice's Consultation to marshal cadres of talented officials directly under his command in much the same manner as Nikolai Miliutin and Zablotskii had used their agencies in the Ministries of Internal Affairs and State Domains. By mid-century, each had assembled a small group of highly trained officials; together they controlled a body of knowledge and experience that made them very necessary resources to their superiors.

If the expectations of Panin, Kiselev, and Perovskii were to be realized, the bureaucratic cadres that Miliutin, Zablotskii, and Zarudnyi commanded were essential to these efforts. Zarudnyi thus pursued the path upon which Miliutin and Zablotskii had embarked a few years before, and he perhaps had even more impact on the procedures and standards of his agency then they. "By working himself harder than anyone else," Shubin-Pozdeev recalled, "Zarudnyi had the rare ability to spur them [his subordinates] not only to work in the bureaucratic sense, but ... [to instill in them] a desire to draft not only conclusions, but to work out every question from every angle and within its proper historical context."[117] His first attempt to direct his new bureaucratic resources toward reform goals came in 1852. Bludov's work on Russia's civil code again provided him with the opportunity.

Throughout the 1840s, Panin raised numerous petty objections to those portions of Bludov's broader proposals for reform of Russia's civil code that he deemed direct attacks upon his position in the bureaucratic hierarchy or threats to his ministerial authority.[118] By 1852, these two senior statesmen had reached a bureaucratic stalemate, and, in an attempt to break the impasse, Nicholas I created a special Imperial Commission to reconcile their conflicts. As an expression of his continued support, the Tsar named Bludov its head and appointed Deputy Minister of Justice P. D. Illichevskii to represent Panin's position. In addition, there were senators A. F. Veimarn, R. M. Gubet, and M. M. Karniolin-Pinskii, as well as a representative from the Ministry of Justice's Consultation, who soon was replaced by Liuboshchinskii, by then Chief Procurator of the Senate's First Department. Liuboshchinskii named Zarudnyi as the committee's chief administrator.[119]

The Committee of 1852 represented both traditionalists and men who favored change. The views advocated by Veimarn and Gubet remain unclear, as do those which Liuboshchinskii's predecessor held during his brief tenure. Karniolin-Pinskii, who had become a Senator just the year before, first had worked with Speranskii in the Second Section. For more than a decade after he transferred to the Ministry of Justice, he had ardently seconded Panin's efforts to recruit talented, well-educated officials, and it was thought that he even could influence his master on occasion. At that moment, however, Karniolin-Pinskii was desperately trying to divorce a wife whose scandalous affairs had produced several unwanted offspring,[120] and his state of mind obviously was not suited to a critical analysis of Russia's civil laws. Nor was that of his colleague Illichevskii, also a protégé of Speranskii, who might have been expected to support reform. But his was a strange and confused mind which, only a few years later, fell prey to madness. One official found Illichevskii utterly bored by the petty tasks Panin heaped upon him but so unassertive that his only protest was to sign his name (which he had begun to abbreviate "Ill. . .") vertically rather than horizontally. He became obsessed with service decorations and spoke of little else.[121] Prince Meshcherskii served with him just a few years later, called him "*nothing* in the fullest meaning of the word," and remarked that "everyone knew that he *in no way* was capable of any thought whatsoever."[122] On those rare occasions when he attended the Senate or the State Council, Illichevskii sat in silence;[123] it seems that he served in much the same manner on the Committee of 1852.[124]

Bludov's voice thus became dominant on the committee. In January 1849, he had told the Emperor that Russia's civil laws demanded "radical transformation" and proposed the introduction of limited adversarial procedure, the use of attorneys (who would hold civil service rank), and the creation of justices of the peace to mediate minor civil disputes.[125] Yet like Kiselev and Perovskii, Bludov's innovations still centered on modifications of procedure. At no time did he propose broader reforms, nor did he ever contemplate challenging the administrative authority of autocracy.[126] Zarudnyi therefore was forced to work for a reform of Russia's civil laws within this very limited framework and to limit his efforts to technical improvements.[127]

Panin's resistance to reforms that might "undermine irreparably the system,"[128] and Bludov's determination to preserve the autocrat's administrative authority, thus confined Zarudnyi's role to one very similar to that which Miliutin and Zablotskii had played in their respective agencies a few years earlier. With no clear alternative to propose and, in any case, unable to implement his conviction that Russia required broader, more fundamental changes, Zarudnyi was reduced to following the path of administrative adjustment. He and his close friends already had concluded, however, that this was insufficient to achieve the sort of "renovation" that Russia required.

The Foundations of a New Service Ethic

From the moment they entered Russia's civil service, such senior Nicholaean statesmen as Panin and Bludov had held elite offices that had allowed them to believe that their "superior sensitivity and taste"[129] immediately could be put at their country's disposal for some worthwhile purpose. Furthermore, they, as well as Kiselev and Perovskii, possessed the supreme self-confidence born of educations based on the teachings of the Enlightenment and early sentimentalism that their enlightened minds could create a superior administrative order in the civil, diplomatic, or military bureaucracies of Russia. Such would not come, they realized, without grief and suffering, but, in their view, that very fact gave deeper meaning to life and reaffirmed their faith that the future somehow would be better than the present. Service to the state transcended individual desires within the context of their sentimentalist service ethic, for they believed they ought not judge the actions of a ruler who stood on a far higher plane than they.[130] Such elite officials gave a sense of purpose to their lives by serving Tsar and country. Because their wealth and high birth had secured them material comforts, they could afford the intellectual luxury of seeking life's deeper meanings, and they formulated their spiritual lives within the framework of a society that had made their daily lives comfortable and satisfying. Count Bludov could extol the "alphabet of service, which is not taught in universities ... and [which is] not elementary, so-called material knowledge,"[131] because such qualities ensured his high position.

Such young men as Miliutin, Zablotskii, and Zarudnyi faced a very different situation. Without serfs or estates, they, and a number of others with similar economic and educational backgrounds, set out to make bureaucratic careers for themselves in order to improve their lives. Although unusually well-educated and untypically energetic, they were not spared a number of painful years in the lower ranks of Russia's pettifogging clerical army before they rose to higher positions. As a consequence of the rigid service system Nicholas I imposed on Russia, their late adolescent years were devoted to the scribe's inky trade, not to those duties that had fostered the self-esteem of their Alexandrine predecessors. Miliutin and Zablotskii knew the boredom of inconsequential chancery work, while Zarudnyi, despite his university degree, was first assigned the menial clerical duty of summarizing reports. A number of their colleagues suffered similar experiences. Future state secretary and member of the Committee of Ministers V. P. Butkov actually devoted his first years as a civilian official in the War Ministry to becoming a living catalogue of his ministry's archives and was promoted five grades in the Table of Ranks in just three years as a reward.[132]

Rather than flattering their self-image and nourishing their aspirations, life in Russia's service in the 1830s and early 1840s crushed the young men who exchanged the security of their elite school classrooms for clerks' stools in offices buried deep within those great chanceries with which the architect Rossi so recently had adorned St. Petersburg. This stark reality pressed upon them from all sides; it condemned them to tasks they thought too menial for men of their elite educations, destroyed their dreams, and oppressed their spirits. Nikolai Miliutin once wrote that a "conflict between life and poetry" faced them,[133] a conflict in which, as his elder brother Dmitrii once reported from the army, everything was "totally at odds with my former conceptions, habits, and studies."[134] These young men could not insulate themselves from reality as did those who remained at the university to immerse themselves in the intellectual currents of the 1830s. For them, life had to take precedence over poetry. "Hard work and a sense of duty"[135] replaced idealism, and while they did not immediately make their peace with the hard reality of service life, they had to become reconciled to it. Periodic lapses into their old language of idealism no longer rang true as they left their world of dreams behind them.[136] For them, "literature" and "poetry" gave way to "politics" as the 1840s dawned.[137]

Just when these young men began to abandon their idealist concerns about beauty and truth in favor of pragmatic concerns, the idealism of their schoolmates who had shunned the bureaucracy was challenged in an equally painful manner. *"I do not know exactly, but something is wrong,"* one worried informant wrote to Count Benkendorf, and that warning led the Chief of Nicholas's Third Section to report that Russians were beginning to exhibit "a state of mind and feelings which is less propitious than at any time during the entire past fifteen years."[138] Benkendorf's apprehensions caused a number of Russia's intellectuals to cease writing; others were driven from their newly won university faculty posts because they failed to praise sufficiently the established order. For some of those who no longer could serve Russia with their pens, the bureaucracy offered a means of support, a refuge from the prominence they had gained as writers, and a limited opportunity to serve their country and its people.

In the moderate intelligentsia's search for havens during the 1840s, Perovskii played an important and unique role. "Perovskii liked to surround himself with individuals who had been educated in the university and were talented in scholarly and literary work," wrote one of his contemporaries,[139] while the novelist Mel'nikov-Pecherskii recalled that he "insisted it was necessary for any truly enlightened minister to conduct himself in such a manner."[140] Given the limited number of graduates emerging from Russia's elite schools and universities, Perovskii rightly viewed those well-educated intellectuals whom the Third Section so feared as an untapped source of talent. He offered them positions in his ministry just when they were seeking some means to withdraw from public view. The philologist Vladimir Dal', whom he named director of his personal chancellery, was merely the first among many.[141] During the next decade, Perovskii recruited Nikolai Nadezhdin, Ivan Aksakov, Ivan Turgenev, Count A. K. Tolstoi, Mikhail Saltykov-Shchedrin, Ivan Panaev, Aleksandr Herzen, and Nikolai Nekrasov, as well as Iuri Samarin, Konstantin Kavelin, Petr Redkin, Count Sollogub, and V. V. Grigor'ev.[142] Slavophiles, Westerners and even former political exiles all found places under his protection as he attempted, with considerable success, to employ their very obvious talents for Russia's welfare.

Perovskii's enlightened recruitment policies, combined with those of Kiselev in the Ministry of State Domains, made it possible to restore that exchange of ideas between the young men who had left their friends in Moscow's university and literary circles to enter Russia's service in the 1830s. This interchange was broadened by a new influx of young men from the Empire's elite schools and universities in the

1840s who, even more than the generation of Miliutin, Zablotskii, and Zarudnyi, felt impelled toward careers in government service. Romanticism had touched both groups but had produced very different effects. When combined with sentimentalism, it produced an exaltation of feeling that was poor preparation for the stark realities of a civil servant's life in St. Petersburg. The conflict between "poetry" and "politics" all but paralyzed Miliutin, Zarudnyi, Aleksandr Girs, and Konstantin Grot during their first year or two in the St. Petersburg bureaucracy, precisely because of the passivity that sentimentalism had instilled in them. Coupled with realism, however, romanticism produced a more positive affirmation of young Russians' abilities to act upon the world around them, and that was very much a part of the experience of those who entered the bureaucracy from Russia's elite schools in the 1840s. Sentimentalism had spawned passivity that could be overcome only at the cost of considerable emotional torment for such youths as Miliutin, Zablotskii, and Zarudnyi, but romanticism tinged with realism gave birth to an adoration of heroic deeds among the young men who followed them to St. Petersburg. They found positive heroes in the novels of Victor Hugo, James Fenimore Cooper, Sir Walter Scott, and, most of all, Alexandre Dumas,[143] and that impelled them to seek a more active course for their lives. As V. R. Zotov, soon to become a civilian official in the War Ministry, wrote in 1840, "Glory is our heart's desire/ To serve our country and our Tsar!"[144] Mixed with readings of Hegel and, later, the writings of the French utopian socialists, such adoration of heroic action led this new "generation" of young officials to become concerned about social problems and to advocate confronting them through positive action.

The generation of the 1840s was disposed by their school-boy intellectual experiences to think about Russia's problems in more action-oriented terms; in the university, their teachers urged them further along that path. Within the context of the Hegelian ideal that Timofei Granovskii, Petr Redkin, and Konstantin Kavelin lauded in their lectures at Moscow University, students came to think of change as a phenomenon taking place over time, and they thus rejected the need for accepting passively that existing order which had been so much a part of the sentimentalist service ethic. Under the influence of their professors' interpretations of Hegel, they began to believe that a heightened consciousness, gained through study and scientific inquiry, could enable them to take part in the great universal process of change, and that in turn affirmed their ability to improve the quality of life in Russia.[145] Their new convictions were reinforced at the Sunday gatherings that Granovskii's close friend Kavelin held for his students. Kavelin passionately argued against serfdom, and the effectiveness of his pleadings can best be judged by noting that a number of those who attended his Sunday gatherings appeared among the liberal minorities on those provincial committees that discussed the problems of emancipation in 1858.[146] At the same time, V. S. Poroshin opened to those who attended his lectures about political economy at St. Petersburg University the teachings of the French utopian socialists, which elevated the dignity of the individual above all else and held the well-being of all members of society, not the interests of a privileged elite, to be of paramount importance.[147]

Adolescent intellectual experiences that led the young men of the 1840s to think in broader terms about society and its welfare were reinforced by formal educations that focused more concretely on Russian reality and prepared them more directly for careers in government service. Dmitrii Miliutin could remark with considerable truth that "we, Moscow youths, had very vague notions in general about service affairs,"[148] because life in Russia's service did not consume his teachers' and classmates' attention. There was more concern with service affairs in the school experiences of Miliutin's contemporaries who attended St. Petersburg's elite schools, but, even there, a number of wealthy young nobles did not think exclusively in those terms. Until the 1840s, Russia's more wealthy noble youths thought it important to have been in state service, but they felt it necessary to devote no more than a few years to such tasks before they could retire *cum dignitate* to pursue other interests. "In the family into which I was born, it was considered a matter of class honor from generation to generation for young noblemen to devote their young adult years to military service," wrote Konstantin Veselovskii. "Because of this," he continued, "they entered the army not for the purpose of making it a lifelong profession, but so that, after spending a few years in it, they could retire with at least the rank of major . . . and, with a feeling of having done his duty, each could return to the bosom of his peaceful estate."[149] By contrast, government service became an all-absorbing concern for most students toward mid-century. "Hearing not only at school, but also at home, about the achievements of our predecessors, we let our thoughts dwell upon what was for us the most understandable and attractive side of our future service careers," Konstantin Arsen'ev recalled in remembering his student days at the Imperial School of Jurisprudence.[150] Unlike some of the youth of the 1830s, these students hastened into the service, as Valuev once explained, "so as not to be delayed in reaching the much-desired rank of *statskii sovetnik*."[151]

The young men who entered the agencies of Zablotskii, Miliutin, and Zarudnyi in St. Petersburg during the mid- to late 1840s had a sense of elite identity that was even more pervasive than that of the men under whom they first chose to serve, and this provided them with a more secure self-image once they had launched their careers. In an effort to improve the quality of provincial civil servants, the Emperor Nicholas had decreed in 1839 that university or elite school graduates must serve at least three years in the provinces before they could be eligible for positions in the capital. Only the handful who had graduated with distinction were exempted from this requirement, and, therefore, those young men who began their careers in St. Petersburg after 1840 had the sense of belonging to a particularly select group.[152] Feelings of eliteness were enhanced for graduates of the Lyceum at Tsarskoe Selo and the Imperial School of Jurisprudence by the intense loyalties which they held toward their classmates and their *alma mater*. "In their midst developed those elements of simple brotherly unanimity, exemplary comradeship, which bound them together after graduation and throughout their lives," explained Aleksei Iakhontov, who added that "there developed among all *litseisty* [Lyceum graduates] a love for their school and for Tsarskoe Selo as their childhood home."[153] *Litseisty* loved their school and forgave it its faults. "It is true that the Lyceum requires changes," Golovnin once confessed. "But as a *litseist,*" he added, "I do not want to lay a hand upon our beloved *alma mater*. Let others do so after I am gone."[154]

The ties that bound *litseisty* as youths endured into later life. Romantic poems written by adolescents about to enter the bureaucracy glorified their common bonds of camaraderie and shared youthful passions:

And do remember when, bewailing youth,
The days we spent in Lyceum's garden,
When you serenely blossomed
And life's grief was yet unknown.
   M. Longinov (1840)[155]

With new strength cement our beauteous union,
Preserve our comradely vows
In sacred communion.
   N. P. Semenov (1841)[156]

Friendships formed at the Lyceum became life-long commitments, and the impact of such school ties on the articulation of state policy later in the nineteenth century remains one of those fascinating questions yet to be studied by historians. Such bonds united the conservative D. A. Tolstoi and the more progressive A. V. Golovnin, M. Kh. Reitern, and A. K. Girs, who diverged sharply on political questions but joined in celebrations held on October 19th every year to commemorate the Lyceum's opening. For that day they set aside political animosities to be rejoined in those ties established during their long-ago adolescence.

Like the *litseisty*, the *pravovedy*, graduates from the Imperial School of Jurisprudence, were acutely conscious of shared comradely experiences which remained treasured memories long after they had gone into the civil service. More than four decades after his graduation, the *pravoved* V. V. Stasov captured the intensity of those feelings when he wrote the following reminiscences:

> Our class, our microcosmic world, was for me, as for many of my comrades, something that was forever dear, treasured, and alluring.... All my love, all my sympathy, and interests ... were transferred to the school and to my classmates. I found there much of that which home and family could not provide.... This was a life among equals with comrades devoted to a common task and occupation.... The conversations and arguments, the lively exchanges of ideas about things we had just read, regardless of whether they were mild and friendly or rude and hostile, were attractive to youths and endlessly treasured in their memories. These were our first guideposts.... Here our opinions were formed and our convictions strengthened.[157]

For *pravovedy*, their school became their *alma mater* in the broadest sense. With their classmates they formed close and lasting fraternal ties based on shared emotional, spiritual, and physical gratifications, and these helped to ease their transition from school to service under Panin's stern regime. Also like the *litseisty*, their common bonds defined to some extent later service relationships. "For him, a comrade from the School [of Jurisprudence] is something like a spiritual brother, who on all occasions, including promotions in service, should be given unquestioned preference over others," explained one observer about the *pravoved* Konstantin Pobedonostsev after he had risen to become one of the most influential men in Russia.[158]

The *pravovedy* thus comprised a corps of experts trained in the law, very conscious of their elite status, and bound together by firm and enduring ties. Some became a part of Zarudnyi's "school" in the Ministry of Justice. Others formed a body of reformist opinion in the Moscow Departments of the Senate, which were less oppressed by Panin's regime than were judicial agencies in St. Petersburg. Still others transferred to different ministries in order to advance their careers more rapidly. Prince Dmitrii Obolenskii and Pavel Glebov moved into the Naval Ministry to join the reformist *konstantinovtsy* in the mid-1850s. Some of their classmates later transferred to the Ministry of Internal

Affairs to serve under Miliutin or to the Ministry of State Domains to serve under Zablotskii. However and wherever they served Russia, *pravovedy* remained faithful to the admonition that their school's patron Prince Oldenburgskii had given at its first graduation ceremony to "preserve that fervent desire with which you long to show your limitless thanks for the inestimable grace of Our August Ruler who gave you such a great means to prepare yourselves for the service."[159] Many also endeavored to win influence and high status as rewards for excelling in their Emperor's service.

When these young men left their schools for the chanceries of St. Petersburg, they did not remain as isolated as Miliutin, Zarudnyi, Zablotskii or those others who had gone into the bureaucracy in the 1830s with elite educations as their only instrument for advancement. Entry into St. Petersburg's impersonal bureaucratic world was eased for the youth of the 1840s because their school ties helped them to obtain civil service positions from older graduates who had risen to head offices and departments. A. K. Girs, who left the Lyceum in 1835, was followed into the Ministry of Internal Affairs in the 1840s by A. V. Golovnin and D. A. Tolstoi, both of them future ministers. Konstantin Grot, who entered the Ministry of State Domains in 1838, was followed by Nikolai Garting and several others. Similar movements can be seen in the War Ministry during the early 1840s[160] and the Admiralty in the early 1850s,[161] where older comrades opened the way for younger ones.

Entrance into the civil service was facilitated further for these young men because Miliutin, Zablotskii, and Zarudnyi had created an institutional apparatus which enabled them to rise more easily, and a number deliberately entered these agencies because their directors were reputed to recognize talent and merit more quickly.[162] This new generation of civil servants was not obliged to struggle for the recognition that would lift them above the gray clerical mass in the central bureaucracy during their first years in Russia's service. Elite school graduates of the 1840s, therefore, did not spend their first years as officials in bitter conflict with the system of which they had become a part but, instead, worked on resolving administrative problems they thought important. Thus, when Nikolai Vtorov entered the Ministry of Internal Affairs in 1844, he found, in sharp contrast to the bitter experiences of Miliutin, Zablotskii, and Zarudnyi, "a friendly and like-minded circle of young men from the universities and lycées who dealt with administrative questions not from a paper-shuffling, purely formalistic, or casuistic perspective, but who sought to see the heart of the matter at hand, trying when possible to decide questions on well-informed bases and to institute a clear-cut system under which . . . [they sought to reach] more solid and broadly based decisions on any given question."[163]

Young men such as Vtorov already were predisposed to think about society and its welfare, for they were trained above all to serve the state and their Emperor. Like their predecessors, they sought models in the service, but they were not obliged to emulate, for want of anything better, those senior statesmen whose sentimentalist service ethic had proved so inhospitable for Zablotskii and his friends a decade before. Vtorov, his friends, and associates found far better models in Zablotskii, Zarudnyi, and Miliutin, whose economic status and career aspirations were similar to their own. "All of us, or almost all of us," Konstantin Arsen'ev once remarked, "regarded the service from the point of view of personal success or personal advantage."[164]

The elite school graduates of the late 1830s and 1840s also were closer to each other in intellectual outlook than Zablotskii, Miliutin, or Zarudnyi had been to their Alexandrine mentors. Both stood relatively close to each other in the service hierarchy and worked closely together to resolve administrative problems and study conditions in Russia. Although the men of the 1830s had by then become office section chiefs and department heads, they did not allow rank and position to separate them from their like-minded subordinates. Young Aleksandr Shumakher later remembered that "younger officials with higher educations began to exchange opinions and to consult with each other on more serious questions that were being dealt with by their various office sections. In doing so, they sought to establish clear principles based on reason and knowledge in the decision of such matters."[165]

These men shared a belief that their knowledge could be used for the benefit of Russia and that this goal could be achieved within the framework of the bureaucracy in which they served. They also shared what Prince Dmitrii Obolenskii once called an "incomprehensible, firm hope that the present order could not continue for very long and that better days soon must come."[166] This was particularly important because experience already had shown such men as Miliutin and Zablotskii that most government officials still were abysmally ignorant about the true state of Russian social and economic life, and they had concluded that progressive officials ought to make a broader knowledge of Russian conditions their first priority. This simply had seemed good administrative practice at first, but the influx into their offices of well-educated young men who believed that the acquisition of such knowledge could become part of a universal process by which they might participate in evolutionary change added a dynamic dimension to their studies. Rather than collect data mechanistically, they began to press for reform itself, as was evident in the shifting priorities of Miliutin's Municipal Section. By 1848, his investigators no longer merely gathered information about abuses of power and administrative malpractices in provincial towns but actually attempted to curtail them.[167]

St. Petersburg's chanceries constituted only one arena in which the interchange of ideas between progressive officials took place during the 1840s. Their discussion was broadened further by their many social encounters. The 1840s and early 1850s saw several interconnected circles emerge in St. Petersburg, and the meetings of bureaucratic colleagues in these informal surroundings were important for broadening their ideas, developing their views about change, and expanding the circle of men able to bring specialized knowledge about Russian conditions to bear on the issues of reform and renovation. As these circles developed, they came to shelter most of the men who drafted the Great Reforms legislation. During the difficult decade that Russians lived through between Europe's revolutions of 1848 and the Crimean War, these men elaborated upon the new service ethic that was beginning to emerge from the agencies of Zablotskii, Miliutin, and Zarudnyi. They reached a broader view of what reform ought to be and how it could be implemented within Russia's conservative, and increasingly outdated, political system.

CHAPTER 3

Forces Assemble

"These young men worked, studied, and read, and they looked upon the pointless, empty life of high society with contempt. . . . [They were sustained by] some incomprehensible hope that the present order could not continue for very long and that better days soon must come."

Prince Dmitrii Obolenskii

During the 1840s, Russia's moderate intellectuals developed a new awareness of their obligation to pursue knowledge, not for itself, but for the benefit of society. This so-called return to reality freed them from those ivory towers to which their intellectual wanderings had confined them during the 1830s and returned them to the mainstream of pragmatic affairs. In those central government offices most concerned with learning more about Russian economic, social, and legal conditions, Miliutin, Zablotskii, and Zarudnyi urged their subordinates to break down those mountains of official papers generated by the bureaucracy's dedication to the rituals of formalistic administration in order to better understand the complexities of Russian life. Having risen to more prestigious positions as directors of office sections, they insisted that the officially accepted portrait of life outside St. Petersburg and Moscow was inaccurate because it had been painted by subordinates bent on pleasing their superiors. A decade spent in the Russian bureaucracy had convinced them that such administrative adjustments as Kiselev, Perovskii, and Panin had advocated no longer could suffice, and they urged responsible officials to learn more about Russia's economic life, social problems, and the failure of her laws to function properly in order to understand the increasingly complex situation the Empire faced as mid-century approached. Such knowledge, they thought, could provide a basis for social and economic changes, although they did not yet

77

perceive the broader dimensions of these changes. During the last decade of Nicholas's reign, their increasingly close relationship with new elite school and university graduates helped to clarify their view. Together, moderate intellectuals and progressive bureaucrats interracted to consider the most fundamental dilemmas of progress and develop the reform view that became so fundamental to the genesis of Russia's Great Reform legislation. Above all, they needed to direct the forces of social change on a positive course and broaden the political role of newly emergent economic groups in order to establish a broader political base for autocracy. This had to be accomplished despite the inevitable opposition of nobles who held high government offices and wielded great political influence.

The return to reality that moderate intellectuals and progressive officials shared during the last decade of the Nicholas era, coupled with their common commitment to change, established a reconciliation between them which partly counteracted the better-known "parting of ways" that had occurred when the paths of progressive opinion and state authority had diverged after 1825.[1] "How could I be lured into government service under the political conditions which prevailed at that time?" asked the young Westerner Boris Chicherin in describing the vast gulf he perceived between the government and public opinion at mid-century. "To become the direct instrument of a government that mercilessly oppressed every thought and all enlightenment and which, as a consequence, I detested from the bottom of my soul," he continued, "was the prospect that lay before me. I turned away from it with indignation."[2] By contrast, experience taught the Slavophile Ivan Aksakov that Chicherin's preference for abandoning the government's path could be even less desirable than service itself. Aksakov retired after two years in the bureaucracy rather than perform the duties he found distasteful; however, he soon realized that his conscience would not permit him to remain apart, even though he, like Chicherin, might have preferred to do so. As he confessed in a remarkably candid letter to Miliutin:

> Having retired from the service, I found myself in a rather unpleasant position. In the first place, it was necessary for me to live . . . from the labor of my serfs. In the second place, any sort of civic activity in literature was impossible under the present conditions. Finally, I now know that I can be neither a serf-owning landlord nor a speculator. I have been forced to recognize that even though one struggles unsuccessfully against the falsehood of contemporary life, one still is obligated, as an honorable man, to carry the heroic struggle to its last extremity.[3]

Aksakov's statement was important for a number of reasons, not the least of which were his desire to hold a useful civic position and his refusal to live from his serfs' labor, even though many of his associates continued to do so. Just two years earlier, in fact, the great revolutionary exile Aleksandr Herzen had managed to sell his serfs at a substantial profit. With the advice of Baron James Rothschild, he reaped lucrative profits from investments in Parisian real estate and American bonds, and became precisely the sort of speculator to whom Aksakov referred.[4] Aksakov's remarks also were noteworthy because they embodied all those diverse elements that comprised the outlook of a man of the 1840s. In his dedication to heroic struggle's "last extremity," he displayed the sort of commitment to positive action that helped bridge the gap between the passivity of Russian intellectuals in the 1830s and their involvement in the reform debate of the late 1850s.

While Chicherin shunned civic action by remaining at Moscow University to work on his doctoral dissertation until 1857,[5] Aksakov sought Miliutin's intercession to find another position in the Petersburg bureaucracy, where he hoped "to serve good and truth with all the talent of my soul."[6] Although each dealt in different ways with his hatred of Nicholas's oppressive authority, both were closely associated with those intellectual circles that shaped the outlook of some of the leading figures among Russia's intelligentsia during the Nicholas era. In Moscow, the Herzen and Stankevich circles were instrumental in the ideological development of those intense young men who emerged as Westerners and Slavophiles in the 1840s, while the circles of Ivan Panaev, Andrei Kraevskii, and, to a lesser degree, Mikhail Petrashevskii, were important in the intellectual life of St. Petersburg a brief decade later. True, there were those like Ivan Turgenev who, in his tale about "Hamlet of Shchigrovskii District," cursed such intellectual circles as "a destruction of any original development [and] . . . a disgraceful substitute for society, women, and real life,"[7] but for many passionate, thinking young men they were, as Chicherin later wrote, "supportive, encouraging, and stimulating." Chicherin readily admitted that these groups had their faults, but he saw no alternative as mid-century approached. "What was one to do when they wouldn't let people out into the open air?" he asked. "These were the only lungs with which Russian thought, being squeezed from all sides at the time, had to breathe at all."[8] So great was the impact of these groups on the intellectual life of Russians that any number of studies about the intelligentsia during the 1830s and 1840s have been formulated in terms of those circles which dominated the lives of their members.[9] The ideas they discussed have been often and well studied and need not occupy our attention here. More important, there were less-studied circles in St. Petersburg that were influenced in important ways by these more illustrious groups.

Progressive Bureaucrats and St. Petersburg's Circles

St. Petersburg's lesser circles did not command such broad loyalties as did those of Herzen, Ogarev, and Stankevich during the 1830s or that of Belinskii and Panaev in the 1840s. Nor did the views of the members of these circles find expression in major journals, as did those of the more famous *Sovremennik* circle. Their members did not confront those cursed questions of the era with such intensity, and their ranks did not include those towering intellectual figures who directed the development of progressive and radical Russian opinion during the 1840s and 1850s. Their members shared interests that were only slightly less binding nonetheless. Concerned with western ideas, literature, and politics, they conceived of change as an evolutionary process, and they advocated reform, not revolution. These broadened views of reform were of major consequence in determining the character of the Great Reforms.

These lesser circles are difficult to study and even more difficult to discuss in the terms that historians have applied to their more illustrious counterparts. Far less conscious of their historical importance, their members were more modest, and intellectual debate was not the central focus of their lives. Because much of their time and attention was taken up with governmental affairs, almost none of these men kept diaries, and very few ever wrote memoirs. "There were times," Miliutin's elder brother Dmitrii once wrote, "when I contemplated keeping a diary in order to remember everything that was somewhat noteworthy that I happened to observe or in which I was myself a participant. But I managed to accomplish this undertaking only . . . at odd moments," he confessed. "After a short-lived effort, I abandoned this attempt for lack of time."[10] Although most conscious of the need to leave a record for posterity, Dmitrii Miliutin began to keep a regular diary only in 1873, as he neared sixty. His brother Nikolai never did so, except during the brief weeks he spent with Zablotskii and Keppen in southern Russia during 1837. The same was true of Zarudnyi, and Zablotskii never made even a first attempt to begin a diary. Valuev, whose caustic remarks we cited at the beginning of this study, kept a lengthy diary between 1847 and 1884 but, before his death, destroyed most of the sections that related to the Nicholas era.[11]

These men also left few memoirs about those difficult years just before and during the Crimean War. Although the indefatigable Dmitrii Miliutin was an exception, he was out of St. Petersburg during most of the 1840s. In any case, he became so cautious about any discussion of reform questions as a professor at the General Staff War Academy toward the end of the decade that he instinctively transferred that circumspection to his memoirs so that they are less reliable about this period than others. Among other enlightened bureaucrats, only Aleksandr Golovnin wrote memoirs, but he emphasized the 1860s, not the 1840s.[12]

Such men were extremely reticent in their letters about matters of a private and intellectual nature. All lived and served in St. Petersburg, saw each other frequently, and had no reason to commit their disputes and discussions to paper. They had begun to occupy positions from which they could hope to influence state affairs and stood to lose a great deal if they roused the suspicion of their superiors or the police. Even when one among them left the capital on an official assignment, or traveled to the West, they avoided any written comment on broader questions of change or matters of an intellectual nature. There are no remarks about political or intellectual issues in the letters that Nikolai Miliutin sent home to friends during his visit to western Europe in 1845 and 1846.[13] The same was true of his lengthy correspondence with his close friend A. K. Girs, who often was away from St. Petersburg on official assignments during the mid-1840s.[14]

The paucity of the types of sources that have figured so prominently in studies about the leading circles of Moscow and St. Petersburg makes it especially difficult to examine those lesser circles in which progressive bureaucrats and moderate intellectuals congregated. Further, we do not have voluminous police reports about them as we do, for example, about the gatherings that Petrashevskii held at his lodgings at about the same time because these groups were careful not to attract the attention of the police. Nonetheless, even a limited discussion of these less visible groups can broaden our picture of the interchange between bureaucrats and moderate intellectuals that occurred during the 1840s and early 1850s as they discussed the ideas of the West, analyzed the failings of Russia's society and government, and grappled with the dilemmas of reform and change.

Like many young officials, Nikolai Miliutin at first lived a poor and lonely life, sharing two poorly heated rooms with a former schoolmate and trying to make ends meet on the miserly salary he received as a *gubernskii sekretar'* in the Ministry of Internal Affairs.[15] During his first year in the capital, his only friends were his elder brother Dmitrii (then a student at the General Staff War Academy) and Mikhail Leks, his kindly middle-aged superior in the ministry's Economic Department.[16]

Early in 1837, however, Miliutin moved to more spacious lodgings on the Ekaterinskii Kanal, and more friends began to gather more frequently at his rooms.[17] At first there was only Ivan Arapetov (another former schoolmate who later served with Miliutin on the Editing Commission), Zablotskii, Konstantin Arsen'ev (Zablotskii's immediate superior), and Grigorii Nebolsin, a statistician at the university. Consumed by romantic notions of comradeship—of which the declarations that Herzen and Ogarev made to each other on Sparrow Hills were not an overly extreme example[18]—they felt isolated during their first years in the capital and attempted to recreate their "schoolboy" circles as an antidote to the loneliness of their new lives. They met only for a few months before Miliutin and Zablotskii joined Keppen to study peasant life in Russia's southern provinces, and it would seem that their discussions centered mainly on service gossip and casual social matters.[19] At that point they still were dedicated to emulating their superiors rather than to seeking paths of their own.

When Miliutin returned, in mid-1838, from his year-long assignment in the South, his evening gatherings began to include a broader sampling of men of progressive views. Dmitrii Miliutin later recalled that his younger brother's long stay in the provinces in the company of Keppen and Zablotskii had left him more sober and that he had become seriously interested in economics, statistics, and problems of state administration.[20] Konstantin Veselovskii, later a member of the Academy of Sciences who struck up a friendship with Miliutin around 1840, recalled that the young men who came to his rooms debated a wide range of political, economic, judicial, and historical questions and discussed how they related to Europe and Russia. These young men were faithful readers of *Journal des Débats, Le Temps,* and *La Siècle,* and they were seriously interested in the parliamentary life of Louis-Philippe's France.[21] By the winter of 1846, Miliutin's weekly gatherings had begun to include members of the Petersburg intelligentsia as well. "In the evenings, I. P. Arapetov, A. P. Zablotskii, Count Ivan Petrovich Tolstoi, Liubimov, Kriukovskii, and other general acquaintances often assembled," Dmitrii Miliutin remembered. "To this intimate circle, others were added gradually," he continued. "Among their number, the most prominent was Nikolai Ivanovich Nadezhdin, with whom my brother Nikolai worked in editing *The Journal of the Ministry of Internal Affairs.*"[22] The former editor of the Moscow weekly *Teleskop,* Nadezhdin only recently had returned from the Siberian exile.

Dmitrii Miliutin remembered only that "there were absorbing discussions about scientific and artistic questions [and] these were always animated, often by a dash of humor or amusing stories," at his brother's lodgings.[23] But debate within Nikolai Miliutin's circle of friends had begun to center on more serious issues than his brother chose to recall. A. E. Tsimmerman, a young army officer who knew both brothers at the time, later wrote that "even during the reign of Nikolai Pavlovich, Dmitrii and, especially, Nikolai Miliutin, were well known for their liberal views," but he added that "the elder brother became frightened by this reputation and conducted himself with extreme caution."[24] The great geographer Petr Semenov, a distant relative and a close acquaintance, added that Dmitrii Miliutin was "the most cautious and circumspect"[25] of his family and feared that the discussions at his brother's lodgings might do harm to the military career he had pursued with such dedication for more than a decade.

There was, of course, good reason for Dmitrii Miliutin's excessive caution. By the mid-1840s, his brother's circle had become very much involved in criticisms of Russia's administration, even though they remained staunch defenders of autocracy. Zablotskii, perhaps the most influential member of the group after Miliutin himself, characterized their friends as "neither revolutionaries nor constitutionalists," but men who favored progress through orderly evolution within the framework of autocracy. Their belief in justice, hard work, and duty—those virtues in which, according to Zablotskii, "they saw not only the means without which it is impossible to improve one's position in society legitimately, but also a necessary requirement for the full enjoyment of life ... and a basic law of morality"—made them sharply critical of the bureaucratic processes in which all were involved.[26] The rare account left by Obolenskii, a *pravoved* who attended Miliutin's gatherings regularly, makes it even more clear that their discussions involved far sharper criticisms than the "absorbing discussions about scientific and artistic questions" which Dmitrii Miliutin later recalled. According to Obolenskii's recollections, written considerably earlier than Miliutin's:

> Service conditions and the highest-ranking statesmen were subjected to bitter and sarcastic criticism. Everyone came with his own anecdote to tell about his minister or director, and hearty laughter greeted the words of each speaker. At that time, liberal ideas did not, in general, have a defined form. Among political and economic works we preferred to read the new books: Proudhon, Fourier, Louis Blanc, and so forth. The French revolution of 1848 animated these young men even more, but this animation was purely platonic. It goes without saying that no one dreamed of standing in the ranks of overt revolutionaries. But, being unable to sympathize with that strict regime in which all society was held, especially beginning with the year 1848, these young men worked, studied, and read, and they looked upon the pointless, empty life of high society with contempt. Fear reigned over everything. In

administration, routine held sway; in the courts, formalism became scandalous. Life lay hidden in the minds and hearts of these young men, but it was sustained by them with some incomprehensible, firm hope that the present order could not continue for very long and that better days soon must come.[27]

Two factors or, more precisely, two individuals helped to stimulate the circle's interest in the French utopian socialists and applauded their more sharply focused criticisms of the Nicholas system in the late 1840s. One was Miliutin's younger brother Vladimir, and the other was Konstantin Kavelin, a well-known professor from Moscow University.

During his student years at the University of St. Petersburg, Vladimir Miliutin shared his brother's lodgings and brought to the Miliutin circle his interest in European political economy.[28] His essays on "The Proletariat and Pauperism in England and in France" and "Malthus and His Opponents," the first critique of Malthus's ideas in Russian, were known to the members of his brother's circle and may well have been discussed at its meetings. During the late 1840s, however, Vladimir Miliutin began to withdraw from their company to associate with the *Petrashevtsy* and with the esoteric, erotic salon that assembled at the home of G. N. Gennadi.[29] More sensitive and thoughtful than his elder brothers, Vladimir, like a number of other intellectuals during the late 1840s and early 1850s, was intellectually, even physically, destroyed by the "censorship terror" that pressed upon him. This was a time when erotic—sometimes simply pornographic—literature enjoyed a surge of popularity among those very men who not so long before had sworn to serve truth, love, and beauty. Ivan Turgenev, who lived in St. Petersburg during these years, attributed this directly to the manner in which these sensitive men reacted to Nicholas I's repressive regime. In discussing Boccaccio's *Decameron* and the manner in which elegant lords and ladies amused each other with obscene tales in order to forget about the terrible plagues that raged around them, he posed the question to his friends: "And really, wasn't the Nicholas oppression its own type of plague for educated society?"[30] Certainly Turgenev had a point. Men who had been (and would again become) some of Russia's most creative and sensitive writers abandoned their nightly debates about Russia's past, present, and future and devoted their evenings to pornographic verse, to whores, and to compulsive gambling and drinking.[31] For Vladimir Miliutin, these years had fatal consequences; most probably at Gennadi's, he contracted syphilis and died before the age of thirty.[32]

More pragamatic, more realistic, and more hopeful, those in Miliutin's circle did not follow the path of his younger brother, and the urgings of Konstantin Kavelin helped to direct their discussions about change toward workable alternatives. As the ominous clouds of political reaction settled over Russia, Kavelin and his close friend on the Moscow University faculty, Petr Redkin, abandoned their professorial chairs to seek refuge in the St. Petersburg bureaucracy. Both took posts in Miliutin's Municipal Section, and Kavelin edited a number of the important new statistical studies that were being compiled in Miliutin's office.[33]

A deeply committed Hegelian, a strong opponent of serfdom, and a thinker well-acquainted with the works of the French utopian socialists, Kavelin soon became the Miliutin circle's mentor, much as he had served as preceptor for students at Moscow University earlier in the decade. Yet the political repression that drove him from his chair at the university did not cause him to reject his belief in the renovating power of autocracy. "I believe completely in the necessity of absolutism in present-day Russia, but it ought to be progressive and enlightened," he wrote to his friend Granovskii soon after he reached the capital.[34]

Because Miliutin's circle believed in orderly, evolutionary change, the publicist Pavel Annenkov dubbed it the "Petersburg Party of Progress."[35] By the late 1840s, their ranks included not only the men we have mentioned, but also Aleksandr Girs (one of Miliutin's closest associates in the Municipal Section), Konstantin Grot (who became Governor of Samara in 1853), Evgenii Korsh (a leading Westerner and friend of Herzen), the young Westerner historian Boris Chicherin (during his visits to St. Petersburg), Petr Redkin, Iakov and Nikolai Khanykov (both *litseisty,* whose brother Aleksandr was an ardent disciple of Fourier and one of Chernyshevskii's intellectual mentors in the late 1840s), V. S. Poroshin (regarded by many as the most exciting professor at St. Petersburg University), and Andrei Kraevskii, editor of *Otechestvennye zapiski.*[36] Together, these men used the Ministries of Internal Affairs and State Domains to improve their knowledge about Russia, and they even seized control of the Russian Geographical Society in order to direct its resources toward the same end. As mid-century approached, they extended their associations, and, by the outbreak of the Crimean War, they had established ties with almost every progressive group in the capital. At the same time, through the efforts of Kavelin, Korsh, and Chicherin, they cemented relations with circles in Moscow and with such leading intellectuals as Granovskii and Mikhail Pogodin.[37] Perhaps most important of all, the Miliutin circle bridged the chasms that had opened between various groups of the intelligentsia earlier in the 1840s. Although in many ways sympathetic to the views of the Westerners in the great debate that tore the ranks of the intelligentsia apart, they also preserved close ties with Slavophiles and proponents of Official Nationality.

Miliutin and his closest friends achieved this seemingly impossible reconciliation of bitter opposites by offering an opportunity to engage in "practical" work within the government to those men whose views had denied them any political role. As a result of these efforts, not only the Westerners Kavelin and Redkin but also the Slavophiles Ivan Aksakov and Iurii Samarin held positions in the Economic Department of the Ministry of Internal Affairs. Here they found it possible to work together productively and effectively despite the acrimonious debates that continued to divide their friends during the last decade of the Nicholas era. In the Economic Department this reconciliation was achieved only on a limited scale, but the effectiveness of meaningful political action as a means of reconciliation soon was proved far more conclusively in the legislative preparations for the Great Reforms themselves. Those Westerners and Slavophiles who participated in the discussions of various government committees hastened to bury their differences and reconciled themselves with each other and with the state. Only among those who were excluded from the reform preparations did the debate of the 1840s continue.

One of the first circles with which Miliutin and his friends became acquainted in St. Petersburg was that of Nikolai Nedezhdin and Konstantin Nevolin. Especially for those among them who had not studied at the university, this broadened their views, for Nadezhdin and Nevolin counted some of Russia's leading scholars among their friends. Born the son of a parish priest in 1804, Nadezhdin had studied at the Moscow Ecclesiastical Academy and then at Moscow University.[38] He soon became a disciple of Kant and Schelling and, after finishing his doctoral dissertation in 1831, received a post at Moscow University. Belinskii, Nikolai Stankevich, and Konstantin Aksakov heard his lectures and were moved by them to devote themselves to the study of Schelling's ideas. During these years, Nadezhdin became a close friend of former Minister of Justice Ivan Dmitriev and of Mikhail Pogodin. A number of aristocratic literary critics resented his sharply worded reviews of Pushkin's work and called Nadezhdin's writing "very common and vulgar."[39] Nonetheless, his career bore every promise of success until he became the editor of *Teleskop*, a journal in which many of the younger generation of Moscow literary community participated. Konstantin Aksakov, Mikhail Zagoskin, the poet Iazykov, Belinskii, Herzen, Ivan Kireevskii, Ivan Panaev, and a number of others all contributed to its pages, and despite opposition from the Moscow "establishment" (including most importantly the powerful Nikolai Grech), *Teleskop* flourished until Nadezhdin published Chaadaev's first "Philosophical letter." Success changed quickly into persecution as the authorities declared Chaadaev insane and sent Nadezhdin to Ust'-Sysol'sk. Thanks to several powerful friends, among them Iakov Rostovtsev, he was freed from Siberian exile after several years and went to live in the Crimea.[40]

Intercession by Perovskii made it possible for Nadezhdin to enter government service in St. Petersburg as editor of *The Journal of the Ministry of Internal Affairs*. As a number of his Moscow friends moved to St. Petersburg, he again became involved with scholarly and literary circles and soon renewed his friendship with Belinskii and Panaev. Most of all, he enjoyed the company of Konstantin Nevolin, also a priest's son, who became perhaps their closest friend during their years in the capital.[41] As one of the three best students at the Moscow Ecclesiastical Academy, Nevolin had been assigned to work on codification in the Second Section, and Speranskii then had sent him to study law at the universities of Berlin, Göttingen, and Heidelberg.[42] He returned to St. Petersburg to receive a doctorate in civil law and then taught for several years at Kiev's University of St. Vladimir. In 1843, the year that Nadezhdin became editor of *The Journal of the Ministry of Internal Affairs*, Nevolin was appointed Professor of Russian Civil Law at St. Petersburg University.[43] Widely regarded as Russia's preeminent authority on civil law during the 1840s, Nevolin shared with Nadezhdin an apartment where a number of prominent academics gathered. Among them were V. V. Grigor'ev, P. S. Savel'ev, I. P. Sakharov, V. V. Skripitsyn, and Vladimir Dal'.[44]

Dal', a close friend of Nevolin and Nadezhdin and already widely acclaimed as an ethnographer and lexicographer, had been the first of Russia's literary figures whom Perovskii brought into the Ministry of Internal Affairs. He had earned a doctorate in medicine at the University of Dorpat, had participated in the famous Khiva expedition led by Pervoskii's younger brother in 1839–1840, and, during most of Perovskii's tenure, directed his personal chancery.[45] Like Nadezhdin, Dal' was a specialist on Russian sectarians and later published several studies about the *khlysty* and the *skoptsy* based on materials he had obtained with Perovskii's help.[46] Perovskii considered Dal' one of his most valuable aides and placed an extraordinary amount of confidence in his judgment.[47]

Like Dal' and Nadezhdin, V. V. Grigor'ev, an orientalist who had studied at St. Petersburg and Moscow Universities between 1831 and 1842, was one of Perovskii's recruits[48] and served as Nadezhdin's assistant until 1851, when he transferred to the provincial capital of Orenburg to be closer to the region upon which his scholarly work had come to focus.[49] His interests in eastern studies were shared in the Nevolin-Nadezhdin circle by his friend P. S. Savel'ev, the son of a Petersburg merchant and also educated at the University of St. Petersburg. Savel'ev was a numismatist, especially interested in Central Asia, and became the secretary of the Committee on Foreign Censorship (1841–1852), where he had access to the latest works published in the West.[50]

The remaining two leading figures in the Nadezhdin-Nevolin circle shared Nadezhdin's interests in Slavic culture and religion. Ivan Petrovich Sakharov, like Nevolin and Nadezhdin the son of a priest, had studied medicine at Moscow University and had come to St. Petersburg in 1836 to serve in the Postal Department. Beginning in the 1830s, and continuing until illness made it impossible for him to continue his work in the mid-1850s, Sakharov published a large scholarly corpus about peasant life. His work added a rare dimension to the experience of friends who were less acquainted with the world outside the community of scholars than he was.[51] Sakharov was deeply patriotic, as were Nadezhdin and V. V. Skripitsyn, the other leading member of the group. Unlike the rest of the Nevolin-Nadezhdin circle, Skripitsyn was a nobleman who had begun his career in the Imperial Guards. As was common in the Nicholaean service, he had exchanged his Guards' epaulettes for the uniform of a civil servant and, by the 1840s, had become director of the Department of Ecclesiastical Affairs of Foreign Faiths in Perovskii's ministry. Skripitsyn, the least scholarly of the group, was known for his russification policies in his dealings with foreign faiths within the Empire.[52]

The Nadezhdin-Nevolin circle was thus unusual in St. Petersburg's intellectual and service milieux because all but one of its early members were of non-noble origin. That single factor may have helped them to bridge the gap between the intelligentsia and the bureaucracy in the mid-1840s. Mavericks in both worlds, they tended not to be bound by the constraints that governed either. Due to the diversity of its membership and its unique connection with the Petersburg worlds of scholarship, intelligentsia, and government service, the Nadezhdin-Nevolin circle served Miliutin, Zablotskii, and some of their closest friends as a means for establishing closer contacts with the intelligentsia and St. Petersburg's scholarly community during the mid-1840s.[53] It also acquainted them with other young officials who shared their views—most notably Aleksandr Golovnin and Iurii Samarin—whom Dal' often brought as his guests to these evening gatherings and who soon became a part of their group.[54]

Contact between the intelligentsia and St. Petersburg's progressive young bureaucrats was facilitated during the 1840s and early 1850s because, as we mentioned earlier, increasing numbers of the intelligentsia entered the bureaucracy in order to withdraw from public view at that time. We already have discussed how this affected the Ministries of Internal Affairs and State Domains, but it also extended to other agencies. The critic and writer A. V. Druzhinin, the young satirist Mikhail Saltykov, the playwright V. R. Zotov, and V. A. Tsie (who later played an important part in discussions about local government reform), served as civilian officials in the War Ministry during the 1840s. Saltykov, Zotov, and Tsie all were *litseisty*, and that bond drew them together in the ministry's offices.[55] Likewise, the writer and editor Panaev, the critic, censor, and editor A. V. Nikitenko, and the novelist Goncharov all served with Nadezhdin's friend Savel'ev, while the *litseisty* Evgenii Lamanskii and Mikhail Reitern served in the Ministry of Finance.

It would be impossible to reconstruct all the interconnecting relationships that tied these men into a loosely knit group, unified in what Prince Obolenskii called "the desire for a better order."[56] Yet the fragmentary sources indicate that there was considerable contact between progressive young officials and the St. Petersburg intelligentsia outside the bureaucracy as well. During the early 1850s, gatherings dominated by such literary figures as Ostrovskii, Pisemskii, and Grigorovich met every Thursday at Kraevskii's lodgings. These also were frequented by Nikolai and Dmitrii Miliutin, Zablotskii, and other "important officials,"[57] according to the scholar and literary critic A. N. Pypin. Zablotskii even reportedly served as the model for one of Goncharov's characters in *Obyknovennaia istoriia.*[58] Other groups met at the lodgings of Prince Odoevskii, who served so ably as Zablotskii's co-editor of *Sel'skoe chtenie,* and at the Zhemchuzhnikovs', where a number of *pravovedy,* including V. A. Artsimovich and Prince Obolenskii, gathered during the late 1840s.[59]

Miliutin, Zablotskii, and their close associates most frequently met the St. Petersburg intelligentsia at the evening gatherings which Ivan Panaev held every week. Panaev had been educated at the Boarding School for Sons of the Nobility at St. Petersburg University, entered the bureaucracy in 1831, and, beginning in 1834, served in the Ministry of Public Instruction. An affluent aristocrat, he moved easily in St. Petersburg's high society and was well acquainted with a number of prominent statesmen, including Minister of Finance Kankrin.[60] He followed the intellectual path of Russia's romantic youth of the 1830s. Like them, he saw "society in eternal struggle with the poet" and concluded that the two were separated by an unbridgeable chasm. "Society will never rise to the poet's level," he once wrote, "and the poet will never descend to the level of society."[61]

Soon after Panaev met Belinskii in 1839, he embarked upon that reconciliation with reality that characterized the intellectual odysseys of Herzen, Belinskii, and others. Herzen's preachings during 1840 convinced Belinskii that reality must be challenged and that the human personality could have meaning only in a struggle against the oppressions of the external world.[62] Following that path, Panaev, too, concluded that the artist must be the conscience of his time and society. Along with Belinskii and Herzen, he had concluded that the artist, as the only effective agent to combat an immoral world, must work to alter society. Panaev expressed his commitment to this view through his active participation in Kraevskii's *Otechestvennye zapiski,* a new journal for which Belinskii served as chief literary critic and which, between 1840 and 1847, published important works by Herzen, Nekrasov, Ogarev, Saltykov, Granovskii, Dostoevskii, Vladimir Miliutin, Zablotskii, and many others.[63] Until Panaev and Nekrasov assumed the editorship of *Sovremennik* in 1846, and took Belinskii, Turgenev, Goncharov, and a number of other leading *intelligenty* with them, *Otechestvennye zapiski* was the leading forum for progressive opinion in Russia.

Panaev's close connection with *Otechestvennye zapiski* made him a central figure in a literary circle that met at his lodgings throughout the 1840s and early 1850s. Its most prominent early members included Belinskii, Nekrasov, Turgenev, Botkin, Kraevskii, Herzen, Ogarev, Count Sollogub, Dal', Kavelin, and Grigorovich.[64] During the early 1840s, Belinskii's passion for the French Revolution became a major preoccupation during many of their evenings as they studied and read together. "Although they did not know French," Panaev later recalled, "Belinskii and many of our friends ... gathered at my lodgings each Saturday and I read to them what I had managed to compile and translate [from *Histoire parlementaire de la révolution française*] in the course of the previous week."[65] During these years, Panaev also translated "whole notebooks of Lamartine, Louis Blanc, and others" for his guests,[66] and not long afterwards, works by Proudhon, Cabet, and Fourier became objects of his circle's enthusiasm.[67]

Zablotskii, Miliutin, and their close friends were not part of Panaev's gatherings during the early 1840s, but they began to appear there during the middle of the decade, as a result of their growing friendship with Kraevskii.[68] During the late 1840s, their associations broadened further as a result of Vladimir Miliutin's close connection with the *Sovremennik* circle and Kavelin's long-standing friendship with Belinskii. Kavelin had known Belinskii ever since 1834, when his parents had hired the young critic as a tutor for their son.[69] During the eleven months he spent in St. Petersburg during 1842, Kavelin had been closely associated with Panaev's circle, and, when he returned to serve in Miliutin's Municipal Section in 1848, he hastened to renew his friendship with his former comrades. In doing so he brought the progressive officials with whom he served into a much more meaningful relationship with Panaev. By mid-century, Ivan Arapetov, Zablotskii, Miliutin, and Prince Obolenskii all became regular visitors at his evening gatherings.[70] No longer were they bureaucrats who stood apart from the society and the debates of the intelligentsia. They had become respected figures in both milieux.

The Imperial Russian Geographical Society

St. Petersburg's progressive young officials carried the exchange of views that they had begun with the circles of Nadezhdin, Nevolin, and Panaev into the more sedate confines of the Imperial Russian Geographical Society during the late 1840s and early 1850s. Between 1845 and 1856, 513 men from St. Petersburg's bureaucratic, literary, and scholarly communities became full members of this organization, in addition to thirty-nine others who were associate members.[71] In the Russian Geographical Society, "modestly housed on the third floor of Utin's residence on the Moika," as one member recalled,[72] these men broadened their ideas about reform and made serious efforts to assemble accurate demographic data and material about social and economic conditions in Russia's countryside. Most important, they tried to make their new knowledge available to more educated Russians. So popular did the society become among educated young men in mid-nineteenth-century Russia that Baron M. A. Korf, a close confidant of the Emperor, feared that it might one day threaten the autocrat's power. The Society, he remarked, "by its unusual collection of young men [who gather] for conversation on subjects about public affairs presents something not easily tolerated in an enlightened autocracy."[73] Contrary to Korf's fears, the Geographical Society actually became an instrument for the defense of enlightened autocracy in Russia. During the last decade of the Nicholas era, when reaction ruled the Empire and oppression lay heavily upon men who favored reform or renovation, it offered an alternative between complete rejection of the State's policies and total acquiescence. It provided men who supported the precepts of autocracy but believed with Kavelin that they "ought to be progressive and enlightened,"[74] with an opportunity to follow a middle path, to broaden their studies of Russian conditions and thereby nourish their hope for a better future.

Much has been written about the oppression that Russian intellectuals suffered during the Nicholas era, and we need not summarize it here. But to portray the second quarter of the nineteenth century as a time of unmitigated oppression and political obscurantism is to repeat only that side of the story told so dramatically by such alienated intellectuals as Herzen, Belinskii, and Panaev, who suffered from tyrannical censors' pens. Without doubt, Nicholas's reign encompassed what the scholar

Mikhail Lemke once called the "epoch of censorship terror," but it also was the Golden Age of Russian Literature. It saw some of Russia's first great composers and painters emerge, and it marked the development of Russian theater to a point where it assumed an identity of its own. Jurists began to be trained in Russia during these years, and the youths educated at the School of Jurisprudence later provided the expertise for making the Judicial Reform Statutes of 1864 perhaps the most successful of the Great Reforms. That so much intellectual and scholarly endeavor flourished during the Nicholas era is evidence that many educated Russians reconciled themselves to its constraints and found it possible to work creatively and successfully within such limits.

Nowhere was the Nicholas system more lavish in support of learning than in the field of applied science, which Uvarov, creator of the trilological doctrine of "Orthodoxy, Autocracy, and Nationality," sought to develop for the welfare of Russians and the glory of their rulers. As its new charter, drafted under Uvarov's supervision, read, the Academy of Sciences "must keep the government posted on all discoveries made by its members or foreign scholars that will abet the safeguarding of public health or lead to improvements in industry, the arts, manufacturing, trade, and shipping."[75] Uvarov also labored to make the Academy of Sciences in St. Petersburg a "showcase of Russia's contribution to modern scientific thought,"[76] and he extended this view into other parts of the scientific establishment. With steadfast dedication, he recruited noted scientists, first from the University of Dorpat, and then from universities throughout Europe.

Uvarov's efforts produced spectacular results. He brought to St. Petersburg, Karl Ernst von Baer, who began his career as an embryologist but broadened the range of his scientific enquiry immensely once he settled in St. Petersburg. In the tradition of Alexander von Humboldt, whom Nicholas personally had invited to explore the Ural, Caspian, and Altai regions of the Empire in 1829, von Baer pioneered a scientific study of the Empire's natural resources based on the work of specialists.[77] In addition to von Baer, Uvarov recruited others: Hermann Heinrich Hess, the founder of thermochemistry; Heinrich F. E. Lenz, the discoverer of Lenz's law on the direction of induced electrical current; Moritz Jacobi, a pioneer in galvanoplastics; the physicist A. T. Kupffer; and the zoologists Alexander Middendorff and Johann Brandt.[78] Such support for applied science led to the establishment of the world-renowned observatory at Pulkovo directed by the great astronomer Friedrich Georg Wilhelm von Struve, who fostered the measurement of the Russo-Scandinavian arc, "one of the greatest scientific undertakings of nineteenth-century Russia."[79]

The Geographical Society provided an important example of Nicholas's support for scientific endeavor. Its founding was the result of urgings by explorers[80] and academicians[81] seeking to pursue scientific interests, energetic Imperial General Staff officers who urged further geographical study of areas into which the Empire was seeking to expand,[82] and a few progressive government officials who realized that more research about Russia's demography and agriculture could be useful in developing better policies.[83] Encouraged by their enthusiasm, Nicholas approved plans to establish the Geographical Society on August 6, 1845. Its temporary charter was modeled on that of Britain's Royal Geographical Society, with the provision that within four years its members would draft a permanent one. Called the Imperial Russian Geographical Society, it was financed by an annual grant of 10,000 rubles from the Imperial Treasury, and Grand Duke Konstantin Nikolaevich, Nicholas's second son, became its first president.[84]

As with the Academy of Sciences, non-Russians dominated the Geographical Society from the beginning and, of its fifty-one founders, the names of thirty-one bespoke foreign or Baltic German origin. Baron Vrangel directed its Section on General Geography; von Struve, that on the Geography of Russia; von Baer headed the Section on Ethnography; and Keppen presided over the Section on Statistics. F. P. Litke, a Baltic German naval officer who was tutor and companion to Grand Duke Konstantin Nikolaevich, became its vice-president. All were part of the Uvarovian scientific establishment in the Academy of Sciences; all were devoted to the Uvarovian principle that applied science should be employed to win international acclaim for Russia; all saw themselves as a part of Russia's social and scientific elite. Undoubtedly, most of them hoped to see the Society rival its British model, just as the Pulkovo Observatory already had begun to rival that at Greenwich.

The Geographical Society was begun as an arm of the Uvarovian scientific establishment designed to pursue science for the greater glory of Russia, although some of its founders disliked Uvarov personally and chafed at the slowness with which he made decisions.[85] Among its founders, only Zablotskii, Dal', Nadezhdin, Arsen'ev, and Prince Odoevskii represented the views of St. Petersburg's progressive young officials.[86] Probably none of its founders, including even Zablotskii, expected that within half a decade the Society would become a major instrument for advancing economic, demographic, and social studies of those regions destined to be touched most directly by the Great Reforms.

The efforts of Aleksandr Golovnin, chosen at the age of twenty-four to serve as the Society's secretary, were particularly important in enabling progressive officials to gain such influence in its affairs.[87] Born into a famous noble family on March 25, 1821, Golovnin was a sickly child who sought refuge in books from a household dominated by women.[88] During his early adolescent years, he immersed himself in the works of Derzhavin, Lomonosov, Kheraskov, Sumarokov, Fonvizin, Batiushkov, and Bariatinskii. He read and re-read Karamzin's *History of the Russian State,* and from it developed a love for Russia, a sense of her potential greatness, and a belief in autocracy.[89] His formal education began as a day student on a state scholarship at the First Petersburg Gymnasium. Accustomed only to the company of his mother and sisters, he suffered cruelly from the taunts of his schoolmates, until his mother was able to enroll him at the Lyceum at Tsarskoe Selo in 1835.[90] There Golovnin found the company of youths committed to the Lyceum's tradition of close comradeship deeply gratifying, for it was not uncommon for adolescent youths to find physical as well as intellectual satisfaction among their comrades at the Empire's elite schools.[91] In this more congenial atmosphere, Golovnin continued to devour the writings of Byron, Goethe, Schiller, Pushkin, and Zhukovskii, and he thus became imbued with the same intellectual and emotional outlook that Miliutin, Zablotskii, Zarudnyi, and others like them carried away from school to their first chancery assignments.[92]

Golovnin at first found it difficult to reconcile his dreams with life in St. Petersburg's chanceries. He had won the Lyceum's gold medal, given only to those who ranked first in their class, and had entered the civil service at the comparatively high rank of *tituliarnyi sovetnik* (grade nine). He first served in the Fourth Section of His Majesty's Own Chancery under N. M. Longinov, a close friend of his deceased father, whom he described as "an honorable and kindly old gentleman."[93] For Golovnin, however, the work was intellectually deadening. As he later described these months (his memoirs are written entirely in the third person), "his service duties were not tiring, but they were devoid of meaning, involving first correspondence and then the task of preparing documents about the administration of girls' schools."[94] When Golovnin transferred to Dal's office in the Ministry of Internal Affairs, he found his place in the service. Dal' assigned him work he considered useful, and he devoted long hours to his new responsibilities. Golovnin found in Dal' a mentor to be respected and admired,[95] much as Miliutin and Zablotskii had found such models in Perovskii and Kiselev. Yet Golovnin's relationship with his superior differed markedly from theirs. Dal' stood only three grades above his protégé in the Table of Ranks, frequently invited him to meetings of the Nadezhdin-Nevolin circle, and introduced him to Nikolai and Dmitrii Miliutin, the Khanykov brothers, and Iurii Samarin.[96]

Dal's confidence in Golovnin's intellectual and administrative talents, and the respect that such explorers as Litke had for his father's memory, led to his appointment as secretary of the Geographical Society in October 1845.[97] Since it was the responsibility of the Society's secretary to serve as the president's assistant, Litke may have supported Golovnin in the hope that he could bridge the gap that separated Grand Duke Konstantin Nikolaevich, who held no official service rank at the time, from St. Petersburg's official world.[98] Perhaps more important, he may have seen Golovnin, so highly recommended by his fellow Baltic German Dal', as someone who would defend the interests of Russia's foreign scholarly establishment within the Society. If that were his purpose, Golovnin at first more than fulfilled his expectations. "News of the Geographical Society interests me greatly. Our meticulous secretary sends me whole notebooks about it and I am extremely grateful to him," he wrote to Baron Vrangel that November.[99]

During the last half of the 1840s, Golovnin worked to bring progressive officials into the Geographical Society. His reasons for doing so are not clear, and he passes over this important question in his memoirs. Certainly, patriotic feelings and the desire of young educated Russians to break the grip of German scholars upon their scientific establishment may have been one reason, and it is one that has received ample attention in the few accounts that have been written about the Geographical Society during the past century.[100] But what historians have so frequently portrayed simply as a nationalistic Russian effort to overcome German dominance in their scientific establishment was, in fact, considerably more complex. Faced by policies of retrenchment that made it difficult for them to continue their studies of Russian conditions after 1848, progressive young officials tried to seize the Society because it was the institution outside the bureaucracy best able to support their work.

One cannot say for certain that this latter purpose was foremost in Golovnin's mind when be began to bring friends from the bureaucracy into the Geographical Society in 1846, but what may have begun as an attempt to increase Russian influence turned into a concerted effort by progressive officials to seize control. Of the 170 new members added to the Society during the next two years, the names of only thirty-nine readily identify them as being of probable foreign or Baltic German origin. Most important, seventeen of Golovnin's new recruits were prominent among those who emerged as the core of Russia's enlightened bureaucracy or were closely allied with them.[101] During the eighteen months after the revolutions of 1848 in Europe, seven more progressive young officials were recruited,[102] and, by 1850, at least thirty were members. That twenty-two of them were in the Section on Russian Statistics offers further evidence for their purpose in joining.

These were talented, energetic men, by that time well schooled in the arena of bureaucratic and academic intrigue. When confronted by their challenge, the middle-aged "German" scholars, undisputed for so long in the preeminent positions which Russia's scholarly and scientific establishment had bestowed upon them, could not parry their attack. Further, when these young men began an offensive in late 1849, Uvarov had been replaced in office by the unassertive Prince Shirinskii-Shikh-matov, who admitted to "neither thought nor will of my own. I am only the blind tool of the Sovereign's will," he proclaimed with misguided pride.[103] When the so-called "German party" in the Society was challenged, the Emperor did not make his will known. Shirinskii-Shikhmatov thus did nothing to defend the influence of the scientific elite which Uvarov had assembled in St. Petersburg and nurtured with such care.

Signs of the coming conflict were evident in April 1846, when Litke wrote at length to Baron Vrangel about the first skirmishes between a few progressive young officials and Russia's scientific establishment:

> What they tell me about the [Geographical Society] meeting of April 9th, I do not like overly much, and if the spirit or, perhaps more precisely, the habit of argument, takes root in the form in which it came to light in that meeting, then the development [of the Society] in a scholarly direction will be completely repressed and factionalism will develop in its place. . . . It is essential that all right-thinking members close ranks around the president and support him. At the April meeting there was no one—or almost no one —of those upon whom he could rely and lean: not you, nor Baer, nor Struve. It would be sinful and sad if our infant (as we call the Geographical Society) at its very birth should suffocate in the fumes of discord.[104]

Although writing to Vrangel about marshaling support for Konstantin Nikolaevich as president, Litke was in fact speaking of mobilizing the senior scholarly and scientific community for its own defense. The conflict remained muted for some eighteen months but broke out sharply when it came time to draw up the Society's permanent charter. Late in 1847, a drafting committee of eight was chosen to work under Litke's direction. Von Baer, Gelmersen, Fuss, and E. K. Meiendorff defended the views of the scholarly establishment, while Nikolai and Dmitrii Miliutin, supported by Poroshin, opposed them.[105] The eighth member, P. N. Musin-Pushkin, stood between the two factions.

Litke and his supporters urged that the Society continue to emulate the Royal Geographical Society, in order to keep most of the decision-making power in the hands of a Council they controlled. Poroshin and the Miliutins insisted that the Council be subordinated to the Society's General Assembly[106] and, as one scholar wrote recently, stood "for the full democratization of the Society."[107] What they advocated, according to Dmitrii Miliutin, was to "extend participation in scholarly activity to a broader circle of members"[108] and, as his brother Nikolai commented further, to make certain that "scholarly questions and proposals concerning the entire Society are decided in its General Assembly [and not in its Council]."[109] What they hoped to achieve, in the view of one observer, was to redirect the Society toward statistical and ethnographic research about European Russia, while the scholarly establishment, in the tradition of such German mentors and colleagues as von Humboldt and Ritter, wanted to employ its resources for exploring uncharted regions of the Empire.[110]

The challengers of the scholarly establishment had not yet gained the power base needed to win control, for Litke had the ear of Konstantin Nikalaevich, and, with his support, the views of the establishment prevailed.[111] St. Petersburg's young progressives did not abandon their struggle but adopted new tactics. Their small, well-planned guerrilla foray to capture the Society's ramparts had shown them a breach in the walls themselves and, in 1849, they found the means to lauch a mass assault that the scholarly establishment could not repel. The Miliutins, Zablotskii, Poroshin, and their friends argued that the Society should be "Russian" in its composition and interests, a point which Nikolai Miliutin had emphasized in April 1847[112] and which Iakov Khanykov had repeated in his arguments for geographical terminology based on Russian rather than foreign words.[113] At a time when the number of Russians in the Society was increasing, but when the vice-president and all four heads of its Sections were of Baltic German or foreign origin, these calls for the Society to become "Russian" struck a sympathetic chord. Continuing to sow these fertile seeds of discontent, the young progressive officials reaped their harvest early the following year.

On February 16, 1850, the Geographical Society held its first elections under a permanent charter, and the progressive bureaucrats' campaign for "Russianness" yielded surprising results. Litke was ousted from his post and replaced as the Society's vice-president by General M. N. Murav'ev, a man of reactionary views and little geographical expertise but one known for being "Russian" in his outlook. Murav'ev's victory was symbolically important, but the election of the Society's Council members and the heads of its four Sections was of more consequence for controlling its direction and resources. "Germans" representing the scholarly establishment were replaced by "Russians." Only von Struve kept his post, while Baron Vrangel, Keppen, and von Baer were replaced by A. D. Ozerskii, Zablotskii, and Nadezhdin. In addition, the Council included F. F. Berg, A. M. Kniazhevich, A. I. Levshin, Baron E. K. Meiendorff, Dmitrii Miliutin, A. S. Norov, P. A. Tuchkov, and I. P.

Shul'gin. The Society's new secretary was A. K. Girs, a close friend of Zablotskii and the Miliutins.

From their position of dominance on the Society's Council, St. Petersburg's enlightened bureaucrats consolidated their control over its resources. At least eleven of the seventeen members of the editorial board of *Geograficheskie izvestiia*—the Society's monthly publication and most important organ for directing its research—were from their ranks or sympathetic to their goal of supporting ethnographic and statistical studies of Russia,[114] and Kraevskii, their friend and associate since the mid-1840s, became its editor. This new editorial board changed the name of their journal, as a signal to the Society's members that they were fulfilling their pledge to make the Geographical Society more "Russian," and *Geograficheskie izvestiia* became *Vestnik Imperatorskago Russkago Geograficheskago Obshchestva* in 1851. To strengthen their control over the Society they recruited more men who they were confident would support their aims. Of 118 new members taken into the Geographical Society between 1851 and 1856, sixty were nominated by eleven progressive officials who drafted the Great Reforms or were very closely associated with those who did.[115] During precisely those years when it was most difficult to pursue studies of provincial social and economic conditions within the regular agencies of the central bureaucracy these men dominated the Society, and then, in 1857, when it became possible to resume their work within the regular bureaucracy, they abandoned it to St. Petersburg's scholarly establishment.[116] In the 1857 elections, Litke was elected vice-president almost unanimously, while von Baer and Gelmersen returned to the Society's Council. Although Russia's enlightened bureaucrats continued to be members after that, the years of their most energetic participation were over.

While they controlled the Geographical Society, the enlightened bureaucrats used it to carry out statistical and ethnographic studies that further prepared them for the role they would play in drafting the Great Reforms. To them, the problems Russia faced at mid-century no longer could be stated in terms of administrative bureaus that functioned ineffectively or of officials who fulfilled their duties imperfectly or improperly. By the late 1840s, they had become convinced that the arbitrary power of nobles and officials must be curbed, that serfdom eventually must be abolished, that the judicial system must be reformed, and that the lives of everyone in Russia must be ruled by law. They must harness the forces of social change and create a broader base of support for autocracy that somehow allowed Russians some amount of participation in their government.

To carry out these complex tasks they faced many difficulties, not the least of which was the need to obtain accurate information about

Russia's population. Even mid-nineteenth-century censuses could be considered only reasonably accurate calculations of males from the tax-paying classes of the Empire because very sizable and significant portions of the population, including women, nobles, and government officials were not regularly inscribed.[117] When Zablotskii and his friends seized control of the Geographical Society, government statisticians were about to begin the ninth official census. They hoped to use their new positions in the Society to implement census procedures that would provide such data about religion, age, nationality, occupation, and family size as modern statisticians and statesmen considered vital to informed policy-making. But control of the census was in the hands of Minister of Finance F. P. Vronchenko, a traditionalist whose reluctance to argue for innovations in the conservative Nicholaean financial establishment had helped his rise to ministerial rank.[118] Because of Vronchenko's opposition, Zablotskii and his supporters in the Society's Statistical Section had to give way. Late in 1856, they tried again, this time with the support of Keppen who, with the backing of the Society's entire Council, urged Konstantin Nikolaevich to support conducting the 1857 census according to more scientific principles.[119] This time the new Minister of Finance P. F. Brok proved just as adamant in opposing change. Even in combination with other scholarly and scientific institutions, Petr Semenov, one of nineteenth-century Russia's greatest statisticians, concluded that it would be impossible for the Geographical Society to attain its goals "so long as the government does not take legislative measures for producing a general and accurate census of the population of the entire Empire."[120] The tsarist government did not heed Semenov's repeated pleas until 1897.

Unsuccessful in compiling more comprehensive information about Russia's population, Zablotskii and his associates in the Geographical Society's Statistical Section turned to less ambitious and controversial undertakings. Data in government files remained too limited to study economic or social problems on an Empire-wide basis. Therefore, they continued those local and regional studies for which they could assemble the necessary data through first-hand observation. Their most successful effort was Ivan Aksakov's study of the eleven commercial fairs in the Ukraine. His study, published in 1858, provided valuable information about Russian internal trade and manufacture that had never been available to the government before and earned the prestigious Konstantinovskii medal for its author. The enlightened bureaucrats also were more successful in their ethnographic researches. Of particular importance was the success of the Society's periodical publication, *Etnograficheskii sbornik,* edited first by Nadezhdin and then by Kavelin, who urged the Ethnographical Section of the Society to pursue provincial, not Empire-wide, studies and to place them in a broader historical context.[121]

Although control of the Geographical Society did not yield all they had hoped for between 1850 and 1857, it provided Russia's enlightened bureaucrats with important opportunities to investigate internal trade, population movements, and local life in the Empire and to transmit their findings to a wider audience.[122] Equally important, it brought together men who had not yet become acquainted in the course of their government assignments. Iu. A. Gagemeister, a graduate of Dorpat University, and E. I. Lamanskii, a *litseist,* both of whom had spent their early careers in the conservative Ministry of Finance, established those common links with Miliutin, Zablotskii, Arapetov, and Girs in the Statistical Section of the Geographical Society, which cemented the alliance they carried into the Editing Commissions of 1859–1860.[123] The same was true of S. M. Zhukovskii, who served on the Editing Commissions, and of Ia. A. Solov'ev, a young official in the Ministry of State Domains who rose to become an important figure in the enlightened bureaucrats' ranks by the mid-1850s. Like Miliutin, Solov'ev helped to prepare the *zemstvo* reforms of 1864 and draft the Emancipation of 1861.

With the exception of Prince V. A. Cherkasskii and the specialists who drafted the Judicial Reform of 1864, every government official who helped to draft and support the Great Reform legislation took an active part in the Geographical Society between 1850 and 1857. "Given the absence of any civic life among us at that time, the existence of such a center [as the Geographical Society] in which people interested in knowledge could gather for general discussions had special value in the eyes of society," recalled F. G. Terner, a young civil servant who was well acquainted with Zablotskii and Miliutin during the last years of the Nicholas era.[124] For exchanging ideas and furthering an understanding of Russia, the Geographical Society thus was of considerable importance in that assembly of forces within the bureaucracy that preceded the beginning of reform work after the end of the Crimean War.

Coupled with their belief that change was an evolutionary process, the work of these progressive, well-educated young officials during these years led them to contemplate a gradual transformation of rural Russia. Through their common labors and continued interaction with the intelligentsia they coalesced into an enlightened bureaucracy: a group of officials who envisioned change in broader terms than the administrative adjustments championed by Perovskii, Kiselev, and Panin, who shared the social conscience of the intelligentsia, and who believed that, as educated men with an ever-broadening understanding of Russian conditions, they could utilize their superior knowledge for the benefit of all Russians. The manner in which they studied Russia's provinces, their initial vision of rural Russia's transformation, and the manner in which they emerged as an enlightened bureaucracy are the subjects of the following chapter.

ChAPTER 4

An Enlightened
Bureaucracy Emerges

*"All that we have done thus far is not yet
ripened fruit but only good seed. It is not yet
a task that is completed, but only a good
beginning."*

Konstantin Arsen'ev

The initial purpose of the studies that Miliutin and Zablotskii fostered during the 1840s was to develop data that could be used to understand provincial conditions and improve the central administration's ability to resolve regional and local problems by drafting more precise regulations. "Survey the existing failings and areas in which practice does not conform to the law in the civic and economic organization of towns and cities," Miliutin instructed his agents of special commisions in 1845. "Lay the groundwork for assembling complete administrative statistics about these areas of concern and . . . seek the means for a better organization of civic and economic affairs in these municipalities."[1] These tasks were very similar to those that Zarudnyi had set for himself within the Ministry of Justice at about the same time as he and his associates set out to find the faults (what he called "imperfections") in Russia's laws.[2]

Although important, statistics were only one of several instruments required to resolve the problems Russia faced, and, as mid-century approached, these men began to look beyond new regulations and more efficient administration to a gradual transformation of the Empire's social and economic life. "Even if they are absolutely accurate, numbers alone cannot provide a full understanding of any given issue," Konstantin Veselovskii admitted in 1847. "A qualitative evaluation of any problem," he added, "also is necessary."[3] Veselovskii's statement was an early expression of the enlightened bureaucrats' perception that no matter how precise or complete, mere information could not serve as an effective instrument for renovating Russia's stagnant social and economic systems. By mid-century they had begun to understand that such data never could be more than an instrument for refining and perpetuating policy. That realization compelled them to confront the most complex dilemma that modern Russian statesmen yet had been obliged to face. No longer was it a question of implementing and perpetuating policy; they had to find the means to change it.

Ever since Peter the Great had abolished the Boiar Council that advised Muscovite tsars, Russia's autocrats had made policy and relied on their chosen agents to execute their will. Peter's monopoly over the process of policy-making in domestic affairs was even more certain because his closest adjutants often were not part of the Empire's civil administration and worked outside that administration to carry out his commissions. Changes in policy thus came as a result of his own perceptions of Russia's needs or, much more rarely, as a consequence of influence exerted upon him by favorites who held his confidence.

Throughout the eighteenth century, Russia's autocrats made policy as circumstances warranted or as their perceptions of the Empire's needs changed. On those few occasions when they felt the need to consult a broader segment of opinion, they created *ad hoc* advisory bodies which ranged from such small groups of Imperial favorites as the Empress Anna Ivanovna's Supreme Privy Council, the Unofficial Committee of Alexander I, and Nicholas I's Committee of December 6th, to such larger bodies as Catherine II's Legislative Commission. None had a place in Russia's regular administrative structure. Their size, membership, and responsibilities were determined by the autocrat's whim, and they served strictly at the ruler's pleasure. Technical expertise or a broad knowledge of Russian affairs never was a prerequisite for membership in these groups. Far more important was loyalty to the autocrat. Individuals or interest groups in Russia thus first had to win the sovereign's favor, if they helped to bring about changes in policy. The only alternative was the eighteenth-century palace revolutions during which disgruntled aristocrats overthrew rulers whose policies were unpopular or seemed ill-advised.

So long as Russia's administration remained relatively unstructured, and the problems facing it reasonably uncomplex, such crude means for implementing and changing policy posed no insurmountable problems. As the Empire's bureaucracy increased in numbers, took on more complex functions, and had to face more complicated problems in the post-Napoleonic era, it became increasingly difficult to implement policy and even more awkward to change it. No sovereign could hope to understand the baffling problems that Russia faced during the second quarter of the nineteenth century. Nicholas I could not propose direct solutions as Peter the Great had done, because the resolution of these problems required more expertise than any single individual could possess. Nicholas I had grown up in a world without the technology that so rapidly entered the lives of men and women in the 1840s and 1850s. An autocrat who had grown up in a world without railroads, steamships, or factories with steam-driven machinery could not easily change state policy to encompass the complex social and political problems that such technology created.

If the Emperor could not confront the problems facing his Empire in the direct manner of the eighteenth-century autocrats, the issue of changing policy was complicated further because the interests of the state and its nobles no longer coincided. Since most statesmen and senior officials still came from aristocratic, serf-owning families, they slowed the implementation of policies that stood against the traditional interests of their class.[4] Furthermore, the so-called "palace revolutions" that eighteenth-century Russian aristocrats had used to change policy no longer were effective in the post-Napoleonic era. There were a number of reasons for that, not the least of which was Paul I's Statute on the Imperial Family. Issued on the day of Paul's coronation, this decree established a firm order of succession and ended the unstable situation that the Empire's nobles had used to extort extensive privileges from eighteenth-century autocrats. The result was a stalemate in which the autocrat found it difficult to implement policies that were against the interests of the aristocracy, while the aristocracy found it even more difficult to force changes in those state policies they opposed.

This situation was complicated further because Russia's growing army of petty clerks, who had learned their narrow duties on the job, opposed any change for fear that such might burden them with new tasks that they might be unable to learn.[5] These thousands of poorly educated, underpaid men, whose lives we described briefly in the first chapter of this study, stood as a mutely passive but immensely effective force against even the slightest policy change. So effective was their resistance that millions of decrees, orders, and requests for information lay unheeded in Russian provincial offices while they continued to perform their mechanical functions in the manner they had learned when they first entered government service.[6]

Between these extremes in Russia's civil service stood those officials who held positions ranging from assistant office section chiefs to department heads. These men implemented policy on a daily basis, knew its flaws from personal observation, and even understood how it might be made more effective or more responsive to particular circumstances. Yet these men feared to make recommendations to their superiors. "They can wipe me from the face of the earth," confessed one such official as he tried to explain why he did not recommend policy changes when he knew they were necessary.[7] Such fears caused men who knew better to tell their superiors only what they thought they wanted to hear. They did not make recommendations that could have made it possible for senior statesmen to propose meaningful changes in policy to the autocrat. And even ministers of state feared to carry criticisms to the Emperor.[8] The result, Valuev confessed in 1855, was that all of Russia's many failings disappeared when one read the official reports. If one believed their contents, he lamented, it seemed that "everything possible has been done everywhere. Success has been achieved everywhere."[9] As Zarudnyi complained at about the same time, the Empire's government was being consumed by a sort of "clerkish rot and ignorance."[10]

A decade before he penned his critique of Russia's administration, Valuev wrote about the officials' obligation to act in a more responsible manner in order to avert a growing paralysis in the Empire's instruments of policy:

> The well-being and domestic success of any state [he wrote to Perovskii in 1845] depends to a significant degree upon the activities of those individuals to whom the more important areas of state administration are entrusted. Their influence on the civil and political life of any country is even more noticeable in an autocratic state, where public opinion stands mute, where citizens are not summoned to participate in discussions of public affairs, and where, finally, great statesmen frequently conceal their personal shortcomings and mistakes behind the impenetrable shield of the autocrat's name.[11]

Although he thought officials should act responsibly, Valuev offered no suggestions about how state policies could be changed, nor did he indicate what new instruments might be created to overcome that near-stalemate between autocracy, aristocracy, and bureaucracy on the issue of changing policy. Like other men who emerged as enlightened bureaucrats in Russia's central administration, Valuev thought it important to assemble information about the government's failings but saw no means for converting those data into new policy.

Failure to convert information into policy was perhaps the most critical issue that progressive officials faced. The most dramatic example was the Committee of December 6th, which failed to institute any changes in policy, even though Nicholas I had given them a broad mandate to survey the entire administration and recommend improvement where they thought necessary.[12] Using especially the testimony of the Decembrists, and admittedly lacking the more accurate data that enlightened bureaucrats assembled two decades later, the committee examined Russia's local and central administration, inquired into the condition of the nobility, and studied the institution of serfdom. Yet they accomplished little. Lack of motivation, far more than lack of information, caused their failure. At Speranskii's urging, they avoided the entire question of changing policy by agreeing that their task was "not the full alteration of the existing order of government, but its refinement by means of a few particular changes and additions."[13] Policy questions thus were transformed into minor administrative issues.

If such august bodies as the Committee of December 6th could not convert new information into new policy, it is not surprising that the bureaucracy as a whole was no more successful. Even on those minor issues about which everyone agreed, it often proved impossible to make policy changes. In a classic case, both St. Petersburg and provincial officials in Zablotskii's agency agreed to improve the quality of sheep that the state peasants raised in southern Russia. Yet some eight years after the work began, the ministry had been unable to put the decision into effect and finally set the entire question aside until some later, unspecified date.[14]

Obviously, some steps had to be taken to create new policy-making instruments in Russia's central administration if the Empire's more crucial and controversial social and economic dilemmas were to be confronted effectively. The need for new policy-making instruments was all the more necessary because the more traditional means for changing policy had proved so ineffective. Both Alexander I's "Unofficial Committee" and Nicholas's Committee of December 6th had been notable failures. Beyond that, Nicholas had convened ten special committees in an attempt to resolve the economic and social crisis posed by serfdom, and all of them had failed.

Miliutin, Zablotskii, and a number of their associates at first perceived only dimly this need for new policy-making instruments. But their efforts to assemble more accurate and comprehensive data about local conditions in Russia created the means for converting information into policy even before they fully realized what they had accomplished. Most important of all, their willingness to seek out expert advice, even when that meant cutting across jealously guarded lines of ministerial authority, established the prototypes for those committees of experts that drafted the Great Reform legislation. Beginning in the mid-1840s, they exchanged information informally.[15] At first such exchanges were confined within a particular department, then broadened to a given ministry, and soon bridged the gap between the ministries that had been created when senior Nicholaean statesmen had refused to sanction formal inter-agency cooperation in a jealous effort to preserve their personal power and authority. The enlightened bureaucrats called this ever-widening process *glasnost'* (literally, publicity), but, as Alexander I and his Young Friends had done with the term "constitution," they endowed it with a meaning quite different from the one it usually bore in the West. At mid-century, the enlightened bureaucrats saw *glasnost'* as a means to involve men who shared their views in a broader discussion of their nation's renovation and transformation. Although limited to specific problems and areas of policy, *glasnost'* became important in bridging the gap between the bureaucracy and educated society which Nicholas I's firm suppression of the Decembrists had opened at the beginning of his reign.

Concern about making qualitative judgments and their increased support of *glasnost'* produced subtle but important changes in the enlightened bureaucrats' attitudes. They no longer emphasized more precise regulations but began to use much more frequently the term "transformation" *(preobrazovanie)* in their discussions of state problems. *Preobrazovanie* had been used by Russian administrators throughout the first half of the nineteenth century, but generally in the narrower sense of administrative or institutional adjustments, even when related to social and economic issues.[16] Zablotskii used it in 1841 to argue that "changes in serfdom ought to change this [present] order of things and should lead to other fundamental transformations in our civic order"[17] but did not describe the transformations to which he alluded, and, from Miliutin's similar usage of the term early in 1844, it seems that both applied it in its traditionally more limited administrative sense. Certainly in his lengthy memorandum "On the Transformation of Municipal Public Administration," Miliutin spoke only of administrative changes in town and city government and did not attach that broader meaning it would have for enlightened bureaucrats a few years later.[18]

V. A. Tsie was probably the first among the enlightened bureaucrats to use *preobrazovanie* in the sense of social or economic transformation, and he did so in the context of his ideas about prison reform. Born in 1820, Tsie graduated from the Lyceum at Tsarskoe Selo the year after Konstantin Veselovskii and entered the civil service as a censor in 1839. In 1847 or 1848 (it is not possible to date the manuscript more precisely), he wrote a brief essay "On Prisons and Their Transformation" in which he urged the rehabilitation of criminals so that valuable human resources would not be lost to the state. "The transformation of prisons is not the consequence of any particular philosophical theory," Tsie wrote. "It is the essential, inevitable requirement of our times . . . [in which] the modernization of our ways, as a result of broader education, urgently requires the abolition of those crude and brutal concepts and customs that have been handed down to us from the middle ages."[19] Tsie argued that the rehabilitation of prisoners was in the best interests of the state and thus specifically tied education and progressive policies to its well-being.

Tsie discussed the transformation of prisons in terms of the state's welfare because the enlightened bureaucrats put the interests of the state before those of any particular group. They used their concern for the welfare of the state to justify much of their statistical work, as Miliutin, Girs, Kavelin, and Redkin characterized their studies of Russia's towns and cities as "a rich collection of practical data and important documents that are essential for the intended transformation [of municipal economy and administration]."[20] Their concern for the state's welfare also led Russia's enlightened bureaucrats, and especially Zablotskii and his associates in the Ministry of State Domains' Academic Committee and Department of Rural Economy, to urge further measures for a gradual transformation of rural Russia during the last decade of the Nicholas era.

For enlightened bureaucrats, the broad issue of rural Russia's transformation during the late 1840s and early 1850s centered on the issue of agricultural improvement; they did not argue for the immediate abolition of serfdom, even though they all considered it an anachronistic and economically unprofitable system. Even to begin the improvement of Russian agriculture was a difficult task because that deepseated conservatism common to all peasants for whom the failure of new crops or techniques could mean starvation led serfs to resist innovation. In the Russian countryside, such conservatism was institutionalized in the repartitional peasant commune in which a timid or conservative majority could bar a more adventurous minority from experimenting with change. Equally important, the vast majority of Russia's serf-owning nobles were unwilling to diversify crops and did not have the capital to acquire modern agricultural implements. In any case, serfs traditionally supplied the implements with which they tilled the land.

Certainly, any innovation was beyond the means of most Russian serf-owners. According to Keppen's calculations, 84 percent of them owned fewer than 100 male serfs in 1834, and 60 percent owned fewer than twenty. Among these 106,637 serf-owners, the average number of male peasants owned was a mere 18.8, far fewer than the number needed to support a nobleman and his family.[21] For such marginally endowed squires, manorial economy was directed toward survival, not profit and growth. They remained buried in their rural nests, for they could afford to live nowhere else. At best, they hoped to keep themselves afloat with the help of state loans for which their few serfs served as collateral.

If any modernization of age-old agricultural techniques was beyond the means of most serf-owners, that small minority of comfortable-to-wealthy lords, that 16 percent of the serf-owners who owned 81 percent of the serfs, also had little motivation to modernize their estate economy during the Nicholas era.[22] These great lords counted their bondsmen in the hundreds and thousands, and serfdom continued to provide them with a comfortable income. In hard times, they readily could supplement their incomes by state loans, and they preferred the certainty of crops and methods proved over centuries to innovations that were as yet untested.[23] A number of the great lords, whose paths the enlightened bureaucrats crossed in the course of their government assignments, spoke knowledgeably about modern principles of agronomy, the wonders of horse- and steam-driven machinery, and even the inevitability of emancipation; but very few had any intention of putting their preachings into practice.[24] Still, the enlightened bureaucrats' early attempts to set a transformation of rural Russia into motion are instructive, not merely for what they attempted immediately but for what these efforts reveal about their attitudes toward change, the peasantry, the nobility, and, most of all, serfdom, as they probed life in Russia's provinces and laid the foundations for the transformations they knew must come.

Studying Russia's Provinces

During the 1840s, Russia's central administration began to concentrate its resources on studies of provincial life. Such originated with Kiselev's surveys of the state peasantry during the late 1830s and in the Statistical Section that Bludov established in the Ministry of Internal Affairs in 1835, even though inadequate funding at first prevented it from functioning properly.[25] Perovskii hastened to allocate more resources to statistical studies, and in March 1842, he established the Provisional Section for the Reorganization of Municipal Government and Economy for studying economic, social, and administrative conditions in Russia's towns and cities. At about the same time, he assigned the task of compiling broader studies about provincial life to another new agency, the Provisional Statistical Committee.[26] The activities of these two agencies were further coordinated in the 1840s by Miliutin, who directed the Provisional Section and served prominently as a member of the Provisional Statistical Committee. Combined with Zablotskii's Department of Rural Economy in the Ministry of State Domains, they produced impressive studies about life in Russia's provinces during the 1840s and 1850s.

In Russia's central administration, the frequent cooperation of these agencies was particularly unique. At a time when government offices generally were extremely sensitive about their prerogatives and jealously guarded their areas of responsibility, these three bureaus exchanged information and personnel on a continuing basis and without rancor. Men who served in Zablotskii's Department of Rural Economy transferred to Miliutin's Municpal Section in the mid-1840s, and, in some cases, moved back a few years later. Because these agencies were instrumental in providing senior officials in Russia's central administration with reliable information about provincial conditions, we should examine their activities more closely.

When Perovskii assumed office late in 1841, his first concern was with Russia's towns and cities. These had presented serious problems to Imperial statesmen since the time of Peter the Great as senior officials struggled to provide the services urban residents required. These problems were made especially difficult because Russian rulers had begun to create a more modern bureaucratic structure in the central government, while town and city administration continued to function as it had in the seventeenth century.[27] When the *nakazy* drafted for the Legislative Commission of 1767 by its urban constituencies revealed how far city government had diverged from the laws, Catherine II had been obliged to give serious attention to its improvement and issued her Municipal Charter on April 21, 1785.[28] Catherine's charter suffered the fate of earlier eighteenth-century municipal legislation. During the next half-century, the problems that she had attempted to resolve grew worse, and, by the 1840s, Russia's municipal administration had ceased to function effectively.[29] The military governor of Kazan reported that many public offices were staffed by untrained, often illiterate men, leaving a handful of inefficient and corrupt clerks to represent the government in public, while reports from the civil governors of Saratov, Tula, and Poltava confirmed that the situation was equally bad in other areas.[30] Clearly, municipal affairs required serious and immediate attention.

Eighteenth- and early nineteenth-century autocrats faced mainly administrative and economic problems in Russia's cities, but Nicholas I also had to confront social, even political, difficulties. Recent Soviet studies have argued that Russian authorities had become concerned about the growth of an urban proletariat as early as 1826 and feared its political consequences.[31] Although such arguments exaggerate the significance of the government's early efforts to restrict industries located in the larger cities of the Empire, there can be no doubt, as Professor Zelnik has shown in his penetrating study about St. Petersburg's factory workers,[32] that senior officials and the Emperor were apprehensive about an urban proletariat, even though it was not a primary factor in determining their attitudes toward industrial development. During the 1830s, their concern about the social problems heralded by even limited industrial development increased, and, in 1840, Nicholas established a commission chaired by Count P. F. Buxhoeveden to study the conditions under which the "working people and artisans" of St. Petersburg lived and worked. Since there was no government policy about factory workers at that time, Buxhoeveden's Commission was to propose "possible ways to improve their situation."[33] Like most attempts to generate policy within the Nicholaean government, the Buxhoeveden Commission proposed nothing beyond administrative adjustments, and never even finished its work.

Since the beginning of the nineteenth century, five special commissions had been established within the Ministry of Internal Affairs to study urban society and investigate the failings of Russia's municipal government institutions. Like the Buxhoeveden Commission, none had completed their assignment because senior statesmen did not understand the sorts of resources needed for such a task. "This commission is made up of *chinovniki* [who are] occupied with other tasks and who do not receive any additional salary for taking on these extra duties," Perovskii wrote in explaining why the last of these commissions, which he was about to close early in 1842, must be considered a failure like its predecessors. He quickly went on to point out that it lacked the minimum personnel and support services needed to carry out assignments. Unless that was changed, Perovskii insisted, there was no reason to expect that any future effort would be more successful.[34]

Realizing that statistical studies ought to be entrusted to experts able to give them their full attention, Perovskii urged Nicholas to establish the Provisional Section for the Reorganization of Municipal Government and Economy in his ministry. Following the example of Kiselev's recent surveys, he planned to send officials from this new agency to carry out on-the-spot studies of local conditions, and he appointed Miliutin to direct its staff of twenty-six with an annual budget of 13,454 silver rubles.[35] Between 1842 and 1846, Miliutin's new agency concentrated on towns and cities in the provinces of Saratov, Voronezh, Iaroslav, Tula, Riazan, Mogilev, Tambov, and the Baltic regions, in addition to Moscow and St. Petersburg.[36] In all, his agents of special commissions assembled data about municipal budgets, property holdings, and administrative problems[37] in 139 towns and cities.[38]

The very basic economic and administrative data that these surveys emphasized proved hard to come by.[39] Miliutin's agents found it difficult to explain how towns and cities might resolve their fiscal difficulties,[40] because sometimes they could not learn even the most elementary facts about what had caused them. Miliutin bombarded his agents with requests for information about the number of merchants, fairs, shops, and warehouses, the average cost of basic goods and services, and, even, accurate population figures for various towns.[41] Even in Dorpat, home of one of the Empire's great universities, Miliutin had to ask his agent of special commissions for "an enumeration of city dwellers according to their economic status" and for information about the number of bookshops, schools, and charity organizations in the city.[42]

Rudimentary though they were, these early surveys provided training experiences for the new type of officials that Russia's first enlightened bureaucrats were trying to assemble in their agencies. Miliutin insisted that his agents of special commissions and the personnel in the central office of the Provisional Section be far better educated than the average Petersburg official, and it is clear that a substantial portion had elite or university educations. Of those who served prominently in the Provisional Section during the 1840s, Aleksandr Girs, Konstantin Grot, and Konstantin Veselovskii were *litseisty*; Count A. K. Sivers was a *pravoved*; A. F. Shtackelberg and G. I. Frolov were graduates of St. Petersburg University; N. P. Bezobrazov had a degree from the University of Kazan; and K. A. Krzhevitskii held a master's degree from the University of Dorpat. Later in the decade, more illustrious names appeared: Konstantin Kavelin, Ivan Aksakov, Iurii Samarin, Petr Redkin, and Ivan Turgenev all served in Miliutin's Provisional Section before 1850.[43]

But Miliutin demanded far more than advanced education from the men who served under him. They had to abandon the Russian bureaucrat's traditional commitment to formalism[44] and be willing to devote long hours to the drudgery of statistical compilations, as Miliutin insisted on initiative and turned an unsympathetic ear to pleas of overwork. For those who shared his dedication, his demands were welcome;[45] for those who did not, his expectations seemed appalling. "I do not ask you, Your Excellency, I implore you to put yourself in my position," the clearly miserable *tituliarnyi sovetnik* N. V. Kopaneishchikov complained to Miliutin's superior. "I hardly have time to sleep. I must see and verify everything myself, prepare reports, deal with local authorities, and, finally, I now am instructed to attend meetings of the Provincial Council."[46] Such a reaction was the opposite from that of Adolf Shtackelberg who, when asked to determine why trade and industry had declined so precipitously in the Baltic provinces, undertook an additional study on his own initiative about the causes and consequences of famine in the same region.[47]

Once these preliminary studies were completed, and after the St. Petersburg Municipal Reform Act had been drafted, Miliutin broadened his agency's inquiries. During his first years as head of the Provisional Section (renamed the Municipal Section in 1847), he had developed basic data about provincial towns and cities and had assembled a cadre of well-trained, energetic officials in his agency. By the mid-1840s, the Municipal Section had begun to project an image among the intelligentsia and educated elites in Russia that was sufficiently appealing to attract some of the most talented entrants into St. Petersburg's official world. In September 1848, Konstantin Kavelin became an editor in the Municipal Section,[48] and in April of the following year, Miliutin chose the jurist P. G. Redkin to be one of his office section chiefs.[49] Two of the men who had so inspired students at Moscow University earlier in the decade thus placed their talents at Miliutin's disposal before the 1840s ended.

An article in an 1844 issue of *The Journal of the Ministry of Internal Affairs* pointed out that "in both the civic and governmental sense, the city has always been the most noble member of the state's body."[50] Throughout the decade, the efforts of the Municipal Section testified to its officials' belief in that axiom. Excluding Poland and Finland, 693 localities in the Empire bore the designation of *"gorod,"*[51] and, by 1849, Miliutin's agents had studied about 300, despite a number of problems caused by the agents' inexperience and even naïveté at the outset. They had been slow to realize that data housed in provincial archives were so unreliable that accurate information had to be assembled only through first-hand observation,[52] and it was not until after he completed draft proposals for the St. Petersburg reform in 1845 that Miliutin had worked out comprehensive instructions for the studies his agency required. These indicated that he and his associates finally had realized the full extent of their task and had reached conclusions about how it should be undertaken. Miliutin assigned three major duties to his agents of special commissions: "to study existing problems and identify areas in the civic and economic organization of towns and cities in which practice does not conform to the law, to lay the groundwork for compiling complete administrative statistics about these areas of concern, . . . and to seek the means for better organizing civic and economic affairs in these municipalities."[53] In contrast to his earlier instructions, he now urged them to cast the nets of their inquiries widely in order to understand better the nature of municipal society, economy, and administration itself.[54]

Such demanding assignments kept Miliutin's agents of special commissions in the provinces for months, even years, in order to complete them. Adolf Shtackelberg, one of the earliest recruits in the Municipal Section, spent nearly all of the decade between 1842 and 1851 in the Baltic provinces,[55] and Girs worked for over two years in Iaroslavl.[56] Konstantin Grot spent five months in Minsk, six in Tver, and shorter periods in Kazan, Saratov, Iaroslavl, Poltava, and Mitau.[57] Nikolai Bezobrazov stayed for nearly three years in Saratov province,[58] K. A. Krzhevitskii was in the provinces of Kiev, Podolia, and Volynia for over a year,[59] and Count A. K. Sivers spent some two years in Iaroslavl and another six months in Tver.[60] Young Count Dmitrii Tolstoi served for three years in the Baltic provinces and spent another two in Voronezh, Riazan, Tambov, and Kaluga,[61] while Konstantin Veselovskii worked for more than a year in Mogilev,[62] as did Ivan Aksakov in Iaroslavl.[63] These men had to work under arduous conditions, and their lives were further complicated by the suspicions—sometimes unconcealed hostility—of local officials who saw these deep probings into local economic and administrative practices as direct threats to their long-held sinecures.[64] Finally, because administrative ties between St. Petersburg and the provinces were so poorly established, some of these men received their salaries irregularly at best and often lived lives of want while they waited for their salaries to arrive.[65]

That men of education and culture took up such arduous tasks bespeaks a devotion to duty that was rare in the Russian bureaucracy. As Zablotskii remarked some years later, his colleagues saw "in the fulfillment of their duty . . . a basic law of morality."[66] They also found an opportunity for worthwhile service to their country at a time when, as Aksakov lamented to Miliutin, "any sort of civic activity in literature is impossible."[67] Equally important, as a Municipal Section report stated in the late 1840s, they had concluded that "these studies will supplement in one of the most critical areas of government, detailed administrative statistics, which represent a rich collection of practical data and important documents, that are essential for the intended transformation of . . . all types of state administration."[68]

Municipal Section officials understood that transformations in any area of Russian life demanded accurate data upon which planners could base recommendations for change, but they had not yet perceived that there were no effective instruments for changing policy in Russia's central bureaucracy. Nonetheless, the more careful allocation of resources and more accurate budgeting procedures that they imposed on those town and city administrations they studied began to turn large budget deficits into surpluses. In 1840, public debts in Russia's town and city governments totalled 260,966 silver rubles and were increasing at the rate of more than 5 percent a year. Many towns and cities could not provide even basic public services without state subsidies and paid such miserable salaries that they could not hope to engage competent personnel to perform essential services. Regular members of fire-fighting units in some towns, for example, received an annual salary of only 2.86 rubles![69] Miliutin's efforts reversed this trend so significantly that the treasuries of Russia's towns and cities reported a surplus of 370,833 silver rubles in 1847.[70] Even such a limited achievement showed Miliutin and his colleagues that small committees of experts might draft effective reform legislation and pave the way for changing policy in a bureaucracy dedicated to perpetuation of existing policy, not its alteration.

Some two decades later, Zablotskii remarked that Miliutin thought statistics were "the key to administration" and added that "all statistical work done . . . under his supervision always had a practical purpose. These studies broadened as the sphere of his administrative activity expanded."[71] The implications of this work thus extended well beyond the Municipal Section's primary concern for Russia's towns and cities. It gave support to the demands of Zarudnyi and his associates in the Ministry of Justice that *zakonnost'* (lawfulness) be instituted in all areas of Russian life. The acute absence of *zakonnost'* in urban administration, Miliutin argued, was due to local officials' lack of training in the law and the incomprehensibility of the *Digest of the Laws* to all but trained specialists. "The system, and even the editing procedures, used in our *Digest of the Laws* and in all other codices," he wrote, "can be understood only if one possesses a considerable level of judicial education."[72] Miliutin insisted that city officials could not be expected to defend *zakonnost'* until they had convenient access to the laws and assigned N. V. Varadinov, an official who held a doctoral degree in law, to prepare a digest of all resolutions and decrees that applied to municipal administration and government.[73] Varadinov also prepared a lengthy work on the theory and practice of administrative affairs *(deloproizvodstvo)* which, for the first time, provided Russian bureaucrats with a practical guide, a theoretical justification, and an historical explanation for the administrative procedures that ruled their lives and the affairs of the Empire.[74]

The work of Miliutin and his agents extended to other areas, which added other important dimensions to the Municipal Section's activities at mid-century. By the mid-1840s, Kavelin, Miliutin, Redkin, and Girs agreed that serfdom was a malignancy that underlay Russia's economic, social, and political problems and hoped for its eventual abolition.[75] As their interest in serfdom grew, these men and their associates used long months spent in Russia's provincial towns to study conditions in the surrounding countryside as well. Although by no means comprehensive,[76] these studies enabled Miliutin to prepare a lengthy report about grain production in which he determined that Russia was the only nation in Europe to produce enough grain for its people and for export.[77] Going a step beyond the work done by Zablotskii two years earlier,[78] he sought measures to eliminate famine and suggested that improved transportation could provide the key.[79] His proposals contained little beyond those recommendations he had made nearly a decade earlier in his more localized study about the region between St. Petersburg and Moscow,[80] but the volume of statistical data he assembled to describe Russia's grain trade and agricultural production was impressive. As such, his report indicated that the growing emphasis on statistical studies in the Ministry of Internal Affairs had begun to yield broader results. These stemmed partly from the studies produced by his Municipal Section, but also from the statistical work undertaken by other agencies. The Statistical Section, which functioned as an adjunct to the Ministry's Council under the directorship of Konstantin Arsen'ev, was particularly important.

The development of such special statistical bureaux within Russia's central administration was a slow and arduous process. Early attempts to establish statistical agencies ended in failure because most senior officials were unenthusiastic about assembling large holdings of statistical data to help in formulating and implementing state policy. At the beginning of the century, only Speranskii called for a statistical section within the Ministry of Internal Affairs, but his effort came to naught because provincial agencies did not submit the necessary data to the ministry's central office. Transfer of Speranskii's Statistical Section to the short-lived Ministry of Police in 1811 brought no improvement, nor did its return to the Ministry of Internal Affairs in 1819. Plans for its reorganization lay unattended in the Committee of Ministers until late 1827, when it was decided to abolish the Statistical Section altogether.[81] The next year that decision was reversed when Nicholas requested the Ministry of Internal Affairs to provide Konstantin Arsen'ev, a professor in the Imperial School of Engineers, with the information needed to prepare a series of lectures about Russian statistics for Nicholas's eldest son and heir. Imperial interest saved the Ministry's Statistical Section, and its future existence was assured.[82]

One historian recently remarked that Minister of Internal Affairs Count Bludov "tried frantically to please [the Emperor], and was in terror of his master's disapproval."[83] Although Nicholas I's interest in statistics compelled him to reorganize his ministry's statistical office and place it under Arsen'ev's direction, Bludov did not understand how it should function, nor did he realize the resources it required. He therefore assigned Arsen'ev a miserly annual budget of just over 7,000 rubles and a miniscule staff of three statisticians and two copyists.[84] Most of the data for the Statistical Section's work were to be supplied by newly established provincial statistical committees, but few ever submitted reports, and those that did so paid scant attention to accuracy.[85]

Between 1835 and 1842, Arsen'ev employed the major publications of his agency to good purpose nonetheless. In particular, he used its two volumes of *Materials for Statistics of the Russian Empire* to argue the case for additional resources to support more research. Professor Karl Herrmann, Arsen'ev's mentor at St. Petersburg's Pedagogical Institute, already had established the framework for such an appeal a decade earlier when he had written that:

> The value of statistics for a government consists in the fact that they indicate what measures it should take in a given situation and, also, hasten their implementation. . . . Without knowing its population, the quality of its fields, the condition of its factories and manufacturies, the bazaars in which its peasants sell their products . . . and, finally, without having a precise understanding of the mores and customs of its peasants, it is impossible to administer a village properly. . . . If such statistical data are needed for the proper administration of a small estate, then just think how essential such data are by comparison for the administration of an entire state.[86]

Arsen'ev elaborated on Herrmann's theme in his plea for an expanded program of statistical research. "Statistics . . . constitute the basis of the state's strength," he wrote in the first volume of *Materials for Statistics of the Russian Empire,* but cautioned that much organization and development needed to be done before such studies could play their intended role. "All we have done thus far," he warned, "is not yet ripened fruit but only good seed. It is not yet a work that is completed, but only a good beginning."[87]

Arsen'ev's plea was repeated in even stronger terms in an unsigned review of the second volume of *Materials.* Appearing in *The Journal of the Ministry of Internal Affairs* in 1842, this essay linked the study of statistics with the precepts of Official Nationality:

> Knowledge of one's homeland [the reviewer wrote] stands much higher than many other types of knowledge and, in view of our present general striving for national character *(narodnost')*, such ought to be required of every statesman, civil servant, soldier, estate owner, industrialist, merchant, and, in general, every educated patriot. We shall go even further and say that without a knowledge of these complex and heterogeneous subjects [i.e., sta-

tistics] which, in their totality, comprise the basis of a state's strength, our very love of our homeland cannot be fully unselfish and fruitful.[88]

By the early 1840s, that small circle which included Arsen'ev, Miliutin, his closest associates, and the editorial board of *The Journal of the Ministry of Internal Affairs* hailed statistics as an essential adjunct to the adjustment and implementation of state policy. Their urgings finally reached the highest levels of government when Perovskii became Minister of Internal Affairs late in 1841.

Perovskii knew that statistics were important for adjusting and implementing state policy. Convinced that broad and vital questions of change could be dealt with by administrative measures, he nevertheless realized that it was necessary to understand how that administration functioned before trying to adjust it. It was important to understand what impact administrative adjustments would have on provincial society and economy, and Perovskii therefore approved plans for detailed statistical studies of several provinces that Arsen'ev had selected as typical of various types of economic conditions in Russia. He did not assign these new duties to Arsen'ev's Statistical Section, but to the Provisional Statistical Committee, a new agency that he established in 1843 under the direction of Miliutin's patron and director of the ministry's Economic Department M. I. Leks. Leks was an indifferent administrator, and his strongest asset probably was his aversion to disagreeing with anyone.[89] His appointment allowed control of the committee's work to fall into the hands of Miliutin and Zablotskii, neither of whom had the rank and seniority needed to head it themselves.

The Provisional Statistical Committee reduced Arsen'ev's agency to an impotent appendage of the ministry's Council, and Arsen'ev was not even named a member. He toured Russia's provinces[90] but remained outside the mainstream of statistical work in the Ministry of Internal Affairs for the next decade, as other agencies began broader investigations.[91] It is difficult to discover the reasons for his eclipse. The leading Soviet expert has attributed his removal to a fear of his "progressive views" on the part of a "reactionary government."[92] But Miliutin and Zablotskii, both of whom served on the Provisional Statistical Committee, were no less "progressive" than was Arsen'ev, and, in fact, were more so. More probably, it was not Arsen'ev's "progressive views," but his public statements about how statistical data should be applied to policy formulations, that made Perovskii wary about involving him in broader statistical studies. Even those few statesmen who recognized the importance of statistical data and would have agreed with Professor

Herrmann's opinion that their value consisted "in the fact that they indicate to [the government] ... what measures to take in a given situation"[93] were reticent about making such information available to men outside their immediate offices. A. I. Artem'ev, an official who served on the Provisional Statistical Committee and its successor, the Statistical Committee, once noted that many of its findings, which had been compiled into five large volumes of "Governmental Statistics about Russia," never were published "because of their extensive nature"[94] and, until the late 1860s, even summary statements of the national budget were considered state secrets by the Emperor and his ministers.[95] Arsen'ev's candidly negative comparisons between Russia and the West in terms of the sophistication of their statistical research could only have made his superiors wary about entrusting him with broader responsibilities.[96] Even more important, he urged greater consultation between government and public opinion and called for the veil of secrecy that shrouded the government's acts to be lifted.

> Until the rural serfowner, the merchant, and the factory owner have come to understand their true interests and have accustomed themselves to publicity (*glasnost'*) which, in the beginning, frightens only those timid, short-sighted, and self-seeking individuals who cannot stop from hiding that which, for the welfare of all, ought to be known to everyone ... it will be impossible for statistics [in Russia] to reach that level of development already achieved in England, France, Prussia, and a few other states of the German Confederation.[97]

Arsen'ev's conspicuous absence notwithstanding, the Provisional Statistical Committee included some of Russia's leading statisticians. Academicians Keppen and von Baer, as well as Nebolsin, Miliutin, Zablotskii, and Nadezhdin, agreed to launch a broad survey of the Empire that would bring together economic, ethnographic, topographic, public health, and administrative data. Each was an expert in at least one of these fields, and they agreed to combine their collective talent to produce an extensive statistical portrait of life in Russia's provinces. They also decided to begin an intensive study of town and country life in the provinces of Iaroslav and Nizhnii-Novgorod.[98]

By 1846, the Provisional Statistical Committee had not even received the allocations needed to send agents of special commissions to Iaroslav and Nizhnii-Novgorod provinces, while its proposed broader survey of the Empire suffered because key committee members had too many other administrative responsibilities. Each assembled considerable data from government sources, but more pressing duties prevented them from compiling the materials into a final report. Once the Petersburg Municipal Reform Act was implemented, Miliutin took over the arduous task of editing his colleagues' data and, in 1850, completed five volumes of "Governmental Statistics about Russia." Reportedly a vast and comprehensive work that interspersed scholarly essays, extensive tables, and a special atlas with detailed data about the nobility, clergy, state peasants, privately owned serfs, and urban residents of Russia,[99] it never emerged from the inner recesses of St. Petersburg's chanceries. Miliutin published a fifty-page summary in the first volume of the Russian Geographical Society's *Collection of Statistical Information about Russia* in 1851,[100] but the rest of this rich statistical description of Russian life at mid-century perished in a fire that destroyed much of the Economic Section archives on May 28, 1862.[101]

The fire of May 1862 also destroyed the Committee's work on Iaroslav and Nizhnii-Novgorod provinces. During 1852 and 1853, two groups of agents of special commissions were sent to these provinces to assemble what official censuses had failed to obtain: a detailed population analysis according to age, sex, class, occupation, and religion, with special attention to Old Believer sects.[102] These so-called "statistical expeditions" included some of Miliutin's closest colleagues in the Municipal Section and some of the ministry's most able officials, especially Count A. K. Sivers, the novelist Melnikov-Pecherskii, and Aleksandr Artem'ev.[103] Those few documents that survived the fire of 1862 are replete with complaints about the problems of locating information in provincial and district offices, but we know very little else about how provincials reacted to these agents. Gogol's portrait of the young noble wastrel Khlestakov, who was mistaken for an agent of the Third Section and was showered with bribes and gifts by corrupt small town officials, comes most readily to mind, but there is little against which one can test this example, except for one rare account that has survived in Artem'ev's diary. This indicates that the reception accorded to the fictional Khlestakov may have been by no means a mere product of Gogol's fertile imagination. As Artem'ev described his arrival in the town of Myshkino on January 15, 1852:

> I stopped at the hotel. After several minutes, the mayor handed me a document which entitled me to lodgings in the home of one Timofei Vasil'evich Chistov, a merchant of the second guild. Another merchant, Oreshnikov, offered me his horses.... They brought me to a lavish residence, parquet, silk, gold—all were scattered everywhere—but utterly without taste. There the mayor met me again: "Ah, so it turns out that I am to lodge with you!" I said. "Just so, little father, Your Excellency, Aleksandr Ivano-

vich!" exclaimed the mayor, as his grey beard thrust itself forward and his eyes twinkled.[104]

Artem'ev's hosts tried to distract his attention but failed, as he assembled information about local officials and the people they governed. Artem'ev's colleagues must have been equally immune to the charms of their provincial hosts because, by 1853, they had assembled a great deal of material. According to Artem'ev, senior officials' principled objections to the release of Miliutin's broader studies did not extend to statistical information about individual provinces,[105] but funds could not be found to publish the first part of their study until 1861. Entitled *On the Composition and Movement of Population in the Provinces of Nizhnii-Novgorod and Iaroslav,* this work and much of the still-unpublished research were destroyed by the fire of 1862 before any of it was put on sale. A summary, entitled *A List of Populated Locations in Iaroslav Province,* was published somewhat later, in 1865.[106]

By the early 1850s, the efforts of a few enlightened bureaucrats had freed Russia's central administration for the first time from the need to rely on information compiled by suspicious and fearful local officials.[107] Data about provincial economic, administrative, and social conditions thus were assembled in those agencies of the central government that could understand and draw conclusions from them. Perhaps even more important, the work of the Municipal Section and Provisional Statistical Committee took highly educated, well-trained men into the provinces for long periods, which allowed them to gain a first-hand understanding of provincial conditions that was rare in the middle levels of the central administration. This proved particularly valuable when some of these men began to draft legislative proposals for emancipating the serfs and reforming local administration a decade later.

Because the Provisional Statistical Committee cut across ministerial organizational lines, with members from the Ministry of Internal Affairs, the Ministry of State Domains, and the Academy of Sciences, it became especially important in the exchange of information about provincial life within the central bureaucracy. The data assembled in Zablotskii's Statistical Section in the Department of Rural Economy in the Ministry of State Domains broadened that exchange still further. Originally named the Third Department, the Department of Rural Economy was organized on January 1, 1838.[108] Other sections of the ministry were concerned primarily with collecting taxes and levying recruits from state peasant villages, but it worked to improve agriculture in Russia and to broaden the ministry's knowledge about rural life. Its areas of responsibility included cadastral surveys and the direction of agencies charged with disseminating information about agriculture.

Particularly important, the Academic Committee of the Ministry, presided over by the department's chief, operated under its aegis.[109]

As one of the first men to serve in it recalled, the Department of Rural Economy was remarkably unencumbered by clerical assignments. From the very first, its officials were known for their knowledge about rural economy and peasant affairs. These included N. A. Zherebtsov (its vice-director from 1841–1844), A. K. Girs, N. I. Tarasenko-Atreshkov (author of several brochures on economic affairs), A. I. Levshin (an important figure in the preliminary emancipation discussions in the Ministry of Internal Affairs), Keppen, and Zablotskii, as head of the department's Statistical Section.[110] One observer remarked that these men caused the Department of Rural Economy to function "not according to general rules of officialdom, but according to principles of knowledge and enlightenment."[111] Using to good advantage the Emperor's decree of 1839, which permitted only the highest ranking graduates to begin their civil service careers in St. Petersburg, these men launched a concerted effort to entice the elite of Russia's university graduates into their department.[112]

We shall discuss further on the efforts of the Department of Rural Economy and the Academic Committee of the Ministry of State Domains to establish peasant schools and model farms, encourage local agricultural societies, and support agricultural exhibitions. What concerns us here are the statistical studies that these bureaux, and especially Zablotskii's Statistical Section, produced during the 1840s and early 1850s. Based on an on-going series of cadastral surveys begun in the early 1840s, these revealed that although state peasants were taxed on the basis of revisional male souls, as Peter the Great had decreed, they had preserved their tradition of distributing their tax obligations according to the amount of land used by each household.[113] In view of this very common practice, Kiselev and his advisers decided to conduct a thorough examination of state peasants' resources, with an eye to shifting the tax base to the land itself. Special cadastral commissions under the jurisdiction of the Department of Rural Economy were sent into the provinces to classify the fertility of peasant lands, to tabulate the number of labor days required to cultivate a *desiatina* of land in various districts of each province, to chart grain prices, and to estimate levels of peasant literacy.[114]

Begun in May 1842, surveys of state peasants' lands continued into the early 1850s. By 1856, studies of 5,022,725 male souls and 24,710,606 *desiatiny* of land had been completed in twenty-five Great Russian provinces.[115] The result equalized the tax burden on all peasants in all provinces and, according to the official history of the Ministry of State Domains, increased state revenues by six million rubles annually without raising the tax rate.[116] Using the data assembled by these cadastral commissions, the Department of Rural Economy studied the causes of poverty among state peasants and attempted to discover ways to alleviate it. Zablotskii's officials also thought accurate statistical data the key to solving economic and administrative problems. "It is most important of all for administrators to know precisely the subject they are dealing with," Keppen wrote in 1846. "For men responsible for finding ways to improve the economic life of Russia, each piece of information has its value." But Keppen also had begun to urge his younger colleagues to look for trends and set their data into broader contexts. "Information of this type," he explained, "is all the more valuable when it is arranged in a systematic manner, such as in the form of a complete survey of some part of the country."[117] Konstantin Veselovskii, who later replaced Zablotskii as head of the Statistical Section, seconded Keppen's urgings. In addition to statistical data, he insisted, "qualitative evaluations" of economic and social questions were important, for only in that way was it possible to obtain "an accurate appraisal of the status of the subject [under consideration] and . . . reach conclusions about the best means for improving it."[118]

Although the Ministry's cadastral surveys were not completed by the middle of the century, they provided the Department of Rural Economy and its sub-sections—the Academic Committee and the Statistical Section—with enough data for its officials to formulate broader generalizations about provincial conditions and to propose limited measures for bettering the economic position of the state peasants. Perhaps most notable among these commentaries was the "Memorandum on the Shortcomings of Communal Landholding and the Advantages of Private Ownership of Land by the Peasants," which Zablotskii prepared in 1851. When any discussion of change could prove dangerous, Zablotskii began his memorandum with bold proclamation:

> A subject such as the improvement of the economy, by its very nature, and especially in view of that special form in which it exists among us, requires . . . that one take into account those *economic* and *moral* conditions which serve as the basis of the present economic way of life among the peasants.
>
> Among these economic conditions, the *means of owning land* occupies a major place. Without the confidence of the peasant in the continual ownership of those lands which he tills, there can never be any successes in agriculture and all other efforts at improvement will be rendered impotent.[119]

Zablotskii now argued more forcefully than he had a decade before that communal use of land lowered agricultural output and insisted that it was the "stumbling block to any attempt at improvement."[120] His de-

The Winter Palace (Courtesy of the Saltykov-Shchedrin Public Library, Leningrad)

partment's cadastral surveys had convinced him that peasant productivity would increase if the peasant could consider the land his own, but he refrained from the fateful word "emancipation" and even warned that it could prove dangerous to abolish suddenly the age-old custom of communal land usage in peasant villages. The first steps toward improvement should include "gradually introducing new customs and lawfulness *(zakonnost')* in place of absolute confusion and arbitrariness."[121] Therefore, without actually proposing emancipation, Zablotskii urged that state peasants be given private ownership of the fields they tilled and the meadows they used for grazing their cattle and harvesting fodder.[122]

Zablotskii was seeking an eventual transformation of rural Russia so that state peasants would have a more direct stake in the existing order. Perhaps most significant, he, Miliutin, and a number of their associates attempted to involve a broader segment of educated opinion in discussing this gradual transformation, and they did so at a time when the domestic policies of the Nicholas state had reached their most reactionary point. Their most obvious ally was the Russian Geographical Society, but the Department of Rural Economy, and especially its Academic Committee, went even further outside the bureaucracy to assemble information about rural life. In a competition designed to draw educated

Russians into a governmental discussion of important economic and social questions, this body invited private individuals to submit "economic-statistical descriptions" of separate provinces or districts in the Empire. "Only greater *glasnost'* can provide a solid basis for future measures for the improvement of this sector of national industry," the Academic Committee announced.[123]

In post-1848 Russia, this bold appeal met with a predictably timid response. Still, it was noteworthy because it occurred at a time when Nicholas and his advisers were especially wary of involving Russia's educated public in any discussion about the peasantry and change. At the same time, the enlightened bureaucrats made further attempts to understand how provincial conditions might be improved. During the last decade of the Nicholas era, they pursued several undertakings designed to further encourage a gradual transformation of rural Russia.

Toward Gradual Transformation of Rural Russia

Throughout the 1830s and 1840s, grain shipments comprised just over 17 percent of Russia's total exports, and, by 1860, they had risen to almost 36 percent. In 1820, only 19.7 percent of Russia's exports were not agricultural products; by 1860, the portion had fallen to a mere 11.1 percent.[124] Given the importance that agricultural products had for Russia's foreign trade, Imperial statesmen found it a matter of some considerable concern that their nation's peasants were actually among the least productive in Europe. During the 1840s, the grain yields averaged 15.7 bushels per acre in France; in Austria, they were 14.1 bushels; in Prussia, 12.2 bushels; but in Russia, a paltry 9.9 bushels.[125] Not only was the average yield very low, but the ratio of grain harvested to seed planted portrayed a tenuous enterprise at best: 7.1 bushels of grain harvested for each bushel sown was the best yield of any state peasant village in the Empire in 1840. The next best was 4.45:1, and only in seven of forty-seven provinces was the ratio 4:1 or better. The average ratio of grain harvested to seed sown in these provinces was a mere 3.21:1, with one province reporting a disastrous 1.9:1.[126]

Problems associated with the low productivity of Russia's peasantry affected not only the Empire's export trade; they also caused serious domestic economic difficulties. Low productivity combined with wretched transportation caused fluctuations in grain prices that were extreme by any standard. The price of grain in 1838 fluctuated between a high of 25 francs 89 centimes and a low of 14 francs 50 centimes per hectolitre in France. The maximum price never was more than twice the minimum anywhere in the West. However, Russia suffered wild price fluctuations throughout the first half of the nineteenth century.[127] In 1804, the fluctuation was 650 percent. In 1843, there was more than a 500 percent variance between the minimum and maximum, and the fluctuations were even more extreme between one part of the Empire and another. In January 1845, one *kul'* (300 pounds) of rye flour cost 7 rubles 50 kopeks in Pskov, while it cost only one ruble in Tambov and Kharkov. Even in the same province, prices soared and plummeted from one year to the next. A *kul'* of rye flour that sold for three rubles in Kursk in 1829 soared to twenty-three rubles by October 1833 and fell to four rubles in 1836.[128]

Any general increase in productivity was of considerable economic and political importance for Russia; yet it was by no means a simple task to modernize agriculture. Serf resistance to innovation stemmed from that deep-seated conservatism common to all peasants for whom the failure of new crops or techniques meant starvation, but it was intensified by the belief that added or different demands on their time and labor violated long-standing tradition. Serfs therefore resisted those few far-seeing noble masters who attempted to introduce new crops, fertilizers, and machinery on their estates. Such efforts were rare because most rural lords made no attempt to alter the medieval tillage of their estates. Few had the capital to finance new crops or machinery, and most nobles were unwilling to risk capital on such ventures if they had it. They did not understand that there were better ways of increasing their estate profits than to decree increases in *obrok* or bring a few additional *desiatiny* of land under cultivation by adding additional *barshchina* to their serfs' labor obligations.

To overcome this widespread aristocratic indifference to agricultural modernization, a number of enlightened bureaucrats joined a few senior officials in the 1840s in launching a two-pronged program for a gradual transformation of rural Russia. On the one hand, they tried to acquaint more nobles with new advances in agricultural techniques, and they encouraged the development of agricultural societies on the district, provincial, and regional levels to publicize such innovations. At the same time, because they were reluctant to interfere directly in the management of the nobles' affairs, they tried to set a progressive example by the way in which they dealt with the peasants who resided upon Treasury lands. This was a major motivation behind Kiselev's administrative reforms in the late 1830s, and it lay behind the educational programs and model farms with which the government tried to educate its peasants in the 1840s and early 1850s.

The study of agriculture and the training of agronomists was one of those rare areas of education that the autocrat left for a long time in private hands, partly because the formal training of agronomists received little attention anywhere in Russia before the 1840s. Serf-owners usually left agricultural matters to estate managers or to the serfs themselves, and, until the 1820s, there was little effort made to alter traditional forms of serf tillage. The Free Economic Society, founded by Catherine II in 1765, often discussed agricultural questions, and a handful of private agricultural societies had been established at the beginning of the nineteenth century. But the first Russian agricultural school, established by Moscow's Imperial Agricultural Society, was not founded until 1821, and it remained a lonely pioneer for almost two decades until the first state-supported agricultural training center opened on August 15, 1840.[129] Located in Mogilëv province on the Treasury estate of Gorygoretsk, it included a school for teaching peasant farmers about modern agricultural techniques and a higher level institution for educating agronomists to manage large estates.[130] Fluctuations in state policy, coupled with Ministry officials' uncertainty about its true purpose, made the existence of the Gorygoretsk school precarious for almost a decade. Only in 1848 was its place in Russia's educational system made clear when the school was divided into an Agricultural Institute, with university status to train agronomists, and an Agricultural School *(uchilishche)* for state peasants and selected serfs.[131]

Although their educations varied markedly, depending on whether they studied at the Institute or the *uchilishche*, all students received practical training, at the insistence of the Academic Committee. Clearly, such Academic Committee members as Zablotskii, Veselovskii, and Keppen wanted to educate agricultural specialists, not noble dilettantes,[132] and they urged that several more schools be founded in other regions of the Empire because "the establishment of new agronomical schools can be so very important to the state."[133] Because they emphasized the value of practical training, the enlightened bureaucrats on the Academic Committee urged the establishment of eight widely dispersed state-directed model farms.[134] The first was organized in Vologda province, some fifty *versty* from the provincial capital, and was followed by others strategically located in the grain-growing provinces of Saratov, Tambov, Mogilëv, Kazan, Kharkov, and Ekaterinoslav.[135]

Peasants between the ages of seventeen and twenty were trained on these model farms in a four-year course of study that included reading and writing, arithmetic, religion, and elementary agricultural theory, in addition to practical training in all aspects of agriculture and animal husbandry. Especially during the winter months, they were trained in a variety of those trades and crafts needed by prosperous peasant farmers, and particular attention was given to blacksmithing and repairing farm implements.[136] Most important, they learned about raising tobacco and fodder crops in addition to the usual grains so that they could practice effective crop rotation when they returned home.[137]

The Academic Committee thus tried to educate at least a small number of peasants in more advanced agricultural techniques. Like most efforts conceived within such bureaucracies, their program suffered from inadequate funding, and they had to develop their model farm program much more slowly than they wished. They had planned to enroll some 75–150 state peasants and 25–50 serfs on each farm in order to train between 800 and 1,600 in any four-year period, but, by mid-century, their limited budget had made it possible to provide housing for only 706.[138] Further, some of the classroom work must have been far too sophisticated for student farmers who had learned to read and write only after they arrived at school. Some of the titles in the farms' student libraries presupposed such advanced education that peasant student farmers could not have even hoped to read them. Apparently, a number of those enlightened bureaucrats who administered Russia's model farm program were unable to comprehend the level at which peasant students must be taught.[139]

Whatever their limitations, the agricultural schools and model farms established by the Ministry of State Domains during the 1840s laid the base for that gradual transformation of rural Russia that enlightened bureaucrats envisioned. These institutions not only taught peasant farmers agricultural techniques and useful trades, but they also trained them in the manufacture of modern farm implements. At the Vologda model farm, for example, more than a dozen different types of farm implements, including steel harrows and self-scouring plows modeled on the design perfected by the Illinois blacksmith John Deere only a few years before, were produced by peasant students at mid-century, and a number of these were taken back to their villages by proud graduates.[140] Small numbers of modern implements thus made their way into the Russian countryside on the eve of the Crimean War; along with them came peasants trained in their manufacture, use, and repair.

That Russia's rural masses were interested in agricultural innovation became even more evident to the enlightened bureaucrats in the Department of Rural Economy as a result of their efforts to organize provincial agricultural exhibitions. Zablotskii and his colleagues saw these as important vehicles for exchanging information, recognizing the accomplishments of able peasants, and improving agricultural productivity. "Public exhibitions of products of the agricultural industry stimulate competition among producers and, at the same time, serve as a means to evaluate the level of development of this or that sector of agricultural labor, as an indication of measures needed for further achievements, and as a means for bringing farmers closer together," the authors of the Department's five-year report wrote in 1849.[141] Their success may well indicate that some of Russia's peasants were considerably less backward than the extremely low overall agricultural productivity figures indicate. This does not mean that the image of primitiveness attached to Russian agriculture in the middle of the nineteenth century lacks validity or that the rural transformation that enlightened bureaucrats envisioned did not lie some considerable distance in the future. But it does indicate that there was enough interest in raising productivity among Russia's rural population to establish the basis for such a transformation. That most exhibitors were state peasants, in whose hamlets the enlightened bureaucrats in the Department of Rural Economy were breaking down the peasant practice of communal land usage,[142] may indicate that the primitive quality of Russian agriculture was more the result of conservatism articulated by the repartitional commune than of individual peasant resistance to innovation and progress.

Russia's first agricultural exhibition was held in Odessa in 1843. When the number of exhibitors increased by nearly 50 percent the following year, officials in the Department of Rural Economy decided that an Empire-wide program of such exhibitions might be successful. They broadened their efforts that same year in Iaroslavl and more than 300 entrants, most of them state peasants and serfs, came to display their exhibits. Again, the number of entrants more than doubled the following year, and the number of exhibits almost reached 7,500.[143]

The successes of these first agricultural exhibitions encouraged the enlightened bureaucrats in the Department of Rural Economy to plan others. During the last decade of the Nicholas era, such exhibitions were held in the provinces of Iaroslav, Tambov, Ekaterinoslav, Kazan, Poltava, Vladimir, Vologda, and Taurida, and each brought entrants from several surrounding provinces. Between 1844 and 1849 alone, they attracted nearly 6,000 exhibitors and had almost three times that number of exhibits.[144] As had been the case in Odessa and Iaroslavl, most entrants were state peasants. As we suggested earlier, this may have indicated a more serious interest in the quality of agricultural production among Russia's masses than historians have realized.

Such enlightened bureaucrats as Zablotskii and his associates in the Department of Rural Economy tried to lay the groundwork for a gradual transformation of rural Russia by training state peasants and serfs and hoped to stimulate interest in modernization through provincial agricultural exhibitions. To support their program further, they encouraged nobles to establish agricultural societies and used them to stimulate discussion about new crops, chemical fertilizers, and agricultural machinery among Russia's provincial lords. They hoped that their effort would help to mechanize Russian agriculture and, in turn, increase crop yields to meet the growing demand for Russian grain in Europe.

Russia's first agricultural society had been founded in 1765, just over a decade after its counterpart had been established in England (1753) and just four years after a similar one had been founded in Paris.[145] Named the Free Economic Society, it included great lords and scientific experts who joined to promote agricultural advancement in Russia.[146] One of their major objectives was to increase the revenues from their estates, but they also hoped to induce smaller proprietors to follow their example.[147] For three decades, they pursued these tasks alone. Then, in 1805, the Baltic lords of Lifland formed an agricultural society; their example was followed in 1818 when the nobility of Moscow founded the Imperial Agricultural Society.[148]

Professor Blackwell has written that the Imperial Agricultural Society at Moscow "particularly reflected the concerns and curiosities of landlords who were turning their production toward commercial markets and who wished to develop and modernize agricultural industries."[149] Their interest was shared by the Free Economic and Lifland Agricultural Societies, but their activities were restricted to the great lords of the Empire, often with close connections at Court. Especially in the case of the Free Economic Society and the Imperial Agricultural Society at Moscow, their endeavors to some extent reflected state policy because they received substantial subsidies from the Ministries of State Domains and Finance.[150] Their leading members often were senior statesmen (Admiral Count N. S. Mordvinov presided over the Free Economic Society for many years, for example), and, although they wrote about their work in journals and scientific texts, even the more prosperous and better educated segments of the Great Russian provincial nobility usually were not closely associated with them.

In an attempt to broaden participation in the improvement of Russian agriculture, Kiselev launched a program to increase the number of agricultural societies even before the Ministry of State Domains was founded. In the late 1830s and early 1840s, the Imperial Economic Society at Kazan (1839), the Iaroslav Agricultural Society (1842), the Estland Agricultural Society (1839), the Kurland Agricultural Society (1839), and the Gol'dingen (Kuldiga) Agricultural Society (1839) were founded, in response to his urging. The latter three centered in the Baltic provinces—an obvious indication of the Baltic German lords' continued interest in agronomy—but the societies at Kazan and Iaroslav, especially when viewed in conjunction with the Imperial Agricultural Society of Southern Russia (founded in 1828), showed that interest in new crops and agricultural techniques had begun to spread among the provincial lords of the South and West.[151]

Enlightened bureaucrats in the Department of Rural Economy encouraged this new interest in agricultural modernization outside the capitals and the Baltic provinces during the late 1840s and early 1850s. Branches of the Imperial Agricultural Society of Southern Russia were established in Ekaterinoslav and Kishinev in 1845, followed by the formation of the Lebedian Agricultural Society (in Tambov province) in 1847 and the Agricultural Society of Southwestern Russia (in Penza) in 1848.[152] But there was strong resistance from many Russian serf-owners, and, although by mid-century there were twenty-one private organizations concerned with agricultural modernization, all but eight were in Moscow, St. Petersburg, or the Baltic provinces.[153]

It is difficult to explain why enlightened bureaucrats in the Department of Rural Economy found it so difficult to win the support of Russia's provincial nobles in their efforts to establish a network of agricultural societies, and they were extremely vague about it in their published remarks. "Unfortunately, it is necessary to note," they wrote in their five-year report in 1849, "that in spite of all the Department's willingness to increase the number of these organizations, obstacles to the formation of local agricultural societies have been encountered in the majority of provinces, the elimination of which does not depend upon the Department."[154] The conservatism of the provincial nobility was undoubtedly a factor in this reluctance, especially when coupled with their very limited capital resources. Still, these factors alone do not adequately explain the reluctance of the provincial lords to form local agricultural societies, and we must look elsewhere for an answer.

There is little archival evidence to suggest to us the process by which enlightened bureaucrats in the Department of Rural Economy initiated debate about the establishment of provincial agricultural societies, and there is even less evidence about local nobles' response. Nonetheless, one can make some inference about the process and the reasons for the reticence of the nobles from events that occurred in Tula in 1846. There, a segment of the nobility fell directly into the group that Professor Blackwell described as "landlords who were turning their production toward commercial markets and who wished to develop and modernize agricultural industries,"[155] and they were quite aware of the economic constraints imposed on their efforts by serfdom.[156] Yet, when urged to organize a provincial agricultural society in 1846, they refused. We have little specific information to explain why they did so, but the proposal itself may provide some accurate clues. When the Tula Provincial Assembly of the Nobility met in 1846, State Councillor Pokhvisnev, Marshal of the Nobility in Venevsk district, suggested that they organize a provincial agricultural society. Pokhvisnev cast his proposal very much in terms of the views held by enlightened bureaucrats in the Department of Rural Economy. Although he spoke about the benefit serf-owners could derive from the information such a society could disseminate, he emphasized how the nobility could serve the throne by forming such a society. "Who among us is not convinced that we are obliged to serve the throne and our homeland to the utmost?" he asked. "Who among the Russian nobility is not prepared to give up his property, even his life, for Tsar and Country?"[157]

A reasonably accurate reply to Pokhvisnev's rhetorical questions might have been "almost no one." In theory, Russia's serf-owners remained the first servants of the throne, but at mid-century reality bore little resemblance to theory. Provincial lords still exalted the virtue of having served as a measure of social respectability rather than as a duty owed to Tsar and Country. Far more important were their estates and their unlimited power over their serfs. "The Emperor can issue his commands to me, and I must obey him, but he issues no commands to you," one observer wrote in recounting a nobleman's speech to his assembled serfs. "I am the Emperor on my estate," he continued. "I am your God in this world and I have to answer for you to the God above."[158] Given this attitude among provincial nobles, one can surmise that the Tula nobility were hardly sympathetic to an appeal that they form an agricultural society to serve Tsar and Country. They probably were even less sympathetic after they learned that one major purpose of the society would be to provide data about their province's serf economy so that government officials could prepare proposals for bettering the conditions under which Tula bondsmen lived.[159] The assembled Tula nobility voted down Pokhvisnev's proposal by a margin of nearly three to one.[160]

Although the evidence is far from conclusive, it suggests that enlightened bureaucrats in the Department of Rural Economy attempted to impose a more responsible view of state service on provincial nobles by urging them to participate in local agricultural societies. That they perceived a purpose in the creation of such societies beyond the betterment of Russia's manorial economy was especially clear in a memorandum that Zablotskii sent to Grand Duke Konstantin Nikolaevich just a few months after the Crimean War ended. After pointing out that they had publicized such issues as new crops, machines, and farming methods but had "accomplished very little in the area of bettering the condition of the serfs,"[161] Zablotskii urged that agricultural societies be brought more closely under the control of his Department of Rural Economy. In that way such societies could play an important part in preparations for an emancipation by "accustoming our society to the idea that the abolition of serfdom is inevitable [and] by ridding this idea of the phantoms and false notions formed by confused imaginations . . . which, until the present time, have clouded the clear understanding of this matter."[162] Zablotskii hoped to initiate a controlled debate on emancipation within Russian society and envisioned agricultural societies, especially those in Moscow and St. Petersburg, as useful instruments through which the government could encourage discussion yet keep it within limits acceptable to the Emperor and his closest advisers. Zablotskii thus saw them as an important element in broadening the process of *glasnost'*.[163]

That these views were not born merely of Zablotskii's concern about Russia's Crimean debacle can be seen from the efforts of the Ministry of State Domains' Academic Committee and Department of Rural Economy to utilize agricultural societies during the first half of the decade. In 1852 and 1853, the Academic Committee invited noble agricultural societies to submit proposals for improving agriculture in Russia, and eleven societies responded at some length. While an overriding concern about the narrowly focused interests of Russia's serf-owners dominated their replies, they exhibited a broad grasp of the agricultural dilemmas their nation faced.[164] Clearly, they viewed the invitation as a far broader mandate for discussion than did the civil servants who initiated the inquiry. Their proposals covered an impressive range of topics and problems, from the need for an "immediate definition of the relations between peasants and their lords," to the shortage of veterinarians in the countryside and the need for cattle insurance,[165] even though Zablotskii and his colleagues thought these societies should confine themselves to providing information needed by the central bureaucracy. As he remarked to Konstantin Nikolaevich, "the cooperation of private individuals, freely given, can be useful and valuable for the government, but, for such private individuals, the support of the government is essential."[166] In his view, that fundamental fact defined the relationship between the two.

Most government officials feared to involve public opinion in discussions of policy, and even such enlightened bureaucrats as Zablotskii and Veselovskii found it difficult to extend their concept of *glasnost'* that far. This was partly because their bureaucratic experience had conditioned them to expect obedience from society, not encourage dialogue with it. The difficult political climate in which they had to work during the first half of the 1850s also was a factor because no one knew just how much discussion of state affairs could be considered legitimate. Finally, enlightened bureaucrats' apprehensions stemmed from their reluctance to discuss solutions when they did not yet fully understand the problem. Fearful that they had gone too far, Zablotskii, Veselovskii, and their colleagues began to parry Russia's agricultural societies with those standard bureaucratic responses they had learned so well. They referred important matters to other agencies and pleaded that they did not have the authority to discuss critical issues. An opportunity to extend *glasnost'* beyond the confines of the bureaucracy thus was lost as a consequence of the enlightened bureaucrats' own inability to pursue a dialogue among groups with whom they were not closely acquainted and whose public statements they could not readily control.

As with Miliutin's timid attempt to extend *glasnost'* to the Petersburg merchantry in 1844, the efforts of Zablotskii and his associates to extend it to Russia's agricultural societies proved unsuccessful. Russian lords proved unwilling to accept the limited role that officials in the Department of Rural Economy offered them, and the enlightened bureaucrats grew uneasy as a result. But it was they, not the nobles willing to discuss policy in concrete terms, who were most responsible for the failure of the attempt. Unfamiliar with the limits to which *glasnost'* could be extended, and unwilling to press their discussions to those limits, the enlightened bureaucrats turned away from the very men whom reasonable debate might have turned into valuable allies.

Enlightened bureaucrats never felt at ease with public opinion, and that produced a growing disenchantment with their programs among the nobility. Many Russian lords would have agreed with General Tsimmerman's statement that enlightened bureaucrats "were in no way advocates of true freedom, which has nothing in common with this stifling sphere of officialistic democracy," and that "once they had obtained power these liberals became unceremonious despots and exercised absolute arbitrariness in their actions."[167] Enlightened bureaucrats' apprehensions stemmed from their conviction that the nobility was selfish and irresponsible. "The nobility is self-interested, unprepared, [and] underdeveloped," Miliutin soon wrote to Kiselev.[168] Based on his own experience, he and his associates had little reason to think otherwise. Therefore, they modified the process of bureaucratic co-optation to extend *glasnost'* beyond the bureaucracy.

Noblemen who entered the bureaucracy and exhibited those abilities that enlightened bureaucrats respected, or those whom they came to know in their Petersburg circles, became the ones with whom they pursued discussions about reform and change. The serf-owner and Slavophile Iurii Samarin in an important sense owed his place on the Editing Commissions to his years of service with enlightened bureaucrats in the Ministry of Internal Affairs, while they withheld such trust from Ivan Aksakov, who had not proved reliable and loyal during his service in Miliutin's Municipal Section. Kavelin won their trust because of his accomplishments in the Municipal Section during the late 1840s and early 1850s, and Prince Cherkasskii gained entry to their inner circle because of his close association with the Grand Duchess Elena Pavlovna, who became a generous patron of the enlightened bureaucrats during the same period.

The efforts of the enlightened bureaucrats to extend *glasnost'* thus took place mainly within the bureaucracy and a few private circles during the last decade of the Nicholas era when they launched the co-optation process that brought a few of the intelligentsia into their ranks. The cadre of reformers whom Miliutin, Zarudnyi, and Zablotskii assembled in their agencies during the mid-1840s had become almost fully developed by 1855, and its ranks expanded very little during the next decade. It was the enlightened bureaucracy, as formed by the end of the Crimean War, that played a major part in planning Russia's Great Reforms, and it was to the men who proved themselves during the last decade of the Nicholas era that they turned to help them draft reform legislation. Especially in the preparations for reform in the Polish Kingdom in 1863–1866, Miliutin first turned not to men with government service experience in Poland but to those who had been tested in the bureaucratic arena during the last decade of the Nicholas era.

During this period of the Nicholas era, Russia's emerging enlightened bureaucrats thus became more deeply involved with problems of transformation and change than one might expect, in view of the reactionary character that has been assigned to that period of the Empire's history. It is true, of course, that they shared apprehensions held almost universally among men who favored reform, and, like their friends among St. Petersburg's intelligentsia, they were reluctant to discuss reform questions openly. Like most educated Russians, they stood ready to condemn the excesses of revolution in western Europe by mid-1848, but they had to be more cautious in expressing their political opinions because the Emperor demanded that government officials set the standard of loyalty by which others were measured. Writers who ran afoul of the censors were dealt with more severely if they were in the civil service, as Dal' and Saltykov-Shchedrin could readily testify. Those who feared to tread that narrow and blurred line between the acceptable and the forbidden retreated for fear of damaging their ability to influence state affairs at a later and more propitious time.[169]

These added risks made it all the more remarkable that some of the enlightened bureaucrats pursued their program for a gradual transformation of rural Russia throughout the dark days after 1848. They could do so because their perceptions about Russian politics were more acute than those who shunned careers in the bureaucracy. Schooled in the hard realities of Petersburg intrigue for more than a decade, the enlightened bureaucrats had acquired highly sensitive political instincts. They had risen in the civil service precisely because their education, talent, and willingness to approach state affairs from a nontraditional outlook had attracted such energetic and less rigid statesmen as Kiselev and Perovskii who, even after 1848, shielded them from the worst dangers of Russia's capricious political climate. At mid-century, they began to attract the attention of even more illustrious protectors. Golovin's privileged position as one of Konstantin Nikolaevich's confidants brought the Grand Duke's protection to his friends, especially after they seized control of the Russian Geographical Society. As President of the Geographical Society, Konstantin Nikolaevich scarcely could deny them his protection, at least by association, so long as they did not violate censorship regulations openly. In that matter, the enlightened bureaucrats were supremely cautious. Between 1848 and 1856, their published writings were exclusively technical or statistical and contained nothing that could be considered objectionable by even the most paranoid of censors.

Grand Duke Konstantin Nikolaevich strengthened the enlightened bureaucrats' defenses, and, as the first half of the 1850s drew to a close, he recruited a number of them into his Naval Ministry. At the same time, Miliutin and Prince Dmitrii Obolenskii found another protector in the person of Grand Duchess Elena Pavlovna, wife of the Emperor's younger brother Grand Duke Mikhail Pavlovich, whose circle, like that of Konstantin Nikolaevich, we shall examine at some length in the next chapter. With support from such highly placed patrons, the political position of the enlightened bureaucrats at the time of the Crimean War was far more secure than that of any other progressive group in Russia.

Enlightened bureaucrats enjoyed patronage in high places not only because of their sharply honed instincts for political survival but because their perspective on state affairs differed from that of other men dedicated to reform and change. Although their outlooks had been influenced by western European idealism, they had become pragmatic and realistic men who understood the futility of proposing theoretical solutions to pressing economic and political problems. They never shared the fascinations with ideal societies—utopian socialist or otherwise—that had so entranced many among Russia's intelligentsia. Necessity had obliged them to jettison such ideological trappings while they struggled to establish themselves in government service. Therefore, they read the works of Proudhon, Fourier, and Louis Blanc,[170] Prince Obolenskii recalled many years later, but their interest was academic. They never seriously thought that such societies could take root in Russia. From their positions within the bureaucracy, they thought that meaningful work in the cause of transformation was possible even after

1848 and could reject theoretical utopias all the more easily. Of course, open political discussion no longer was permitted, but they found it relatively easy to forego as their sphere of activity grew more extensive.

Enlightened bureaucrats' sphere of activity broadened during the decade after 1848 for several reasons. They no longer were junior officials but had attained middle- to high-level administrative positions, with ranks that put them in the top 5 percent of the Russian bureaucracy. Their service grades generally ranged between seven and four, at a time when most still were under the age of thirty-five; by the end of the reign, nearly all had won the coveted rank of *statskii sovetnik* and the hereditary noble status it conferred.[171] With such rank, and the protection of powerful statesmen, their considerable influence extended beyond their agencies to interdepartmental and interministerial committees.[172] Perhaps even more important, they held especially critical positions in the state administration. Zarudnyi had gained a senior and influential position in the Ministry of Justice's Consultation, where he could assemble young men of outstanding talent and education and train them in the practical processes of the law. Miliutin controlled the Ministry of Internal Affairs' Municipal Section and soon headed its entire Economic Department. Zablotskii held a similar position in the Department of Rural Economy and the Ministry of State Domains' Academic Committee, although he did not formally head either until after the accession of Alexander II. A. I. Levshin directed both, but because he frequently was away from the capital, Zablotskii often served as his deputy.[173] Likewise, although Leks was its nominal head, Miliutin and Zablotskii controlled the Provisional Statistical Committee during the entire last decade of the Nicholas era.

Such agencies were not major offices, and they are scarcely mentioned in general studies about Russia's central administration.[174] Yet they acquired unusual importance after the Crimean War ended, and the men who controlled them gained important positions in policy-making circles because they alone had access to that information about conditions in Russia's provinces and about the Empire's legal processes that were essential for drafting the Great Reform legislation. Senior Russian statesmen came to see clearly the value of accurate statistical data at just the time when these men reached positions which gave them control of such information. Because they were the possessors of statistical "truth" at the moment when the Emperor's advisers finally began to perceive the value of such "truth," their role in planning the Great Reforms was assured.

As the Crimean era dawned, Russia's enlightened bureaucrats still had not found the means to change policy in order to resolve the dilemmas that they and all Russian officials faced during the 1840s and early 1850s. They realized that new instruments were needed and even had begun to see that committees of experts such as Zablotskii, Miliutin, and Zarudnyi had assembled could best serve that purpose. What they had not yet learned was how to connect such middle-level agencies with the highest echelons of Russia's administration that stood at the apex of the autocratic legislative process. Nonetheless, with their cadres of loyal, efficient, and talented officials, and with a command of information about the state of the Empire that few in the central bureaucracy could equal, Russia's enlightened bureaucrats were in a position to begin testing the path to reform once the Crimean War ended. This is not to say that they had foreseen such an opportunity during the last decade of the Nicholas era, or even that they envisioned the possibility of the Great Reforms in 1855. If Kavelin's testimony is accurate, they saw little in the way of reform opportunities during the first months of Alexander II's reign, but, when the path to reform began to open in 1856, they tested it. They stepped with caution but then grew more bold. Very quickly they gained control of the most critical aspects of the reform processes and began to prepare legislative drafts for the Great Reforms. That they were able to do so was the result, in large measure, of their preparations during the war years themselves.

chapter 5

Preparing for Reform

"If one separates the essential from the covering of paper—that which is from that which only seems to be—and sifts out the truth from the half-truths and the falsehoods, then everywhere the brilliance will rise to the top and the rot will sink to the bottom."

Grand Duke Konstantin Nikolaevich

Although they had not found the means to create administrative instruments to shape policy at mid-century, the enlightened bureaucrats nonetheless had begun to assemble the personnel resources to staff them. Their effort to initiate a gradual transformation in Russia had enabled them to assemble data of a quality and quantity previously unseen in the Empire's central administration. It also had enabled Miliutin, Zablotskii, Zarudnyi, and their closest associates to test well-educated junior officials in St. Petersburg's ministries and draw those who best met their standards of efficiency, talent, and loyalty into their agencies. Above all, however, their endeavors during the late 1840s and early 1850s created an effective means for bridging the gap that separated the work of one ministry from another. This enabled them to overcome a serious failing of Russian administrative practice that had been instrumental in barring the way to change and reform in the Empire.

Perhaps one of the most glaring flaws in the administrative apparatus that evolved in Russia during the eighteenth and early nineteenth centuries was that senior statesmen had become extremely sensitive about their prerogatives as a consequence of on-going efforts to expand their areas of responsibility and to restrict those of their colleagues. Especially during the reign of Nicholas I, when secrecy became an integral part of administrative practice, these men grew intensely proprietary about their ministries' duties and the information they controlled. It often was all but impossible for one ministry to obtain important information from another, and those agencies that dealt with Russia's domestic affairs could not gain access to the information needed to resolve important questions. Even so progressive a statesman as Kiselev barred Miliutin from a group of officials sent by his Ministry of State Domains to study life in peasant villages in 1839 because the nephew he had helped to educate and place in Russia's government service served in a rival ministry.[1]

Close personal ties, dedication to learning more about town and country life, and a rare willingness to move from one agency to another allowed the enlightened bureaucrats to approach the complexities of Imperial administration in a manner very different from their superiors'. Anxious to resolve problems rather than perpetuate established practice, they shared information readily and established effective networks for communicating within the bureaucracy. At first, they shared information and advice informally,[2] but, knowing the special expertise that each possessed, they began to request each other's participation on special inter-agency and inter-ministerial committees where the knowledge of one could serve the needs of them all.[3] These special committees of experts cut across departmental and ministerial lines and became models for the administrative instruments they created to alter policy and initiate a social and economic transformation in Russia after the Crimean War.

Although none of these committees had been particularly effective, the precedent for involving special committees in Russia's legislative process had been set by such *ad hoc* bodies as Alexander I's Unofficial Committee, Nicholas's Committee of December 6th, and the secret committees convened to discuss serfdom during the second quarter of the nineteenth century. For their committees of "experts" to be effective, however, it was necessary for the enlightened bureaucrats to connect them to the highest levels of Russia's administrative structure and gain experience in the Imperial legislative process themselves. Most of them knew a great deal about Russia's economic and social problems, and that was vital in planning the broad transformation that would be remembered in history as the Great Reforms. But they had little experience in the equally critical area of legislative action, and such experience was essential if their reform proposals were to be transformed into law. During the early 1850s, a few enlightened bureaucrats took part in Russia's legislative process under the tutelage of Grand Duke Konstantin Nikolaevich in the very unlikely arena of the Imperial Naval Ministry. A few years later, others gained further experience when they drafted an emancipation for the serfs who lived on the Grand Duchess Elena Pavlovna's estate at Karlovka.

These undertakings were important for Russia's enlightened bureaucrats because they were supported—in fact initiated—by members of the Imperial family. Both Konstantin Nikolaevich and Elena Pavlovna thus played an unexpected role in preparations for the Great Reforms and helped the enlightened bureaucrats meet those awesome challenges they faced during the decade after Russia's Crimean defeat. These two Imperial patrons had still greater influence because they encouraged broader discussion of reform in their circles, where such issues could be debated more candidly and with more safety than elsewhere. Composed of men who became known as *konstantinovtsy*, Konstantin Nikolaevich's circle retained a more official character, for it was centered within Russia's Naval Ministry itself. Elena Pavlovna's circle functioned more as a salon in which she encouraged debate about state problems and urged her carefully chosen guests to propose innovative solutions. Further study of both groups can add to our understanding about the manner in which Russia's enlightened bureaucrats prepared to embark on the path to the Great Reforms. Equally important, it was through their associations with their two Imperial benefactors that they were able to connect their inter-agency committees of experts—those potentially effective instruments for changing policy they had created during the previous decade—with the highest levels of the Imperial political and administrative process.

Konstantin Nikolaevich and the *"Konstantinovtsy"*

Of all Grand Dukes of the nineteenth century, Konstantin Nikolaevich played the most active sustained political role. Born on September 9, 1827, he began to take part in state affairs in the mid-1840s, and continued for almost four decades. From the beginning, his course in life was set by his father, Nicholas I, who dedicated him to service in the Imperial navy. Nicholas did so to realize one of his fondest dreams, which was to restore Russia's navy to the glory it had enjoyed during the reigns of Peter the Great and Catherine II. Throughout his son's childhood and youth, he left that task in the hands of one of his most trusted adjutants, Prince A. S. Menshikov. Menshikov's appointment as an admiral in 1827 (at the time, he had never once commanded a ship at sea) signaled the beginning of his control over Russian naval affairs for almost a quarter-century.[4] Toward the end of Menshikov's tenure as Russia's naval chief, Konstantin Nikolaevich reached maturity and became one of his most important deputies.

Before Konstantin Nikolaevich reached the age of four, he was named General-Admiral and Chief of the Naval Guards.[5] Just more than a year later, in November 1832, Nicholas placed him in the charge of Captain F. P. Litke, a Baltic German seaman who had won acclaim for his four-year circumnavigation of the globe in the sloop *Seniavin*.[6] During the next sixteen years, it became Litke's responsibility to turn his pupil into a dedicated and efficient seaman with a passion for the sea.[7] An explorer, geographer, physicist, and, above all, a devoted naval officer, Litke nonetheless was not well suited to the task, nor did he find its demands particularly pleasant. "At nine in the morning, I begin my duties as tutor and continue them until nine in the evening when the Grand Duke goes to bed . . . but, in another year, it appears that he will be placed completely in my charge and then I shall have to spend the nights with him as well," he lamented to his fellow scientist and friend Baron Vrangel at the beginning of 1834. "Thus are my 365 days to be spent each year without any change whatsoever."[8] Although he did not enjoy them, Litke took his responsibilities seriously. "The will of the Emperor is for me a law and, as His Majesty commands, it is my duty to obey," he told a friend at the time of his appointment.[9] He therefore set out to shape the young Grand Duke's character and left an indelible mark. Konstantin Nikolaevich developed a deep love for the navy and a lasting sense of duty to his native Russia. Russian history was to remember him, however, as a statesman and a reformer, not as a great naval captain.

By most accounts, Konstantin Nikolaevich was a willful but gifted child. Under Litke's firm supervision, he grew into a well-educated, talented young man who showed great promise as a statesman. He was taught by some of Russia's finest scholars and was far more receptive to their offerings than was his elder brother. The academician Heinrich F. E. Lenz taught him mathematics and physics, the poet Zhukovskii schooled him in Russian grammar and literature, and Baron Korf introduced him to statistics and jurisprudence.[10] Korf thought it his task "not to make of him a legal scholar nor a doctor of laws, but a man well-versed on all state questions,"[11] and the Grand Duke greeted his efforts with enthusiasm. "Today we began [a study of] state institutions and [Korf] lectured on the history of the State Council," Konstantin Nikolaevich confided to his diary on December 23, 1847, and added that "these studies always interest me immensely."[12] In all but parade drills, he proved more able than any of his brothers, and, although stubborn, he proved more amenable to discipline and regimentation. Despite the firm regime which Litke imposed on him, he thought of his companion as a second father with whom he could express "all my feelings, even my soul."[13] "I now have three fathers," he wrote to Litke in late 1841. "The omnipresent Heavenly Father, Papa who at the same time is my sovereign, and you who always look after my happiness. How can one not be happy in such a family!!!"[14]

Litke saw as his main task the training of his charge as a naval officer, and by all accounts he succeeded. Under his direction, Konstantin Nikolaevich received his first command, the brig *Ulysses,* in 1843. In the spring of 1845, he went on maneuvers with the Black Sea Fleet and served under Admiral A. V. Kornilov on the frigate *Flora.* From that moment, his passion for the navy was forever established, and, in pursuit of his love, he sailed on some fifty voyages in the course of his life. By 1878, he had spent 1,375 days at sea, more than had any other Romanov prince.[15]

The navy was Konstantin Nikolaevich's first love, but other tasks began to claim his attention as he grew to manhood. In 1845, his appointment as the honorary president of the Russian Geographical Society marked the beginning of a deepening involvement with Russian internal affairs that eventually saw him emerge as a leading advocate of the Great Reforms. Most important initially, his new duties brought him into contact with Russia's emerging enlightened bureaucracy and provided him with what Golovnin described as "the means for obtaining very diverse information about various areas of Russia and . . . the means to direct intellectual activity."[16]

When he was appointed as chairman of the Naval Ministry's commission to revise the Empire's century-old Naval Regulations, Konstantin Nikolaevich began to draw some of these enlightened bureaucrats directly into the service of the reform cause.[17] First among them was Golovnin, whom Litke had praised so highly as secretary of the Geographical Society in the mid-1840s[18] and who had impressed Admiral Menshikov with his careful reports about the political situation in the Duchy of Finland in late 1849 and early 1850.[19] When Konstantin Nikolaevich became head of the commission to revise the Naval Regulations in September 1850, Menshikov named Golovnin to be his secretary.[20] The appointment marked the beginning of a deep emotional bond between the two young men that endured for the rest of their lives. On New Year's Day, 1852, Konstantin Nikolaevich confided to his diary that the previous year had been made especially notable by "the development of friendship with my heartfelt comrade Golovnin."[21]

The substance of Konstantin Nikolaevich's reform of Russia's antiquated Naval Regulations need not concern us because it dealt only with internal naval affairs. Far more significant was the group of enlightened bureaucrats he assembled to improve the administration of the Empire's naval establishment, while he served as acting chief of the Naval Ministry during the Crimean War, and the legislative tactics they developed. A talented administrator among Russian statesmen, the Grand Duke placed great confidence in his deputies, delegated authority to subordinates, and gave department heads rare freedom to make policy decisions.[22] Such attitudes may have stemmed from his training in naval command which, by its very nature, was more decentralized than that of the army. Further, he did not need to fear that the advancement of others within his administration might one day imperil his own position in the Empire's power structure. Konstantin Nikolaevich owed his position to his Imperial birth; others owed theirs to the influence they had won through craft, intrigue, and ability. For all but the most self-confident, encouragement of talented subordinates meant opening the way for a younger statesman who might one day become a dangerous rival. For a Grand Duke, that threat did not exist, and Konstantin Nikolaevich was intelligent enough to perceive that comforting fact.

Willingness to delegate authority and seek out the talented men who served under his command enabled Konstantin Nikolaevich to initiate a debate about the reform of Russia's Naval Regulations that was remarkable in the Empire's central administration for its breadth and candor. As Golovnin explained in a brief essay about his patron, Konstantin Nikolaevich perceived that "in drafting legislation, it was essential to create, so to speak, artificial publicity *(iskusstvennaia glasnost')*, to encourage debates and disputes, and elicit the views of the entire group for which a law was being drafted, rather than being satisfied with the opinions of a narrow circle." As a result of the broad discussion that Konstantin Nikolaevich encouraged within the navy, Golovnin went on, "there was formed in the fleet a body of opinion [about reforming the Naval Regulations] and, when the new Naval Regulations appeared, it seemed as if they were only an expression and a reflection of that opinion."[23] The Grand Duke thus extended *glasnost'* beyond the narrow circle of the central bureaucracy, but found a means to avoid the difficulties the enlightened bureaucrats faced when they attempted to extend the same process to aristocratic provincial agricultural societies. His version of *glasnost'* was indeed "artificial," but it was *glasnost'* nonetheless. Some enlightened bureaucrats, and especially Golovnin, lost sight of the fact that its limits were very discrete because of the agency within which it was employed and the statesman who had initiated it. Golovnin, as Minister of Public Instruction, later attempted to repeat the Grand Duke's success in an effort to reform Russia's censorship regulations, but he produced far less effective results.

Konstantin Nikolaevich's reform of Russia's Naval Regulations began his broader involvement in the Naval Ministry's administration.

When Nicholas detailed Menshikov on a special diplomatic mission to Constantinople in January 1853, he became acting head of the Naval Ministry and held that post throughout the Crimean War. Because he found that many officials within the Admiralty could not meet his standards because of "age, physical weakness, and being accustomed to the former system they had followed for so many years," he decided that a wholesale importation of young, energetic, and innovative officials able to "understand and assist each other" was necessary. In a flash of insight that was rare among Russian statesmen, Konstantin Nikolaevich understood that such changes in personnel must come at the departmental level.[24] Because senior officials stood so distant from the level of the bureaucratic hierarchy at which policy was implemented, it was middle-level officials—department heads and *stolonachal'niki*—who played the most direct part in determining the quality of administration that any particular bureau could provide.[25] Konstantin Nikolaevich therefore set out to recruit departmental heads and their deputies.

An impressive group of young officials who were unusual in Russia's central administration because they sought added responsibility and thrived on independence in a milieu where most bureaucrats preferred the reverse answered Konstantin Nikolaevich's summons. Among them were Golovnin, Prince Dmitrii Obolenskii (Chief of the Naval Commissariat), Count Dmitrii Tolstoi (Head of the Naval Ministry's Chancery), Prince Fedor L'vov (Obolenskii's comrade from the School of Jurisprudence), Mikhail Reitern (a *litseist* who already had earned a considerable reputation as an expert on state finances), Dmitrii Nabokov, Boris Mansurov, and several others.[26] All were younger than thirty-five (Mansurov was only twenty-five); all had elite or university educations; several (Obolenskii, Tolstoi, Reitern, Golovnin, and Nabokov) would receive ministerial appointments later in the century. Together they became known as the *konstantinovtsy*, the protégés of Konstantin Nikolaevich.

The *konstantinovtsy* gained valuable experience in the tasks of administrative reorganization and in the rationalization of bureaucratic functions under Konstantin Nikolaevich's protection. Unlike most senior Russian statesmen, Konstantin Nikolaevich possessed the will to experiment with innovations in administrative theory and practice. His education, the innovative, independent, fighting sea captains with whom he had served in his naval training and who were so unlike the parade-ground commanders of the army, the urgings of the progressive officials he met in the Russian Geographical Society, and his unique position as a Grand Duke in a ministerial setting, all left him with little sympathy for the *deloproizvodstvo* that consumed time and energy to no effective purpose. Because he regarded *deloproizvodstvo* as a major hindrance to effective administration, he insisted on its reduction. He increased the powers of office section chiefs and department heads, delegated more authority, and assigned greater responsibility to a number of other subordinates.[27] This embodied a bold new approach to state administration in Russia. The academician G. F. Parrot once had spoken in favor of delegating authority when, in one of his many letters to Nicholas in the late 1820s, he urged that the principle of individual responsibility be instituted throughout Russia's central administration.[28] None was bold enough to pursue his suggestion at the time, and no statesman had dared attempt it afterward.

Nor would Konstantin Nikolaevich tolerate officials who were slow to reduce administrative formalities and strip excess verbiage from the reports they submitted. "The multiplicity of forms smothers the true essence of administrative activity among us and gives security to a universal official falsehood," he warned in a circular dated November 1855. "If one separates the essential from the covering of paper—that which *is* from that which only *seems* to be—and sifts out the truth from the half-truths and falsehoods, then everywhere the brilliance will rise to the top and the rot will sink to the bottom."[29] He pressed his view upon his *konstantinovtsy* as they attempted to rationalize administration in the Naval Ministry's central offices. "I require not fulsome praise," he once wrote, "but truth and, especially, honest and well-reasoned reports about shortcomings in every area of administration."[30]

To broaden discussion about the dilemmas posed by the demands of modernization in all areas of Russian life and government, Konstantin Nikolaevich urged the *konstantinovtsy* to publicize their views in the journal *Morskoi sbornik*. A creation of Litke's, *Morskoi sbornik* was founded in 1848 as an instrument for broadening the education of Russian naval officers, and, until 1853, it had enjoyed a very limited circulation, even within the navy itself.[31] In that year, Golovnin reorganized its composition and format, and it soon became one of the most widely read periodicals in the Empire. *Morskoi sbornik* was the only Russian journal that had published details about the fighting in the Crimea,[32] but its surging popularity was more a consequence of the startling fact that, under the patronage of Konstantin Nikolaevich and the energetic editorship of Golovnin, its list of contributors became the most brilliant of any Russian journal. From the world of *belles lettres*, it published works by Ostrovskii, Dal', Goncharov, Pisemskii, Maikov, Grigorovich, and Mikhailov. The Empire's leading scholars and scientists—Nikolai Pirogov, Lenz, von Baer, Struve, and Jacobi—contributed to it, as did such educators as K. D. Ushinskii and F. G. Tol'. All of the *konstantinovtsy* publicized their views about reform and change in its pages, and that was another significant reason for its popularity. When the Crimean War ended, its list of subscribers stood at 5,565, as compared with the 3,100 that the liberal journal *Sovremennik* had boasted in its heyday a decade earlier.[33] No less a figure than the radical publicist Nikolai Chernyshevskii once called *Morskoi sbornik* "one of the most remarkable phenomena in our literature—perhaps the most remarkable in many ways."[34]

Konstantin Nikolaevich took very much to heart the lines his tutor Zhukovskii once penned in defense of progress.

> Progress is a *sacred affair* [Zhukovskii wrote to him in 1841]. Everything on God's earth *develops, goes forward,* cannot and, indeed, ought not to stand still. *Immobility is death,* imperceptible, calm, but all the same it is death, producing only decay. *Progress,* the gradual development of the existing order, without shocks, but *continually,* is life. To stop progress, or to force it ahead too rapidly . . . is equally ruinous. This applies equally in the life of individuals and in the life of a people.[35]

A deep belief in progress and his ability to protect its contributors were the major reasons that the Grand Duke succeeded in making *Morskoi sbornik* into a rare vehicle of reform when state policy was directed toward preserving the *status quo* in the mid-1850s. The fact that *Morskoi sbornik* was left free of censorship until 1858 made his task notably easier because the first decision about what it would publish rested with Golovnin and Konstantin Nikolaevich themselves.[36]

Konstantin Nikolaevich's advocacy of reform had been so worrisome to Russia's senior statesmen that the Third Section assigned a secret agent to report about his activities as early as 1852,[37] and although he did not learn until 1859 that such a spy had served in his private office, Konstantin Nikolaevich nonetheless exercised circumspection in his behavior and in the materials he published in *Morskoi sbornik.* Even when he found manuscripts too critical to be published by his Naval Ministry, he sometimes encouraged their publication elsewhere if he thought they accurately portrayed Russian conditions. He wrote to one author, who described in "vivid examples the terrible and woeful conditions of our military courts," that *Morskoi sbornik* could not publish his essay, but that Herzen's émigré journal "*Kolokol,* I think, would accept it with pleasure."[38]

With the support of Konstantin Nikolaevich and his *konstantinovtsy, Morskoi sbornik* called for the reform of public education, encouraged early debate about judicial reform, urged that corporal punishment be abolished, and discussed many other important issues during the 1850s. The extent to which it expressed a broad range of public opinion can be seen not only from the impressive list of contributors we mentioned earlier, but also from the increase in their numbers. In 1848, *Morskoi sbornik* published the work of only six contributors, and when Golovnin began to reorganize it in 1853, the number had risen to a mere thirteen. Only three years later, the number of annual contributors had reached 109, and, in 1857, it reached a peak of 122. Even after the debate about emancipation became public in late 1857 and the dilemmas of reform and change could be debated in print elsewhere, the number of contributors for the following year still stood at 106.[39]

Thus, it was under the patronage of Grand Duke Konstantin Nikolaevich that a number of enlightened bureaucrats—the *konstantinovtsy*—gained both practical experience in the autocratic legislative process and were provided with an opportunity to discuss in print their views about the broader transformation Russia required. Others among them found an opportunity to test the practicality of their reformist views under the patronage of the Grand Duchess Elena Pavlovna, another member of the Imperial family who openly supported the enlightened bureaucrats in the Crimean era. Unlike anyone else in Russia, she provided them with the means for testing their ideas about the emancipation of Russia's serfs, and her salon became an important complement to the efforts of Konstantin Nikolaevich and the *konstantinovtsy*. Together they helped to stimulate the reform debate during the first months of Alexander II's reign.

Elena Pavlovna and Her Salon

While experimenting with their mentor's concept of *iskusstvennaia glasnost'* and discussing broader issues in the pages of *Morskoi sbornik,* the *konstantinovtsy* were restrained in their discussions because they took place within a government agency and in the pages of an official journal. Beginning in 1847, and continuing into the 1860s, others among Russia's enlightened bureaucrats enjoyed a unique opportunity to discuss many economic, social, and even political issues at the "morganatic evenings" of the Grand Duchess Elena Pavlovna, sister-in-law of Nicholas I and aunt of Alexander II.

Elena Pavlovna was born Frederike Charlotte Marie of Württemberg in Stuttgart on January 9, 1806. Her father, younger son of the Württemberg royal family, found it distasteful to live under his elder brother's rule and took his wife and children to Paris soon after the Napoleonic wars ended. There, Frederike Charlotte Marie attended the elite finishing school of Madame Campan, an educator soon to become famous for her publication of *Conseils aux jeunes filles, ouvrage destiné aux écoles élémentaires* in 1824, and she even studied with the renowned Georges Cuvier, the leading antagonist of Geoffroy Saint-Hilaire in the debate over the origins of man. Frederike Charlotte Marie returned to Stuttgart late in 1820 to learn that she had been chosen by the Russian Dowager Empress Mariia Feodorovna as a bride for her youngest son Grand Duke Mikhail Pavlovich.[40]

When she arrived in St. Petersburg at the end of September 1823, the young princess brought a firm resolve to become part of her new homeland and proclaimed to her new countrymen, "I feel that here I have set foot upon my true native soil."[41] She studied Russian before she arrived and even had read parts of Karamzin's *History of the Russian State* in Russian.[42] Despite her best hopes and efforts, her life in Russia was not to be happy. Married on December 5, 1823, she shared none of her husband's fascination with the rigid and sterile militarism that pervaded Russia's army, and she endured perverse abuses at his hands, which reportedly shocked even other members of the Imperial family.[43] Her education had done little to prepare her to face the intrigues of a court dominated by the aging Dowager Empress Mariia Feodorovna, and she suffered the woman's sharp-tongued criticism in silence. To this was added the burden of family grief. All but one of her children died before they reached adulthood.[44]

Unhappy in her personal life, the Grand Duchess sought solace in books, the arts, and works of charity. She became the patron of the artists Ivanov and Gorbunov and was instrumental in launching the great Anton Rubinstein upon his career. From her personal fortune she financed the publication of Radlov's early work about Turkish dialects and supported the Russian Asiatic explorer Potanin.[45] She supported other scholarly endeavors, including Skrebitskii's voluminous work on the emancipation of 1861[46] and the Slavophile Ivan Beliaev's studies about the genesis of representative government institutions in Russia.[47] After her husband died, she became patron of the Holy Cross Community, a forerunner of the Russian Red Cross, whose Sisters of Mercy cared for the sick and wounded during the dark days of the Crimean War.[48] Later she helped to found the Russian Musical Society and continued her interest in the care of the sick by establishing the Eleninskii Clinical Institute, where provincial doctors could come to study modern medical practices.[49]

Elena Pavlovna lavished wealth and attention on the arts, sciences, and good works, but these by no means encompassed the whole of her interests. That probing mind and wide-ranging intellectual curiosity which had led her to study with Cuvier as a young Württemberg princess in Paris made her deeply interested in state affairs and those "cursed questions" which so preoccupied the Russian intelligentsia. She was an ardent admirer of Gogol, followed closely the Slavophile-Westerner debates of the 1840s and early 1850s,[50] read extensively about Russia's geography, and had long discussions about statistics with Arsen'ev.[51] "She always sought the company of scholars," one historian remarked. "Moving in professorial circles when she visited Moscow, she at first occasioned them no small uneasiness because she was a woman from the world of the Court, the society of which they scorned."[52]

Men were attracted by Elena Pavlovna's beauty and captivated by her stormy nature and passion for intellectual debate. Nicholas called her "the scholar in our family circle"[53] and sent the Marquis de Custine and Baron von Haxthausen to discuss Russian politics with her in the hope that these foreign visitors would be impressed.[54] She discussed affairs of state with the Emperor's closest advisers and won their respect for her broad understanding of complex problems. Kiselev, Bludov, Lanskoi, Prince A. M. Gorchakov, Baron Korf, and a number of other statesmen were her frequent guests at dinners and evening gatherings. From them she learned about the problems Russia faced and posed questions they found provocative and impressive.[55] Count Bludov reportedly remarked that "she has the mind of a man and the soul of a woman,"[56] and Kiselev described her as "a woman with a wide-ranging intellect and a superlative heart." "After an audience with her," he concluded, "everyone would be left amazed by her ability and her remarkable perceptiveness."[57] Marquis de Custine, who made many an acid comment about the Russians he encountered during 1839, admitted that although "her obligation of doing the honors for French literature at the Court of the Emperor Nicholas makes me afraid of the Grand Duchess Helena," he found her to be both "beautiful and intellectual" and concluded that, in her case, "celebrity as a woman of wit and high intellectual attainment must be a heavy burden in a royal court."[58] Baron Korf, a dutiful and industrious commentator on Russian high society, perhaps described her best in his diary account of their meeting in October 1847.

> We sat for a long time *tête-à-tête*, in a serious conversation about legislation and, among other things, about the peasants. On all matters, she spoke like a true statesman, of course not like many of our present-day statesmen, for that would be for her a poor compliment indeed. . . . Listening to the conversation and the thoughts of the Grand Duchess on such matters, one realized that Salic Law is not well founded everywhere, at least, and one laments the fact that [people such as she] cannot sit on our State Council.[59]

Elena Pavlovna

Konstantin Nikolaevich

Mikhailovskii Palace (Courtesy of the Saltykov-Shchedrin Public Library, Leningrad)

Because many of her papers disappeared during the 1870s,[60] we have few of Elena Pavlovna's own writings to shed light on her attitudes about politics and reform, and it therefore must be her actions, not her written words, that speak for her views. From the very brief diary that she kept in 1849, we know that she perceived three "truths"—religious, philosophical, and political—to be a continuing phenomenon in the experience of mankind and that she regarded the essence of "political truth" to be "*la liberté,*" which, she confided to her diary, must be the prime objective of all government. Yet in her view *la liberté* was not the exclusive domain of "*la démocratie*" or "*la république*"; it also could be achieved through the institution of monarchy and ought, in fact, to be every monarch's prime objective. To attain liberty, and to extend it to all men, she insisted, was "*le but de la monarchie, de l'aristocratie, comme de la République.*"[61]

During the first two decades of her life in Russia, Elena Pavlovna attempted to draw on the knowledge of statesmen rather than influence them with her own opinions. For her, as for the enlightened bureaucrats whom she soon would come to patronize, the 1830s and early 1840s were a time of preparation and study in which she endeavored to learn about Russia's problems before attempting to influence the course of events in the Empire. Beginning in the mid-1840s, however, she began to seek ways to develop a body of opinion in St. Petersburg which could influence the views of Russian statesmen and the course of events in the Empire. To supplement the information received from the Empire's senior statesmen about Russian affairs, she began to seek out young officials known for their administrative ability and sympathy for change. Cautious, timid, and constrained by the rigid prejudices of her husband, she first organized a salon dominated by Court society. Within a decade, it became one of St. Petersburg's major centers of progressive opinion, where enlightened bureaucrats and their allies among the intelligentsia played a prominent role.

Elena Pavlovna's salon began as a "circle" of Court figures who met weekly in the apartments of her ladies-in-waiting.[62] Almost from the beginning, it included a few men who were little known in high society but whom statesmen such as Kiselev, Perovskii, and Bludov valued as officials of outstanding talent and great promise. First to be invited was Prince Obolenskii, a young *pravoved* then serving as deputy to the President of the First Department of St. Petersburg's Civil Court of Justice,[63] who was unusual among Russia's enlightened bureaucrats because he came from an ancient princely family that still held title to some 500 male serfs and was closely connected at Court.[64] His father had married a lady-in-waiting to the Dowager Empress, and he recently had wed a lady-in-waiting to the Princess Dariia Trubetskaia.[65] Despite this background, Obolenskii's views were very different from what one would expect from the scion of a great and wealthy noble family. By the mid-1840s, he had become a close friend of Miliutin and Zablotskii and occupied a prominent place in those circles dominated by progressive officials and was about to enter the Russian Geographical Society as an ally of those who seized control of it at mid-century. Early in the 1850s, he became one of the first enlightened bureaucrats Konstantin Nikolaevich drafted for service in his Naval Ministry.[66] Because one of his closest comrades at the School of Jurisprudence was Prince L'vov, whose sister was governess to Elena Pavlovna's only surviving daughter,[67] Obolenskii was the obvious candidate among the enlightened bureaucrats to receive the first invitation to the Mikhailovskii Palace in late 1847. He accepted it with some trepidation, for the Grand Duchess's home also was the residence of Mikhail Pavlovich who, Obolenskii recalled in his memoirs, "represented something truly terrible, like some sort of wild beast, in the eyes of us civil officials."[68]

Obolenskii's fears proved groundless. "From her very first words," he later wrote, "the Grand Duchess impressed me with the straightforward nature of her questions and the liveliness of her conversation."[69] But it was not until the summer of 1848 that she began to discuss state affairs seriously with her young guest. Between their first and second meetings, revolutions swept through western Europe, and reaction intensified in Russia. Obolenskii's friends were very sensitive to this changing political climate, and, as we mentioned earlier, it had traumatic consequences for some. It was with surprise, and perhaps even some hope, that the young prince heard Elena Pavlovna express her views about the state of affairs in Russia. Her comments made such a deep impression on him that nearly three decades later his recollection of them remained sharp and clear. Their meeting occurred on a summer day at Pavlovsk, and Elena Pavlovna had summoned him to a sitting room filled with flowers and greenery:

> In order to encourage me to be candid [Obolenskii recalled], she launched into a critical evaluation of the entire present course of state policy and, in doing so, exhibited such a knowledge of the real condition of our civic life that I involuntarily expressed my own views.... Speaking of the younger generation, she told me of her sympathy for its noble impulses and aspirations. With indignation she spoke of the emptiness and triviality of Court life, of the absence of thought and of any desire to recognize and understand the needs of the country, of the general indifference, and of the empty, lifeless formalism.[70]

Such sentiments reflected some of the enlightened bureaucrats' most bitter complaints, and even a few senior statesmen shared some of their opinions. Perovskii had warned the Emperor on one occasion that bureaucratic formalities had crippled effective administration.[71] Less than a decade later, the noted economist and statistician L. V. Tengoborskii lamented that "records and letters seem to reproduce themselves, one might say, in geometrical proportions."[72] But what Perovskii and Tengoborskii reported to the Emperor, they did not pursue in open discussion with subordinates, although they tacitly encouraged them in such views. Therefore, it was an unheard-of experience for Obolenskii to find a sympathetic ear within the bosom of the Imperial family in the midst of the political reaction that descended on Russia after 1848. When Elena Pavlovna asked him about others who shared his views and hopes, he was anxious to speak on their behalf.[73]

The first of Obolenskii's friends to join him in Elena Pavlovna's salon was Miliutin, in whom the Grand Duchess became interested when Perovskii and Kiselev sang his praises at several of her private dinner gatherings.[74] At some point in 1847 she invited Miliutin to visit her, and at least one account has it that Kiselev told his apprehensive nephew that it was because "she wants to see a Russian liberal, a rare beast if ever there was one."[75] Like Obolenskii, Miliutin found the same warm reception. On several occasions in late 1848 and early 1849, they visited the Mikhailovskii Palace and, although constrained by the presence of Grand Duke Mikhail Pavlovich, who sat playing chess in another corner of the room, they discussed with their newfound patron the problems facing Russia.[76]

Until his death in 1849, Mikhail Pavlovich's presence loomed over Elena Pavlovna's efforts to extend her inquiries about Russian problems beyond that narrow circle of Nicholaean courtiers who regularly crossed her path. Her contacts with the enlightened bureaucrats remained limited to Obolenskii, whose family background made him an inconspicuous guest, and Miliutin, whose less exalted background was somewhat compensated for by his family ties to Kiselev. After her husband's death, however, she began to invite more men not connected with the Court to her "morganatic evenings," and every Thursday the Mikhailovskii Palace was transformed into one of the most brilliant salons in St. Petersburg. Her salon was notable for the wide variety of views and interests represented. The artists Aivazovskii and Pimenev; the academicians von Baer and Nikolai Pirogov; the writer P. A. Viazemskii; the historian Stepan Shevyrev; the statesmen Bludov, Protasov, Uvarov, Kiselev, Perovskii, and Korf; and such enlightened bureaucrats as Prince Obolenskii, Nikolai and Dmitrii Miliutin, Prince Odoevskii, and Dmitrii Khrushchov all were frequent visitors. They discussed everything from art, music, and historical scholarship to the unpublished works of Gogol' and the Slavophile-Westerner controversy.[77] Yet, as her desire to influence state policy increased, Elena Pavlovna's ability to do so grew more limited because many of the statesmen upon whom she relied for information about state affairs in the past no longer were in a position to serve her interests. Uvarov left the Ministry of Public Instruction in 1849; Perovski had resigned as Minister of Internal Affairs in 1852; and Kiselev, probably her closest confidant among the advisers of Nicholas I, was named Russia's first post-war ambassador to Paris early in 1856. The Grand Duchess was not on close terms with any of their immediate successors; and that left her contacts with the inner circle of Russia's senior statesmen considerably eroded, especially because she had devoted much of her attention during the war years to improving medical services in the Crimea and had drifted further away from direct contact with the Empire's internal affairs. On the eve of the Great Reform era, Elena Pavlovna's influence in St. Petersburg's centers of high politics thus was considerably less than it had been a half-decade earlier, for she had woven her first web of political connections among men whose careers were nearly past.

Although her connections with Imperial statesmen had been weakened by resignations, retirements, and replacements, Elena Pavlovna had the means at her command to construct new instruments for influencing state policy, which were more potent than the ones she had lost. With the death of Nicholas, she became the senior member of the Imperial family and, especially during the first months of his reign, that gave her an added measure of influence with her nephew Alexander II. More important, her new status increased her influence with Konstantin Nikolaevich, whose Naval Ministry became the center of reformist sentiment during the final months of the war,[78] and she had a loyal following among the leading enlightened bureaucrats. While many of the senior statesmen upon whom she had relied for information and influence no longer were on the scene, these younger men began to gain positions of importance at the war's end. Finally, when Alexander II replaced Minister of Internal Affairs Bibikov with Count S. S. Lanskoi, an aging statesman who had been a frequent dinner guest at the Mikhailovskii Palace since the mid-1840s,[79] Elena Pavlovna re-established her close connection with the very ministry in which the early work on drafting the emancipation decrees was concentrated.

Elena Pavlovna therefore had at her command the means to play a role in Russian affairs, and she resolved to press for the reforms she thought important. Like many others, she had not earlier perceived the inner rottenness of the system her brother-in-law forged and realized the full extent of its failure only after the Crimean reversals, when her nephew, a man she thought weak and indecisive, mounted Russia's throne as Alexander II.[80] Alexander was less self-assured than his father. He was much less dynamic, and far more petty in the defense of his Imperial prerogatives. *'Il est jaloux de son pouvoir,'* the Grand Duchess once confided to a favorite,[81] and her apprehensions about his ability to resolve Russia's crises increased when he made his first appointments. Because Elena Pavlovna feared the growing influence of General Iakov Rostovtsev, her husband's former confidant, she resolved to take up the political role she had shunned a decade before.[82] "I have become Russian in spirit and in all my habits," she once told Baron Korf. "I cannot feel happy except in Russia."[83] Now she dedicated her energy to those reforms she considered essential for Russia's preservation as a Great Power. She explained her decision to Obolenskii on the first day of the new reign:

> I was invited to the Grand Duchess [Obolenskii wrote in his brief memoirs] and had a very lengthy conversation with her, out of which the conclusion emerged that she had resolved to seek further influence in order to paralyze the influence of those individuals whom she considered especially dangerous. In this she hoped for the cooperation of Grand Duke Konstantin Nikolaevich. She asked me, for my part, to try to prevail upon him not to refuse to play a major part in the affairs of general administration and not to limit his conversations with his brother to the narrow interests of the Naval Ministry. . . . I told the Grand Duchess that . . . [his broader influence] was fully possible if the Grand Duke were to be offered a position that would impose upon him the duty to . . . become involved with more general administrative matters such as, for example, a position as President of the State Council.[84]

In association with Konstantin Nikolaevich, Elena Pavlovna worked to make the collective wisdom of educated Russian opinion available to senior statesmen by assembling the many reform proposals which she and the Grand Duke received during the early months of the new reign. Most of all, however, she used her salon evenings to encourage an exchange of ideas between enlightened bureaucrats and the moderate intelligentsia at a time when discussions of reform and, particularly, emancipation, were not yet permitted in the Russian press. Even before peace had been made in the Crimea, her salon became a center in which Russia's enlightened bureaucrats assembled regularly. Not only Miliutin and Obolenskii attended her evening gatherings but also Golovnin, Deputy Minister of State Domains Khrushchov, Miliutin's brother-in-law A. A. Abaza (later to become Minister of Finance), Zablotskii, M. Kh. Reitern, another future Minister of Finance, and Iakov Solov'ev, a young cadastral expert who had transferred from Zablotskii's Department of Rural Economy to the Ministry of Internal Affairs.[85] Although they knew each other well and obviously discussed questions of reform among themselves, the Grand Duchess's salon provided these men with their first semi-public forum. It enabled them to turn away from a narrow study of local conditions and, by drawing on their collective knowledge, to develop broader reform programs.

Elena Pavlovna's encouragement of reformist opinion came to a temporary halt in October 1856, when she became ill and had to undergo a series of complex treatments that kept her at Europe's spas for nearly two years. Yet she never abandoned her concern for Russia's future while she lived in the West. She used every opportunity to assemble comparative data and encouraged discussion between Russian and European experts. During the summer of 1857, she organized a conference at Wildbad-im-Schwarzwald, to which she invited men who were especially known for their expertise about the problems posed by serfdom in Russia. Among them were Kiselev, Kavelin, Prince Obolenskii, Abaza, V. V. Tarnovskii (who owned large estates in the Ukraine and had won Elena Pavlovna's trust as a lord who supported an equitable emancipation settlement), and Baron von Haxthausen, a German expert on rural problems whose three-volume *Studies on the Interior of Russia* had earned him a European-wide reputation as an expert on Russian peasant life.[86] These men discussed at considerable length the proposals that Miliutin and Kavelin had drafted the previous fall for emancipating the serfs at Karlovka. We shall return to a discussion of the Karlovka reform; here it is important to note that the discussions at Wildbad had implications that reached far beyond the question of emancipating the 15,000 serfs who tilled Karlovka's quarter-million acres. As Professor Bakhrushin once wrote:

> At Wildbad, in essence, not only the bases of the future reform [i.e., the emancipation of 1861], but also the plan for implementing it were proposed and firmly established: (1) an emancipation with land by means of a redemption plan; (2) peasant self-government based on the peasant commune; (3) a tax based on land; (4) the organization of provincial committees for the preliminary discussion of important questions; (5) the creation of rural mediators [*mirovye posredniki*]—all these questions were not only raised but fully worked out in the discussions about the matter of [emancipation at] Karlovka.[87]

Such principles were very much in keeping with Haxthausen's views, and the final report of the Wildbad Conference echoed almost exactly the conclusions he had set down a few weeks before in the preliminary working paper, "Observations on the Broader Development and Extension of the Present Provincial Order in Russia, Especially in Relation to the Imminent Abolition of Serfdom."[88] Indeed, the memoranda that Haxthausen prepared at Elena Pavlovna's urging in 1856 and 1857 quite accurately anticipated much of the form in which the Russian emancipation acts emerged in 1861.[89]

The Wildbad Conference was less important for its emancipation program (for such was not so very different from plans circulating among the Russian intelligentsia at the time)[90] than for the fact that its proposals bore the imprimatur of a Russian Grand Duchess, the man who had served for two decades as Nicholas I's Chief of Staff for Peasant Affairs, two great lords who owned large estates in the Ukraine, and a scholar who enjoyed European-wide acclaim and had enjoyed the generous patronage of Nicholas I in his efforts to study peasant life in Russia. Yet, whatever their similarities or differences, all theoretical programs for emancipation were untried and untested, and their implementation seemed very unlikely. Throughout 1856 and most of 1857, Russia's nobles continued to greet with stubborn silence the Emperor's request that they consider how to accomplish an emancipation. Likewise, by the summer of 1857, the Secret Committee Alexander II convened to discuss the problem had produced nothing beyond timid statements that urged caution and restraint. Elena Pavlovna thus decided to test current theory by implementing a full-scale emancipation at Karlovka.

Throughout the 1840s Elena Pavlovna had discussed the problems that serfdom posed for Russia's future development with Kiselev and other statesmen, and, very soon after the death of her husband, she began to consider practical ways to improve the conditions under which Russia's serfs lived. She began with the purchase of Karlovka from Countess Razumovskaia for the immense sum of 2,800,000 rubles.[91] Consisting of some 250,000 acres (90,904 *desiatiny*) in the province of Poltava, Karlovka was home to 7,397 male and 7,625 female serfs living in twelve separate villages and hamlets.[92] Less than two years after she purchased the estate, Elena Pavlovna launched her first attempt to improve the conditions under which her serfs lived. She was influenced particularly by the principle Kiselev had defended since 1816 that the first step in bettering the serfs' daily lives was to curb the arbitrary and despotic powers that masters wielded over them and that this could best be accomplished by establishing in law the obligations which lord and peasant owed to each other.[93] In 1851, she therefore issued a charter which specified the amount of *barshchina* required from each peasant household and established the important principle that aside from these required labor duties, the remainder of the serfs' time was their own.[94]

Elena Pavlovna's charter of 1851 was only a beginning. At the start of the new reign, she instructed Baron Engelhardt, the estate's manager, to draft a plan to free its serfs. Engelhardt recommended that they be allowed to rent one sixth of the estate's lands at a fixed annual fee of two rubles per *desiatina* and that they be encouraged to purchase these lands in freehold.[95] Engelhardt's land allotments averaged out to a scant two *desiatiny* per male serf, hardly enough to provide even a minimal level of subsistence. His proposal marked, nonetheless, a beginning, and Elena Pavlovna turned to Miliutin and Kavelin for suggestions about improving it.[96]

When she asked Miliutin and Kavelin for advice about emancipating her serfs in the fall of 1855, Elena Pavlovna still viewed her plan mainly as a philanthropic act that others might be encouraged to follow.[97] Given her close relationship with Kiselev and Nicholas I, Elena Pavlovna may have shared their view that the government ought to set examples for the Empire's serf-owners, but Miliutin saw an opportunity to give her effort broader significance. He hoped to use discussions about freeing the serfs at Karlovka as a means to broaden debate about emancipation in general. Although she continued to respect Kiselev and other Nicholaean statesmen with whom years of mutual interests had cemented a lasting friendship, Elena Pavlovna began to espouse the less cautious tactics of the younger generation by late 1855. Therefore, despite Kiselev's strong objections, Miliutin convinced her to follow his more ambitious and adventurous course.[98] Henceforth, the tone and tempo of her efforts on behalf of reform became more attuned to the views of Russia's enlightened bureaucrats than to those of her friends among Russia's former senior statesmen.

In March 1856, Elena Pavlovna petitioned for permission to discuss her emancipation plans with neighboring lords for Poltava and Chernigov. Based upon a memorandum to which Miliutin had assigned the innocuous title, "A Plan of Action for Emancipating the Serfs of those Estate Owners Who Wish to Do So in Poltava and Adjacent Provinces," the Grand Duchess's request hardly reflected the broader importance that its authors hoped it might assume. Serf-owners wishing to free their bondsmen were to meet at Karlovka, work their ideas into a general plan in which the interests of nobles, peasants, and government were equally protected, and the final result, to serve as "an example and a guide," would be submitted for Imperial approval.[99] Since Alexander intended to urge the assembled nobility in Moscow to "give some thought to how this [i.e., an emancipation] can be accomplished" just a few days later, he gave his blessing to his aunt's apparently similar request.[100]

During the summer of 1856, Miliutin and Kavelin discussed the Karlovka emancipation, and, by the beginning of October, Miliutin delivered to his Imperial patroness their "Preliminary Ideas about the Organization of Relationships between the Nobility and Their Serfs." This document advocated full and unconditional emancipation and urged that a state-supported redemption plan be developed to help peasants purchase land from their former masters at prices to be set on the recommendation of committees made up of provincial lords.[101] This latter suggestion most probably originated with Kavelin, who was more optimistic about the value of participation by nobles in the legislative process than was Miliutin. Further, Kavelin was convinced that prosperity of the state and that of the nobility were closely connected and, in a yet-unpublished essay, had argued that the fresh capital which a government-sponsored redemption plan could inject into Russia's economy would benefit state and nobility alike.[102]

On October 7, 1856, Elena Pavlovna presented these "Preliminary Ideas" to Alexander II and urged that the government provide guidelines for an emancipation in order to win the support of the nobility for its reform program.[103] She realized too late that she had gone too far. Her nephew commended her good intentions and urged her to discuss the Karlovka emancipation with Poltava's lords, but he insisted that the nobility must take the initiative in proposing broader emancipation schemes. Such was not the government's task in his view.

> The resolution of this question [the Tsar wrote to Elena Pavlovna on October 26] is affected by many and varied conditions, the significance of which can be determined only through experience. Rather than hasten to outline general legislation for a new order among the most numerous estate in the realm, I am waiting for well-intentioned proprietors of serf-populated estates to express their views about the extent to which they think it possible to improve the lot of their peasants according to principles which, for both sides, will be humanitarian and not onerous.[104]

Whatever hopes Elena Pavlovna, Miliutin, Kavelin, and their friends may have had for spurring the central government to produce a general emancipation thus were dashed by a single Imperial pronouncement. In search of more illustrious backing for her proposals, the Grand Duchess convoked the Wildbad Conference the following summer.

Pronouncements by the conference's experts impressed Alexander II, especially when Haxthausen and Elena Pavlovna convinced Prince Aleksandr Gorchakov, Russia's new Foreign Minister, to join them in urging the Wildbad proposals upon him at Bad Kissingen in late June 1857.[105] But the urgings of this august group still could not overcome the Tsar's hesitation,[106] and even Kiselev soon qualified his support for the Wildbad proposals by warning Alexander that "to give *complete freedom* to twenty-two million peasants of both sexes is *undesir-*

able and *impossible.*"[107] While confessing that "the question of the serfs does not cease to trouble me; it ought to be resolved,"[108] Alexander did not press his Secret Committee in St. Petersburg to resolve the issue, although he appointed Konstantin Nikolaevich a member at that point. Of Konstantin Nikolaevich's commitment to an emancipation there can be no doubt. But, like the enlightened bureaucrats who looked to him as their patron, he had little practical experience in deflecting the delaying tactics of St. Petersburg's great lords. By mid-August, "the temporizing policy the regime had pursued for more than a generation" had been affirmed once again.[109]

The Secret Committee returned the serf question to the Ministry of Internal Affairs.[110] Soon afterward, the emancipation process was set in motion unexpectedly when Minister of Internal Affairs Lanskoi induced the nobility of the northwestern provinces to take a formal stand on the side of emancipation. The famous Nazimov Rescript of late November 1857 was the result of Lanskoi's behind-the-scene efforts, and work on a full-scale emancipation began to move more decisively than anyone had foreseen when the Wildbad Conference had concluded its meetings.[111] By the time that Miliutin and Kavelin completed their revisions of the Karlovka emancipation charter early in 1858, there no longer was any need to stimulate a broader debate on emancipation because it already was in full bloom.[112] The final importance of the Karlovka reform thus lay in the practical experience that Miliutin, Kavelin, Solov'ev, Abaza, Tarnovskii, Cherkasskii, and Samarin gained from the task.[113] For them, it provided a practical introduction to some of the problems they encountered on a far greater scale as members of the Editing Commissions of 1859–1860.[114]

In the autumn of 1858, when Elena Pavlovna returned to Russia after an absence of almost two years, entirely different attitudes prevailed in St. Petersburg. Discussions of reform gripped all levels of educated society, and the emancipation debate was on everyone's lips. A Russian statesman returning to St. Petersburg described the capital's changed mood in a letter to a friend:

> Arriving in Russia now, one runs the risk of not recognizing her. On the surface, everything seems the same, but one feels an internal renovation in everything. One feels that a new era is beginning. The most despairing skeptics, the most obstinate opponents of progress, should recognize that in the past two years civic opinion has achieved great successes in Russia. . . . From all sides, ideas and lucid views are gradually ousting the old routine which, taking pride in its ignorance and stupidity, was ashamed of nothing before and during the war.[115]

In this altered atmosphere, the Grand Duchess's salon assumed a new role. No longer needed as a haven to shelter reformist opinion from hostile surroundings, it became an instrument for broadening discussion about reform among men whose duties in the bureaucracy often associated them with only narrow parts of Russia's legislative process. It further increased the contact between St. Petersburg's statesmen, bureaucrats, and the intelligentsia as views frowned on by the Empire's censors, including those from Herzen's illegal *émigré* journal *Kolokol*, were discussed freely. Perhaps most important of all, the salon established informal and unofficial liaisons between the Emperor and the men charged with drafting reform legislation within the bureaucracy. With Elena Pavlovna's encouragement, such men of modest background as Miliutin, Zablotskii, and Solov'ev found a rare opportunity to argue the case for their views in person before the Emperor.[116]

We shall have occasion to refer again to Elena Pavlovna and her salon during the years between 1858 and 1861 in our discussion about the enlightened bureaucrats' role in drafting the Great Reform legislation itself. In preparing them for that task, Elena Pavlovna and her salon had been important for the practical experience that the Karlovka reform had provided and for the broader contacts with senior statesmen the salon had encouraged. Elena Pavlovna had served well in her role as their patron and protector during the years between the revolutions of 1848 and the opening of public debate about reform a decade later.

On the Eve of the Great Reforms

The months of November and December 1857 marked a critical milestone along the road that led from the fall of Sevastopol to the Great Reforms. During those two months, Alexander II's government published rescripts and directives that removed the debate about reform from the inner recesses of St. Petersburg's chanceries and placed it in the public domain. Equally important, although the debate became public and men spoke more freely about the changes needed in Russia, its substance was altered dramatically when the government assumed full responsibility for the substance of the reforms and left only matters of form and procedure to be debated by the nobility and the educated public.[117] Because the enlightened bureaucrats would play a crucial part in determining the substance of these reforms, we should summarize the attitudes, experience, and collective wisdom they brought to the many

and complex tasks of drafting that body of legislation destined to receive the collective title of the Great Reforms.

Because the shadings in the political spectrum that encompassed
educated opinion in Russia became clearly defined only in the 1860s,
there were numbers of officials who stood in the ranks of the enlightened bureaucracy for brief periods during the mid- to late 1850s before
moving on to occupy political positions that were more clearly identifi-
able as "left" and "right." Indeed, this amorphous quality of political
views was shared by much of Russian educated opinion during the two
decades before the Great Reforms. Portions of the intelligentsia in Moscow became polarized earlier as a consequence of the theoretical concerns and artificial atmosphere fostered by the Slavophile-Westerner
controversy of the 1840s, but in St. Petersburg the intellectual atmosphere remained notably more fluid. Throughout the 1840s there was
a rich banquet of ideas and systems—the entire body of political, social,
and economic thought produced in the West during the previous two
decades, in fact—that was sampled quite eclectically by the capital's
intelligentsia. Lines of intellectual conflict were not drawn so clearly
here as in Moscow, nor would they be for some time. Even the magis-
terial presence of "furious Vissarion" Belinskii in St. Petersburg did not
drive the intelligentsia of Russia's capital into the ideological bloodlet-
ting that consumed Moscow's educated society.

Political antipodes such as those that developed in Russia during the
1860s could be generated only when educated opinion became gripped
by some truly monumental issue, such as the debate about the Great
Reforms. It was debate over what the Great Reforms ought to be, what
they should accomplish, how desired ends should be achieved, and,
perhaps most important, what the final product, in fact, really was that
polarized educated opinion and drove Russians into more clearly defined political groupings during the 1860s. But even the polarization
during the early to mid-1860s applied most particularly to those segments of educated opinion willing to take up extreme political positions,
and what some have called "liberal" opinion remained quite undefined.
Nikolai Miliutin characterized this phenomenon in a letter to his
brother Dmitrii, only recently appointed Minister of War, in December
1861. "It seems to me that two characteristic traits distinguish our
Russian opposition," he wrote from Rome. "In the first place, it mani-
fests itself only in extreme political views which, if one wished to use
a western analogy, could be called *extreme Right* and *far Left*. In the
second place, liberal tendencies have not yet assumed a clearly defined
form. Everything remains hazy, confused, unsteady, and full of contradictions."[118]

Among these ever-shifting sands of political opinion, a number of men passed through the ranks of Russia's enlightened bureaucracy during the Great Reform era before moving on to defend either more radical or conservative positions. The famous writer Saltykov-Shchedrin first worked for change from within the bureaucracy only to reject that course later, as did the Slavophile Iurii Samarin and the Westerner Konstantin Kavelin. The *litseist* Count D. A. Tolstoi stood prominently among the *konstantinovtsy* before he rose to become Russia's conservative Minister of Public Instruction (1866–1880) and reactionary Minister of Internal Affairs (1882–1889). Likewise, P. A. Valuev held many attitudes common to enlightened bureaucrats during the 1840s and 1850s, and his "Thoughts of Russian" is a classic critique about the failings of the Russian administration at the time of Nicholas I's death.[119] Valuev, however, is better remembered as a conservative Minister of Internal Affairs (1861–1867), an even more conservative Minister of State Domains (1872–1879), and President of the Committee of Ministers (1879–1881). Even though they sailed different courses as they tacked before the uncertain political winds of the late 1850s and early 1860s, the views of all these men constitute important elements in any composite of the attitudes held by Russia's enlightened bureaucracy at the dawn of the Great Reform era.

On the eve of the Great Reforms, Russia's enlightened bureaucrats thus did not hold an integrated political and social philosophy in common. In addition to such men as Miliutin, Zablotskii, Golovnin, and Zarudnyi, whose views remained reasonably constant throughout their careers, there were among them Westerners and Slavophiles, as well as future conservatives and radicals. They all shared, however, certain views and aspirations. "Despite sharp differences in their basic beliefs," Prince Obolenskii recalled in his memoirs, "all agreed upon one general feeling. All shared a desire for a better order of things."[120] By 1855, they agreed that the Nicholas system could not continue unchanged. What should replace it was the thorny question that divided Valuev from Miliutin, Golovnin from Count Tolstoi, and Zarudnyi from Konstantin Pobedonostsev as the sixties moved toward their end.

In stating their "desire for a better order of things," these men were unanimous in condemning the procedures that Imperial bureaucrats employed. Russia's army of officials had increased by almost 34 percent during the last decade of the Nicholas era, and in 1850 alone, more than 12,000 men had entered the bureaucracy at rank fourteen or above in the Table of Ranks.[121] When we recall that Russia's universities graduated fewer than 1,000 students each year[122] and that the graduating classes at the Tsarskoe Selo Lyceum and the Imperial School of Jurisprudence each numbered less than thirty,[123] it becomes obvious that the vast majority of these new officials were not well educated. Their major task was not to solve problems or make decisions but to guide the rising flood of papers through the bureaucratic hierarchy. The vast majority saw in those many inconsequential documents they processed the true essence of administration and would have agreed with young Mikhail Veselovskii, who once confessed that "each new document that was produced seemed to me to be a new current of benevolence flowing from [our office near] Chernyshev Bridge into the vastness of Russia."[124] Appearance, not substance, was their chief concern, and it was this administrative domain of petition, applications, inquiries, and reports that formed the elegant veneer that overlay what Zarudnyi termed "a kind of clerkish rot and ignorance" which the enlightened bureaucrats so bitterly opposed.[125]

Valuev best summarized the enlightened bureaucrats' criticisms of such men and their work when he wrote that "all the centralization and formalism of administration, all the measures of legislative precaution, the hierarchical surveillance . . . display their impotence daily . . . [while] increasingly mechanistic *deloproizvodstvo* more and more prevents us from achieving results in various areas of state administration. . . . All governmental agencies nowadays," he concluded, "are more occupied with each other than with the essence of those matters for which they are responsible." At the end of the Crimean War, only Konstantin Nikolaevich's Naval Ministry stood as a rare and lonely exception to that gloomy generalization.[126]

To such men as Valuev, and the enlightened bureaucrats generally, Konstantin Nikolaevich's administrative regime, which emphasized substance over form and delegated authority to departmental directors and other subordinates, seemed an ideal for which to strive. Beyond that, they urged that two other qualities—*glasnost'* (publicity) and *zakonnost'* (lawfulness)—be embodied in Russia's administration to eradicate the scourge of *proizvol* (the uncontrolled exercise of arbitrary authority) which they perceived to be at the root of many of Russia's failings.[127] In particular, they opposed the *proizvol* that aristocratic lords exercised over their serfs, and their transfer of such attitudes to Russia's civil service. Yet, as much as they professed to despise the abuses of *proizvol,* none of the enlightened bureaucrats contemplated altering its most intitutionalized and long-lasting Russian form—the manner in which autocracy itself functioned. For them, it was the autocracy's ability to exercise *proizvol* benevolently that constituted a major instrument through which important social and economic transformations could be achieved. Only a benevolent autocrat acting on recommendations carefully prepared by expert officials, they insisted, could transcend the narrowly conceived, particularistic interests of Russia's fragmented, semi-caste society and formulate effective changes in state policy.

The flaw in such reasoning was that theirs was an ideal, not reality. No autocrat since Peter the Great had succeeded in exercising *proizvol* to transform Russia, and there was no indication in 1855 that Alexander II would prove the exception to that unfortunate rule. There was nothing in his first acts as Emperor to indicate that he would not follow precisely in his father's footsteps. His removal of D. G. Bibikov, one of the few progressive statesmen to serve Nicholas during the years of the Crimean Wars, seemed to bode ill for any reformist program, especially when he named as Bibikov's successor S. S. Lanskoi, a statesman educated at the turn of the century and nearing seventy at the time of his appointment. Lanskoi's first official act was to issue a circular stating that "our most gracious Sovereign has ordered me to preserve inviolate the rights granted to the nobility by His August Predecessor,"[128] and the Empire's lords joyfully seized upon it as a reaffirmation of serfdom. Nor did the situation seem improved by Alexander's choice of M. N. Murav'ev, a man well known for his reactionary views, to succeed Kiselev as Minister of State Domains. In 1856, it scarcely seemed credible that such appointees, especially in combination with such conservative Nicholaean statesmen as Prince A. F. Orlov (President of the State Council), P. F. Brok (Minister of Finance), Count V. F. Adlerberg (Minister of the Imperial Court), and Count Panin would permit reform proposals to reach their new Emperor.

During the mid- to late 1850s, an unfounded vision of a benevolent autocratic application of *proizvol* thus goverened the enlightened bureaucrats' efforts to broaden the transformation they had begun to envision a decade earlier. They tempered their advocacy of *glasnost'* and *zakonnost'* to accommodate that vision and the role they reserved for themselves in such a process. Especially important, they thought that their superior knowledge about Russian conditions permitted them to bend such concepts whenever it seemed that the result could benefit Russia. Even their respect for the law was set aside as they labored to advance the renovation of autocracy and the transformation of society. Anxious to remove the most onerous aspects of Nicholaean censorship, they nonetheless urged that critical debates about the substance of draft legislation be kept within St. Petersburg's chanceries. They had become convinced that their newly created instruments for changing policy could be effective only if they remained unencumbered by public opinion, not obliged to function in conjunction with its broader development and articulation.

Only during the early months of Alexander II's reign, when any progress toward reform seemed utterly out of the question, were the enlightened bureaucrats willing to make common cause with those elements of public opinion that had begun to emerge outside the bureaucracy. Once preparations for reform began, and once they established those groups of experts that they had chosen as their instruments for initiating changes in state policy, they abandoned such momentary radical allies as Aleksandr Herzen and labored to exclude public opinion from any decisive influence on their work. Most important of all, they devoted a great deal of effort to barring educated aristocratic opinion from effective participation in the legislative debates that preceded the emancipation. As they had done during the last decade of the Nicholas era, they drew only upon those segments of public opinion they particularly trusted by employing that time-honored bureaucratic technique of co-optation, which had proved effective not only in Russia but also in other states at critical moments in their history.

Once Alexander II made clear that he would not rely on such instruments of aristocratic opinion as provincial noble assemblies to draft reform legislation, the enlightened bureaucrats' influence upon the Great Reforms was all but assured. When senior statesmen realized that such legislative work demanded expert knowledge about local conditions in Russia, their participation was guaranteed. Throughout the ensuing decade they played the central role in drafting Russia's Great Reform legislation, but they acted quite unlike the liberals and constitutionalists that historians of the late nineteenth and early twentieth centuries thought them to be.[129] Although dedicated to renovating and transforming the Russian Empire, they remained autocratic servants of an autocratic master, and their approach to the Great Reforms was dominated by that single characteristic.

chapter 6

The Enlightened Bureaucrats in the Great Reform Era

"In an era of civic awakening, it is more important than ever for the government to seize control of the social movement. . . . For this, acts of notable boldness are needed in order to astonish the masses and impress them."

P. A. Valuev

At mid-day on February 18, 1855, the people of St. Petersburg learned that Nicholas I, whose powerful personality had ruled their lives for three decades, was dead. What Konstantin Kavelin branded as "a thirty-year tyranny of madness, brutality, and misfortunes" had come to an end.[1] Whether or not they shared Kavelin's bitter view, Russians could not remain indifferent to Nicholas's passing, for his system had left a lasting imprint upon their lives. As Emperor, he had labored to establish the epitome of a rationalist police-state, an anachronism reminiscent of Europe's *anciens régimes,* and, in the manner of his European predecessors, he had endeavored to take all power, and focus the resolution of all problems, into his hands alone. Such had been a difficult task within the relatively manageable geographical confines of Western states; it proved utterly impossible in Russia. For the Empire was too vast, and especially in the nineteenth century, its problems too complex, for any man to comprehend, let alone resolve. As Mikhail Pogodin wrote of Nicholas, "he did not realize that since the time of Peter [the Great] conditions had changed and that Petrine activities transposed into our era simply became an optical illusion."[2] Russia paid a high price for Nicholas's belief in that illusion. When it became clear in mid-1855 that she could neither supply nor even properly arm her army in the Crimea, defeat in a war that Nicholas had never expected to begin became inevitable. Russia faced her greatest failure and the greatest

168

challenge in her never-ending competition with the West since Charles XII had driven Peter the Great's armies in headlong flight from the battlefield at Narva in November 1700.

Political and economic events of the first half of the nineteenth century altered dramatically the nature of Russia's competition with the nations of Europe and that left an enduring imprint upon the state Nicholas had ruled. No longer did the key to Russia's successful competition with the West lie in her ability to develop effective counterparts to those social and political institutions that had aided Europe's rise to preeminence in the sixteenth and seventeenth centuries. In the eighteenth century, traditional Russian institutions—including the aristocracy, serfdom, certain Muscovite administrative traditions, and, above all, autocracy itself—all could be marshaled to support the sovereign's effort to strengthen Russia politically, militarily, even economically. The problem for eighteenth-century Russian autocrats had been to bring their nation's institutions and society to their highest level of development and to speed up the process from gradual evolution to rapid transformation. Much of their achievement stemmed from the elaboration of their nation's traditional social and political institutions while imposing upon them the more sophisticated, rationalist culture of Europe. The achievement of Peter the Great and his eighteenth-century successors thus lay not in turning Russia upon a new course, but in transforming her along social and political lines that preserved at least basic ties to her traditions. Russia's successful transformation in the eighteenth century therefore saw her become successful in competition with the West, while preserving her traditional social and political institutions intact and even strengthening them in the process. In a number of important ways, autocracy, aristocracy, and serfdom all were stronger in 1789, for example, than they had been when Peter the Great had overthrown his half-sister Sofia's regency in 1689.[3]

As Nicholas and his chief advisers eventually learned, the imperatives of the competition between Russia and nineteenth-century Europe were very different from those their predecessors had encountered. Most of all, to develop Russia's traditional institutions still further along the lines followed by eighteenth-century autocrats—to bring them to that level of perfection implied in Uvarov's slogan "Orthodoxy, Autocracy, and Nationality" and proclaimed as accomplished fact by the defenders of Official Nationality—meant, in fact, to weaken her, not prepare her, to face the new and dangerous challenges posed by the industrializing nations of the West. For "Orthodoxy, Autocracy, and Nationality" described a social order and articulated a political outlook that had all but disappeared in Europe. Further efforts to develop the institutions and values that underlay that slogan could only carry Russia further away from the new achievements of the West. Yet Russia's traditions, as expressed so succinctly in Uvarov's triad formula, could not be abandoned utterly and instantly. Russia's very existence first had been defined by the Orthodox Church,[4] and that was closely tied with autocracy and, even, nationality. Further, Russia's Emperor was sworn to defend autocracy, and the Empire's administrative institutions had been built upon a commitment to serve that same mission.

As important as it seemed to preserve the political, social, and religious traditions that originally had defined her existence and had helped her to rise to a position of international authority under Peter the Great, it was even more imperative that Russia meet the challenge that Western nations posed to that international position in the middle of the nineteenth century. To be sure, defeat in the Crimea in no way menaced Russia's national security, for the Anglo-French armies, even if joined by Austria, had no intention of marching upon Moscow or St. Petersburg. The Allies had not gone to war to conquer Nicholas's Empire, but only to foil what they had thought to be his improper designs upon the lands of the Sultan, and their defeat of Russia's armies in the Crimea had achieved that aim. But defeat in the Crimea posed a threat to Russia, nonetheless, because her claim to European Great Power status had rested solely upon her military might ever since Peter the Great had thrust her upon the European political scene with his dramatic defeat of Charles XII and his Swedish armies at Poltava in 1709.[5] Because the Crimean debacle challenged that claim, Russia stood at a fateful crossroads. Either she must reenter the competition with her European rivals into which Peter had cast her, or slip back into Asia, and the second alternative was a very real possibility in the minds of some European statesmen at the time. Count Reiset, a former First Secretary of the French Embassy in St. Petersburg, made the point with remarkable candor early in 1854 when he told a Russian acquaintance in Paris that:

> I am resolved to direct all my efforts toward a struggle against your influence in European affairs and to drive you back into Asia whence you came. You are not a European Power; you ought not to be one, and you will not continue to be one if France remembers the part she ought to play in Europe. Our government knows very well your weak points, and they are precisely the ones by which you are tied to Europe. Let those ties be weakened and, of your own accord, you will flow back toward the East, and you will become once again an Asiatic Power.[6]

If Russia were to preserve her position and reenter international competition with Europe's Great Powers, solutions to a multitude of complex problems had to be found. With perhaps the exception of the cotton textile industry, her industrial forces were underdeveloped, her economy stagnant and backward. State finances were in a parlous state, the fragile balance of Kankrin's fiscal reforms of the late 1830s and early 1840s having been destroyed by the financial drain of the Crimean struggle. In the post-Crimean era, no nation could hope to bear the cost of maintaining an army of nearly one and a half million in peacetime. And to create a smaller standing army that could be augmented in time of war by a system of reserves remained impossible so long as the military rank and file were drawn from a servile class. Dmitrii Miliutin made that argument with unprecedented force in a memorandum to Alexander II in March 1856.[7] Serfdom also underlay every other major social, political, and economic dilemma Russia faced, and some means for eliminating the barriers it raised to social and economic progress had to be found.

To resolve such problems would have presented immense difficulties in any state, but in Russia they seemed even more overwhelming because of the broader failures of the Nicholas System. "Administration is in a chaos, moral feelings are crushed, intellectual development has been abandoned, and corruption has grown to prodigious dimensions. . . . All this is the fruit of contempt for truth and a blind, barbaric faith in material force alone," one Russian remarked in September 1855.[8] Such were only external symptoms of a deeper and more malignant disease, for one of the most critical failings of the Nicholas System had been its failure to produce any politically or socially responsible group outside the government upon which the autocrat could rely for assistance in carrying out a broad program of reform. "Our qualities as responsible citizens," the censor Nikitenko confided to his diary in April 1855, "have not yet been formed because we do not yet have those essential elements without which there can be only civic co-habitation but not civic virtue: namely, public-spiritedness, a sense of lawfulness (zakonnost'), and honor."[9] Nor were there any means for communicating with such a body of opinion had it existed. Russia lacked any national consultative or legislative body, for such was inconsistent with the premises upon which autocracy and, particularly the Nicholas System, had been based. At the same time, rigid censorship meant that public commentary about her pressing problems remained impossible. A major dilemma Alexander II confronted at the beginning of his reign, therefore, was whether it was possible to stimulate such a body of opinion into being and create the means for a dialogue with it but keep the ensuing debate within limits traditionally acceptable to autocracy.

A course thus had to be found that would preserve autocracy and its traditional instruments but, at the same time, allow Russia to reenter the competition with Europe on a more advantageous, viable footing. Russia's economy—especially her industry—must develop as had that of Europe (although not necessarily with all the problems that the emergence of an industrial proletariat had brought to Western states), and her social order must be adjusted to meet the needs that reasonably stemmed from that course of action. This meant that serfdom must be changed and, with it, the nature of the social and economic life of the Russian nobility. At the same time, the autocracy, and the institutions that supported it, must be protected. By the middle of the nineteenth century, these institutions included first and foremost the bureaucracy, which offered a viable alternative to Russia's privileged aristocracy as a base of social support for autocracy in the Empire.

Whether they stood among the vast conservative majority of civil servants or the minority of enlightened officials who supported Russia's transformation, all bureaucrats shared a commitment to preservation of the autocracy. Yet any attempt to tie autocracy's future to the bureaucracy in Russia posed other serious problems, for, as we indicated at the beginning of this study, the bureaucracy was an imperfect instrument at best. In addition to the many other failings from which the bureaucracy suffered, most of its members expressed their support for autocracy through a stubborn, passive resistance to any change in the *status quo*, and this unfortunate characteristic posed a very effective barrier to any sort of reform or change. The enlightened bureaucrats thus had to find some means to overcome both the inertia of the vast majority of their fellows and the opposition of the Empire's ultra-conservative great lords, if the necessary changes in Russia—what Daniel Orlovsky has called "renovations"—could be undertaken effectively.[10]

Alexander's turn to the bureaucracy as a social base of support and as a source of public opinion that could comment upon proposed reform legislation thus was more complex than it appeared at first. The result was to spur a unique interaction between enlightened bureaucrats, a handful of progressive aristocrats, and segments of the moderate intelligentsia to advance the cause of state-controlled renovation within the Russian Empire. With the help of the enlightened bureaucrats, Alexander drew upon those segments of the nobility and intelligentsia that he thought least threatening to his autocratic prerogatives and then co-opted them into bureaucratic bodies, thereby controlling them further through the natural (and essentially limiting) forces of bureaucratic caution. At the same time, by splitting the intelligentsia, which had joined ranks to advance the cause of reform in 1857, Alexander's actions ensured that they would not succeed in presenting a united front to the autocratic power he guarded so jealously. The result was to identify a small group of reliable men dedicated to the cause of progress in Russia and separate them from those broader social and intellectual groups they might have led in protest against the Emperor's refusal to grant them such means of political expression as had accompanied the emergence of an economic and social order dominated by the middle class in the West.

Alexander's efforts to stimulate discussion about social and economic renovation within the bureaucracy brought the enlightened bureaucrats into positions from which they could influence the content of the reforms promulgated in Russia between 1861 and 1874. They were the possessors of the new sorts of information needed to draft the legislation for Russia's new transformation, the guardians of a treasure house of knowledge about conditions in an Empire so vast that no one could comprehend the full extent of its diversity. Such knowledge about life in Russia's provinces became especially vital to the reform process once Alexander rejected as inadequate the proposals offered by the last secret committee to consider the serf question in 1857. After he brought Konstantin Nikolaevich into the legislative discussion in August 1857, and once publication of the Nazimov Rescripts brought discussion of emancipation and the reforms that must stem from it into the public arena, accurate information about local conditions took on new importance. If the government were to evaluate the materials assembled by committees of the provincial nobility throughout 1858, officials with some statistical expertise and some knowledge about conditions in Russia's provinces must be assembled in the central bureaucracy. Further, if effective institutions were to be created to replace serf-owners' judicial and administrative authority in the countryside, officials with broad knowledge about such matters also must be assembled to draft the necessary legislation.

Alexander himself understood from the first that such expertise could come only from within the bureaucracy. Early in April 1856, a full nine months before he established Russia's last secret committee of senior statesmen to discuss the dilemmas of serfdom, he instructed Minister of Internal Affairs Lanskoi to concentrate in his ministry the work of all government agencies that related to the "organization of the serfs of the nobility," to prepare recommendations about what principles ought to be incorporated in an emancipation, and to determine how they might best be implemented.[11] Long before the provincial nobility had begun to draft proposals to free their serfs, and even before the Secret Committee of 1857 began to discuss the question, the Ministry of Internal Affairs thus had assumed effective control over legislative preparations for an emancipation and the other reforms that must follow in its wake. Of particular importance, Lanskoi's deputy, Aleksei Levshin, had brought with him from the Department of Rural Economy in the Ministry of State Domains Iakov Solov'ev, an official who already had won for himself a considerable reputation as a statistical expert. Soon to be named head of the *Zemskii Otdel*, a special section of the Central Statistical Committee that assumed full control over drafting Russia's forthcoming *zemstvo* reform, Solov'ev had just completed a brilliant study of Russia's rural economy that won the coveted Zhukovskii Prize from the Geographical Society in 1856, and a citation from the Academy of Sciences a year later.[12] Solov'ev was virtually the last addition to the enlightened bureaucrats' ranks before they began to draft the Great Reform legislation. Convinced by late 1857 that their superior expertise and dedication to their nation's welfare entitled them to a major role in drafting Russia's forthcoming reform legislation, the enlightened bureaucrats set out to assume the part for which they had prepared for so long.

In advocating reform, the enlightened bureaucrats accepted the institution of autocracy as sacrosanct and were convinced that it would exercise its great authority for benevolent purposes. In that sense, they shared the values of their seventeenth- and eighteenth-century European counterparts. But they clearly understood that the social and economic order which the slogan "Orthodoxy, Autocracy, and Nationality" defended was an anachronism and that its perpetuation threatened Russia's survival as a Great Power. Therefore, Zablotskii had condemned Russia's serf order as early as 1841. Convinced that it impeded Russia's economic and industrial development, he also saw it as a blatant violation of his ideal of a society based on law and governed by law.[13] Later in the same decade, Miliutin had indicted serfdom in equally harsh terms and thus had joined Zablotskii as one of its bureaucratic opponents. "Serfdom serves as the main—perhaps even the only —hindrance to any development in Russia at the present time," he wrote in February 1847. "No amount of government solicitude, no efforts by private individuals, can improve it," he added. "Only with the emancipation of the serfs will the betterment of our rural economy become possible."[14]

In their condemnation of serfdom for its retrograde impact upon Russia's economy, the enlightened bureaucrats diverged from those senior statesmen such as Kiselev and Perovskii, who preserved a formal commitment to emancipation (although always accompanied by practical reservations that postponed immediate action), but had little to say about why serfdom ought to be abolished, beyond remarking upon its moral evils.[15] By contrast, the enlightened bureaucrats advanced what they viewed as solid economic reasons for serfdom's demise, although they shared some of the apprehensions that their Emperor and his closest counselors expressed about the dangers that might follow in the wake of an emancipation.[16] Most important, however, while recognizing that the economic welfare of Russia's serf-owning nobles ought to be a consideration in developing new state policies, they did not propose to make it a fundamental precondition for any emancipation settlement, and their arguments always proceeded from what they considered to be the state's best interests.[17] If pressed to do so, they were prepared to argue that the nobility no longer need be cherished as Russia's premier service class and that the interests of the bureaucracy and nobility no longer needed to coincide.[18]

Because the enlightened bureaucrats defended neither the perpetuation of Russia's privileged aristocracy nor the serf-based economic order that supported it, they could seek other paths to Russia's renovation than could the Empire's most senior statesmen. Clearly, any perpetuation of the traditional social and economic order that underlay serfdom stood in the way of Russia's effort to reaffirm her claim to Great Power status after the Crimean War. Therefore, her eighteenth-century experience could not be repeated in the sense of accelerating the pace at which her traditional institutions emulated the more advanced level that their counterparts had attained in Europe. Europe's experience since the French Revolution of 1789 stood in opposition to Russia's course since that time, and any repetition of the principles inherent in the Petrine transformation of the early eighteenth century could only carry their rival systems further apart. As in Peter's time, Russia needed once again to emulate the more rapid economic progress that Europe had achieved, but, in contrast to the Petrine transformation, her political institutions and traditions had to be set apart from those of the West. While Peter had been able to enlist the ideology of the rationalist police state in the cause of strengthening Russia's traditional institution of autocracy, any turn to nineteenth-century Western political theories obviously promised just the opposite effect.

By 1856, the political ideologies of the West stood in unflinching, hostile array against those very precepts and institutions of autocracy that Alexander II was sworn to defend and to which the enlightened bureaucrats were committed by necessity and conviction. Europeans unhesitatingly saw in Russian autocracy the personification of that tyranny they had fought to destroy in the revolutions of 1789, 1830, and 1848, and the survival of autocracy only strengthened some of them in their opposition to Russia's claims for recognition as a European power. "I went to Russia to seek for arguments against representative government, I return a partisan of constitutions," confessed the Marquis de Custine in 1839. "Liberty is wanted in every thing Russian," he concluded. "Whoever has well examined that country will be content to live anywhere else."[19]

Few in Europe disagreed with de Custine's crushing condemnation. Nor was the condemnation by European public opinion the only thing that Alexander had to fear from the ideologies of the West. For there were growing numbers of men and women within his domains who also adhered to the political precepts to which Europeans swore allegiance and who urged their implementation in Russia. Thus, while Peter the Great had been free to urge upon his reluctant subjects ever-greater use of European ideas and political theories, for such promised the further strengthening of autocracy itself, Alexander II was obliged to exclude the ideologies of nineteenth-century Europe from Russia because they threatened destruction of autocracy. Any expression of such principles within his domains carried with it an ever-present threat of greater European hostility to the political precepts he was sworn to defend and the promise of European support for their destruction. Miliutin clearly recognized that threat in 1863, when he warned Alexander that revolt must be crushed quickly in Tsarist Poland. "It is necessary to act immediately, and we have no more than six months left [in which to do it]," he told the Tsar during an audience at Tsarskoe Selo. "If . . . we have taken no measures [within that time]," he warned, "we not only will lose Poland, but we shall have all of Europe on our hands as well."[20] Miliutin's apprehensions about European public opinion were well advised and fully justified from the point of view of effective Tsarist politics. Shaken by the Crimean defeat, and still in search of a means to resolve the problems that Russia's economic backwardness posed in such stark terms, the institutions of Russian autocracy were at no point during the Great Reform era prepared to sustain a full-scale ideological assault from the West. That became an issue of overwhelming significance in determining the path Russia would follow during the 1860s and 1870s.

Even though the political options were more restricted than they had been at the opening of the Petrine era, mid-nineteenth-century Russians still had to seek some pattern of transformation that could enable their nation to incorporate Europe's economic achievements while defending autocracy. The alternative to effective transformation remained nothing less than revolution, as the experience of Europe had shown so dramatically since 1789. Thus, a new transformation based on Russian experience and tradition, whenever possible, had to be generated, and this became the enlightened bureaucrats' chief concern once the Crimean War was ended. The transformation they sought had to preserve autocracy and its institutional supports while altering its outlook. Put another way, the autocracy and its bureaucratic defenders had to assume a broader concern for society's needs and foster economic progress in order to fulfill the mission that progressive Russians, schooled in the principles of Germany's *Aufklärung,* had first perceived as a function of legitimate government as the eighteenth century drew to a close.[21] Well before the demise of serfdom became certain, it had been clear that the autocracy could not rely on the nobility's supposedly paternalistic concern for the well-being of their serfs to meet the needs of Russia's masses. Nor had the merchantry or the nobility engaged in manufacturing on their estates proved to be the bearers of economic progress and industrial development, as had the middle class in the West. From the perspective of the enlightened bureaucrats, both of these functions had to be shouldered by the autocracy and the bureaucracy which, they hoped, would serve the interests of Russia, not those of particular classes or interest groups.[22] "The well-being and domestic success of any state depends in large measure on the activities of those individuals to whom the more important areas of state administration are entrusted," Valuev wrote in 1845. State officials must bear greater responsibility in an autocratic state, he insisted, because "public opinion stands mute [and] . . . citizens are not summoned to participate in discussions of public affairs."[23]

Although they labored under few illusions about its failings, the enlightened bureaucrats thus thought the bureaucracy potentially more promising as an instrument to formulate and to direct Russia's new transformation than were any of the other seemingly limited alternatives. Above all, they feared that the nobility would be motivated only by self-interest, and therefore they endeavored to exclude them from the legislative debates of the first decade of Alexander's reign. "The nobility is self-interested, unprepared, [and] underdeveloped," Nikolai Miliutin concluded early in 1858,[24] and he and his associates had continued to apply that blanket condemnation to Russia's lords throughout the legislative preparations for the reforms. This view was tragically misconceived in the case of that minority of serf-owners who displayed a sense of political responsibility from the beginning of the reform debate. The enlightened bureaucrats were not unaware of that sentiment, but they were inclined to regard it as an aberration in aristocratic opinion rather than as a sincere response by a portion of Russia's lords to their Emperor's invitation to debate the nature and course of Russia's transformation. For that reason, the enlightened bureaucrats sought to co-opt only the small segment of this body of responsible sentiment that appeared to accord with their own views most closely; and, as a result, such serf-owning nobles as Samarin, Cherkasskii, and Tarnovskii were brought into the Editing Commission. But these men were far from being representative of those lords who responded to Alexander's summons in 1856. Rather, they usually enjoyed a special connection with the enlightened bureaucrats or their Imperial patrons that made Miliutin, Zablotskii, and their colleagues confident that they could become trustworthy associates.

During the late 1850s, the enlightened bureaucrats' negative attitude toward nobles' participation in Russia's legislative process alienated that segment of aristocratic opinion that had endeavored to respond in a politically responsible manner to the new imperatives Russia faced at the beginning of Alexander's reign. Perhaps their most outstanding representative was Aleksei Mikhailovich Unkovskii, a nobleman from the province of Tver, who had studied with Granovskii and Kavelin at Moscow University and had been a regular visitor at those Sunday gatherings where Kavelin had subjected serfdom to continuing and penetrating attack.[25] After serving briefly in the Ministry of Foreign Affairs, Unkovskii had retired in 1852 to manage his family estates and, within a year, was elected to an important provincial commisission.[26] In 1853, he also became a district judge; in 1857, his fellow nobles elected him to the office of provincial marshal, and he became their spokesman.[27]

During the first years of Alexander's reign, Unkovskii's activities revealed his serious sense of responsibility to Russia and his deep concern for the welfare of his native province. Along with his close associate, A. A. Golovachev, he criticized the corruption and dishonesty of provincial officials and complained about them to the Ministry of Internal Affairs, with some effect.[28] By 1858, he had concluded that the patriarchal authority of the nobles over their serfs must be abolished, that the serfs must be freed with sufficient land to support themselves, and that the nobility should be compensated for the loss of lands and serfs by some sort of government-financed program.[29] In this he shared the views that the enlightened bureaucrats and such of their close allies as Kavelin and Boris Chicherin had articulated in 1856 and 1857.[30] But he diverged sharply from them over such vital issues as the nobility's future role in local administration and the extent to which the bureaucracy ought to direct Russia's transformation. Unkovskii thought the bureaucracy too corrupt and incompetent to implement reforms and urged that the nobility be entrusted with responsibility for directing local affairs after the serfs were freed and the manor lords' legal control over them abolished. "Only the nobility, the most enlightened of all rural classes," he insisted, "can direct and instruct the masses in fulfilling government decrees."[31] He spoke with little effect. By early 1862, he and a number of like-minded Tver lords concluded that the Emancipation Acts of February 19, 1861, had "raised the question of emancipating the peasants but did not finally solve it" and that the government was "not capable of realizing" further transformations in Russian life.[32]

If the enlightened bureaucrats opposed the participation in Russia's legislative and political processes that such responsible lords as Unkovskii and Golovachev demanded, they were equally unsympathetic to those broader demands for political participation that arose in the course of what one modern scholar has called the "constitutionalist campaign" of 1861–1862.[33] Such arose in part as a consequence of their refusal to concede a role in Russia's legislative process to responsible aristocratic representatives, and the campaign's ultimate failure therefore increased the alienation between educated opinion and Russia's central administration. The years 1861 and 1862 witnessed a widespread call for what many thought of as a reestablishment of the Muscovite *zemskie sobory,*[34] but neither Alexander nor his advisers would contemplate such concessions. They were supported in their refusal by a number of the enlightened bureaucrats' closest allies.

Konstantin Kavelin, mentor of the youth of the 1840s at Moscow University, Miliutin's close friend and his associate in drafting the Karlovka reform project, insisted in 1861 that any representative national body such as a *zemskii sobor* could only institutionalize the reactionary views of the nobility and exclude the newly emancipated peasantry from participation in Russia's political processes. "Political rights for one class, without political rights for all others," he wrote, "are something unthinkable, something that should encounter unanimous opposition, not only from the government, but from the masses and every enlightened, liberal person in Russia."[35] Kavelin was supported in his views not only by Cherkasskii and Samarin[36] but also by the westerner Boris Chicherin. "Sheltering themselves beneath the mantle of liberalism and longing for the return of the old order," Chicherin recalled, "the nobility thought to use this instrument of constitutionalism to take power into its hands and turn affairs to its advantage once again."[37]

The dilemma that the "constitutionalist campaign" posed for men such as Samarin, Kavelin, and Chicherin was how to incorporate into the political process that minority of lords who expressed a clear sense of political responsibility, yet exclude that majority, embittered by the emancipation and anxious to regain their former economic and social power, from a voice in the formulation of policy legislation. "The assembly of elected representatives of the entire Russian land represents the only means for the satisfactory resolution of those questions stimulated, but not resolved, by the statute of February 19th," the nobility of Tver insisted.[38] "Russia is still a dismal wasteland," Kavelin replied. "It is necessary to begin at the bottom, not the top, to cultivate this soil," he continued. "Self-government, that treasured dream of every enlightened and liberal person in Russia, can only begin to come true in the provinces with the energetic assistance of the nobility. In this fertile school, it will prepare itself for those broader political activities which, without such preparation, always will remain nothing but an unrealized fantasy."[39] Thus, Kavelin and his associates thought that Russia's nobles could begin to play a larger role in the Empire's ongoing transformation only after a long period of study in the practical school of local affairs. For the moment, the reform process must remain in the hands of the enlightened bureaucrats and the men they had co-opted from the intelligentsia and the nobility.

If the enlightened bureaucrats thought the nobles unprepared to assume a responsible role in Russia's transformation, they thought the peasantry even more so. Mass illiteracy, of course, was only the first and most obvious difficulty that barred the rural masses from taking an active part in public affairs. In their broad studies during the 1840s and 1850s, Zablotskii and his Department of Rural Economy had found the peasantry demoralized, irresponsible, and so primitive in their understanding of agriculture that they did not even know how to match seed to soil and climate.[40] Yet perhaps even more than among the nobility, the enlightened bureaucrats saw in the newly freed peasants a source of conservative support for autocracy and its enlightened bureaucratic instruments. In discussing reforms for the peasants in Tsarist Poland, Miliutin told Iakov Solov'ev of his conviction that the masses were an untapped reservoir of talent that would one day serve as a source of enlightened officials.[41] To a British diplomat, he once confided that "in Russia and in Poland, the elements of conservatism . . . [are] to be found rather amongst the peasant class than amongst the nobles," and went on to identify the peasantry as "a counter-balance to the revolutionary elements" that Russian authorities faced.[42] Yet the potential of the peasantry could be realized only after long years of education. Until they became literate citizens with whom the government could establish effective communications, Miliutin warned in describing the peasants in Russia's Polish lands, these men and women would be denied the "full advantage of the benefits of the new order and the very future of the civil government . . . [would] be poorly ensured."[43]

Convinced that neither nobles nor peasants could properly define the initial course of Russia's transformation in the 1860s, the enlightened bureaucrats attempted to turn the inadequate instruments and personnel of the bureaucracy to their purposes. In the most direct sense, they set out to use specially created bureaucratic instruments to undertake tasks similar to those that Peter the Great had assigned personally selected men to accomplish. To serve his purposes, Peter had chosen men who shared his views and enthusiasms, although it had been no easy matter to find them in sufficient numbers. Yet the task had been made somewhat easier because the Petrine transformation preserved important elements of continuity with Russia's social and institutional traditions.[44] Autocracy, a service aristocracy, serfdom, and administration by men who bore the Tsar's personal commission, all were traditional concepts comprehensible to the men who served Peter the Great, although their frame of reference often was skewed because they envisioned them in their seventeenth-century Russian forms, not the more advanced European ones that Peter wanted to apply.

For the enlightened bureaucrats, the task of plotting Russia's transformation in the middle of the nineteenth century was notably more complex precisely because traditional frames of reference applied far less to their efforts than they had to those of Peter the Great. Although it had become necessary to break with Russia's traditional institution of serfdom and to alter significantly the nature of her privileged aristocracy, the bureaucratic instruments at their disposal were staffed by men whose views were very traditional indeed. Further, the strength of the ideological opposition to Peter's transformation had been significantly eroded by many events that had occurred during the seventeenth century,[45] but Russia's historical experiences since Peter's time often had strengthened the attitudes that defended the broad social and political order that encompassed serfdom. This defense had been most ardently expressed by the proponents of Official Nationality throughout the Nicholas era, and Uvarov's slogan of "Orthodoxy, Autocracy, and Nationality" had found such broad support precisely because it expressed traditional values with which Russians were familiar and in which very many of them believed.[46] On the eve of the Crimean War, very few Russians had any reason to doubt the view that theirs was the best of all worlds. "There is no country in all of Europe which can pride itself on possessing such a harmonious political existence as our own," Shevyrev had proclaimed from Moscow a decade earlier,[47] and others echoed and re-echoed his view as Russia approached mid-century. Concluded one writer: "In Russia, there exists everything necessary for the national welfare."[48]

The key to this self-satisfaction for all but the alienated intelligentsia was the institution of autocracy. "Under the sacred, beneficial protection of autocracy, this fortunate land of Russia blossoms," one prominent official wrote.[49] "You need a superior mercy so as to soften the law, and this can only come to us in the form of absolute monarchy," the great novelist Gogol added. "Without an absolute monarch, a state is an automaton. . . . A state without an absolute monarch is like an orchestra without a conductor."[50] To be sure, the Crimean War had shaken Russians' confidence, and had shaken it all the more severely because it had been so certain. Yet in times of crisis, men and women tend to turn to the tried and the true, toward solid traditional values, not away from them. Although Nikitenko could remark that "the main shortcoming in the reign of Nikolai Pavlovich consisted in the fact that it was all a mistake,"[51] and Kavelin could curse the Tsar as a sovereign whose reign had been a "thirty-year tyranny of madness,"[52] their loyalty to the institution of autocracy itself remained unwavering. During the cruel, dark days of 1848, Kavelin lamented "the disgrace, the humiliation, and the shameful slavery" in which Russians were held by their ruler; yet even then, and in the very same breath, he confessed that "I believe in ... absolutism for present-day Russia."[53]

Even so harsh a critic of Nicholas as Kavelin thus was not prepared to turn onto a totally new and uncharted course. Just a few weeks after the Tsar's death, he wrote that "if, bit by bit, the voice of public opinion will reach [the new Tsar] then ten or even fifteen years of this alone will suffice without any further reforms or transformations."[54] During the days of doubt and searching that Russians lived through in 1855 and 1856, autocracy thus remained the political beacon upon which each and every one of them—from the radical exiled publicist Aleksandr Herzen, to the great lords at Court, to the lesser nobles in the distant provinces, to the enlightened bureaucrats, to the petty officials in St. Petersburg's chanceries—tried to set his bearings. "Our common people love to see in their ruler a powerful and stern sovereign," wrote one of them in his memoirs about these years, and his was an opinion widely shared.[55] "People point to the severity, the despotism, of the deceased Emperor," Aleksandr Artem'ev wrote from deep within the inner offices of the Ministry of Internal Affairs in 1856. "Nonsense!" he exclaimed, as he went on to insist that Nicholas "believed in the power of the Russian spirit and hoped that this spirit, already sufficiently acquainted with the enlightenment of the West, would concern itself with the creation and development of native Russian principles."[56]

"Native Russian principles," or, perhaps more precisely, Russian principles into which were integrated those elements of the European experience that were thought necessary for Russia's transformation, were the keys that the enlightened bureaucrats sought at the end of the Crimean War. They searched for precepts that at one and the same time preserved comforting elements of tradition but also pointed the way to the economic and social changes that Russia required. "Decisive measures appear to be difficult," Artem'ev wrote at that time. "But were the reforms of Peter the Great easy?"[57] What Artem'ev called "enlightenment, a true, devout, enlightenment not based [solely] upon western principles"[58] had to be defined in such a way as to add new, more dynamic dimensions to Uvarov's triad formula. At first, these were the virtues and talents the enlightened bureaucrats had sought among elite school and university graduates of the 1840s and 1850s, and they were best expressed by what Zablotskii called "guideposts" that he once defined as "hard work and a sense of duty" in which these men "saw a basic law of morality."[59] By the beginning of Alexander's reign, these attitudes had become more refined and more easily defined as precepts with which the enlightened bureaucrats hoped to direct the bureaucracy. These new principles upon which they hoped to base Russia's transformation in the 1860s were *glasnost'* (publicity) and *zakonnost'* (lawfulness). Both drew upon European experience but, as Alexander I, his Young Friends, and Speranskii had done with the term "constitution" at the beginning of the century, the enlightened bureaucrats tempered their meaning by the dictates of Russian administrative and political tradition.

Even in the Russian context, *zakonnost'* and *glasnost'* encompassed a variety of meanings, and disagreement over their content was a prominent element in the Great Reform debates. Above all, *zakonnost'* was seen as a counterbalance to the arbitrary behavior of bureaucrats who traditionally bore the personal commission of the autocrat or one of his agents. In the recent words of one historian, it was the "keystone" of the outlook of men who wanted "the further rationalization of the autocracy and supported the admission of responsible members of 'society' into the machinery of the Imperial government to help formulate state policy."[60] Zablotskii once defined it as "the first condition by which . . . the success of all administration is guaranteed."[61] Yet it was a condition that even enlightened men found hard to establish. "The necessity of *zakonnost'*, unfortunately, is rarely recognized by our administrators," wrote Privy Councillor Nikolai Bakhtin in 1856. "Many people in authority think that if their intentions are pure and their goal useful for society, then any means are acceptable so long as they lead toward the proposed end."[62] Not only must *zakonnost'* limit the unfettered arbitrariness of state officials, but it also must define the legal procedures that would eliminate the pervasive system of administrative surveillance *(nadzor)* that senior officials used to control the behavior of their subordinates. *Zakonnost'* thus could help to control the abuses of arbitrary power *(proizvol)* within Russia, could help to break down the rigid system of estates (in which the privileged aristocracy was the most prominent), and, in the future, could create a society in which all citizens enjoyed equality under the law.[63] As such, it was a vital element in the principles that the enlightened bureaucrats endeavored to introduce into the bureaucracy, and, through that institution, into Russian society as a whole.

Although the function of *zakonnost'* could be readily defined, the nature and meaning of *glasnost'* was the subject of more dispute, the resolution of which was very important in defining the ultimate heritage of the Great Reforms. As we saw in earlier chapters, the nature of *glasnost'* had begun to be defined, during the last years of Nicholas's reign, within the broadened circle of the enlightened bureaucrats' activities in St. Petersburg. Ideally, they thought that *glasnost'* should serve as a check upon *proizvol* and corruption in the bureaucracy and in society and that it should serve as a means for holding up to public scrutiny the actions of those who served the people and the state.[64] Soon after the Crimean War ended, they began to refine their definition significantly. One of the first to do so was V. A. Tsie, perhaps the first of the enlightened bureaucrats to use the term transformation in a broader social sense, who now saw *glasnost'* as a fundamental guarantee of *zakonnost'*. In a memorandum in which he argued for administrative decentralization in 1856, he wrote:

> It is necessary to note that, with the expansion of [administrative] authority [on the local level], it is essential to resort to a single device, namely *glasnost'*, in order to retain it within lawful limits. This is the most reliable, one can even say the only, means for ensuring that the beneficial plans of the central government will not become a dead letter but will become fully beneficial in their consequences.[65]

Not only did Tsie see *glasnost'* as a very important instrument with which the enlightened bureaucrats could induce the bureaucracy to abandon its long-standing passive resistance to change, and thereby implement the administrative and social transformation of Russia in the Great Reform era, but he also viewed it as the most effective means for eliminating corruption at all levels of government. "Nowhere does *glasnost'* have such a fundamental and undoubted utility as in legal proceedings," he wrote. "It provides the oppressed with an opportunity to enjoy the protection of the law, and it alone, with its all-shattering power, can shake and finally eradicate the most shameful ulcer of our society—corruption."[66]

Tsie saw the extreme centralization of Russia's government as an impediment to effective administration, and he cursed corruption as one of its major by-products. But there were others who saw centralization and such corresponding abuses as *nadzor* and *proizvol* as even more pernicious. Prince Petr Dolgorukov, a controversial and tempestuous figure during the first years of Alexander II's reign, extolled *glasnost'* as the chief antidote to the arbitrariness of Russia's bureaucrats. "*Glasnost'* is the fiercest enemy of [administrative] abuses, and secrecy is their ally and protector," he proclaimed in November 1857.[67] For Dolgorukov, *glasnost'* could uncover the corruption and abuses of authority that flourished at all levels of Russia's administration. He wrote:

> Without the broad development of *glasnost'* the government will never have the opportunity to recognize all the abuses [in its administration] and thus will never have the opportunity to eradicate them. . . . *Glasnost'* is the best physician for the ulcers of the state. . . . A wise use of *glasnost'* is the best weapon for destroying false rumors, secret schemes, absurd and evil hearsay. By permitting all civic interest groups to express themselves openly, but peacefully and properly, the government will give peaceful and calm expression to all legal demands. A reasonable and proper discussion of various questions will supply the government with information about the needs and requirements of Russia.[68]

Dolgorukov held no position in Russia's service and was virulently antibureaucratic in his attitudes. Indeed, he lauded the virtues of *glasnost'* defined in broad terms because, in his view, bureaucrats had "no more acquaintance with the internal life of Russia than with that on the Isle of Ceylon."[69] Thus, for Dolgorukov, neither a well-meaning autocrat, nor well-intentioned officials, could initiate a transformation in Russia. Unlike the enlightened bureaucrats of the 1850s, he advocated not *"glasnost'* within reasonable limits,"[70] but a full and open public debate about Russia's needs. For men such as he, *glasnost'* could become the mortar to bind Tsar, educated opinion, and the masses into an invincible force that could overcome all reactionary sentiment and all self-interested opposition to reform in Russia. As Aleksandr Herzen proclaimed in much the same vein in 1858:

> When there is arrayed against them power and freedom, the educated minority and the entire masses, the will of the Tsar and public opinion, what can they [i.e., the serf-owners of Russia] raise against it? . . . *Glasnost'* will punish [the serf-owners] long before the lash of the government or the axe of the peasant will reach them.[71]

Although the enlightened bureaucrats disagreed with the definition and function of *glasnost'* advocated by Dolgorukov and Herzen, the political events immediately following the promulgation of the Emancipation Acts led some of them to reconsider their views and recast their own definition. Most important, the virulent sentiment which emerged at the extremes of the political spectrum, expressed both in the serf-owners' antipathy to the Emancipation Acts and in the university riots later in 1861, led them to reconsider the need for broadening that circle among educated society in which the issue of transformation should be debated. As Nikolai Miliutin wrote in December 1861:

> It will be essential to create a body of opinion or, if you will, a middle-of-the-road party (in parliamentary terms, a center party) such as does not exist in Russia at the moment, but for which the necessary elements certainly are not lacking. The government alone can do this ... by making timely concessions, *but they must be made publicly, with dignity ... and without administrative subterfuges.* [72]

Miliutin thus called for broader participation by educated people in local affairs, and he saw that as a means by which the state could blunt the force of radicalism. As a result, he insisted, "the activity of our society will take on a practical direction that will all the better serve to counteract anarchistic intellectual ferment."[73] As he wrote in a memorandum dated May 22, 1862:

> The most vital state interests with which, perhaps, are connected the entire future development of Russia, urgently demand that the new rural institutions [i.e., the *zemstva*], to which, one can hope, a significant portion of the energetic elements in our society are fated to be attracted ... be given, insofar as possible, an effective and serious meaning.[74]

Most important, in terms of giving "effective and serious meaning" to the *zemstva*, Miliutin insisted, they must deal with important local issues and not simply be submerged under a flood of bureaucratic tasks. "The application of the elective principle to administration," he warned Russia's senior statesmen, "can only be meaningful and useful when elected officials are empowered by law to undertake independent and serious activity."[75]

Such a view of *glasnost'* as Miliutin, Golovnin, Solov'ev, and Konstantin Nikolaevich championed in the discussions about the forthcoming *zemstvo* reform that took place in 1862[76] marked an important broadening of those definitions and that significance which they had attached to the term a few years earlier. Yet even their earlier and narrower definition was not shared by more conservative Russian policy-makers. This was especially so because Russian statesmen faced a fundamental dilemma on the issue of censorship and how it related to *glasnost'* during the early years of Alexander's reign. Indeed, the problem of how to control discussions of public policy once they had been initiated in the press was one of the most troublesome that Alexander and his advisers faced, and their efforts to resolve it finally produced a narrow definition of *glasnost'* that had very important effects on curtailing the debates about Russia's transformation as the middle of the 1860s approached.

Alexander II unknowingly articulated the dichotomy in his understanding of *glasnost'* when, in 1857, he insisted that censorship must continue, that there must be "a judicious vigilance" exercised over the press,[77] but that such ought not to "inhibit thinking."[78] Implicit in that view was the conviction that everyone in Russia should think as the government did and that any public debate about policy should be directed toward developing the views he and his chief statesmen set forth, unclear and vacillating though they might be. Censorship was to be governed by moral imperatives, not administrative regulations, a view based on those precepts of Official Nationality that had been such an integral part of Alexander's education and early political experience. Alexander's view was given an articulate and lengthy elaboration by O. A. Przhetslavskii, a member of the Main Censorship Administration, who wrote an important memorandum entitled "On *Glasnost'* in Russian Journalistic Literature" in 1860.

Przhetslavskii began his memorandum with a description of what he considered to be *glasnost'*, in its broadest and most extreme form:

> During the past few years the conviction has appeared, and quickly taken root among all levels of Russian society, that *glasnost'*, that is, the transmission by the press of private opinions about all issues ... is the most effective means for ... the correction of shortcomings in our system of legislation and administration, and, finally, for putting an end to all abuses of power and derelictions of duty among state officials. According to this view, *glasnost'* alone should be enough to attain all those results that honorable men so passionately desire, and toward which a benevolent government continually strives.[79]

Przhetslavskii argued that although *glasnost'*, in theory, could help to develop "conscientious, healthy tastes and feelings of decency at many levels of society [and] could have real value in stimulating discussions about serious issues within a framework permissible to the government,"[80] it had achieved just the opposite effect in Russia. "Such *glasnost'* as has established itself in the Russian periodical press in recent years," he warned, "stands in opposition to the spirit and the bases of state institutions, and to Russia's system of administration and legislation. It does not conform to our civic order, the peculiarities of our national character, the level of our present development, or our future requirements."[81] If it were to achieve positive results, he insisted, "glasnost" must be in an inviolable harmony with the circumstances of time and place. In other words, it always must have an indissoluble link with, and conform to, the bases and forms of the state and civic structure; it must never work in conflict with them."[82] The nature of glasnost' also must be related to the peculiarities of national character and the level of education among the nation's masses. Therefore, "glasnost", as it exists in one country, can never be fully and unconditionally transplanted to another."[83] Russia, Przhetslavskii insisted, must follow her own path.[84]

Przhetslavskii thought that moral imperatives must establish the sort of glasnost' that could preserve the prerogatives of autocracy and still allow legitimate expressions of public opinion to serve the state. Guided by moral imperatives established by the government, public opinion then could serve autocracy in a manner defined by the autocrat himself, and Przhetslavskii was certain that public opinion would be willing to assume such a role because it could be confident that the government would formulate and implement policies that served only the best interests of all Russians.[85] He thus proposed a form of glasnost' that defined public opinion as public support for the government. "We want improvements, and we think that we can attain them without the help of public opinion by means of a bureaucracy that is sunk up to its very eyeballs in thievery!" an amazed Nikitenko exclaimed when he read Przhetslavskii's proposals.[86] Yet it was Przhetslavskii's view that defined the role of glasnost' in Russian administration and, hence, Russian politics, by the mid-1860s. In opposition to the urgings of the enlightened bureaucrats, glasnost' became little more than a partial removal of the cloak of secrecy that had shrouded the punishment of corrupt officials in the 1830s and 1840s, while public opinion was expected to adhere to those same moral precepts as it had for the past half-century. By that point, the enlightened bureaucrats had drawn out the main outlines of Russia's transformation, but, by failing to prevail in the debate about glasnost', they had confined any further elaboration of that transformation to St. Petersburg's inner chanceries. Because politics continued to be inseparably linked with administration in Russia, the traditional pressures that had blocked the way to the Empire's renovation during the Nicholas era once again could reassert themselves with overwhelming force. It had been very difficult for the enlightened bureaucrats to cast their views into concrete legislative proposals for Russia's transformation between 1856 and 1865. It became even more difficult to defend that body of legislation once the forces of tradition found effective institutional means for reasserting themselves.

The instruments with which the enlightened bureaucrats had cast their views about reform and change into draft legislation during the first decade of Alexander's reign were special committees of "experts" drawn from the ranks of their most able fellows and supplemented by those representatives of the moderate intelligentsia and progressive nobility with whom they had personal ties and in whom they placed particular trust. The prototypes of such special bodies had been those interdepartmental and interministerial committees in which the enlightened bureaucrats and their allies had discussed administrative policy issues during the late 1840s and early 1850s. In them, they already had practiced the methods of co-optation best suited to bringing men with unique experience or knowledge into their discussions from outside St. Petersburg's chanceries. This was especially the case in the Ministry of Internal Affairs, by mid-century the dominant institution of Russian domestic administration, in which the authority of the ministry to actually make law was attested to by a dramatic increase in the number of circulars and instructions that the minister issued independently of the Tsar's direct approval[87] and where Perovskii and his successor Bibikov had allowed Miliutin and other middle-level officials a wide range of opportunities to use such advisory bodies. Thus, it was no accident that responsibility for preparing legislative drafts for the emancipation and a number of other important reforms had settled in that ministry within a week of Alexander's famous speech of March 30, 1856, in which he told the assembled Moscow nobility that "it is better to abolish serfdom from above than to await the time when it will begin to abolish itself from below" and urged them "to give some thought to how this can be accomplished."[88]

For some two years after Alexander delivered his speech to the Moscow lords, the preparations for drafting the first acts of the Great Reforms remained centered within the Ministry of Internal Affairs. During that time, a number of enlightened bureaucrats assembled important data about serfdom, local administration, and a variety of other questions that related to rural life. Debate about transforming Russia's economic, social, and judicial order offered them compelling opportunities for action, after more than a decade of confinement to the arena of small and inconspicuous deeds. Although the emancipation preparations were more dramatic and exciting, a number of the enlightened bureaucrats, and especially Miliutin, Girs, and Solov'ev, were better prepared for the equally vital debate about the renovation of local administration and government that paralleled the emancipation discussions. From experience, they knew all too well the sterile routines of *deloproizvodstvo,* and they continued to assemble information about how these paralyzed life and government in the Empire. Like few others in

Russia, they understood how completely the Nicholaean effort to intensify administrative centralization had failed. Without rapid and effective communications, it had proved impossible to concentrate effective decision-making authority at the center of Russia's government.[89] At mid-century, such critical public services as fire-fighting, public health care, and police protection all were grossly inadequate for the needs of the Empire's provincials at a time when the impending emancipation was about to increase by more than 30 percent the number of Russians for whom public administration was directly responsible.[90]

The enlightened bureaucrats' studies of provincial life in the late 1840s and 1850s now became the starting point for their efforts to transform local government. Early in 1856, Nikolai Bakhtin urged his superiors to use such statistical studies in their efforts to formulate administrative reforms,[91] and others soon began to seek more specific reform programs. One important means for transforming local government, Golovnin's classmate V. A. Tsie wrote in mid-1856, was by "an extension of the level of power and the circle of authority of local and subordinate powers, that is, by a limitation of centralization." For Tsie, the curse of centralization lay at the root of Russia's administrative failings. "Almost the only reason for the continued growth of *deloproizvodstvo* among us," he wrote, "is the vast, all-consuming process of centralization."[92] A turning-away from the Nicholaean precepts of extreme centralization could reduce bureaucratic formalism, and it could provide Russia's local administration with "that importance and freedom of movement without which it is impossible to expect the necessary enthusiasm for civic affairs [from private citizens]."[93] Like Zarudnyi, Miliutin, Bakhtin, and a number of their lesser-known colleagues, Tsie argued that a defense of the law was essential to the success of any program of administrative reform, and he extolled *glasnost'* as one of its best guarantees.[94]

Tsie never was obliged to test his theoretical commitments and, in fact, never translated them into concrete proposals for reform. It remained for Lanskoi and a number of enlightened bureaucrats in whom he placed particular confidence to translate the generalities of the debate about local government from the realm of theory into concrete legislative action.[95] During the first year of Alexander's reign, growing numbers of progressive officials raised their voices to criticize centralization, bureaucratic formalism, and the pervasive system of administrative surveillance as obstacles that virtually paralyzed provincial administration in Russia. Such was one of the central points in Valuev's famous "Thoughts of a Russian,"[96] and his sentiments were echoed by numbers of his colleagues. "It is a wonder that there is any government left here at all," Senator Kastor Lebedev confessed, aghast at what he had seen in Vladimir province.[97] A growing body of such sentiment among senior officials, and especially the enlightened bureaucrats in the Ministry of Internal Affairs, impelled Lanskoi to press a program of decentralization upon Alexander.[98]

More aware of his limitations as an administrator and reformer than were most ministers in mid-nineteenth-century Russia, Lanskoi was more willing to delegate authority. "He relied upon his subordinates and opened the way to direct influence upon the course and direction of state affairs for men in secondary positions of authority who . . . ranked higher than their superiors in terms of intellect and ability," Valuev once explained.[99] Most importantly, Lanskoi turned to Solov'ev, Miliutin, Girs, and Mikhail Saltykov, those enlightened bureaucrats in his ministry from whom he already had begun to seek advice about peasant affairs, for recommendations about the reform of Russia's local government.[100] Before they could begin to draft legislation, however, they had to confront the efforts of other statesmen to limit the involvement of the Minister of Internal Affairs in the preparation of reform legislation.

Perhaps the most energetic supporter of this counter-effort was Minister of State Domains M. N. Murav'ev, who, in 1858, tried to limit the authority of the Minister of Internal Affairs and to usurp the powers of those provincial governors who recently had come forward and boldly urged further decentralization in Russia's administration. He urged that governors-general, until that time assigned only to govern far-flung or particularly troublesome regions, be appointed throughout the Empire.[101] In the spring of 1858, only Grand Duke Konstantin Nikolaevich stood with Lanskoi against those great lords in the Main Committee on Peasant Affairs who supported Murav'ev's plan. Among the enlightened bureaucrats, Miliutin condemned Murav'ev's proposed governors-general as "pashas or satraps,"[102] and Solov'ev insisted that the faults of provincial administration could be better corrected by granting more independence to civil governors than by creating new officials to usurp their power.[103] Aided by V. A. Artsimovich, who recently had resigned as governor of Tobolsk to protest interference by western Siberia's governor-general in his administration,[104] Miliutin, Solov'ev, and Lanskoi condemned Murav'ev's plan as a violation of *zakonnost'* and proper administrative order.[105] Alexander at first rejected their statement as "a chancery view . . . completely in opposition to my own,"[106] but, when faced with Lanskoi's firm intention to resign rather than alter his stand, he reversed his position and withdrew his support of Murav'ev's proposals.[107]

As President of the Main Committee on Peasant Affairs, which had been formed early in 1858 out of the secret committee that Alexander had established a year before, Konstantin Nikolaevich was vitally interested not only in the issues of emancipation and local administration but also in judicial reform. As he had done on several earlier occasions, he endeavored to broaden the reform debate by a controlled form of *glasnost'*. As usual, it was one of the *konstantinovtsy*, Prince Dmitrii Obolenskii, whose writings formed the core of his effort. After serving as Chief of the Naval Commissariat in the early 1850s, Obolenskii was assigned to reform Russia's naval judicial regulations.[108] Among other things, he prepared for Konstantin Nikolaevich a lengthy criticism of the modest recommendations that Count Bludov, as the leading voice of the 1852 commission on judicial reform, had just completed. The Grand Duke immediately sent Obolenskii's critique to some thirty leading Russia statesmen, in the hope that their replies could stir a broad debate within the Empire's central administration about judicial reform.[109]

Obolenskii's critique urged a broad transformation. "The transformation of the judicial sphere in Russia," he wrote, "cannot be postponed, for upon this reform depends the success of improvements in all other sectors of the state's administration."[110] Russia's lack of an independent judiciary, he insisted, was the most critical flaw in her state structure.

> The absence of [an independent] judiciary was, until the present time, an insurmountable obstacle, destroying and rendering futile all the government's efforts to improve the internal organization of Russia, to better her administration, to develop trade and industry, [and] to improve her morality. Finally, the matter of defining the [new] relationship between the serfs and their masters shall remain unresolved in practice so long as the mediating power between these two classes, that is, the *courts*, is not given any sort of proper organization.[111]

Because it was necessary to "change the fundamental principles of civil court procedure" in Russia, Obolenskii urged reformers either to adopt foreign systems *in toto* or to seek "through the paths of theory" new principles for constructing an "entirely new, unique, and original judicial order." The lengthy written legal processes of the Nicholaean court system that effectively denied all illiterates access to civil courts must be replaced by a more open system in which specialists could interpret the law, not merely administer it. "This is the most fundamental reason why a proper judicial order does not exist among us," Obolenskii exclaimed. "We have no lawyers!"[112]

Such glaring flaws in Russia's judicial system, Obolenskii argued, must be obvious to "anyone who has studied it not merely on paper, and not in the highest spheres of state administration, but in the realm of practice and at its level of application where the disparity between the law and reality is not concealed by lifeless forms." He thus challenged the ability of men such as Bludov to formulate the new juridical principles Russia required and urged that reform legislation be drafted by experts who had seen the conflict between law and reality "in all its scandalous nakedness" at first hand.[113] With more than a decade of experience as a senior juridical consultant in the Ministry of Justice's influential Consultation, and presently serving as deputy to V. P. Butkov, a State Secretary in the State Council's Department of Civil and Spiritual Affairs,[114] Zarudnyi was eminently qualified for precisely such an assignment. During the late 1850s, he had begun to urge Russia's jurists to study the judicial systems of Europe as models; yet he also understood the damage that the wholesale and uncritical application of such models to Russian conditions could produce.[115] Unlike Obolenskii, who urged the adoption "*in toto* of the principles of the French, Prussian, British, or some other judicial process or, through the paths of theory, to arrive at the formation of new, as yet unknown, principles,"[116] Zarudnyi recommended a more modest and moderate approach. A study of Russia's judicial needs should be set against the background of western European legal systems in an effort to produce a reform uniquely responsive to Russia's requirements.[117] To that end he began to assemble commentary by Russian specialists. Like Konstantin Nikolaevich and Obolenskii, he encouraged them to use Bludov's proposals as a foil for their critiques.[118]

Although he was occupied with helping to draft the emancipation legislation during most of 1860 and early 1861,[119] Zarudnyi's efforts to stimulate discussion among Russia's small cadre of learned jurists proved successful. The debate was stimulated further by new leadership within the Ministry of Justice and by a new call for a judicial transformation that issued from Konstantin Nikolaevich's Naval Ministry. In his search for reform models after the Crimean War, Obolenskii had dispatched the young *pravovedy* P. N. Glebov and K. S. Varrand to France and England.[120] These two young men drew important conclusions from their observations in the West, and Glebov hastened to publicize them in a serialized article on "Naval Judicial Proceedings in France" in the pages of *Morskoi sbornik.*[121] Glebov's essay struck at the very heart of the autocrat's traditional view that the judiciary was an integral part of the state's administrative apparatus and that jurists were administrators, not interpreters, of the law.[122] By urging that Russia's judicial administration and structure be made independent of the regular state administration, as in France, he also struck yet another blow against Bludov's proposals and against the foundations of Russia's privileged aristocracy and the serf order that supported it.[123]

Debate within bureaucratic agencies and among a limited number of men not in state service, whose motives and judgment they trusted, thus helped the enlightened bureaucrats to clarify their views about reform and transformation in Russia. To translate their views into legislative proposals, however, required other instruments. At the beginning of 1859, the special committees of experts that we mentioned earlier therefore assumed the leading role in the transformation debate. These would give legislative form to the enlightened bureaucrats' aspirations of transforming Russia's society and economy through administrative means. After testing these instruments in the legislative preparations for the emancipation of 1861, the enlightened bureaucrats went on to use them to prepare the *zemstvo* acts, the judicial reform statutes, reforms in Tsarist Poland, certain modifications in Russia's censorship codes, and a variety of other important legislative ventures that collectively became known as the Great Reforms.

In sharp contrast to the secret committees that Nicholas I had summoned to discuss serfdom and various administrative reforms, these bodies were made up largely of men who shared certain aspirations, attitudes, and commitments about administration and reform. There was not that effort to balance moderate and extremist positions that had been such an integral feature of earlier committees, as autocrats had endeavored to create situations in which they could ensure their direct personal authority by mediating the disputes of their servants. For a brief moment, institutions served that mediatory function themselves. As Daniel Orlovsky recently wrote, Russia's ministries "were the only possible executor of an activist reform movement from above. . . . Bureaucratic momentum and the Tsar's will reinforced each other, and the result was the Great Reforms."[124] The recently established power of the Ministry of Internal Affairs as the dominant authority in domestic political-administrative affairs alloted an especially influential role to the enlightened bureaucrats who had the minister's favor and controlled the information and the departments needed to prepare such reform legislation.

Even before Alexander created the Editing Commission to prepare the emancipation acts, he placed the direction of the legislative work firmly in the hands of bureaucrats guided by his special adjutant General Ia. I. Rostovtsev. Because he was not well acquainted with personnel in the middle and upper levels of Russia's central administration, Rostovtsev turned to Petr Semenov, a distant relative, explorer, and geographer, who, as someone who had stood apart from the hotly contested and emotional issues surrounding the emancipation discussions, had become his confidant and assistant during the fall of 1858.[125] Rostovtsev was convinced of Semenov's impartiality, his deep commitment to support the Emperor's desire for an emancipation, and his talent for organizing and summarizing complex materials. Probably for those reasons, Rostovtsev asked his young relative to find a means to integrate into draft legislation the information contained in the emancipation proposals being sent to St. Petersburg by the provincial nobility.[126]

What Semenov proposed in response to Rostovtsev's request reflected the views of Miliutin, Kavelin, and Solov'ev, all of whom he had come to know as friends in the Geographical Society. All of them warned that the proposals prepared by committees of serf-owning lords could serve only as raw materials for the preparation of a single, comprehensive emancipation statute that should be drafted by a commission of experts and enlightened bureaucrats. Kavelin, in fact, had proposed just such a commission more than a year before.[127] Semenov also urged one emancipation statute for the entire Empire, but recommended that it be divided into legal, administrative, and economic sections in order to better clarify the new relationship that must emerge between former serfs, government, and nobility.[128] Together with a memorandum drafted by Miliutin as a statement of the Ministry of Internal Affairs' position, Semenov's recommendations became the basis for Alexander's decision to create the Editing Commission on February 17, 1859.[129]

At Rostovtsev's urging, Semenov prepared nominations for the Editing Commission, and he drew his choices from the areas of St. Petersburg life he knew best. At least twelve of the names he proposed were men whose work he knew and respected in the Geographical Society, and nearly all could be counted among the enlightened bureaucrats.[130] So could the other nominations he made from the men who served in the central government: Mark Liuboshchinskii (Zarudnyi's senior colleague), K. I. Domontovich (a close associate of Zablotskii), Nikolai Stoianovskii (one of Zarudnyi's protégés), and Dmitrii Khrushchov, who was Miliutin's close friend and an early member of Elena Pavlovna's circle.[131] The aristocrats chosen to serve on the Editing Commission boasted backgrounds very similar to Semenov's choices from the central administration. As "member-experts" known for their expertise about conditions in their native provinces, he named Prince Cherkasskii, Samarin, A. N. Tatarinov, G. P. Galagan, N. I. Zheleznov, A. M. Unkovskii, N. Kh. Bunge, A. I. Koshelev, and, with great reservations, Count P. P. Shuvalov. He had become acquainted with these men in the progressive salons of the capital or as a consequence of his friendship with prominent enlightened bureaucrats. Their combined experience about Russian conditions was unequalled in the central government because their departments in the Ministries of State Domains and Internal Affairs held a near monopoly on such information.

Rostovtsev agreed to accept all of his young relative's nominations except for Koshelev (whom he rejected because of his involvement in the liquor trade), Unkovskii (whom he condemned as a political agitator), and Shuvalov (whom he rightly feared as an opponent of any emancipation that would allow former serfs to purchase land).[132] Most of the Editing Commission members knew each other at the time of their appointments, and that made them more effective as advocates of the enlightened bureaucrats' position. Eight had been a part of Miliutin's circle at some point before 1858,[133] six had been associated with Slavophile circles,[134] and three (Zablotskii, Miliutin, and Ivan Arapetov) had stood on the outer fringes of the *Sovremennik* circle in the mid- to late 1840s. Six members of the Editing Commission—Tarnovskii, Cherkasskii, Samarin, Petr Semenov, Galagan, and Miliutin—had been associated with the Grand Duchess Elena Pavlovna's salon before 1858,[135] but it was in the Geographical Society that the largest number had met before 1859. Fourteen Editing Commission members came from that group of young Russians who had joined the Society in the late 1840s and early 1850s when the enlightened bureaucrats had seized control.[136] Most of these men immediately joined together to urge a landed emancipation upon those conservative serf-owners and statesmen who made up the remainder of the Editing Commission. Led by Miliutin, Solov'ev, Samarin, and Cherkasskii, they formed a bloc of eighteen which, with the frequent support of a satellite group of four sympathizers, controlled the direction of the emancipation debates between March 1859 and October 1860.[137]

Only one member of this bloc (N. Kh. Bunge, a professor from St. Vladimir University in Kiev) had not been associated with the enlightened bureaucrats in some manner during the decade before 1859. All but three were in state service at the time of their appointment, and two of that number (Samarin and Tarnovskii) had only recently retired. Only Prince Cherkasskii never had been in state service before he became a member of the Editing Commission. In addition to their experience as state officials, these men also boasted a far more impressive educational profile than did the Empire's most senior statesmen. Only 53.8 percent of Nicholas I's ministers had attended a university, elite school, private boarding school, or gymnasium, and, although Alexander II's ministers were better educated (88 percent had some formal schooling), only 18 percent had graduated from the university.[138] By contrast, 66.7 percent of the enlightened bureaucrats and their allies on the Editing Commission were university graduates; of the remaining 33.3 percent, all had elite educations. Eleven among them had traveled or studied in the West, often on assignments commissioned by the government.[139]

Organizational sessions in the Editing Commission began in March 1859, but the actual preparation of the legislative drafts took place in a number of special section meetings. As Semenov had proposed, there were administrative, legal, and economic sections to which financial and codification sections later were added. In each, enlightened bureaucrats and their allies wielded decisive influence. Four of them (Kalachov, Zhukovskii, Domontovich, and Solov'ev) served on the legal section, as did Liuboshchinskii, a man very supportive of their views, while only two members (Apraksin and Bulygin) strongly opposed them. The economic section contained ten members from the enlightened bureaucrats' bloc,[140] in addition to three who often supported their position (Prince Golitsyn, Zalesskii, and Zheleznov). Together, these thirteen men faced six opponents.[141] In the administrative section, five supporters of the enlightened bureaucrats,[142] in addition to Prince Golitsyn, had to face five opponents,[143] while seven of the nine members of the financial section were from the enlightened ranks.[144] Finally, twelve of the thirteen codification section members supported the enlightened bureaucrats' program, while only Galagan saw it as his duty to oppose what he once called "the unlawful demands of theory."[145]

Because the Editing Commission was discussing an issue that directly involved the lives and fortunes of more than a hundred thousand noble families who owned serfs, and because Alexander had committed himself publicly to involving the nobility in the emancipation discussions, Rostovtsev insisted that his committee hold discussions with representatives of Russia's serf-owning lords. Under the enlightened bureaucrats' urging, and in large measure because of their intense efforts, the Editing Commission produced a substantial draft of the Emancipation Acts in less than six months.[146] Another year was required, however, for its members to defend their work against the serf-owners' attacks. Nonetheless, the beginnings of Russia's transformation had been laid, and the enlightened bureaucrats pressed on to continue that process.

Zablotskii once had written that "any change in the serf order . . . will bring with it other essential transformations in our civic administration,"[147] and, even before the defense of their draft Emancipation Acts was complete, the enlightened bureaucrats on the Editing Commission had begun to move on to other tasks. At the urging of Lanskoi, who was struggling against Murav'ev's efforts on the Main Committee to undermine the institutional authority of the Ministry of Internal

Affairs, Alexander had established the Commission on Provincial and District Institutions on March 27, 1859. Its purpose was to prepare draft legislation for a transformation of Russia's local administration, to create new institutions that would replace the serf-owners' administrative authority in village life once the Emancipation Acts had abolished it, and to reform the police forces that functioned in Russia's provinces and districts. Alexander left the Commission's composition largely in Lanskoi's hands, and, even more than the Editing Commission, it was dominated by enlightened bureaucrats and their allies. Headed by Miliutin (at Lanskoi's insistence), it included Zarudnyi, Konstantin Grot, Solov'ev, Girs, Stoianovskii, Artsimovich, and Nikolai Kalachov among its leading figures.[148]

The Commission on Provincial and District Institutions moved more slowly than the Editing Commission. In the administrative and political sense, its tasks were perhaps even more complex because the entire future of Russia's provincial development, and the effectiveness of the ties between a renovating central administration and its outlying regions depended on its success. Five of its key members—Miliutin, Solov'ev, Girs, Kalachov, and Zarudnyi—were deeply involved in the emancipation work at the same time, and Miliutin especially had little time for directing discussions about local affairs while his economic section on the Editing Commission wrestled with the complexities of the emancipation settlement. Further, important materials from other government agencies were not transferred to the Commission for more than a year, and its entire operating budget was not released until mid-1860.[149] By that time, it had prepared a program for police reform, part of which drew upon the work of the Editing Commission's administrative section, and the main aim of which was to introduce a much-needed professionalism into Russia's local police forces.[150] Before the first draft of the *zemstvo* legislation was completed, however, Miliutin was forced into retirement, and the full responsibility for completing the task was left with Solov'ev. Not until March 9, 1862, did he place his proposals in the hands of Valuev, who had shifted to a more conservative view of local affairs and had recently succeeded Lanskoi as Minister of Internal Affairs.[151] Valuev confidently modified Solov'ev's proposals in order to provide Russia's provincial lords with a more substantial role in *zemstvo* affairs, despite efforts by Konstantin Nikolaevich and such enlightened bureaucrats as Reitern and Golovnin to defend them in a select committee that was established to resolve the debate.[152] The balance shifted when Miliutin unexpectedly reentered the fray that spring.

In the seclusion of his Roman retreat during the winter of 1861–1862, Miliutin had made dramatic modifications in his narrow view of *glasnost'.* He now favored encouraging a much broader segment of society to take part in local affairs and saw such participation as an important device for weakening extremist opinion on the left and right.[153] During a brief visit to St. Petersburg in May of 1862, he argued that responsible local government could free Russia's central administration from "moral responsibility for petty and distant abuses, a responsibility not in keeping with the true meaning and dignity of the state power."[154] Had Valuev continued to command the Emperor's unquestioned support, Miliutin's defense of Solov'ev's proposed new *zemstvo* institutions hardly could have made any notable impact upon the legislative process in St. Petersburg. Yet Konstantin Nikolaevich, Golovnin, and Reitern had begun to enjoy some modest success in their effort to undermine the Emperor's support for Valuev's more conservative position on the question of the *zemstva,* and, when the Council of Ministers met in May and June to review his modifications of Solov'ev's drafts, they agreed to a broader definition of the *zemstva's* role in local affairs.[155]

Yet the outcome remained far from certain. During the next year, these draft statutes were attacked by advocates of gentry constitutionalism, by those who feared the growing revolutionary movement in Poland, and, most critically, by Valuev himself. Only when former Minister of Public Instruction, E. P. Kovalevskii, and Nikolai Bakhtin, whose memorandum in 1856 had helped to launch the early debate on *glasnost'* and administrative decentralization, entered the fray against Valuev in the State Council's Combined Departments of Law and State Economy, did Solov'ev's recommendations prevail and become the basis for the *zemstvo* statutes that were promulgated on January 1, 1864.[156] New local administrative and self-government institutions, the *zemstva,* thus were enacted into law, and, by the end of the century, these would emerge as an important political instrument for advancing the cause of progress and reform in the Russian countryside. Not only had emancipation been accomplished, but new institutions embodying the enlightened bureaucrats' precepts of local self-government and administrative decentralization had been established to replace the arbitrary patrimonial authority of the serf-owning nobility.

Administration based on the laws and legal authority thus began to replace *nadzor* and the capricious abuse of power in Russia's provincial and district administration. The growing debate about judicial reform, in which the enlightened bureaucrats and their allies played an important part, helped to further institutionalize and defend those new principles. That the path to European judicial models which Glebov, Zarudnyi, and Obolenskii had blazed soon after the Crimean War became a well-worn trail by the early 1860s was in large measure due to the efforts of Dmitrii Zamiatnin, who succeeded Panin as Minister of Justice in 1862. A *litseist,* and a student of the great jurist A. P. Kunitsyn, Zamiatnin had been part of that elite circle of young men who had received their first practical training in law under Speranskii. As Deputy Minister of Justice, beginning in 1858, Zamiatnin's deep respect for expert opinion about questions of legal theory and judicial practice led him to foster artificial *glasnost'* in his ministry during the last years of Panin's tenure.[157] In July 1859, he was directly responsible for founding *The Journal of the Ministry of Justice,* which supplied the enlightened men in his ministry with a forum comparable to that which their counterparts in the Ministries of State Domains and Internal Affairs had enjoyed for more than two decades.

What was especially significant about the debate that Zamiatnin fostered between 1859 and 1862 was that it molded important segments of educated society, professional jurists, and enlightened bureaucrats into a united front that supported broad reform of Russia's court structure and judicial procedure. Outside the bureaucracy, calls for more comprehensive reform came not only from progressive noblemen but also from many conservative assemblies of the provincial nobility who began to speak out in defense of private property once they had lost their serfs. This removed the issue of judicial reform from the realm of radical transformation and endowed it with a significant conservative appeal that influenced Alexander to support a broader reform of Russia's judicial system than that which he originally had envisioned.[158] Again, a committee of experts became the instrument for preparing the necessary legislative drafts. When Alexander entrusted the task to V. P. Butkov and the State Chancellery in October 1861,[159] work on judicial reform passed directly into the hands of Zarudnyi and a cadre of eight jurists, some of whom had studied at his "school" in the Ministry of Justice for more than a decade.[160]

Zarudnyi and his associates hoped to base their reform proposals on European judicial models, but approval for such a radical departure from Russian legal practice had to be secured at the highest level of the Imperial administration. In January 1862, they received it from Prince P. P. Gagarin, the recently appointed president of the State Council's Department of Laws, who instructed Zarudnyi to set forth "those basic principles, the *undoubted merit* of which is recognized at the present time as the *knowledge and experience of European states* and according to which the judicial sphere in Russia ought to be transformed."[161] By doing so, he paved the way for a fundamental change in Russian institutional attitudes that neither Zarudnyi nor his immediate associates had the authority to achieve. Left free to employ western precepts, Zarudnyi and his associates completed a digest of "Basic Principles for the Transformation of the Courts" by the beginning of April 1862.[162] These judicial and legislative milestones proposed that the application of Russian law be brought under the control of professional jurists who practiced according to the precepts of adversarial procedure in an independent and public court system.[163] These were principles that Alexander II and his advisers, at that point, were prepared to accept. What remained was the painstaking labor of transforming the "Basic Principles" into the draft legislation that became the judicial reform statutes of November 20, 1864. For that task a larger commission composed only of men noted for their technical expertise was created under the auspices of the State Chancellery. Of its thirty-one members, at least twelve were *pravovedy*, another twelve had university degrees, and seven had worked with Zarudnyi to draft the "Basic Principles."[164]

Working under the direction of Zarudnyi and Butkov, this commission sent its draft proposals to the State Council in December 1863, and, on November 20, 1864, the new statutes were promulgated by the Senate. These transformed the practice of law in Russia, and they were perhaps the most successful of all the Great Reforms. Russia's courts were set apart from the regular framework of state administration for the first time, and, except on the local level, where the Justices of the Peace were elected by the *zemstva,* the remainder of Russia's courts were placed in the hands of trained and professional jurists. Judges no longer held tenure at the Emperor's pleasure, but enjoyed life tenure. Trials became public, incorporating Zarudnyi's belief that *glasnost'* was the most effective guarantee of honesty in legal proceedings, and, although the State Council excluded political crimes from their jurisdiction, trials by jury became the rule in other criminal cases.[165] In the view of Alexander II, these statutes made possible legal proceedings that were "swift, just, merciful, and equal for all."[166] The labors of Zarudnyi and other enlightened bureaucrats had induced the Emperor to relinquish absolute control over the dispensation of justice in his domains, one of autocracy's most cherished prerogatives. The Emancipation Acts and the *zemstvo* reform had transformed social, administrative, and economic relationships in Russia; the judicial reform statutes set the stage for transforming the very nature of autocracy.

An effort to realize their vision of *zakonnost'*—an administration and a society that observed the law and functioned according to legal procedures—underlay the enlightened bureaucrats' first efforts to establish in legislation their view of Russia's new course. Their chief instruments were specially created commissions of "experts," men who by education, training, and experience were extremely well versed in a particular aspect of Russia's social, economic, or administrative condition. By their very nature, these special commissions stood outside the framework of the regular Tsarist administration, and that had the very positive result of enabling their members to circumvent many of the bureaucratic procedures and constraints that had served to paralyze the efforts of even the best-intentioned reformers during the Nicholas era. At the same time, the extra-institutional nature of these commissions carried a liability that eventually proved to be every bit as serious as those they had circumvented with such success. Because they functioned outside the established framework of ministerial institutions, they proved unable to construct institutional defenses for their positions.

This liability became all the more serious because so many of the enlightened bureaucrats relinquished their regular institutional assignments during the course of their work on special Imperial commissions. As early as March 1859, Zablotskii had relinquished his positions as Director of the Department of Rural Economy, member of the Ministry's Council, and President of the Academic Committee in the Ministry of State Domains. Between 1859 and 1875 (when he was appointed to the State Council), Zablotskii's only regular position in the higher administration was State Secretary in the Department of State Economy in the State Council.[167] This was not an inconsequential appointment, but it was not a position from which a bureaucrat could develop a strong base of institutional support within the ministerial administration. Likewise, once Nikolai Miliutin was removed from his post as Deputy Minister of Internal Affairs in April 1861, he did not hold another regular position at the highest administrative level until his appointment to the State Council in 1865, the year before he was paralyzed by a stroke.[168] The same situation was true for Obolenskii, Liuboshchinskii, and Konstantin Grot.[169] Until Zarudnyi was appointed to the Senate (which was not a policy-making body in any case) in 1869, he never held a regular administrative appointment higher than a deputy State Secretary in the State Council. Other enlightened bureaucrats who played major roles in drafting the Great Reform legislation, such as Solov'ev, Gagemeister, Domontovich, and Tsie, held even lower positions until their senatorial appointments, and, despite the major role he played in drafting the Emancipation Acts and the reforms in Tsarist Poland between 1864 and 1866, Prince Cherkasskii never once held a senior position in St. Petersburg's central administration.

So long as Lanskoi served as Minister of Internal Affairs, an office which, by the late 1850s, was the most powerful ministerial position in the Empire, the enlightened bureaucrats could remain confident of their ability to influence the direction of Russia's post-Crimean transformation. Indeed, they may have been sufficiently naïve in their political perceptions of the new administrative order that was emerging as a partial consequence of their actions that they were unaware a serious threat existed. The unexpected ouster of Lanskoi and Miliutin in the spring of 1861 showed them the precarious nature of their position. Because they already had relinquished most of their regular institutional positions, they had very few resources with which to reinforce this newly opened breach in their defenses against their opponents. Thus it was not mere coincidence that Miliutin began to broaden his view of *glasnost'* during the last months of 1861. Nor was it accidental that the enlightened bureaucrats turned to Golovnin, now Minister of Public Instruction and the only one among them to retain a position at the peak of Russia's civil administration, to help win official support for that broader view.

Like his colleagues in the ranks of Russia's enlightened bureaucracy, Golovnin believed in *zakonnost'*, and his experience in Konstantin Nikolaevich's Naval Ministry had convinced him of the value of *glasnost'*, provided that its limits were defined.[170] In recalling the views he held at this time, he insisted that he "desired all possible liberty, freedom, and the fullest *zakonnost'* with the complete absence of any *proizvol.*" He later wrote that "the first and essential condition for the successful activity of man's higher nature, that is, his spiritual nature, is *complete* liberty and freedom—that is the end toward which a government which truly desires success in enlightenment ought to strive first of all."[171] These were ideals, not programs to be implemented immediately, however. At the end of 1861, Golovnin regarded the emancipation, and the judicial and *zemstvo* reforms that soon would follow, as important steps in achieving "greater freedom, a lessening of that *proizvol* that formerly weighed so heavily upon society, [and] the introduction of greater *zakonnost'.*"[172] He insisted, however, that conditions would not permit the immediate introduction of those broader freedoms enjoyed by citizens in European nations. "Our major task is to struggle against the impending revolution," he wrote to Konstantin Nikolaevich in May 1862.[173]

At the beginning of 1862, Golovnin thus sought first to "struggle against the impending revolution," which he saw in new disorders in Russia's universities and in the ever-increasing tension in Tsarist Poland, and to introduce a somewhat broader form of *glasnost'* than that which had served the *konstantinovtsy* so well in the Naval Ministry a decade before. He soon found that *glasnost'* might be controlled with relative ease in discussions of naval or military affairs,[174] but that it was far more difficult to encourage discussion of state policies in the press and keep the debates within limits acceptable to the Emperor and his senior statesmen. Golovnin therefore attempted to manipulate the press by subsidizing journals whose editors were willing to publish pro-government articles,[175] and, fearful that the press might become an instrument for spreading revolutionary ideas, he instituted stricter controls until new censorship statutes could be drafted. On March 8, 1862, he named Prince Obolenskii as president of a special commission to accomplish that task. The commission's other two leading figures were Konstantin Veselovskii and Tsie, both prominent enlightened bureaucrats, as we have seen.[176] All were defenders of *zakonnost'* and thought that *glasnost'* could serve as a substitute for *nadzor* and the ubiquitous practice of reading private correspondence by the police *(perliustratsiia)* in order to ensure that the "beneficial plans of the central government," as Tsie once had written, were effectively implemented.[177] Ideally, they thought that *glasnost'* should provide society with the means to criticize the improper or ineffective implementation of state policies, but not the content of the policies themselves.[178]

Obolenskii's commission set out to draft new censorship regulations that would, in effect, institutionalize the commission's views about society, the government, and the manner in which the two should interract on questions of policy. Very quickly, however, Golovnin found himself in an institutional power struggle with Valuev for control of Russia's censorship apparatus. By the beginning of 1863, Valuev had won what proved to be an uneven contest, and the Ministry of Internal Affairs held full control over censorship in the Empire. Because Valuev was determined to encourage limited participation by other groups in the autocratic legislative process,[179] he established a second commission, again under Obolenskii's presidency, but with a much more diverse membership than before. A series of more restrictive regulations that institutionalized the more narrow version of *glasnost'* which Przhetslavskii had championed was the result. When these regulations were sent to the State Council in January 1865, the best efforts of Nikolai and Dmitrii Miliutin, although strongly supported by Konstantin Nikolaevich, only succeeded in having the legislation termed "temporary."[180] At best, it was a Pyrrhic victory; the "temporary" regulations of April 6, 1865, controlled Russian censorship for the next thirty-eight years. By establishing a more centralized and effective censorship apparatus in Russia, and by concentrating all responsibility for it in the Ministry of Internal Affairs, these regulations gave the Russian government a more powerful weapon against the press and a more effective instrument for controlling *glasnost'* than it had ever held before.[181]

Confronted by administrative instruments that defended a form of *glasnost'* which, in effect, equated public opinion with public support of the government's policies, and with no position in the regular administration from which to launch a counterattack against the growing authority of conservative opinion, the enlightened bureaucrats were reduced to becoming defenders of the Great Reform legislation and moral guardians of the Great Reform *mentalité*. After Golovnin was forced from office in 1866, the only one of the enlightened bureaucrats' number to remain at the center of the Russian government was Dmitrii Miliutin. Yet Dmitrii Miliutin's chief concerns at that point had to be with domestic affairs only as they related to the monumental task of reforming Russia's land forces. The Great Reforms of 1861–1864 had transformed the social and administrative order upon which the Russian army had been based since the time of Peter the Great, for Russia no longer could maintain an army based upon serfdom and aristocratic privilege alone. *De jure*, Russians had become citizens, and the Empire now required a citizen army.[182] It was not until Dmitrii Miliutin had established the legislative framework for transforming Russia's servile military forces into a citizen army in 1874 that he could become more deeply involved in broader questions of domestic policy and politics.[183] By that time, the political climate, and the nature of administrative politics in Russia, were very different from what they had been a brief decade before.

If the underlying purpose of the enlightened bureaucrats' efforts during the Great Reform era was to establish a society based upon *zakonnost'* in which it would be possible for responsible elements in Russian society to become involved in the autocratic legislative process over time, some institutional guarantees had to be established. In their failure to do so—perhaps even to perceive that such was essential to their broader purpose—lay the enlightened bureaucrats' chief failure during the Great Reform era. That it was possible to establish such an institutional base, and from that to develop a broad program for Russia's transformation, was very evident in the political career of Petr Valuev, Russia's immensely powerful Minister of Internal Affairs from 1861–1868, and a man who had stood with the enlightened bureaucrats throughout most of the 1840s and 1850s. It was Valuev who, in June 1862, made the first concrete proposal to establish an institutional framework for increasing the political participation of Russian society in the autocratic legislative process.[184]

Perhaps more clearly than any other statesman of the 1860s, Valuev perceived that those new social and economic forces that the emancipation had unleashed must be harnessed to ensure the survival of an autocracy that, by its very nature, stood in conflict with those forces that had created modern industrial systems in the West. Like Nikolai Miliutin, he hoped to co-opt the social and intellectual elements that formed the basis of the opposition's support, but, unlike Miliutin and other enlightened bureaucrats, he realized that new institutional instruments were necessary to achieve that end. For the enlightened bureaucrats during the 1850s and early 1860s, it had been sufficient to co-opt

Alexander II

P. A. Valuev

those figures of the "opposition" whom they thought most reliable by bringing them into the government committees engaged in drafting reform legislation. Valuev realized that in order to create that "center party" which Miliutin had advocated at the end of 1861, more was needed than mere "concessions [which] would consist of a broad development of the elective principle for local administration (excluding police officials), and a doubling of the budget for education."[185] Some form of co-optation that would enable opposition groups to participate in the autocratic political process was required if the government were "to seize control of the social movement" in the manner Valuev thought necessary. Valuev therefore advocated a "reform of the State Council on bases analogous to the Austrian *Reichsrat.*" "This measure," he argued, "will have the advantage of not posing any threat to the sovereignty of the ruler, and will preserve all of his legislative and administrative power, but, at the same time, will create a central institution which would be a kind of representative of the nation."[186] In just more than a year, Valuev began to envision this institution as a "Congress of State Representatives," elected mainly by the *zemstva,* that would serve as a consultative department in the State Council.[187]

Valuev's proposals stood in dramatic contrast to Miliutin's pious hopes that a "center party" could be brought into being by "a broad development of the elective principle for local administration," and Kavelin's belief that only in the "fertile school" of local self-government could public opinion "prepare itself . . . for further, broader political activities."[188] This difference represented in microcosm the major dilemma that confronted most enlightened bureaucrats during the

1860s and 1870s. In view of the new social and economic forces unleashed by the Great Reforms, it had become essential to create the
means for broader participation in autocratic politics. Yet, as men of the
1840s, most enlightened bureaucrats could not envision instruments
which could accomplish that end without undermining autocracy. Their
inability to do so became even more evident in the mid-1860s when
their patron Konstantin Nikolaevich proposed summoning elected representatives "for participation in the legislative process."[189] Supported
by such enlightened bureaucrats as Golovnin and Reitern,[190] Konstantin Nikolaevich's proposals urged only that consultations take place
"when and in such a manner as may be found useful," with representatives chosen by the corporate bodies of the *zemstva* and the nobility.[191]
On the question of institutionalized participation by society in the
Empire's political processes, these proved far more timid and cautious
than Valuev's programs.[192]

The new social and economic order that had begun to emerge in
Russia posed a further dilemma for Russian statesmen in the 1870s.
Although the Emperor's support remained critical in officials' efforts to
maintain power and influence, it had become necessary for ambitious
statesmen to establish an institutional base for their power as well.
Nowhere was this more evident than in the political career of Valuev
who, from the powerful base of patronage and influence he had created
as Minister of Internal Affairs between 1861 and 1868, continued to
influence state affairs until the end of the reign. Failure to emulate
Valuev's example was a critical factor in Golovnin's fall as Minister of
Public Instruction in 1866, although he did not fully perceive it at the
time and blamed the Emperor's caprice instead.[193] What Golovnin
failed to understand was that the minister who constructed an institutional base for his power could preserve his influence on state affairs
even if he were removed from office. A fundamental part of this institutional base had to be public opinion. Obviously, Valuev was disliked
and feared by many, but he also maintained the support of a significant
portion of the nobility, which served to solidify his power in Russia's
government and ensure his influence on state policy.

If the enlightened bureaucrats had become nearly isolated from the
nerve centers of Russian administrative politics by the mid-1860s, they
were even more sharply separated from Russia's radical intelligentsia.
As men of the 1840s, they had defined Russia's transformation in terms
of the aspirations held by the moderately dissident opinion of their
generation, not in terms of the demands set forth by that revolutionary
intelligentsia that had been spawned by disillusionment with the Emancipation Acts. For them, *zakonnost'*, *glasnost'*, within properly defined
limits, and the lessening of *proizvol* were the prime goals, and they saw

the legislation of the early 1860s as a dramatic major first step toward achieving those ends. They failed to understand that the aspirations of Russia's radicals had taken immense strides during the decade after 1855. "Thou has conquered, O Galilean!" Herzen had proclaimed in 1858, and went on to express his confidence in *glasnost'* as the instrument that would right the wrongs that plagued Russian life.[194] By 1861, such phrases echoed like a voice from the distant past, as Herzen cursed the emancipation as "an act of Judas" and warned that "the peasant community, the will of the people, and the rights of man [will be raised] against the Tsar and the great lords."[195] What the enlightened bureaucrats regarded as major accomplishments, the revolutionary intelligentsia viewed as mere palliatives or, even, betrayals. To the radical intelligentsia's call for revolutionary action, such enlightened bureaucrats as Miliutin posed the alternative of "timely concessions."[196]

The enlightened bureaucrats' inability to confront effectively either the nobility's demand for participation in autocratic politics or the demands of Russia's nascent revolutionary intelligentsia during the 1860s was glossed over temporarily by what the Menshevik writer Feodor Dan has called the "bourgeoisification" of that minority of upper-class Russians who invested wisely the funds they received for lands surrendered to their former serfs.[197] Railroad construction, the development of new industrial enterprises, and increased investment of Russian and European capital during the early and mid-1860s established a new sense of common interest between the government and the more energetic sectors of the Russian economy. This was facilitated even further by the outbreak of revolution in Russian Poland in January 1863, which encouraged still greater reconciliation between the government and nonrevolutionary educated opinion in Russia. Conjuring up visions of the expulsion of the Poles from Moscow in 1612, and of the great victory over Napoleon just two centuries later, the journalist Mikhail Katkov urged the re-creation of that national unity that had carried Russia to victory in those days of national tribulation.[198] Much of the public opinion that had split away from Alexander's government in 1861 and early 1862 thus reentered its camp to pose a united front against Poland's revolutionary forces. By late 1863, any danger that the revolutionary intelligentsia in Russia would join forces with other sectors of public opinion was past. Pressure for increased political participation by the new social and economic forces created by the first wave of Great Reform legislation was reduced in proportion.

The response of Tsarist authorities to the revolution of 1863–1864 in Poland further reconciled potentially dissident elements in Russia with the autocracy, because their policies created an inflated demand for Russian officials, and those who answered the summons of Nikolai

Miliutin and Cherkasskii from Warsaw enjoyed vastly broadened pros-
pects that promised far more successful service careers.[199] This stood in
sharp contrast to the experiences that young men of similar backgrounds had encountered a decade or so earlier when they had faced
years of deadening clerical routines in St. Petersburg's chanceries before
they could hope to rise to higher ranks. Their younger counterparts
found it possible to gain promotion much more quickly in the expanding chanceries of the Russian administration in Warsaw, and they
became reconciled to the government as a result.

Widespread reconciliation between educated opinion and the government in the mid-1860s provided Alexander II and his senior advisers
with opportunities to consolidate the transformation that the enlightened bureaucrats had begun and to reestablish the social harmony that
the Great Reforms had disrupted. The enlightened bureaucrats, however, were not a central part of that process because they had failed to
establish a base within either the bureaucracy or public opinion in order
to perpetuate their influence in state affairs. In 1879, Dmitrii Miliutin,
the last to remain in a policy-making post, described the dilemma that
he and those who shared the enlightened bureaucrats' outlook faced. In
his diary, he wrote:

> It is impossible not to recognize that our entire state structure
> demands fundamental reform from top to bottom. . . . Everything
> ought to be given new forms in agreement with the Great Reforms
> undertaken in the 1860s. It is lamentable indeed that such a colos-
> sal task cannot be undertaken by our present-day statesmen, who
> are not in a position to raise themselves above the point of view
> of a local chief of police. . . . In expressing these melancholy
> thoughts, you involuntarily pose for yourself the question: "Do
> you act honorably, having these convictions, to remain in that
> very government itself?" Often, almost continually, this question
> weighs upon me, but what is to be done? —You may as well knock
> your head against a wall. . . . I am convinced that not only are
> present-day statesmen unable to resolve the crisis that confronts
> them; they cannot even understand it.[200]

"If only we had independent people at the top of our administration,
we would produce an unprecedented example of an autocratic, but, at
the same time, the most free, country on earth," Kavelin wrote a few
years later in a similar vein. "But they do not listen to us now," he
lamented. "We are 'traitors' to our motherland, secret 'enemies' of
autocracy, pathetic Utopians, and dangerous dreamers."[201]

When the enlightened bureaucrats lost much of their ability to influence state affairs in the 1870s, they left few successors to perpetuate

their vision. Much as Aleksandr Herzen, a man of the 1840s, lost his influence on the revolutionary intelligentsia as the 1860s passed their mid-point, so had the enlightened bureaucrats, also as men of the 1840s, lost their influence on succeeding generations of state officials. What separated them from later generations, Golovnin wrote, was that they had endured the almost crippling psychological experience of living through the last decade of the Nicholas era. The younger generation "did not know the atmosphere of the preceding reign," he explained. "To them, the privileges with which our own disappearing genera- tion satisfied itself already seemed insignificant."[202] Toward the end of Alexander's reign, Golovnin and Dmitrii Miliutin finally turned to that very timid constitutionalism that might have enabled the enlightened bureaucrats to establish a broader political base had they espoused such views two decades earlier. "In general, it is necessary to say that for Russia the moment already has come when . . . the government . . . should summon representatives of society to take part in deciding important state affairs so as to lessen the central administration's burden of responsibility," Golovnin wrote in the mid-1870s.[203] Yet having made that concession, he could propose nothing beyond those cautious urgings for *ad hoc* consultations with elected representatives that Konstantin Nikolaevich had proposed in 1866.[204]

At best, such a proposal was sadly anachronistic. It came from that earlier time, the era of the "immortal Statute of 19 February 1861," as Kavelin called it, which those enlightened bureaucrats who had lived until the end of Alexander's reign had begun to idealize in romantic terms.[205] The survivors of the enlightened bureaucracy—Zablotskii, Golovnin, Grot, Shumakher, Dmitrii Miliutin, Domontovich, Stoianov- skii, Kavelin, Liuboshchinskii, and Petr Semenov—still gathered to dis- cuss autocratic politics, as they had for almost half a century,[206] but, with perhaps the exception of Kavelin, they stood well outside the mainstream of opinion in Russia:

> Now more than ever before [Golovnin wrote], I have begun to notice how far I have become separated in my views . . . from the dominant currents of opinion expressed at Court and at the salons. Likewise, I rarely share the opinions of our literary circles, views emanating from the provinces, the obstinate stubbornness of our conservatives, or the crude enthusiasms of our so-called liberals and progressives. . . . In earlier years, I was more willing to make concessions, more easily influenced by others or, at least, I got along with others more easily. But now, recognizing that my own convictions are correct, I refuse to give them up.[207]

Unable—in some cases unwilling—to make concessions to changed conditions, these men repeated the beliefs and formulae that had served them a quarter-century before. The assassination of Alexander II, the Tsar with whom they had worked in what they now remembered as the "sacred undertaking" of the Great Reforms, severed the last tie that bound them to the inner circles of Russia's government.

The terrorist bomb that claimed the life of Alexander II on the afternoon of March 1, 1881, brought a new atmosphere to Russia. That Alexander III's reign, like that of his grandfather Nicholas I, opened in an atmosphere of repression was predictable and understandable, given the circumstances of his father's death. But, while Nicholas had turned to questions of reform within a year after his accession, his grandson continued on a repressive course in administration and politics. Within a week, it was clear to Russia's senior statesmen that Konstantin Pobedonostsev, who as a young *pravoved* had aided Zarudnyi in preparing the Judicial Reform Statutes, was to be a dominant influence in the new Emperor's circle. Yet Pobedonostsev preserved few of the convictions he had espoused as a young jurist. He had become a passionate chauvinist, a staunch defender of unlimited (and unchecked) autocratic power, and an avowed enemy of that very order he once had helped to bring into being. While Dmitrii Miliutin called for further reform to defuse Russia's revolutionary violence,[208] Pobedonostsev urged upon Alexander III a rigid political and social program that would earn for his reign the unenviable epithet: the Era of Counterreforms. Faced with the certainty of Pobedonostsev's influence, Loris-Melikov and Miliutin's brother-in-law Minister of Finance Abaza, resigned at the end of April. Less than two weeks later, Dmitrii Miliutin himself followed them into retirement.[209]

When Russia's new Emperor accepted Dmitrii Miliutin's resignation as Minister of War on May 12, 1881, the era of the enlightened bureaucrats' participation in state affairs came to an end. A few of them continued to sit on the State Council and in the Senate, but without Miliutin and Konstantin Nikolaevich, their Imperial patron who relinquished his presidency of the State Council in July, theirs were to be voices from the past that often went unheeded. At best, these men continued to fight a rear-guard action to defend the Great Reforms from dismemberment during the 1880s and, in that, they enjoyed some modest success.[210] More generally, they lived among themselves, dining, visiting, and corresponding with one another, remembering those comrades already claimed by death, and criticizing the policies of Russia's new generation of statesmen who, they fervently believed, had failed utterly to build upon those principles to which they had devoted their careers in Russia's service for the past half-century.[211]

Notes

Preface

1. A. A. Kornilov, *Kurs istorii Rossii XIX veke,* 3 vols. (Moscow, 1918), II: 125–37.

2. Iu. I. Gerasimova, "Krizis pravitel'stvennoi politiki v gody revoliutsionnoi situatsii i Aleksandr II," in M. V. Nechkina, ed., *Revoliutsionnaia situatsiia v Rossii v 1859–1861gg.* (Moscow, 1962), pp. 93–106. See also M. V. Nechkina, "Reform 1861 goda kak pobochnyi produkt revoliutsionnoi bor'by," in ibid., pp. 7–17.

3. P. A. Zaionchkovskii, *Otmena krepostnago prava v Rossii,* 3rd ed. (Moscow, 1968), pp. 60–62.

4. Terence Emmons, *The Russian Landed Gentry and the Peasant Emancipation of 1861* (Cambridge, 1968), p. 48.

5. Alfred J. Rieber, ed., *The Politics of Autocracy: The Letters of Alexander II to Prince A. I. Bariatinskii, 1857–1864* (Paris, 1966), pp. 24–27.

6. Daniel Field, *The End of Serfdom: Nobility and Bureaucracy in Russia, 1855–1861* (Cambridge, Mass., 1976), p. 100.

7. Ibid., p. 52.

8. See, for example, Pis'mo K. D. Kavelina k T. N. Granovskomu, 4 marta 1855g., in Sh. M. Levin, ed., "K. D. Kavelin o smerti Nikolaia I," *LN,* LXVII (1959): 610.

9. It is important to remember that Alexander did not initially propose an emancipation of the serfs but, to quote the so-called Nazimov Rescript, only an "organization and amelioration of the way of life of the proprietary peasantry," *Materialy dlia istorii uprazdneniia krepostnago sostoianiia pomeshchich'ikh krest'ian v Rossii v tsarstvovanie Imperatora Aleksandra II,* 3 vols. (Berlin, 1860), I: 140. Likewise, the Emperor did not initially contemplate a fundamental alteration in

Russia's judicial administration and court system, see Richard S. Wortman, *The Development of a Russian Legal Consciousness* (Chicago, 1976), p. 244.

10. For a first-rate discussion about the immensely complex question of rank, see Helju Aulik Bennett, "Evolution of the Meanings of *Chin:* An Introduction to the Russian Institution of Rank Ordering and Niche Assignment from the Time of Peter the Great's Table of Rank to the Bolshevik Revolution," *California Slavic Studies,* X (1977): 1–44.

Chapter 1

1. P. A. Valuev, "Duma russkago vo vtoroi polovine 1855g.," *RS,* LXX (May 1891): 354–55.

2. S. M. Troitskii, *Russkii absoliutizm i dvorianstvo v XVIII v. Formirovanie biurokratii* (Moscow, 1974), pp. 274–85; A. D. Gradovskii, "Vysshaia administratsiia Rossii XVIII stoletiia i general-prokurory," in *Sobranie sochinenii A. D. Gradovskago,* 9 vols. (St. Petersburg, 1899), I: 126–34; Reinhard Wittram, *Peter I: Czar und Kaiser,* 2 vols. (Göttingen, 1964), II: 114–18; S. M. Solov'ev, *Istoriia Rossii s drevneishikh vremen,* 15 vols. (Moscow, 1963), VIII: 457–58; Walter M. Pintner, "Civil Officialdom and the Nobility in the 1850s," in Walter M. Pintner and Don Karl Rowney, eds., *Russian Officialdom: The Bureaucratization of Russian Society from the Seventeenth to the Twentieth Century* (Chapel Hill, 1980), pp. 245–49; N. F. Demidova, "Biurokratizatsiia gosudarstvennogo apparata absoliutizma v XVII–XVIII vv.," in *Absoliutizm v Rossii XVII–XVIII vv. Sbornik statei* (Moscow, 1964), pp. 206–42.

3. Iu. V. Got'e, *Istoriia oblastnago upravleniia v Rossii ot Petra I do Ekateriny II* (Moscow, 1913), pp. 71–74, 130–35; Marc Raeff, "The Russian Autocracy and Its Officials," *Harvard Slavic Studies,* IV (1957): 78–79; Daniel T. Orlovsky, "Ministerial Power and Russian Autocracy: The Ministry of Internal Affairs, 1802–1881," Ph.D. dissertation, Harvard University, 1976, pp. 16–17. Orlovsky's dissertation has recently appeared as *The Limits of Reform: The Ministry of Internal Affairs in Imperial Russia, 1802–1881* (Cambridge, Mass., 1981). The citations to Orlovsky's work in this volume are to his dissertation, unless otherwise indicated.

4. Walter M. Pintner and Don Karl Rowney, "Officialdom and Bureaucratization," in Pintner and Rowney, eds., *Russian Officialdom,* p. 371.

5. *Istoriia pravitel'stvuiushchago senata za dvesti let,* 5 vols. (St. Petersburg, 1911), I: 57; George L. Yaney, *The Systematization of Russian Government: Social Evolution in the Domestic Administration of Imperial Russia, 1711–1905* (Urbana, 1973), pp. 63–66.

6. Yaney, *Systematization,* p. 86.

7. Quoted in ibid., pp. 86–87, note 13.

8. Raeff, "Russian Autocracy and Its Officials," pp. 78–79.

9. Gradovskii, "Vysshaia administratsiia Rossii," pp. 126–32; Wittram, *Czar und Kaiser,* II: 115–17.

10. Demidova, "Biurokratizatsiia gosudarstvennogo apparata absoliutizma," pp. 206–42, as well as other essays in this volume. See also Orlovsky, "Ministerial Power," p. 17.

11. A. N. Filippov, "Istoricheskii ocherk obrazovaniia ministerstv v Rossii," *ZhMIu,* No. 9 (November 1902), p. 40.

12. See, for example, S. N. Troitskii, *Finansovaia politika russkogo absoliutizma v XVIII veke* (Moscow, 1966), pp. 30–34, and *passim*.

13. Yaney, *Systematization*, pp. 63–68. See also Marc Raeff, "The Well-Ordered Police State and the Development of Modernity in Seventeenth- and Eighteenth-Century Europe: An Attempt at a Comparative Approach," *The American Historical Review*, LXXX (December 1975): 1235–42.

14. *Istoriia pravitel'stvuiushchago senata*, II: 365; N. M. Korkunov, *Russkoe gosudarstvennoe pravo*, 2 vols. (St. Petersburg, 1903), II: 305–8; Yaney, *Systematization*, pp. 75–76; N. D. Chechulin, *Ocherki po istorii russkikh finansov v tsarstvovanie Ekateriny II* (St. Petersburg, 1906), pp. 282–89.

15. Troitskii, *Russkii absoliutizm*, pp. 169–76; P. A. Zaionchkovskii, *Pravitel'stvennyi apparat samoderzhavnoi Rossii v XIX v.* (Moscow, 1978), pp. 66–67; M. V. Klochkov, *Ocherk pravitel'stvennoi deiatel'nosti vremeni Pavla I* (Petrograd, 1916), pp. 95–108; D. F. Troshchinskii, "Zapiska Dmitriia Prokof'evicha Troshchinskago o Ministerstvakh," *SIRIO*, III (St. Petersburg, 1868): 30–31.

16. Yaney, *Systematization*, pp. 81–85; Wortman, *Development of a Russian Legal Consciousness*, pp. 91–95.

17. M. M. Speranskii, "Otryvok o komissii ulozheniia," in S. N. Valk, ed., *M. M. Speranskii: Proekty i zapiski* (Moscow-Leningrad, 1961), p. 27.

18. L. A. Perovskii, "O prichinakh umnozheniia deloproizvodstva vo vnutrennem upravlenii (mart, 1851g.)," TsGIAL, fond 1287, opis' 36, delo No. 137/15.

19. M. P. Veselovskii, "Zapiski M. P. Veselovskago s 1828 po 1882," GPB, fond 550.F.IV.861/389.

20. "Svod osnovykh gosudarstvennykh zakonov," *Svod zakonov rossiiskoi imperii* (St. Petersburg, 1897), I, pt. 1, articles 47, 1.

21. A. E. Presniakov, *Apogei samoderzhaviia: Nikolai I* (Leningrad, 1925), pp. 3–14.

22. *PSZ*, sobranie 1-oe, No. 20406.

23. W. Bruce Lincoln, *Nicholas I: Emperor and Autocrat of All the Russias* (Bloomington, Ind., 1978), pp. 166–70.

24. A. P. Zablotskii-Desiatovskii, *Graf P. D. Kiselev i ego vremia*, 4 vols. (St. Petersburg, 1881), II: 11.

25. Quoted in Presniakov, *Apogei samoderzhaviia*, p. 14.

26. Lincoln, *Nicholas I*, pp. 86–88.

27. N. M. Karamzin, *Karamzin's Memoir on Ancient and Modern Russia*, Richard Pipes, trans. and ed. (Cambridge, Mass., 1959), pp. 196–204.

28. See especially Baron M. A. Korf, "Materialy i cherty k biografii Imperatora Nikolaia I i k istorii ego tsarstvovanie. Rozhdenie i pervye dvadtsat' let zhizni (1796–1817)," in N. F. Dubrovin, ed., *Materialy i cherty k biografii Imperatora Nikolaia I i k istorii ego tsarstvovanie* (St. Petersburg, 1896), pp. 79–80.

29. *PSZ*, sobranie 2-oe, IX, section 2, pp. 277–80.

30. Orlovsky, "Ministerial Power," p. 79.

31. W. Bruce Lincoln, "Daily Life of St. Petersburg Officials in the Mid-Nineteenth Century," *Oxford Slavonic Papers*, VIII (1975): 85–87.

32. "Zhurnaly komiteta uchrezhdennago Vysochaishim reskriptom 6 dekabria 1826 goda," *SIRIO*, LXXIV (1891), p. 264.

33. For two particularly striking examples, see the statistics about the civil service compiled annually by the *Inspektorskii Department*, in TsGIAL, fond 1409, opis' 2, delo No. 6829, and the statistics on crimes committed by civil servants compiled annually by the Ministry of Justice, in TsGIAL, fond 1405, opis' 52.

34. Quoted in N. V. Riasanovsky, *Nicholas I and Official Nationality in Russia, 1825–1855* (Berkeley and Los Angeles, 1959), p. 101.

35. S. I. Zarudnyi, "Pis'mo opytnago chinovnika sorokovykh godov mladshemu ego sobratu postupaiushchemu na sluzhbu," A. S. Zarudnyi, ed., *RS, C* (1899): 544.

36. See, for example, "Otchet za 1847 god po statisticheskomu otdeleniiu Soveta Ministerstva Vnutrennikh Del," TsGIAL, fond 1290, opis' 1, delo No. 155/10–17.

37. Perovskii, "O prichinakh umnozheniia deloproizvodstva," TsGIAL, fond 1287, opis' 36, delo No. 137/15.

38. Pis'mo N. A. Miliutina k D. A. Miliutinu, 10 avgusta 1838g., ORGBL, fond 169, kartonka 69, papka 6.

39. I. A. Blinov, *Gubernatory: Istoriko-iuridicheskii ocherk* (St. Petersburg, 1905), pp. 161–63.

40. A. V. Golovnin, "Zapiski Aleksandra Vasil'evicha Golovnina s marta 1867g.," TsGIAL, fond 851, opis' 1, delo No. 7/2.

41. A. I. Artem'ev, "Dnevnik, 1 iiulia–31 dekabria 1856g.," GPB, fond 37, delo No. 159/138.

42. I. N. Borozdin, "Universitety v Rossii v pervoi polovine XIX veka," in *Istoriia Rossi v XIX veke*, 9 vols. (St. Petersburg, 1907), II: 352–56.

43. D. F. Kobeko, *Imperatorskii tsarskosel'skii litsei, 1811–1843gg.* (St. Petersburg, 1911), p. 16; I. Ia. Seleznev, *Istoricheskii ocherk Imperatorskago, byvshego tsarskosel'skago, nyne Aleksandrovskago, litseia* (St. Petersburg, 1861), pp. 147–48.

44. Kobeko, *Tsarskosel'skii litsei*, pp. 6–7.

45. *PSZ*, sobranie 1-oe, No. 20597.

46. *PSZ*, sobranie 2-oe, No. 2377.

47. Karamzin, *Karamzin's Memoir*, pp. 160–61.

48. *PSZ*, sobranie 2-oe, No. 7224.

49. W. Bruce Lincoln, "A Profile of the Russian Bureaucracy on the Eve of the Great Reforms," *Jahrbücher für Geschichte Osteuropas*, XXVII (1979): 182–83; Zaionchkovskii, *Pravitel'stvennyi apparat*, p. 69.

50. S. Frederick Starr, *Decentralization and Self-Government in Russia, 1830–1870* (Princeton, 1972), p. 48.

51. "Otchety po Inspektorskomu Departamentu Grazhdanskago Vedomstva za 1847–1857gg.," TsGIAL, fond 1409, opis' 2, delo No. 6829.

52. "Delo o sluzhbe P. A. Valueva," TsGIAL, fond 908, opis' 1, delo No. 4.

53. P. A. Valuev, "Otryvok iz zamechanii o poriadke grazhdanskoi sluzhby v Rossii (1845g.)," TsGIAL, fond 908, opis' 1, delo No. 24/29.

54. Officials in the first category were obliged to have a certificate of graduation from an elite school (such as the Lyceum at Tsarskoe Selo or the Imperial School of Jurisprudence) or a university. Graduation from one of the Empire's *gimnazii* entitled an official to inclusion in the second category, while those with only elementary or home educations were inscribed in the third. Third category officials could become registered in a higher category if they passed an examination to certify that they had the equivalent of a *gimnaziia* or university education.

55. *PSZ*, sobranie 2-oe, No. 7224.

56. Ibid.

57. Ibid.

58. Quoted by Baron M. A. Korf in "Dnevnik za 1840g.," TsGAOR, fond 728, opis' 1, delo No. 1817/iii/264.

59. W. Bruce Lincoln, "The Ministers of Nicholas I: A Brief Inquiry into Their Backgrounds and Service Careers," *The Russian Review,* XXXIV (1975): 319–20.

60. For detailed data on the frequency of promotions in Russia's major bureaucratic agencies, see Tables 4 and 5 in Lincoln, "A Profile," pp. 188–91.

61. A. E. Tsimmerman, "Vospominaniia Generala A. E. Tsimmermana, 1825–1855gg.," ORGBL, fond 325, kartonka 1, papka 1/176–77.

62. Zarudnyi, "Pis'mo opytnago chinovnika," p. 543.

63. "Obshchaia vedomost'. Otchet ... za 1847g.," TsGIAL, fond 1409, opis' 2, delo No. 6829–86/44–45.

64. In the Ministry of Public Instruction, for example, none of the 985 promotions in 1847 were for merit, and a decade later only ten promotions out of 1,375 fell into that category. For detailed data on merit promotions between 1847–1857, see Lincoln, "A Profile," Table 5, pp. 190–92.

65. See, for example, I. V. Roskovshenko, "Peterburg v. 1831–1832gg.," *RS,* CI (February 1900): 477–79.

66. M. E. Saltykov-Shchedrin, *Sobranie sochinenii,* 20 vols. (Moscow, 1970), X: 271.

67. A. I. Artem'ev, "Dnevnik 1 ianvaria–31 iiulia 1856g.," GPB, fond 37, delo No. 158/8. Entry for January 11, 1856.

68. N. V. Gogol', "Nevskii Prospekt," in N. V. Gogol', *Sobranie sochinenii N. V. Gogolia,* 6 vols. (Moscow, 1959), III: 42.

69. Roskovshenko, "Peterburg v 1831–1832gg.," p. 479.

70. K. S. Veselovskii, "Vospominaniia," *RS,* CVIII (December 1901): 16–17.

71. A. V. Golovnin, "Kratkii ocherk deistvii velikago kniazia Konstantina Nikolaevicha po Morskomu vedomstvu so vremeni vstupleniia v upravlenie onym po ianvar' 1858g.," GPB, fond 208, delo No. 2/269.

72. A. I. Artem'ev, "Dnevnik, 1 ianvaria–31 iiulia 1856g.," GPB, fond 37, delo No. 158/9. Entry for January 11, 1856; A. A. Kharytonov, "Iz vospominanii A. A. Kharytonova," *RS,* LXXXI (January 1894): 116.

73. Roskovshenko, "Peterburg v 1831–1832gg.," p. 487; P. I. Nebolsin, "Biudzhety peterburgskikh chinovnikov," *Ekonomicheskii ukazatel',* No. 11 (16 March 1857), pp. 241–50.

74. See especially "Otchet po Inspektorskomu Departamentu Grazhdanskago Vedomstva za 1847g.," TsGIAL, fond 1409, opis' 2, delo No. 6829–86/44–45; "Extraits du Mémoire secret du Conseiller Privé Actuel Tengoborski (janvier 1857)," TsGIAL, fond 851, opis' 1, delo No. 50/289–290; L. V. Tengoborskii, "Kratkoe izlozhenie nashego finansovago polozheniia (mai 1856g.)," TsGIAL, fond 958, opis' 1, delo No. 742/3.

75. Even a quick survey of the annual volumes of *Spisok grazhdanskim chinam pervykh IV klassov* provides dramatic evidence of this phenomenon.

76. F. G. Terner, *Vospominaniia zhizni F. G. Ternera,* 2 vols. (St. Petersburg, 1910), I: 68; Kharytonov, "Iz vospominanii," pp. 116–17; Nebolsin, "Biudzhety peterburgskikh chinovnikov," pp. 241–50.

77. *Stolonachal'nik* was a position, not a rank, but it usually was given to men with at least the rank of *kollezhskii asessor.*

78. The salary for a *stolonachal'nik* varied from ministry to ministry. This figure is for the Ministry of Internal Affairs and can be considered close to average for the 1840s and 1850s. For a brief indication of the standard of living a *stolonachal'nik* might enjoy with this salary and how it would improve if he

could raise his income by various means, see Nebolsin, "Biudzhety peterburg-skikh chinovnikov," pp. 241–50.

79. Among the most prominent editors or deputy editors of such journals were A. P. Zablotskii-Desiatovskii, N. A. Miliutin, and N. I. Nadezhdin *(Zhurnal Ministerstva Vnutrennikh Del)*; A. P. Zablotskii-Desiatovskii *(Zhurnal Ministerstva Gosudarstvennykh Imushchestv)*; and A. V. Nikitenko *(Zhurnal Ministerstva Narodnago Prosveshcheniia)*.

80. M. P. Veselovskii, "Zapiski M. P. Veselovskago s 1828 po 1882," GPB, fond 550.F.IV.861/420.

81. Valuev, "Duma russkago," p. 355.

82. *Opis' del arkhiva Gosudarstvennago Soveta,* 21 vols. (St. Petersburg, 1908), III: 443.

83. "Perepiski po delam o podriadakh (mart 1851g.)," TsGIAL, fond 1284, opis' 36, delo No. 137/24–27.

84. L. A. Perovskii, "O prichinakh umnozheniia deloproizvodstva vo vnu-trennem upravlenii (mart 1851g.)," TsGIAL, fond 1287, opis' 36, delo No. 137/15.

85. Ibid.

86. Tengoborskii, "Extraits," TsGIAL, fond 851, opis' 1, delo No. 289–90.

87. Veselovskii, "Zapiski," GPB, fond 550.F.IV.861/389.

88. For some striking examples, see the title page of "Obozrenie vsekh chastei gosudarstvennago upravleniia. Chast' tret'ia: Politsiia (1831g.)," GPB, fond 380, delo No. 67/1, and "Perepiski po sluchaiu assignovaniia i otpuska gorodskikh summ na soderzhanie politseiskikh sluzhitelei po kazhdomu gorodu (1851g.)," TsGIAL, fond 1284, opis' 36, delo No. 137.

89. Veselovskii, "Zapiski," GPB, fond 550.F.IV.861/390.

90. Ibid., 861/420.

91. Perovskii, "O prichinakh umnozheniia deloproizvodstva," TsGIAL, fond 1287, opis' 36, delo No. 137/15.

92. Artem'ev, "Dnevnik, 1 ianvaria–31 iiulia 1856g.," GPB, fond 37, delo No. 158/48.

93. Perovskii, "O prichinakh umnozheniia deloproizvodstva," delo No. 137/16.

94. Examples of such bureaucratic paralysis are numerous. See especially, "Doklady uchenago komiteta Ministerstva Gosudarstvennykh Imushchestv, 22 iiulia 1850g., i 2 maia 1852g.," and other documents in TsGIAL, fond 398, opis' 14, delo No. 4774/9–88.

95. H.-J. Torke, "Das russische Beamtentum in der ersten Hälfte des 19 Jahrhunderts," *Forschungen zur osteuropäischen Geschichte,* XIII (1967): 214–15.

96. According to A. V. Nikitenko's account, in mid-December 1850, a new regulation was issued which gave superiors the right to remove a subordinate from the civil service for political unreliability or for unspecified transgressions. Particularly significant, an official's superior neither had to prove that such behavior had in fact occurred nor provide the official in question with an explanation for his removal. A. V. Nikitenko, *Dnevnik,* 3 vols. (Moscow, 1955), I: 338.

97. Artem'ev, "Dnevnik, 1 iiunia–31 dekabria 1855g.," GPB, fond 37, delo No. 157/83–84.

98. A. V. Golovnin, "Raznitsa v napravlenii gosudarstvennoi deiatel'nosti v pervoi i vo vtoroi polovine nyneshnego tsarstvovaniia (mart 1867g.)," GPB, fond 208, delo No. 236/12.

99. See, for example, W. Bruce Lincoln, "The Genesis of an 'Enlightened' Bureaucracy in Russia, 1825–1855," *Jahrbücher für Geschichte Osteuropas,* XX (September 1972): 321–22; Field, *The End of Serfdom,* pp. 35–50.

100. Orlovsky, *The Limits of Reform,* p. 51.

101. P. A. Stroganov, "Essai sur le système à suivre dans la réformation de l'administration de l'Empire," in Velikii kniaz' Nikolai Mikhailovich, *Graf P. A. Stroganov (1774–1817): Istoricheskoe izsledovanie epokhi Imperatora Aleksandra I,* 3 vols. (St. Petersburg, 1903), II: 20.

102. The significance of this problem, the weakness of family ties, and the role of education in the outlooks of elite noble youth in the eighteenth century are discussed by Marc Raeff in *Origins of the Russian Intelligentsia: The Eighteenth-Century Nobility* (New York, 1966), pp. 122–47.

103. A. E. Presniakov, *Apogei samoderzhaviia: Nikolai I* (Leningrad, 1925), pp. 3–14.

104. Marc Raeff, *Michael Speransky: Statesman of Imperial Russia, 1772–1839,* 2nd ed. (The Hague, 1969), pp. 44–45.

105. M. V. Klochkov, *General-Prokurory pri Pavle I* (St. Petersburg, 1912), pp. 1–55; "Zapiska Imperatora Pavla I ob ustroistve raznykh chastei gosudarstvennago upravleniia," *SIRIO,* XC (1894): 1–2; Filippov, "Istoricheskii ocherk," pp. 46–48; Kniaz' A. Czartoryski, *Memuary kniazia Adama Chartorizhskago,* 2 vols. (Moscow, 1912), I: 140–43; Nikolai Mikhailovich, *Graf P. A. Stroganov,* I: 88.

106. Raeff, *Speransky,* pp. 41–42.

107. Count P. A. Stroganov, "Essai sur un réglement organique de toutes les branches du gouvernement de Russie," in Nikolai Mikhailovich, *Graf P. A. Stroganov,* II: 254–56.

108. Raeff, *Speransky,* pp. 1–15, 49–51; Korkunov, *Russkoe gosudarstvennoe pravo,* II: 239–45.

109. *PSZ,* sobranie 1-oe, No. 29852, pp. 769–70.

110. *PSZ,* sobranie 1-oe, No. 24686, articles 206, 209, 208, 220. See also M. M. Speranskii, "Vvedenie k Ulozheniiu gosudarstvennykh zakonov," in S. N. Valk, ed., *M. M. Speranskii: Proekty i zapiski* (Moscow-Leningrad, 1961), pp. 201–2.

111. *PSZ,* sobranie 1-oe, No. 24686, article 241.

112. A. P. Zablotskii-Desiatovskii, "Statisticheskoe obozrenie gosudarstvennykh i obshchestvennykh povinnostei, dokhodov, i raskhodov v Kievskoi gubernii, 1850–1851gg.," TsGIAL, fond 940, opis' 1, delo No. 69/3.

113. P. P. Semenov-Tian-Shanskii, *Memuary,* 3 vols. (Petrograd, 1916), III: 22.

114. M. A. Korf, "Vypiska o P. D. Kiseleve," (1845g.), TsGIAL, fond 940, opis' 1, delo No. 303/31.

115. A. P. Zablotskii-Desiatovskii, *Graf P. D. Kiselev i ego vremia,* 4 vols. (St. Petersburg, 1882), I: 1–3.

116. Ibid., p. 3.

117. N. M. Druzhinin, *Gosudarstvennye krest'iane i reformy P. D. Kiseleva,* 2 vols. (Moscow, 1946), I: 257; "Graf P. D. Kiselev," *Russkii biograficheskii slovar',* 25 vols. VIII: 703.

118. Druzhinin, *Gosudarstvennye krest'iane,* I: 260–63; Zablotskii-Desiatovskii, *Graf P. D. Kiselev,* I: 47–152; "Graf P. D. Kiselev, *RBS,* VIII: 706.

119. Druzhinin, *Gosudarstvennye krest'iane,* I: 262–63.

120. P. D. Kiselev, "Zapiska predstavelennaia Gosudariu v 1816 godu o postepennom unichtozhenii rabstva v Rossii," in Zablotskii-Desiatovskii, *Graf P. D. Kiselev,* IV: 197–99.

121. Ibid., I: 324.

122. For a comprehensive discussion of the general state of affairs in Wallachia and Moldavia at this time see V. Ia. Grosul, *Reformy v dunaiskikh kniazhestvakh i Rossiia* (Moscow, 1966), pp. 44–90.

123. W. Bruce Lincoln, "Count P. D. Kiselev: A Reformer in Imperial Russia," *The Australian Journal of Politics and History*, XVI (August 1970): 180–82.

124. P. D. Kiselev, "Vospominaniia," quoted in Zablotskii-Desiatovskii, *Graf P. D. Kiselev*, II: 212–13.

125. Ibid., p. 182.

126. For a summary of the work of those Secret Committees appointed to discuss the peasant question during the reign of Nicholas I, see "Istoricheskaia zapiska o raznykh predpolozheniiakh po predmetu osvobozhdeniia krest'ian," in P. Bartenev, ed., *Deviatnadtsatyi vek: Istoricheskii sbornik*, 2 vols. (Moscow, 1872), II: 145–208; Druzhinin, *Gosudarstvennye krest'iane*, I: 165–96, 280–99.

127. Druzhinin, *Gosudarstvennye krest'iane*, I: 295.

128. The Fifth Section was transformed into the Ministry of State Domains on December 26, 1837; *PSZ*, sobranie 2-oe, No. 10834.

129. Lincoln, "Count P. D. Kiselev," pp. 184–85.

130. Quoted in "Graf P. D. Kiselev," *RBS*, VIII: 713.

131. Druzhinin, *Gosudarstvennye krest'iane*, I: 476.

132. Ibid., pp. 182–83, 480–81.

133. For a detailed account of the work of these investigators, see ibid., pp. 299–475.

134. See, for example, K. S. Veselovskii, "Vospominaniia," *RS*, CXVI (October 1903), pp. 16–17; D. A. Miliutin, "Moi starcheskie vospominaniia za 1816–1873gg.," ORGBL, fond 169, kartonka 12, papka 1/120–22; V. A. Insarskii, *Zapiski V. A. Insarskago*, 2 vols. (St. Petersburg, 1898), I: 65; and the service records of V. A. Insarskii (TsGIAL, fond 1284, opis' 50, delo No. 260), I. P. Arapetov, (TsGIAL, fond 1349, opis' 3, delo No. 94), A. K. Girs (TsGIAL, fond 1284, opis' 31, delo No. 52), A. P. Zablotskii-Desiatovskii (TsGIAL, fond 1162, opis' 6, delo No. 196), and K. K. Grot (TsGIAL, fond 1162, opis' 6, delo No. 154).

135. "Graf Aleksei Kirillovich Razumovskii," *Sovetskaia Istoricheskaia Entsiklopediia* (Moscow, 1968), XI, col. 857; P. P. Semenov, *Geografichesko-statisticheskii slovar' rossiiskoi imperii*, 5 vols. (St. Petersburg, 1863–1885), I: 682; P. Maikov, "Graf Lev Alekseevich Perovskii," *RBS*, vol. Pav-Pet, pp. 541, 550; F. F. Vigel', *Zapiski*, S. Ia. Shtraikh, ed., 2 vols. (Moscow, 1928), I: 227–28.

136. *Vosstanie dekabristov. Materialy*, B. L. Mozdalevskii and A. A. Sivers, eds., Vol. VIII (Leningrad, 1925), pp. 149, 374; *Istoriia udelov za stoletie ikh sushchestvovaniia, 1797–1897gg.*, 2 vols. (St. Petersburg, 1902), I: 66–67; Count Otto de Bray, "Imperator Nikolai I i ego spodvizhniki," *RS*, CIX (January 1902): 132.

137. N. P. Eroshkin, *Istoriia gosudarstvennykh uchrezhdenii dorevoliutsionnoi Rossii* (Moscow, 1968), pp. 172–73; *Istoriia udelov*, I, see graph facing p. 664.

138. *Istoriia udelov*, I: 68, 663. For brief summaries of Perovskii's reforms, see W. M. Pintner, *Russian Economic Policy under Nicholas I* (Ithaca, 1967), pp. 74–76; Jerome Blum, *Lord and Peasant in Russia from the Ninth to the Nineteenth Centuries* (Princeton, 1961), pp. 496–99.

139. *Istoriia udelov*, I: 76–79; *Istoricheskoe obozrenie piatidesiatiletnei deiatel'nosti Ministerstva Gosudarstvennykh Imushchestv, 1837–1887gg.*, 5 vols. (St. Petersburg, 1888), II (pt. 2): 47–49; "Programma sel-sko-khoziaistvennoi statistiki," 17 maia 1847g., TsGIAL, fond 398, opis' 10, delo No. 3152.

140. K. N. Shchepetov, *Krepostnoe pravo v votchinakh Sheremeth'evykh (1708–1885)*, (Moscow, 1947), p. 28; Druzhinin, *Gosudarstvennye krest'iane*, I: 45.

141. L. A. Perovskii, "Dokladnaia zapiska o neobkhodimosti uluchshenii po gubernskim pravleniiam" (1843g.), TsGIAL, fond 1149, opis' 3 (1843), delo No. 94a/6–7, 12.

142. L. A. Perovskii, "O prichinakh umnozheniia deloproizvodstva," TsGIAL, fond 1287, opis' 36, delo No. 137/15.

143. Perovskii, "Dokladnaia zapiska," TsGIAL, fond 1149, opis' 3 (1843), delo No. 94a/7; *PSZ*, sobranie 2-oe, No. 15634; S. A. Adrianov, *Ministerstvo vnutrennikh del*, 3 vols. (St. Petersburg, 1901), I: 54–55; N. V. Varadinov, *Istoriia Ministerstva vnutrennikh del*, 8 bks. (St. Petersburg, 1858–1863), III (bk. 2): 81–82.

144. "Delo o sluzhbe V. I. Dalia," TsGIAL, fond 1349, opis' 3, delo No. 646; "Vladimir Ivanovich Dal'," *RBS*, VI, p. 43; P. Bartenev, "V. I. Dal'," *RA*, I (1872): 2029; P. I. Mel'nikov-Pecherskii, "Vospominaniia o V. I. Dale," *RV*, CIV (1873): 311–12.

145. Lincoln, "Daily Life of St. Petersburg Officials," pp. 90–92; Lincoln, "Genesis of An 'Enlightened' Bureaucracy," pp. 326–27; Varadinov, *Istoriia*, III (bk. 3): 20–24.

146. "Po Vysochaishemu poveleniiu ob ispravlenii nedostatok nashego grazhdanskago sudoproizvodstva: po delu ob imenii i dolgakh kollezhskago registratora Ivana Balasheva," TsGIAL, fond 1261, opis' 1, delo No. 162/190. By far the best account of Panin's views and attitudes in any language is in R. S. Wortman, *Development of a Russian Legal Consciousness*, pp. 168–96.

147. Quoted in Wortman, *Development of a Russian Legal Consciousness*, p. 174.

148. Quoted in A. K. Dzhivelegov, "Graf V. N. Panin," *Velikaia reforma* (Moscow, 1911), Vol. V, p. 70.

149. P. Maikov, "Graf Viktor Nikitich Panin," *RBS*, vol. Pav-Pet, pp. 178–81.

150. A. K. Dzhivelegov, "Graf V. N. Panin," p. 151.

151. N. P. Semenov, "Graf Viktor Nikitich Panin," *RA*, bk. 3 (1887), pp. 538, 546.

152. Dzhivelegov, "Graf V. N. Panin," p. 150.

153. Quoted in S. Rozhdestvenskii, "Posledniaia stranitsa iz istorii politiki narodnago prosveshcheniia Imperatora Nikolaia I," *Russkii istoricheskii zhurnal*, Nos. 3–4 (1917), p. 49.

154. Ibid.; N. M. Kolmakov, "Ocherki i vospominaniia N. M. Kolmakova," *RS*, LXXI (July 1891): 128; Semenov, "Graf V. N. Panin," p. 528.

155. Semenov, "Graf V. N. Panin," p. 546; Wortman, *Development of a Russian Legal Consciousness*, p. 219, table 8.2.

156. See chapter 2.

157. Karamzin, *Karamzin's Memoir*, pp. 195, 197.

158. See, for example, Rozhdestvenskii, "Posledniaia stranitsa," pp. 49–50; N. M. Kolmakov, "Ocherki i vospominaniia N. M. Kolmakova," LXXI (July 1891): 128; Veselovskii, "Vospominaniia," pp. 16–17; D. A. Miliutin, "Moi starcheskie vospominaniia za 1816–1873gg.," ORGBL, fond 169, kartonka 12, papka 1/120–122; Mel'nikov-Pecherskii, "Vospominaniia o Dale," pp. 310–11; "Svedeniia o N. I. Vtorove," GPB, fond 163, delo No. 56/1–2; and A. D. Shumakher, "Pozdnie vospominaniia o davno minuvshikh vremenakh," *VE*, CXCVI (March 1899): 112–14; Druzhinin, *Gosudarstvennye krest'iane*, I: 260–62;

and L. A. Perovskii, "Dokladnaia zapiska," TsGIAL, fond 1149, opis' 3, delo No. 94a/5–9.

159. For an explanation of this term, see Orlovsky, *Limits of Reform*, p. 3.

Chapter 2

1. A. D. Shumakher, "Pozdnie vospominaniia," pp. 112–13.

2. I. A. Goncharov, *Obyknovennaia istoriia* (Moscow, 1960), pp. 62 ff.

3. A. K. Girs, for example, spent several years in the province of Iaroslav studying the economic and administrative affairs of its towns and cities, while A. V. Golovnin spent more than a year in Finland to complete a broad survey of conditions in that area of the Empire. See "Formuliarnyi spisok A. K. Girsa," TsGIAL, fond 1284, opis' 31, delo No. 52; "Delo o sluzhbe A. V. Golovnina," TsGIAL, fond 1162, opis' 6, delo No. 133.

4. This was the case, for example, with Iu. A. Gagemeister, who spent so much time in the provinces between 1833 and 1839 that he was for a time forgotten by his superiors and went for seven years without a promotion. In Gagemeister's case, his superiors tried to set the matter right by giving him two retroactive promotions in the space of two years. "Formuliarnyi spisok Iu. A. Gagemeistera," TsGIAL, fond 1349, opis' 3, delo No. 478.

5. To give a few examples, see the cases of N. P. Bezobrazov, G. I. Frolov, N. M. Garting, K. A. Krzhivitskii, A. F. Shtakel'berg, and A. K. Sivers.

6. A. P. Zablotskii-Desiatovskii, "O krepostnom sostoianii v Rossii," in Zablotskii-Desiatovskii, *Graf P. D. Kiselev*, IV: 342.

7. V. I. Semevskii, *Krest'ianskii vopros v Rossi v XVIII i pervoi polovine XIX stoletiia*, 2 vols. (St. Petersburg, 1888), II: 137–38.

8. Ibid., p. 138.

9. Quoted in Field, *End of Serfdom*, p. 59.

10. Druzhinin, *Gosudarstvennye krest'iane*, I: 295.

11. "Delo o sluzhbe A. P. Zablotskago-Desiatovskago," TsGIAL, fond 1162, opis' 6, delo No. 196; V. P. Semenov-Tian-Shanskii, "Stranitsy semeinoi khroniki: moi ded i babushka so storony materi i ikh rodstvenniki," CU/AREEHC, No. 21.2.4.1; and "Stranitsy semeinoi khroniki," CU/AREEHC, No. 0232.

12. I. Miklashevskii, "Statistika," *Entsiklopedicheskii slovar' Brokgauza-Eifrona* (St. Petersburg, 1901), Vol. XXXI, p. 497; M. V. Ptukha, "Statiskika v Rossi v nachale XIX veka," in *Ocherki po istorii statistiki SSSR. Sbornik statei* (Moscow, 1955), pp. 98–100. On the state of early Russian statistical studies, see also M. V. Ptukha, *Ocherki po istorii statistiki v SSSR*, 2 vols. (Moscow, 1959), II: 9–55, 111–29, and *passim*; K. F. German, *Istoricheskoe obozrenie literatury statistiki, v osobennosti Rossiiskago gosudarstva* (St. Petersburg, 1817), especially pp. 74–77.

13. K. I. Arsen'ev, "Zapiska o sostava i deistviiakh Statisticheskago Otdeleniia Soveta Ministerstva Vnutrennikh Del," 15 noiabria 1852g., TsGIAL, fond 869, opis' 1, delo No. 91/5–7; "Delo o sluzhbe A. P. Zablotskago-Desiatovskago," TsGIAL, fond 1162, opis' 6, delo No. 196.

14. Veselovskii, "Vospominaniia," pp. 16–17; Pis'mo A. P. Zablotskago-Desiatovskago k Grafu P. D. Kiselevu, 29 iiulia 1839g., TsGIAL, fond 958, opis' 1, delo No. 223/1; Pis'mo A. P. Zablotskago-Desiatovskago k M. P. Pogodinu, 3 marta 1841g., ORGBL, fond M. P. Pogodina/II, kartonka 12, papka 26.

15. D. A. Miliutin, "Moi starcheskie vospominaniia," ORGBL, fond 169, kartonka 12, papka 1/120–122.

16. Raeff, *Speransky*, pp. 320–44.

17. Wortman, *Development of a Russian Legal Consciousness*, p. 121.

18. A. P. Zablotskii-Desiatovskii, "Statisticheskoe obozrenie gosudarst-vennykh i obshchestvennykh povinnostei dokhodov i raskhodov Kievskoi gubernii," (1851–1852gg.), TsGIAL, fond 940, opis' 1, delo No. 69/1.

19. Ibid., delo No. 69/2.

20. "Delo o sluzhbe I. P. Arapetova," TsGIAL, fond 1349, opis' 3, delo No. 94.

21. "Delo o sluzhbe A. K. Girsa," TsGIAL, fond 1284, opis' 31, delo No. 52.

22. "Delo o sluzhbe K. K. Grota," TsGIAL, fond 1162, opis' 6, delo No. 154.

23. "Delo o sluzhbe V. A. Insarskago," TsGIAL, fond 1284, opis' 50, delo No. 260.

24. "Delo o sluzhbe A. F. Shtakel'berga," TsGIAL, fond 1349, opis' 3, delo No. 2535.

25. "Delo o sluzhbe K. S. Veselovskago," TsGIAL, fond 1349, opis' 3, delo No. 391; Veselovskii, "Vospominaniia," pp. 16–19.

26. Insarskii, *Zapiski*, I: 65.

27. "Pamiati A. P. Zablotskago," *RS*, XXXIII (1882): 540.

28. Zablotskii-Desiatovskii, "Statisticheskoe obozrenie," TsGIAL, fond 940, opis' 1, delo No. 62/3.

29. Ibid.

30. For a detailed summary of these laws see Druzhinin, *Gosudarstvennye krest'iane*, I: 476–610.

31. Quoted in "Graf P. D. Kiselev," *RBS*, VIII: 713.

32. "Delo o sluzhbe A. P. Zablotskago-Desiatovskago," TsGIAL, fond 1162, opis' 6, delo No. 196; "Delo o sluzhbe N. A. Miliutina," TsGIAL, fond 1162, opis' 6, delo No. 335; Veselovskii, "Vospominaniia," pp. 20–21; Druzhi-nin, *Gosudarstvennye krest'iane*, I: 323.

33. Zablotskii-Desiatovskii, "Vzgliad na istoriiu gosudarstvennykh imu-shchestv v Rossii," (1856g.), TsGIAL, fond 940, opis' 1, delo No. 12/66.

34. Zablotskii-Desiatovskii, "O krepostnom sostoianii v Rossii," in *Graf P. D. Kiselev*, IV: 317.

35. Ibid., pp. 291, 287, 327.

36. Ibid., pp. 322–25.

37. Ibid., p. 308.

38. Ibid., p. 309–11.

39. Zablotskii-Desiatovskii, "Statisticheskoe obozrenie," TsGIAL, fond 940, opis' 1, delo No. 69/4.

40. "Otpusk s otnosheniia k redaktoru *Zemledel'cheskoi Gazety* E. A. Engel'-gardtu ot Tret'ego Departamenta Ministerstva Gosudarstvennykh Imushchestv, ot 31 dekabria 1840g." TsGIAL, fond 398, opis' 16, delo No. 4852/1.

41. "Vypiska iz zhurnala Uchenago Komiteta Ministerstva Gosudarstven-nykh Imushchestv, ot 26 oktiabria 1854g." TsGIAL, fond 398, opis' 16, delo No. 4852/68–70.

42. A. P. Zablotskii-Desiatovskii and Prince V. F. Odoevskii, eds., *Sel'skoe chtenie*, 4 vols., 7th ed. (St. Petersburg, 1843–1848), I: 17–18, 27–28, 54, 111.

43. A. G. Demen'tev, A. V. Zapadov, and M. S. Cherepakhov, eds., *Rus-skaia periodicheskaia pechat' (1702–1894)*, (Moscow, 1959), p. 307.

44. A. P. Zablotskii-Desiatovskii, "Khoziaistvennye aforizmy," *OZ,* LXII (January 1849), sect. 4, pp. 1–16; LXIII (April 1849), sect. 4, pp. 1–14.
45. *PSZ,* sobranie 1-oe, No. 24686, article 220.
46. D. A. Miliutin, *Vospominaniia Generala Fel'dmarshala Grafa Dmitriia Alekseevicha Miliutina* (Tomsk, 1919), pp. 4–6.
47. *Pamiatnaia knizhka kaluzhskoi gubernii za 1861g.* (Kaluga, 1861), p. 165.
48. W. Bruce Lincoln, *Nikolai Miliutin: An Enlightened Russian Bureaucrat of the Nineteenth Century* (Newtonville, Mass., 1977), pp. 4–5.
49. Pis'mo N. A. Miliutina k D. A. Miliutinu, 17 avgusta 1834g., ORGBL, fond 169, kartonka 69, papka No. 3.
50. Lincoln, *Nikolai Miliutin,* pp. 4–6.
51. Pis'mo P. D. Kiseleva k E. D. Kiselevoi, 1815g., ORGBL, fond 129, kartonka 11, papka 42; D. A. Miliutin, "Moi starcheskie vospominaniia," ORGBL, fond 169, kartonka 12, papka 1/13–14.
52. Lincoln, *Nikolai Miliutin,* pp. 63–68.
53. Ibid., p. 15.
54. Pis'mo N. A. Miliutina k D. A. Miliutinu, 10 avgusta 1839g., ORGBL, fond 169, kartonka 69, papka 5.
55. A. E. Tsimmerman, "Vospominaniia Generala A. E. Tsimmermana," ORGBL, fond 325, kartonka 1, papka 1/176–77.
56. Pis'mo N. A. Miliutina k D. A. Miliutinu, 14 fevralia 1837g., ORGBL, fond 169, kartonka 69, papka 5.
57. Miliutin's inability to engage in this sort of charming, vicious intrigue always helped to set him apart from the inner circle of Russian policy-makers, even at the height of his career. Indeed, it nearly cost him his position at one point in 1858, when he could not fight Court intriguers with their own weapons.
58. Kniaz' P. A. Viazemskii, *Zapisnye knizhki* (Moscow, 1963), p. 283.
59. Wortman, *Development of a Russian Legal Consciousness,* p. 156.
60. Quoted in ibid., p. 152.
61. Lincoln, *Nikolai Miliutin,* pp. 16–19.
62. "Delo o sluzhbe N. A. Miliutina," TsGIAL, fond 1162, opis' 6, delo No. 335; *PSZ,* sobranie 2-oe, No. 15432.
63. N. A. Miliutin, "O preobrazovanii gorodovago obshchestvennago ustroistva," 7 aprelia 1844g., TsGIAL, fond 1287, opis' 37, delo No. 738/3.
64. Ibid., delo No. 738/3; Lincoln, "Genesis of an 'Enlightened' Bureaucracy," p. 326.
65. N. A. Miliutin, "Ob ustroistve gorodskikh obshchestv v Rossii, 1842–1846gg.," TsGIAL, fond 869, opis' 1, delo No. 258/81–83.
66. "Ofitsial'noe otnoshenie Ministra Vnutrennikh Del, 14 oktiabria 1843g.," TsGIAL, fond 1287, opis' 37, delo No. 737/283.
67. Miliutin, "Ob ustroistve gorodskikh obshchestv v Rossii," delo No. 258/77–78
68. N. A. Miliutin, "Glavnye osnovaniia dlia nachertaniia proekta ob obshchestvennom ustroistve stolichnago goroda Sanktpeterburga," 7 aprelia 1844g., TsGIAL, fond 1287, opis' 1, delo No. 738/54; Miliutin, "O preobrazovanii gorodovago obshchestvennago ustroistva," delo No. 738/26.
69. Lincoln, *Nikolai Miliutin,* pp. 25–27.
70. W. Bruce Lincoln, "N. A. Miliutin and the St. Petersburg Municipal Act of 1846: A Study in Reform under Nicholas I," *Slavic Review,* XXXIII (March 1974): 60–63.

71. "Vedomost' o deistviiakh otsenochnykh komissiiakh uchrezhdennykh v Sanktpeterburge," (1843g.), TsGIAL, fond 869, opis' 1, delo No. 343/34–36.

72. Lincoln, *Nikolai Miliutin*, pp. 45–47.

73. "Zamechanie Sanktpeterburgskago gorodskago golovy i pervostateinykh kuptsov na proekt komiteta ob obshchestvennom ustroistve stolitsy," TsGIAL, fond 1287, opis' 37, delo No. 738/118–22.

74. Pis'mo N. A. Miliutina k P. D. Kiselevu, 4 marta 1858g., ORGBL, fond 129, kartonka 17, papka 55; Pis'mo N. A. Miliutina k D. A. Miliutinu, 19 aprelia 1858g., ORGBL, fond 169, kartonka 69, papka 10.

75. "Po proektu ob ustroistve S.-Peterburgskoi stolitsy," TsGIAL, fond 1287, opis' 37, delo No. 738a/277–81.

76. Ibid., delo No. 738a/281–86.

77. "Ob"iasnenie k zamechaniiam pred"iavlennym v Obshchem Sobranii Gosudarstvennago Soveta," 1 aprelia 1845g., TsGIAL, fond 1287, opis' 37, delo No. 738a/288–89.

78. "Vypiska iz Zhurnala Soedinennykh Departamentov Zakonov i Ekonomii Gosudarstvennago Soveta, 5-go maia 1845-go goda," TsGIAL, fond 1287, opis' 37, delo No. 738a/372–78.

79. I. I. Mikhailov, "Kazanskaia starina (iz vospominanii Iv. Iv. Mikhailova)," *RS,* C (October 1899): 102.

80. Michel Crozier, *The Bureaucratic Phenomenon* (Chicago, 1967), p. 195.

81. N. D. Chechulin, ed., *Nakaz Imperatritsy Ekateriny II, dannyi komissii o sochinenii proekta novago ulozheniia* (St. Petersburg, 1907), articles 148, 153.

82. N. M. Kolmakov, "Staryi sud," *RS,* LII (December 1866): 533–34.

83. G. A. Dzhanshiev, *Epokha velikikh reform* (St. Petersburg, 1905), p. 604.

84. Ibid.

85. Ibid., p. 602.

86. "Sergei Ivanovich Zarudnyi," *RBS,* VII, p. 241; Dzhanshiev, *Epokha velikikh reform,* p. 602.

87. "Sergei Ivanovich Zarudnyi," *RBS,* p. 241.

88. Quoted in Wortman, *Development of a Russian Legal Consciousness,* p. 232.

89. Dzhanshiev, *Epokha velikikh reform,* p. 602.

90. Quotes from Wortman, *Development of a Russian Legal Consciousness,* p. 232.

91. "Delo o sluzhbe S. I. Zarudnago," TsGIAL, fond 1405, opis' 528, delo No. 83.

92. D. Shubin-Pozdeev, "K kharacteristike lichnosti i sluzhebnoi deiatel'nosti S. I. Zarudnago," *RS,* LVII (February 1888): 479.

93. Dzhanshiev, *Epokha velikikh reform,* p. 603.

94. Quoted in Wortman, *Development of a Russian Legal Consciousness,* p. 183.

95. "Delo o sluzhbe S. I. Zarudnago," TsGIAL, fond 1405, opis 528, delo No. 83.

96. P. M. Maikov, *Vtoroe otdelenie sobstvennoi e. i. v. kantseliarii, 1826–1882: Istoricheskii ocherk* (St. Petersburg, 1906), pp. 332–36.

97. Quoted in Dzhanshiev, *Epokha velikikh reform,* p. 604.

98. Quoted in ibid.

99. "Delo o sluzhbe M. Kh. Reiterna," TsGIAL, fond 1162, opis' 6, delo No. 448; "Delo o sluzhbe S. I. Zarudnago," TsGIAL, fond 1405, opis' 528, delo No. 83.

100. "Delo o sluzhbe M. N. Liuboshchinskago," TsGIAL, fond 1162, opis' 6, delo No. 305.
101. "Pamiati A. P. Zablotskago," *RS,* XXXIII (1882): 520.
102. Kolmakov, "Ocherki i vospominaniia," LXXI, p. 131.
103. Quoted in "Sergei Ivanovich Zarudnyi," *RBS,* p. 242.
104. Ibid.
105. Quoted in G. A. Dzhanshiev, *S. I. Zarudnyi i sudebnaia reforma. Istoriko-biograficheskii eskiz* (Moscow, 1889), p. 13.
106. Prince D. A. Obolenskii, "Moi vospominaniia o velikoi kniagine Elene Pavlovne," *RS,* CXXXVII (March 1909): 505.
107. Zarudnyi, "Pis'mo opytnago chinovnika," pp. 543–46.
108. Ibid., p. 543.
109. Quoted in Wortman, *Development of a Russian Legal Consciousness,* p. 152.
110. Quoted in ibid.
111. Zarudnyi, "Pis'mo opytnago chinovnika," p. 543.
112. Ibid., pp. 543–45.
113. "Sergei Ivanovich Zarudnyi," *RBS,* p. 242; Shubin-Pozdeev, "K kharakteristike lichnosti," p. 481.
114. Kolmakov, "Ocherki i vospominaniia," p. 130.
115. Wortman, *Development of a Russian Legal Consciousness,* p. 184.
116. Shubin-Pozdeev, "K kharakteristike lichnosti," p. 481.
117. Ibid.
118. Wortman, *Development of a Russian Legal Consciousness,* pp. 192–93.
119. Dzhanshiev, *S. I. Zarudnyi i sudebnaia reforma,* p. 25.
120. Kolmakov, "Ocherki i vospominaiia," pp. 125–29.
121. Ibid., pp. 122–23.
122. Prince V. P. Meshcherskii, *Moi vospominaniia,* 2 vols. (St. Petersburg, 1897), I: 96–97.
123. Wortman, *Development of a Russian Legal Consciousness,* p. 188.
124. For a discussion of this, see "Obshchaia ob"iasnitel'naia zapiska k proektu novago ustava sudoproizvodstva grazhdanskago," *Materialy po preobrazovaniiu sudebnoi chasti* (copies in TsGIAL, GPB, and ORGBL), No. 2, pt. 1, pp. 74–78.
125. Ibid., pp. 194–95; Wortman, *Development of a Russian Legal Consciousness,* pp. 160–61; F. B. Kaiser, *Die russische Justizreform von 1864: Zur Geschichte der russischen Justiz von Katherina II bis 1917* (Leiden, 1972), pp. 155–268.
126. Wortman, *Development of a Russian Legal Consciousness,* pp. 162–63.
127. "Sergei Ivanovich Zarudnyi," *RBS,* p. 143.
128. Wortman, *Development of a Russian Legal Consciousness,* p. 194.
129. Ibid., p. 121.
130. Ibid., p. 148.
131. Quoted in ibid. p. 152.
132. Kharytonov, "Iz vospominanii," p. 117.
133. Pis'mo N. A. Miliutina k D. A. Miliutinu, 25 marta 1837g., ORBGL, fond 169, kartonka 69, papka 5.
134. D. A. Miliutin, *Vospominaniia,* p. 81.
135. "Pamiati A. P. Zablotskago," p. 540.
136. See, for example, Nikolai Miliutin's very brief diary, "Dnevnik N. A. Miliutina," TsGIAL, fond 869, opis' 1, delo No. 64/1–3.

137. Pis'mo N. A. Miliutina k D. A. Miliutinu, 25 marta 1837g., ORGBL, fond 169, kartonka 69, papka 5.

138. Quoted in N. V. Riasanovsky, *A Parting of Ways: Government and the Educated Public in Russia, 1801–1855* (Oxford, 1976), pp. 249–50.

139. M. F. de Pule, "Nikolai Ivanovich Vtorov," *RA*, No. 8 (August 1877), p. 428.

140. P. I. Mel'nikov-Pecherskii, "Vospominaniia o V. I. Dale," *RV*, CIV (1873): 310.

141. "Delo o sluzhbe V. I. Dalia," TsGIAL, fond 1349, opis' 3, delo No. 646.

142. See *Adres'-Kalendar ili obshchii shtat rossiiskoi imperii* (St. Petersburg, 1842–1852), for a full listing of the personnel in the central offices of the Ministry of Internal Affairs.

143. V. V. Stasov, "Uchilische pravovedeniia sorok let tomu nazad, v 1836–1842gg.," *RS*, XXX (February 1881): 421.

144. Quoted in Seleznev, *Istoricheskii ocherk* (St. Petersburg, 1861), p. 386.

145. V. N. Rozental', "Moskovskii kruzhok A. V. Stankevicha v 1855–1857gg.," in Nechkina, *Revoliutsionnaia situatsiia v Rossii v 1857–1861gg.*, p. 374.

146. Semevskii, *Krest'ianskii vopros*, II: 347.

147. W. Bruce Lincoln, "The Circle of M. V. Butashevich-Petrashevskii: Some Comments about the Social and Intellectual Climate of St. Petersburg in the 1840s," *The Australian Journal of Politics and History*, XIX (December 1973): 368.

148. D. A. Miliutin, *Vospominaniia*, p. 66.

149. K. S. Veselovskii, "Vospominaniia o tsarskosel'skom litsee, 1832–1838," *RS*, CIV (October 1900): 4.

150. K. K. Arsen'ev, "Vospominaniia K. K. Arsen'eva ob uchilishche pravovedeniia, 1849–1855gg.," *RS*, L (April 1886): 215.

151. Valuev, "Otryvok iz zamechanii," TsGIAL, fond 908, opis' 1, delo No. 24/29.

152. Terner, *Vospominaniia*, I: 67–69; Shumakher, "Pozdnie vospominaniia," *VE*, CXCVI: 113.

153. A. N. Iakhontov, "Vospominaniia tsarskosel'skago litseista 1832–1838gg.," *RS*, LX (October 1888): 103.

154. Quoted in Veselovskii, "Vospominaniia," p. 21.

155. Published in Kobeko, *Imperatorskii tsarskosel'skii litsei,* p. 420.

156. Published in Seleznev, *Istoricheskii ocherk,* pp. 387–88.

157. V. V. Stasov, "Uchilishche pravovedeniia sorok let tomu nazad, 1836–1842gg.," *RS*, XXIX (December 1880): 1036.

158. Quoted in Wortman, *Development of a Russian Legal Consciousness,* p. 211.

159. Quoted in Georgii Siuzor, *Ko dniu LXXV iubileia imperatorskago uchilishcha pravovedeniia, 1835–1910* (St. Petersburg, 1910), p. 35.

160. Kharytonov, "Iz vospominanii," pp. 113–14.

161. Ibid., p. 114; A. V. Golovnin, "Kratkii ocherk deistvii velikago kniazia Konstantina Nikolaevicha po Morskomu Vedomstvu so vremeni vstupleniia v upravlenie onym po ianvar' 1858g.," GPB, fond 208, delo No. 2/271.

162. "Dnevnik A. I. Artem'eva, l iiunia–31 dekabria 1855g.," GPB, fond 37, delo No. 157/71; Kolmakov, "Ocherki i vospominaniia," LXXI (July 1891): 130; Shubin-Pozdeev, "K kharakteristike lichnosti," p. 481.

163. "Svedeniia o N. I. Vtorove za vremia sluzhby ego v Ministerstve Vnutrennikh Del s 1844 po 1862gg.," GPB, fond 163, delo No. 56/2.

164. Arsen'ev, "Vospominaniia," p. 215.

165. Shumakher, "Pozdnie vospominaniia," p. 114.

166. Obolenskii, "Moi vospominaniia," *RS*, CXXXVII: 506.

167. See especially "Ofitsial'nye pis'ma nachal'nika mogilevskoi gubernii po gubernskomu pravlenii Gospodinu Ministru Vnutrennikh Del, 26 iiunia i 30 noiabria 1846g., i 14 ianvaria, 20 sentiabria, i 31 oktiabria 1848g.," TsGIAL, fond 1287, opis' 39, delo No. 28/23–25, 28–31, 36–41, 42–43, 48–40.

Chapter 3

1. Riasanovsky, *A Parting of Ways*, pp. 248–90.

2. B. N. Chicherin, *Moskva sorokovykh godov: Vospominaniia Borisa Nikolaevicha Chicherina* (Moscow, 1929), p. 114.

3. Pis'mo I. S. Aksakova k N. A. Miliutinu, 6 oktiabria 1852g., TsGIAL, fond 869, opis' 1, delo No. 818/30.

4. Martin Malia, *Alexander Herzen and the Birth of Russian Socialism, 1812–1855* (Cambridge, Mass., 1961), pp. 389–90.

5. B. N. Chicherin, *Moskovskii Universitet: Vospominaniia Borisa Nikolaevicha Chicherina* (Moscow, 1929), p. 5.

6. Pis'mo I. S. Aksakova k N. A. Miliutinu, 6 oktiabria 1852g., TsGIAL, fond 869, opis' 1, delo No. 818/30.

7. I. S. Turgenev, *Sobranie sochinenii*, 10 vols. (Moscow, 1961–1962), I: 224.

8. Chicherin, *Moskva sorokovykh godov*, p. 6.

9. See, for example, E. Brown, *Stankevich and His Moscow Circle, 1830–1840* (Stanford, 1961), and numerous Soviet studies of the *Sovremennik* and Petrashevskii circles, especially M. Aronson and S. Reiser, *Literaturnye kruzhki i salony* (Leningrad, 1929).

10. D. A. Miliutin, *Vospominaniia*, p. xxi.

11. P. A. Valuev, *Dnevnik P. A. Valueva, Ministra vnutrennikh del*, P. A. Zaionchkovskii, ed., 2 vols. (Moscow, 1961), I: 10–11.

12. Nikolai Miliutin died before he could write memoirs, and Zablotskii devoted his twilight years to a lengthy biography of Kiselev which appeared as *Graf P. D. Kiselev i ego vremia*, 4 vols. (St. Petersburg, 1882).

13. See, for example, Miliutin's letters to his brother Dmitrii in ORGBL, fond 169, kartonka 169, papka No. 9.

14. Pis'ma N. A. Miliutina k A. K. Girsu, 1842–1854gg., TsGIAL, fond 869, opis' 1, delo No. 880.

15. For comments about the standard of living among low-level civil servants, see P. I. Nebolsin, "Biudzhety peterburgskikh chinovnikov," pp. 244–50; Kharytonov, "Iz vospominanii," pp. 116–17; Terner, *Vospominaniia*, I: 68.

16. D. A. Miliutin, "Moi starcheskie vospominaniia," ORGBL, fond 169, kartonka 12, papka No. 1/122.

17. Pis'mo N. A. Miliutina k D. A. Miliutinu, 8 ianvaria 1837g., ORGBL, fond 169, kartonka 69, papka 5.

18. Malia, *Alexander Herzen*, pp. 49–52.

19. Pis'mo N. A. Miliutina k D. A. Miliutinu, 14 fevralia 1837g., ORGBL, fond 169, kartonka 69, papka No. 5.

20. D. A. Miliutin, "Moi starcheskie vospominaniia," ORGBL, fond 169, kartonka 12, papka 1/155.
21. Veselovskii, "Vospominaniia," pp. 27–29.
22. D. A. Miliutin, "Moi starcheskie vospominaniia," ORGBL, fond 169, kartonka 12, papka No. 4/91–92.
23. Ibid., papka No. 4/174–75.
24. A. E. Tsimmerman, "Vospominaniia," ORGBL, fond 325, kartonka 1, papka 1/210.
25. Semenov-Tian-Shanskii, *Memuary*, I: 207.
26. "Pamiati A. P. Zablotskago," p. 540.
27. Obolenskii, "Moi vospominaniia," CXXXVII: 505–6.
28. D. A. Miliutin, "Moi starcheskie vospominaniia," ORGBL, fond 169, kartonka 12, papka 4/45.
29. Ibid., papka 4/60; A. E. Tsimmerman, "Vospominaniia," ORGBL, fond 325, kartonka 1, papka No. 1/209.
30. Quoted in P. S. Popov, ed., *Pis'ma k A. V. Druzhininu, 1850–1863gg.* (Moscow, 1948), p. 11.
31. Ibid., p. 10; Tsimmerman, "Vospominaniia," ORGBL, fond 325, kartonka 1, papka No. 1/209.
32. Tsimmerman, "Vospominaniia," ORGBL, fond 325, kartonka 1, papka No. 1/209.
33. "Formuliarnyi spisok o sluzhbe Redaktora Gorodskago Otdeleniia Khoziaistvennago Departamenta Ministerstva Vnutrennikh Del Nadvornago Sovetnika K. D. Kavelina," TsGALI, fond 264, opis' 1, delo No. 1/8–9.
34. Pis'mo K. D. Kavelina k T. N. Granovskomu, 5 sentiabria 1848g., in Levin, "K. D. Kavelin," p. 596.
35. P. V. Annenkov, *Literaturnye vospominaniia* (Moscow, 1960), p. 532.
36. D. A. Miliutin, "Moi starcheskie vospominaniia," ORGBL, fond 169, kartonka 12, papka No. 4/91–92; Annenkov, *Literaturnye vospominaniia*, p. 532; Chicherin, *Moskva sorokovykh godov*, pp. 125–26.
37. "Pis'ma K. D. Kavelina k T. N. Granovskomu," *LN*, LXVII (1959): 591–614; Pis'ma N. A. Miliutina k M. Pogodinu, ORGBL, fond 231, kartonka 2, papka 2; Pis'ma K. D. Kavelina k M. Pogodinu, ORGBL, fond 231, kartonka 2, papka 14.
38. "Nikolai Ivanovich Nadezhdin," *RBS*, IX, pp. 19–20.
39. Ibid., p. 24.
40. Ibid.
41. "Konstantin Alekseevich Nevolin," *RBS*, IX, p. 179.
42. Siuzor, *Ko dniu LXXV iubileia*, p. 15.
43. V. V. Grigor'ev, *Imperatorskii S.-Peterburgskii Universitet v techenii pervykh piatidesiati let ego sushchestvovaniia* (St. Petersburg, 1870), pp. 155–57.
44. D. A. Miliutin, "Moi starcheskie vospominaniia," ORGBL, fond 169, kartonka 12, papka 4/92.
45. "Vladimir Ivanovich Dal'," *RBS*, VI, pp. 42–43.
46. V. I. Dal', "Materialy dlia istorii khlystovskoi i skopicheskoi eresei," *Chtenie obshchestva istorii i drevnostei Rossiiskikh*, bk. 4 (1872).
47. Mel'nikov-Pecherskii, "Vospominaniia o V. I. Dale," p. 312.
48. Grigor'ev, *Imperatorskii S.-Peterburgskii Universitet*, pp. 379–80.
49. N. P. Barsukov, *Zhizn' i trudy M. P. Pogodina*, 22 vols. (St. Petersburg, 1888–1906), VII: 320; "Vasilii Vasil'evich Grigor'ev," *Entsiklopedicheskii slovar' Brokgauza-Eifrona*, Vol. IXa, pp. 723–24.

50. "Pavel Stepanovich Savel'ev," *RBS,* XVII, pp. 25–27.

51. "Ivan Petrovich Sakharov," *RBS,* XVIII, pp. 211–14.

52. "Valerian Valerievich Skripitsyn," *RBS,* XVIII, pp. 618–19.

53. D. A. Miliutin, "Moi starcheskie vospominaniia," ORGBL, fond 169, kartonka 12, papka No. 4/92.

54. A. V. Golovnin, "Zapiski i primechaniia (ot vospominanii detstva do oseni 1850g.)," GPB, fond 208, delo No. 1/89–91.

55. Zotov, "Peterburg v sorokovykh godakh," XXXIX: 33; Kharytonov, "Iz vospominanii," p. 114.

56. Obolenskii, "Moi vospominaniia," CXXXVII: 505.

57. D. A. Miliutin, "Moi starcheskie vospominaniia," ORGBL, fond 169, kartonka 12, papka 4/91–92; A. N. Pypin, "U A. A. Kraevskago," in N. L. Brodskii, ed., *Literaturnye salony i kruzhki: Pervaia polovina XIX veka* (Moscow-Leningrad, 1930), pp. 536–37.

58. A. V. Starchevskii, "Odin iz zabytykh zhurnalistov (iz vospominanii starago literatora)," *IV,* XXIII (1886): 379.

59. K. D. Kavelin, "Vospominaniia o Belinskom," in *Sobranie sochinenii K. D. Kavelina,* 4 vols. (St. Petersburg, 1898–1899), III: col. 1097.

60. A. Ia. Panaeva, *Vospominaniia* (Moscow, 1956), p. 360.

61. Quoted in I. Iampol'skii, "Literaturnye deiatel'nosti I. I. Panaeva," in I. I. Panaeva, *Literaturnye vospominaniia* (Moscow, 1950), p. vii.

62. Malia, *Alexander Herzen,* p. 211; Herbert Bowman, *Vissarion Belinskii, 1811–1848: A Study in the Origins of Social Criticism in Russia* (Cambridge, Mass., 1954), pp. 127–30.

63. A. G. Dement'ev, *Ocherki po istorii russkoi zhurnalistiki, 1840–1850gg.* (Moscow-Leningrad, 1951), p. 61.

64. For a more complete listing of those who attended Panaev's Saturday gatherings during the early 1840s, see I. I. Panaev's *Literaturnye vospominaniia* (Leningrad, 1928), pp. 390–446; Panaeva, *Vospominaniia,* pp. 75–125; K. D. Kavelin, "Vospominaniia o V. G. Belinskom," cols. 1084–94.

65. Panaev, *Literaturnye vospominaniia,* p. 392.

66. Panaeva, *Vospominaniia,* p. 97.

67. Annenkov, *Literaturnye vospominaniia,* pp. 209–13.

68. D. A. Miliutin, "Moi starcheskie vospominaniia," ORGBL, fond 169, kartonka 12, papka 4/91–92.

69. K. D. Kavelin, "Vospominaniia o V. G. Belinskom," col. 1084.

70. Panaeva, *Vospominaniia,* pp. 188, 200–202.

71. *Zapiski imperatorskago russkago geograficheskogo obshchestva,* Vol. II (1847): 324–35; Vol. III (1849): 2–14; *Vestnik imperatorskago russkago geograficheskago obshchestva, 1851–1855gg., passim.*

72. Tsimmerman, "Vospominaniia," ORGBL, fond 325, kartonka 1, papka No. 2/67.

73. Baron M. A. Korf, "Dnevnik barona M. A. Korfa za 1848g.," TsGAOR, fond 728, opis' 1, delo No. 1817/xi/186.

74. "Pis'mo K. D. Kavelina k T. N. Granovskomu, 5 sentiabria 1848g.," *LN,* LXVII (1959): 596.

75. Quoted in A. S. Vucinich, *Science and Russian Culture: A History to 1860* (Stanford, 1960), p. 295.

76. Ibid.

77. Ibid., pp. 296–99.

78. Ibid., pp. 299–305.

79. Ibid., p. 301.
80. Especially F. P. Litke, I. F. Kruzenstern, and Baron F. P. Vrangel.
81. Most prominent among them were von Baer, Struve, G. P. Gelmersen, and P. I. Keppen.
82. Including especially F. F. Berg, M. P. Vronchenko, and M. N. Murav'ev.
83. K. I. Arsen'ev, A. I. Levshin, Prince V. F. Odoevskii, and V. I. Dal'.
84. P. P. Semenov-Tian-Shanskii, *Istoriia poluvekovoi deiatel'nosti imperatorskago russkago geograficheskago obshchestva, 1845–1895gg.*, 3 vols. (St. Petersburg, 1896), I: 4–5; L. S. Berg, *Vsesoiuznoe geograficheskoe obshchestvo za sto let* (Moscow-Leningrad, 1946), pp. 24–29.
85. See Litke's letter of September 1845 to Baron Vrangel, quoted in A. I. Alekseev, *Fedor Petrovich Litke* (Moscow, 1970), p. 197.
86. Semenov, *Istoriia poluvekovoi deiatel'nosti*, I: 1–3.
87. Dmitrii Miliutin discusses the importance of Golovnin's role in "Moi starcheskie vospominaniia," ORGBL, fond 169, kartonka 12, papka 4/92–93.
88. Golovnin, "Zapiski i primechaniia," GPB, fond 208, delo No. 1/2–5.
89. Golovnin, "Zapiski i primechaniia," GPB, fond 208, delo No. 1/8–9.
90. Ibid., delo No. 1/11–16.
91. These practices are vividly described in "Pesn' pravovedov," dating from the 1840s:

> Venera, Venera
> Skazhi ty skorei
> Kakaia manera
> Chtob et' veselei?—
> Proshla vsiu Evropu
> Skazali vezde:
> Davat' cherez zhopu
> Priatnei pizde!—
> Tak nuzhno-l' s pizdami
> Znakomit'sia tut?
> Tovarishchi sami
> Daiut i ebut,
> Priiatnoe delo
> Drug drugu davat'
> I zhopkoiu smelo
> Pred khuem viliat'

Published in *Russkii erot. Ne dlia dam* (Geneva, 1879), p. 65.
92. Golovnin, "Zapiski i primechaniia," GPB, fond 208, delo No. 1/17–20.
93. "Delo o sluzhbe A. V. Golovnina," TsGIAL, fond 1162, opis' 6, delo No. 133; Golovnin, "Zapiski i primechaniia," GPB, fond 208, delo No. 1/32.
94. Golovnin, "Zapiski i primechaniia," GPB, fond 208, delo No. 1/32.
95. Ibid., delo No. 1/57–59.
96. Ibid., delo No. 1/89–92.
97. Semenov, *Istoriia poluvekovoi deiatel'nosti*, I: 8.
98. Alekseev, *Fedor Petrovich Litke*, p. 197.
99. Quoted in ibid., pp. 200–201.
100. See, for example, Semenov, *Istoriia poluvekovoi deiatel'nosti*, I: 57–63; Alekseev, *Fedor Petrovich Litke*, pp. 203–16; Berg, *Vsesoiuznoe geograficheskoe obshchestvo*, pp. 49–51.
101. These were D. A. Miliutin, N. A. Miliutin, I. P. Arapetov, K. S. Veselovskii, Iu. A. Gagemeister, A. K. Girs, A. A. Kraevskii, P. I. Mel'nikov,

I. I. Panaev, V. S. Poroshin, Ia. V. Khanykov, D. P. Khrushchov, V. V. Grigor'ev, K. A. Nevolin, P. S. Savel'ev, I. P. Sakharov, and S. M. Usov. All were members of the circles of Miliutin or of Nadezhdin and Nevolin, or they were friendly with them. These names are taken from *Zapiski imperatorskago russkago geograficheskago obshchestva* (1847), Vol. II, *passim*.

102. V. A. Miliutin, K. D. Kavelin, N. A. Zherebtsov, S. M. Zhukovskii, Prince D. A. Obolenskii, A. N. Popov, and M. Kh. Reitern. *Zapiski imperatorskago russkago geograficheskago obshchestva* (1849), Vol. III, *passim*.

103. A. V. Nikitenko, *Zapiski i dnevnik, 1826–1877*, 2 vols. (St. Petersburg, 1892), I: 577.

104. Quoted in Alekseev, *Fedor Petrovich Litke*, p. 203.

105. Originally, M. N. Murav'ev had been named to the committee, but he had resigned. Poroshin was named in his stead.

106. See "Otdel'noe mnenie D. A. i N. A. Miliutinykh i V. S. Poroshina na proekt Ustava Obshchestva," i "Doklad Soveta Russkago Geograficheskago Obshchestva," in Semenov, *Istoriia poluvekovoi deiatel'nosti*, III: 1320–22.

107. Alekseev, *Fedor Petrovich Litke*, p. 210.

108. D. A. Miliutin, "Moi starcheskie vospominaniia," ORGBL, fond 169, kartonka 12, papka 4/98.

109. N. A. Miliutin, "Predmety, na koi preimushchestvenno sleduet obratit' vnimaniia pri predstoiashchem peresmotre Ustava Russkago Geograficheskago Obshchestva," TsGIAL, fond 869, opis' 1, delo No. 769/37.

110. Tsimmerman, "Vospominaniia," ORGBL, fond 325, kartonka 1, papka 2/66.

111. Alekseev, *Fedor Petrovich Litke*, p. 211.

112. N. A. Miliutin, "O pozhertvovanii v pol'zi Russkago Geograficheskago Obshchestva," (aprel' 1847g.), TsGIAL, fond 869, opis' 1, delo No. 770/1–2.

113. D. A. Miliutin, "Vospominaniia," ORGBL, fond 169, kartonka 12, papka 4/93–94.

114. These were K. S. Veselovskii, V. V. Grigor'ev, Zablotskii, M. A. Korkunov, N. I. Nadezhdin, D. A. Miliutin, N. A. Miliutin, A. D. Ozerskii, V. S. Poroshin, I. I. Sreznevskii, and Ia. V. Khanykov.

115. These were N. A. Miliutin, D. A. Miliutin, Zablotskii, A. K Girs, A. V. Golovnin, V. S. Poroshin, Iu. A. Gagemeister, I. P. Arapetov, K. D. Kavelin, E. I. Lamanskii, D. P. Khrushchov. *Vestnik imperatorskago russkago geograficheskago obshchestva, 1852–1855gg., passim*.

116. Senior scholars of the Uvarovian establishment never again would gain the dominance they had enjoyed when the society was founded, however. By the late 1850s, a number of Russians had achieved considerable reputations in scholarly circles and continued to hold positions of importance in the Society after 1857.

117. V. M. Kabuzan, "Revizii," *Sovetskaia istoricheskaia entsiklopediia*, Vol. XI, cols. 914–15; P. P. Semenov, *Istoriia poluvekovoi deiatel'nosti*, I: 124.

118. See Pintner, *Russian Economic Policy under Nicholas I*, for a study of Russian economic policy during this period.

119. P. P. Semenov, *Istoriia poluvekovoi deiatel'nosti*, I: 126–27.

120. Ibid., p. 129.

121. I. S. Aksakov, *Izsledovaniia o torgovle na ukrainskikh iarmakakh* (St. Petersburg, 1858); Semenov, *Istoriia poluvekovoi deiatel'nosti*, I: 108–15, 133–36.

122. Especially the two volumes of *Sbornik statisticheskikh svedenii o Rossii*, which appeared in 1851 and 1854, included a number of their most important

studies: Konstantin Veselovskii's "Prostranstvo i stepen' naselennosti Evropei-skoi Rossii," Mikhail Zablotskii's "Svedeniia o chisle zhitelei Rossii po sos-toianiiam," Andrei Zablotskii's lengthy study about "Dvizhenie narodonasele-niia Rossii s 1838 po 1847 goda," Nikolai Miliutin's "Chislo gorodskikh i zemledel'cheskikh poseleniia v Rossii," as well as his "Statisticheskaia karta, s oznacheniem stepeni naselennosti Evropeiskoi Rossii," Evgenii Lamanskii's studies about state credit, and Valuev's statistical studies about the Empire's Baltic provinces.

123. "Delo o sluzhbe Iu. A Gagemeistera," TsGIAL, fond 1349, opis' 3, delo No. 478; "Delo o sluzhbe E. I. Lamanskago," TsGIAL, fond 1349, opis' 3, delo No. 1234.

124. Terner, *Vospominaniia,* I: 169.

Chapter 4

1. "Obshchaia instruktsiia chinovnikam otriazhaemym dlia obozreniia gorodov," 12 maia 1845g., TsGIAL, fond 1287, opis' 39, delo No. 156/2–3.

2. Dzhanshiev, *Epokha velikikh reform,* p. 604.

3. K. S. Veselovskii, "Plan statisticheskago opisaniia Gosudarstvennykh Imushchestv i sosloviia sel'skikh zhitelei, sostoiashchago pod popechitel'-stvom Ministerstva Gosudarstvennykh Imushchestv," 1847g., TsGIAL, fond 398, opis' 11, delo No. 3635/35–36.

4. See, for example, Zaionchkovskii, *Pravitel'stvennyi apparat,* pp. 90–94, 132–33, 152–53.

5. Raeff, "Russian Autocracy and Its Officials," pp. 78–79.

6. Torke, "Das Russische Beamtentum," pp. 214–15.

7. Artem'ev, "Dnevnik, 1 iiunia–31 dekabria 1855g.," GPB, fond 37, delo No. 157–84.

8. A. V. Golovnin, "Raznitsa v napravlenii gosudarstvennoi deiatel'nosti v pervoi i vo vtoroi polovine nyneshnego tsarstvovaniia," mart, 1867g., GPB, fond 208, delo No. 236/12.

9. Valuev, "Duma russkago," p. 355.

10. Quoted in Wortman, *Development of a Russian Legal Consciousness,* p. 183.

11. Valuev, "Otryvok iz zamechanii o poriadke grazhdanskoi sluzhby," TsGIAL, fond 908, opis' 1, delo No. 24/26.

12. Lincoln, *Nicholas I,* pp. 92–98.

13. "Zhurnaly komiteta uchrezhdennago Vysochaishim reskriptom 6 de-kabria 1826 goda," *SIRIO,* LXXIV (1891): 264.

14. See especially "Doklady uchenago komiteta ministerstva gosudarst-vennykh imushchestv, 22 iiulia 1850g. i 2 maia 1852g.," and other documents in TsGIAL, fond 398, opis' 14, delo No. 4774/9–88.

15. Shumakher, "Pozdnie vospominaniia," p. 114.

16. See, for example, Kiselev's use of the term in 1816, and his recollections of Nicholas I's use of it in 1835. Zablotskii-Desiatovskii, *Graf P. D. Kiselev,* II: 208, IV: 197–98.

17. Zablotskii-Desiatovskii, "O krepostnom sostoianii v Rossii," in *Graf P. D. Kiselev,* IV: 271.

18. N. A. Miliutin, "O preobrazovanii gorodovago obshchestvennago us-troistva," 7 aprelia 1844g., TsGIAL, fond 1287, opis' 37, delo No. 738.

19. V. A. Tsie, "O tiurmakh i ikh preobrazovanii," (1847–1848gg.), GPB, fond 833, delo No. 259/2–3.

20. "O merakh k uspeshnemu proizvodstvu del po ustroistvu gorodskago khoziaistva," 4 fevralia 1849g., TsGIAL, fond 1152, opis' 4, delo No. 160/654.

21. Blum, *Lord and Peasant in Russia,* pp. 367–68.

22. Ibid., p. 368.

23. Field, *End of Serfdom,* pp. 32–35.

24. Zablotskii-Desiatovskii, "O krepostnom sostoianii v Rossii," p. 342; Emmons, *Russian Landed Gentry and the Emancipation of 1861,* pp. 30–39; Field, *End of Serfdom,* pp. 96–101.

25. K. I. Arsen'ev, "Zapiska o sostave i deistviiakh Statisticheskago Otdeleniia Soveta Ministerstva Vnutrennikh Del," 15 noiabria 1852g., TsGIAL, fond 869, opis 1, delo No. 91/2–3.

26. N. A. Miliutin, "Zapiska po vremennomu statisticheskomu komitetu," fevral', 1848g., TsGIAL, fond 869, opis 1, delo No. 90/5–7.

27. This point is convincingly demonstrated by A. A. Kizevetter in "Posadskaia obshchina v Rossii XVIII stoletiia," *Istoricheskie ocherki* (Moscow, 1912), pp. 242–43.

28. *PSZ,* sobranie 1-oe, No. 16188.

29. N. A. Miliutin, "O preobrazovanii gorodovago obshchestvennago ustroistva," 7 aprelia 1844g., TsGIAL, fond 1287, opis' 37, delo No. 738/10.

30. "Vsepoddanneishii raport Kazanskago Voennago Gubernatora o sdelannom im obozrenii vverennoi upravlenii ego gubernii"; "Vsepoddanneishie raporty Saratovskago, Tul'skago, i Poltavskago Gubernatorov o sdelannom imi obozrenii vverennoi upravlenii ikh guberniiakh," TsGIAL, fond 1287, opis' 37, delo No. 120/1–2, 6–7.

31. N. S. Kiniapina, *Politika russkago samoderzhaviia v oblasti promyshlennosti (20–50kh gody XIX v.)* (Moscow, 1968), pp. 414–15; P. G. Ryndziunskii, *Gorodskoe grazhdanstvo doreformennoi Rossii* (Moscow, 1958), pp. 182–84.

32. Reginald Zelnik, *Labor and Society in Tsarist Russia: The Factory Workers of St. Petersburg, 1855–1870* (Stanford, 1971), p. 24. See also Pintner, *Russian Economic Policy under Nicholas I,* pp. 98–101.

33. Quoted in Zelnik, *Labor and Society,* p. 64.

34. Varadinov, *Istoriia,* III (bk. 2): 703.

35. Ibid.

36. Ibid., pp. 703–5.

37. N. A. Miliutin, "Ob ustroistve gorodskikh obshchestv v Rossii 1842–1846gg.," TsGIAL, fond 869, opis' 1, delo No. 258/77–78.

38. Ibid., delo No. 258/94–97.

39. "Delo po otnosheniiu Khoziaistvennago Departamenta v Statisticheskoe Otdelenie, o tom, kakie goroda i kogda imenno poluchili Vysochaishe utverzhdennye plany," sentiabr'–oktiabr', 1849g., TsGIAL, fond 1287, opis' 39, delo No. 824; "Donesenie chinovnika osobykh poruchenii Nadvornago Sovetnika A. K. Girsa Ego Vysokoprevoskhoditel'stvu Gospodinu Ministru Vnutrennikh Del," 17 avgusta 1844g., TsGIAL, fond 1287, opis' 39, delo No. 25/53–55.

40. See, for example, "Donesenie chinovnika khoziaistvennago departamenta Kollezhskago Asessora Veselovskago Ego Vysokoprevoskhoditel'stvu Gospodinu Ministru Vnutrennikh Del, 16 maia 1843g.," TsGIAL, fond 1287, opis' 39, delo No. 28/4–6.

41. See, for example, "Ofitsial'noe pis'mo ot N. A. Miliutina chinovniku

osobykh poruchenii Nadvornomu Sovetniku Girsu," 30 oktiabria 1843g., TsGIAL, fond 1287, opis' 39, delo No. 25/34–37.

42. "Ofitsial'noe pis'mo N. A. Miliutina chinovniku osobykh poruchenii Gospodinu Nadvornomu Sovetniku Shtakel'bergu ot Khoziaistvennago Departamenta, Vremennago Otdeleniia," 4 noiabria 1843g.," TsGIAL, fond 1287, opis' 39, delo No. 22/48–51.

43. See *Adres'-Kalendar* for the years 1842–1856, and the service records of these men, in TsGIAL, fond 1349.

44. One of Miliutin's most frequent admonitions to his agents of special commissions was to find a way to reduce useless official paperwork.

45. See Veselovskii, "Vospominaniia," pp. 30–32; Pis'ma A. K. Girsa k N. A. Miliutinu, 1842–1854gg., TsGIAL, fond 869, opis' 1, delo No. 880; Pis'ma N. P. Bezobrazova k N. A. Miliutinu, TsGIAL, fond 869, opis' 1, delo No. 833; Pis'ma E. I. Baranovskago k N. A. Miliutinu, TsGIAL, fond 869, opis' 1, delo No. 828.

46. Pis'mo N. V. Kompaneishchikova k M. I. Leksu, 29 oktiabria 1843g., TsGIAL, fond 1287, opis' 39, delo No. 24/30.

47. "Rapport chinovnika osobykh poruchenii pri khoziaistvennom departamente kollezhskago asessora Shtakel'berga," 2 sentiabria 1842g., TsGIAL, fond 1287, opis' 39, delo No. 30/14–15; A. F. Shtakel'berg, "Zapiska o prichinakh i sledstviiakh neurozhaev v Lifliandskoi gubernii i o sredstvakh preduprezhdeniia onykh," (iiun' 1844g.), TsGIAL, fond 1287, opis' 2, delo No. 970/3–8.

48. "Formuliarnyi spisok o sluzhbe Redaktora Gorodskago Otdeleniia Khoziaistvennago Departamenta Ministerstva Vnutrennikh Del Nadvornago Sovetnika Kavelina," TsGALI, fond 264, opis' 1, delo No. 1.

49. "Ofitsial'noe pis'mo N. A. Miliutina k Ministru Vnutrennikh Del," 23 aprelia 1849g., TsGIAL, fond 1287, opis' 37, delo No. 666/4–5.

50. "Izsledovaniia o gorodakh russkikh," *ZhMVD,* VI (1844): 5.

51. Ibid., p. 8.

52. See Miliutin's comments in "Ofitsial'noe pis'mo chinovniku osobykh poruchenii Nadvornomu Sovetniku Grafu Tolstomu," 23 aprelia 1849g., TsGIAL, fond 1287, opis' 39, delo No. 745/1–2.

53. "Obshchaia instruktsiia chinovnikam otriazhaemym dlia obozreniia gorodov," 12 maia 1845g., TsGIAL, fond 1287, opis' 39, delo No. 156/2–3.

54. "O merakh k uspeshnemu proizvodstvu del po ustroistvu gorodskago khoziaistva," 4 fevralia 1849g., TsGIAL, fond 1152, opis' 4, delo No. 160/652.

55. "Formuliarnyi spisok A. F. Shtakel'berga," TsGIAL, fond 1349, opis' 3, delo No. 2535.

56. "Formuliarnyi spisok A. K. Girsa," TsGIAL, fond 1284, opis' 31, delo No. 52. On Shtakel'berg, see also materials in TsGIAL, fond 1287, opis' 39, dela Nos. 22 and 30, and in opis' 2, delo No. 970. (This latter includes his "Zapiska o prichinakh i sledstviiakh neurozhaev v Lifliandskoi gubernii i o sredstvakh preduprezhdeniia onym," [iiun' 1844g.].) On Girs's lengthy studies of the towns and cities in Iaroslav province, which went on intermittently for more than a decade, see the materials in TsGIAL, fond 1287, opis' 39, dela Nos. 25 and 45, and Pis'ma A. K. Girsa k N. A. Miliutinu, 1842–1854gg., TsGIAL, fond 869, opis' 1, delo No. 880.

57. "Delo o sluzhbe K. K. Grota," TsGIAL, fond 1162, opis' 6, delo No. 154.

58. "Formuliarnyi spisok N. P. Bezobrazova," TsGIAL, fond 1349, opis' 3, delo No. 171.

59. "Formuliarnyi spisok K. A. Krizhivitskago," TsGIAL, fond 1349, opis' 3, delo No. 1157.

60. "Formuliarnyi spisok grafa A. K. Siversa," TsGIAL, fond 1284, opis' 75, delo No. 2.

61. "Formuliarnyi spisok Grafa D. N. Tolstago," TsGIAL, fond 1284, opis' 32, delo No. 192.

62. "Formuliarnyi spisok K. S. Veselovskago," TsGIAL, fond 1349, opis' 3, delo No. 391.

63. Pis'ma N. A. Miliutina k I. S. Aksakovu, 1849–1850gg., PD, fond 3, opis' 4, delo No. 384; Pis'ma I. S. Aksakova k N. A. Miliutinu, 1849–1850gg., TsGIAL, fond 869, opis' 1, delo No. 818.

64. N. A. Miliutin, "Zametki," 1 fevralia 1844g., TsGIAL, fond 1287, opis' 39, delo No. 22/57; Pis'mo L. A. Perovskago k P. I. Keppenu, 14 dekabria 1846g., TsGIAL, fond 1287, opis' 39, delo No. 386/1–2; a wide variety of materials in TsGIAL, fond 1287 (the collection of the Municipal Section) and letters of these agents to Miliutin in his personal archive (TsGIAL, fond 869).

65. See, for example, "O komandirovanii A. Ia. Stobeusa i N. P. Bezobrazova dlia obozrenii gorodov Saratovskoi gubernii," TsGIAL, fond 1287, opis' 39, delo No. 23/196–99 (Stobeus and Bezobrazov received no pay or allowances for more than two years); and Pis'mo ot komissii dlia revizii obshchestvennago i khoziaistvennago upravleniia goroda Rigi, 31 ianvaria 1847g., which indicates that some eight officials, including Samarin, Khanykov, Golovnin, and Shtakel'berg, had received no salary for many months.

66. "Pamiati A. P. Zablotskago," p. 540.

67. Pis'mo I. S. Aksakova k N. A. Miliutinu, 6 oktiabria 1852g., TsGIAL, fond 869, opis' 1, delo No. 818/30.

68. "O merakh k uspeshnemu proizvodstvu del po ustroistvu gorodskago khoziaistva," 4 fevralia 1849g., TsGIAL, fond 1152, opis' 4, delo No. 160/654.

69. N. A. Miliutin, "Dokladnaia zapiska o blagoustroistve gorodov" (1840-ye gg.), TsGIAL, fond 869, opis' 1, delo No. 319/19.

70. "O merakh k uspeshnemu proizvodstvu del," TsGIAL, fond 1152, opis' 4, delo No. 160/655.

71. *Na konchinu Nikolaia Alekseevicha Miliutina. Sbornik nekrologicheskikh statei* (Moscow, 1872), pp. 67–68.

72. "O sostavlenii svoda postanovlenii dlia mest gorodskago upravleniia," 26 aprelia 1851g., TsGIAL, fond 1287, opis' 37, delo No. 1000/1–2.

73. Ibid., delo No. 1000/5.

74. See N. V. Varadinov, *Deloproizvodstvo ili teoreticheskoe i prakticheskoe rukovodstvo k grazhdanskomu i ugolovnomu, kollegial'nomu i odnolichnomu pis'-movodstvu, k sostavleniiu vsekh pravitel'stvennykh i chastnykh delovykh bumag i k vedeniiu samykh del, s prilozheniem k onym obraztsov i form,* 2 vols. (St. Petersburg, 1857).

75. In addition to the materials on this question cited earlier in this study, see also N. A. Miliutin, "Mysli o sposobakh unichtozheniia krepostnago prava v Rossii," fevral' 1847g., TsGIAL, fond 869, opis' 1, delo No. 449.

76. See, for example, A. F. Shtakel'berg, "Zapiska o prichinakh neurozhaev v Lifliandskoi gubernii," TsGIAL, fond 1287, opis' 2, delo No. 970.

77. N. A. Miliutin, "Obozrenie khlebnoi promyshlennosti i torgovli v vidakh narodnago prodovol'stviia," 1849g., TsGIAL, fond 869, opis' 1, delo No. 69/87–88.

78. See Zablotskii-Desiatovskii, "Prichiny kolebaniia tsen na khleb v Rossii," *OZ,* LII (May 1847): 1–30.

79. N. A. Miliutin, "Obrazovanie khlebnoi promyshlennosti," TsGIAL, fond 869, opis' 1, delo No. 69/180–83.

80. N. A. Miliutin, "Donesenie gospodinu Upravliaiushchemu Ministerstvom Vnutrennikh Del (aprel', 1841g.)," TsGIAL, fond 869, opis' 1, delo No. 725.

81. Ptukha, *Ocherki po istorii statistiki,* II: 358–62.

82. Ibid., pp. 299, 362.

83. Wortman, *Development of a Russian Legal Consciousness,* p. 151.

84. K. I. Arsen'ev, "Zapiska o sostave i deistviiakh Statisticheskago Otdeleniia Soveta Ministerstva Vnutrennikh Del," 5 noiabria 1852g., TsGIAL, fond 869, opis' 1, delo No. 91/5–7.

85. See, for example, ibid., delo No. 91/1–2, 5–8.

86. K. F. German, "Vzgliad na nyneshnee sostoianii statistiki v prosveshchennykh gosudarstvakh Evropy," *ZhMVD,* I (1829): 103–4.

87. *Materialy dlia statistiki Rossiiskoi imperii, izdavaemye s Vysochaishego soizvoleniia, pri statisticheskom otdelenii Soveta Ministerstva Vnutrennikh Del,* 2 vols. (St. Petersburg, 1839), I: i–iii.

88. *ZhMVD* (1842), p. 263; Ptukha, *Ocherki po istorii statistiki,* II: 368.

89. The poet Pushkin, who knew Leks as a young official serving in the office of the Governor of New Russia, once wrote: "Mikhail Ivanovich Leks/ Prekrasnyi chelovek-s" as a comment upon Leks's servile manner. A. I. Artem'ev, "Dnevnik, 1 avgusta–31 dekabria 1856g.," GPB, fond 37, delo No. 156/137. Entry for December 8, 1856.

90. Arsen'ev, "Zapiska o sostave i deistviiakh," TsGIAL, fond 869, opis' 1, delo No. 91/10–15.

91. An indication of the passive role to which Arsen'ev's statistical section was reduced during the 1840s can be seen in its annual report for 1847 (the only one from the 1843–1853 period which has survived). In 1847, his agency received for official consideration only forty-six files *(dela),* plus an additional 574 miscellaneous papers, or a weekly average of less than one official file and eleven miscellaneous papers. "Otchet za 1847 god po statisticheskomu otdeleniiu Soveta Ministerstva Vnutrennikh Del," TsGIAL, fond 1290, opis' 1, delo No. 155/17.

92. Ptukha, *Ocherki po istorii statistiki,* II: 300.

93. German, "Vzgliad na nyneshnee sostoianie statistiki," p. 103.

94. Artem'ev, "Zapiska o statisticheskikh trudakh N. A. Miliutina," TsGIAL, fond 869, opis' 1, delo No. 83/2.

95. Semenov, *Istoriia poluvekovoi deiatel'nosti,* I: 415–16.

96. *Materialy dlia statistiki rossiiskoi imperii,* I: ii.

97. Ibid., pp. i–ii.

98. "Pervoe zasedenie Vremennago Statisticheskago Komiteta," 16 noiabria 1843g., TsGIAL, fond 869, opis' 1, delo No. 90/9–10.

99. N. A. Miliutin, "Proekt programmy izdaniia "Pravitel'stvennaia Statistika Rossii," TsGIAL, fond 869, opis' 1, delo No. 777/1–10.

100. N. A. Miliutin, "Chislo gorodskikh i zemledel'cheskikh poselenii v Rossii," *Sbornik statisticheskikh svedenii o Rossii* (St. Petersburg, 1851), pp. 228–76.

101. Artem'ev, "Zapiska o statisticheskikh trudakh N. A. Miliutina," TsGIAL, fond 869, opis' 1, delo No. 83/2.

102. Ibid., delo No. 83/3–4; Artem'ev, "Dnevnik, iiun'–19 avgusta 1852g.," GPB, fond 37, delo No. 155/1.

103. Artem'ev, "Zapiska o statisticheskikh trudakh N. A. Miliutina," TsGIAL, fond 869, opis' 1, delo No. 83/3.

104. Artem'ev, "Dnevnik, iiun'–19 avgusta 1852g.," GPB, fond 37, delo No. 155/3.

105. Artem'ev, "Zapiska o statisticheskikh trudakh N. A. Miliutina," TsGIAL, fond 869, opis' 1, delo No. 83/3–5.

106. *Spisok naselennykh mest iaroslavskoi gubernii* (St. Petersburg, 1865). Artem'ev indicates that a few copies of *O sostave i dvizhenii naseleniia po guberniiam Nizhegorodskoi i Iaroslavskoi* may have survived the fire of 1862, but I have been unable to locate a copy either in the Soviet Union or in the West. See Artem'ev, "Zapiska o statisticheskikh trudakh N. A. Miliutina," TsGIAL, fond 869, opis' 1, delo No. 83/3.

107. Resistance by Russian provincial officials to requests for information from the central administration was unending and widespread. Throughout the Nicholas era, provincial officials waged a campaign of passive resistance against senior statesmen's efforts to make Russia's administration more effective. In terms of statistical reporting in the Ministry of Internal Affairs, a report stated in 1853 that in a number of provinces the statistical committees, which each governor had been instructed to form in 1834, still had not been established ("O poriadke sobraniia i obrabotki statisticheskikh svedenii, kak v statisticheskom komitete ministerstva, tak i v guberniiakh," 5 dekabria 1853g., TsGIAL, fond 1290, opis' 1, delo No. 193/5–6).

108. The designation of the Third Department was changed to the Department of Rural Economy in 1845.

109. *Istoricheskie obozrenie . . . Ministerstva Gosudarstvennykh Imushchestv, 1837–1877gg.* I: 34–35.

110. Insarskii, *Zapiski,* I: 46–53.

111. Ibid., p. 65.

112. Ibid., p. 66.

113. *Istoricheskoe obozrenie . . . Ministerstva Gosudarstvennykh Imushchestv,* II, (pt. 2): 47.

114. "Programma sel'sko-khoziaistvennoi statistiki 17 maia 1847g.," TsGIAL, fond 398, opis' 10, delo No. 3152; *Istoricheskoe obozrenie,* II (pt. 2): 48–50.

115. The provinces of St. Petersburg, Voronezh, Penza, Tambov, Tula, Riazan, Kursk, Orël, Pskov, Moscow, Ekaterinoslav, Smolensk, Kharkov, Saratov, Novgorod, Tver, Kaluga, Nizhnii-Novgorod, Vladimir, Kherson, Taurida, Iaroslav, Kostroma, Kazan, and Samara were surveyed. In the first nineteen, the tax base was shifted from souls to land and industry by 1856.

116. *Istoricheskoe obozrenie,* II (pt. 2): 58–59.

117. "Doklad P. I. Keppena uchenomu komitetu MGI," 6 maia 1846g., TsGIAL, fond 398, opis' 10, delo No. 3378/1.

118. K. Veselovskii, "Plan statisticheskago opisaniia Gosudarstvennykh Imushchestv i sosloviia sel'skikh zhitelei, sostoiashchago pod popechitel'stvom Ministerstva Gosudarstvennykh Imushchestv," 1847g., TsGIAL, fond 398, opis 11, delo No. 3652/35–36.

119. Zablotskii-Desiatovskii, "Zapiska o nedostatkakh obshchestvennago i o vygodakh lichnago vladeniia krest'ian zemleiu," 1851g., TsGIAL, fond 940, opis' 1, delo No. 16/1.

120. Ibid., delo No. 16/3.

121. Ibid.

122. Zablotskii-Desiatovskii, "Zapiska o nedostatkakh," TsGIAL, fond 940, opis' 1, delo No. 16/3–5.

123. "O prisuzhdennykh Uchenym Komitetom MGI po konkursu khoziaistvenno-statisticheskikh opisanii nagradakh," 10 noiabria 1850g., TsGIAL, fond 398, opis' 1, delo No. 4475/52.

124. W. H. Blackwell, *The Beginnings of Russian Industrialization, 1800–1860* (Princeton, 1968), p. 431.

125. L. Tęgoborski, *Commentaries on the Productive Forces of Russia,* 3 vols. (London, 1855), I: 140–41.

126. Ibid., p. 143.

127. Zablotskii-Desiatovskii, "Prichiny kolebaniia tsen na khleb v Rossii," p. 11.

128. Ibid., pp. 12–13.

129. *Ocherk piatidesiatiletnei deiatel'nosti Ministerstva Gosudarstvennykh Imushchestv, 1837–1887gg.* (St. Petersburg, 1887), pp. 58–59.

130. "Obzor deistvii Departamenta Sel'skago Khoziaistva v techenii piati let, s 1844 po 1849 goda," *ZhMGI,* XXXIII (1849), sect. 1, pp. 212–14.

131. Ibid., pp. 218–19.

132. "Doklad uchenago komiteta Ministerstva Gosudarstvennykh Imushchestv po predmetu preobrazovanii uchilishcha sel'skago khoziaistva, sushchestvuiushchago v vedenii Imperatorskago S.-Peterburgskago Vol'nago Ekonomicheskago Obshchestva," 15 fevralia 1847g., TsGIAL, fond 398, opis' 11, delo No. 3736/14–15.

133. Ibid., delo No. 3736/27.

134. Ibid., delo No. 3736/19.

135. Each farm drew its students from a particular area: the *Vologda farm:* Vologda, Arkhangel'sk, Olonets, Iaroslav, and the northern part of Novgorod provinces; the *Kazan farm:* Kazan, Viatka, Perm, Nizhnii-Novgorod, and Kostroma provinces; the two *Saratov farms:* Saratov, Astrakhan, Orenburg, and parts of Penza provinces; the *Tambov farm:* the provinces of Tambov, Voronezh, Penza, Orël, Riazan, and Tula; the *Kharkov farm:* the provinces of Kharkov, Kursk, Poltava, Chernigov, and part of Kiev; the *Ekaterinoslav farm:* Ekaterinoslav, Kherson, Taurida, Stavropol' provinces and the lands of the Don Cossack Host; the *Gorygoretsk farm:* the provinces of Pskov, Smolensk, Vitebsk, Mogilev, Minsk, Vilno, Grodno, Kovno, and parts of Volynia, Podolia, and Kiev. The provinces of Moscow, Tver, Vladimir, and Kaluga were to be served by the model farm maintained by the Moscow Agricultural Society. "Obzor deistvii Departamenta Sel'skago Khoziaistva," XXXIII: 226–28.

136. Pis'mo A. I. Levshina (direktor Departamenta Sel'skago Khoziaistva MGI), k Uchenomu Komitetu MGI, 25 aprelia 1852g., TsGIAL, fond 398, opis' 16, delo No. 5533/1–2; "Doklad ot nachal'nika statisticheskago otdeleniia Departamenta Sel'skago Khoziaistva K. Veselovskago," 17 iiunia 1853g., TsGIAL, fond 398, opis' 16, delo No. 5533/16–36; "Doklad Uchenago Komiteta Ministerstva Gosudarstvennykh Imushchestv," 28 maia 1855g., TsGIAL, fond 398, opis' 16, delo No. 5533/46–48.

137. "Obzor deistvii Departamenta Sel'skago Khoziaistva," XXXIII: 229–32; "Otchet o sostoianii i deistviiakh Iugovostochnoi uchebnoi fermy," TsGIAL, fond 398, opis' 10, delo No. 3208/4–35.

138. "Obzor deistvii Departamenta Sel'skago Khoziaistva," XXXIII: 228–29.

139. "Katalog knigam nakhodiashchimsia v bibliotekakh uchebnykh ferm, sostoiashchikh v vedomstve Ministerstva Gosudarstvennykh Imushchestv," (1853g.), TsGIAL, fond 398, opis' 16, delo No. 5537/134–35.

140. "Vedomost' zemledel'cheskim i drugim orudiiam, izgotovlennym na Vologodskoi uchebnoi ferme v 1849 godu," TsGIAL, fond 398, opis' 12–13, delo No. 4288/16.

141. "Obzor deistvii Departamenta Sel'skago Khoziaistva," XXXI (pt. 1): 36.

142. Zablotskii-Desiatovskii, "Zapiska o nedostatkakh obshchestvennago i o vygodakh lichnago vladeniia krest'ian zemleiu," TsGIAL, fond 940, opis' 1, delo No. 16.

143. Approximately 95 percent of the exhibitors at the first Iaroslavl agricultural exhibition were state peasants and serfs. "Obzor deistvii Departamenta Sel'skago Khoziaistva," XXXI: 37–39.

144. Ibid., pp. 36–38.

145. A. I. Khodnev, Istoriia Imperatorskago Vol'nago Ekonomicheskago Obshchestva, s 1765 do 1865 goda (St. Petersburg, 1865), p. 2.

146. Ibid., pp. 2–3.

147. Blum, Lord and Peasant in Russia, p. 404.

148. "Obzor deistvii Departamenta Sel'skago Khoziaistva," XXXI: 23.

149. Blackwell, Beginnings of Russian Industrialization, p. 348.

150. By the mid-1840s, the Free Economic Society received an annual appropriation of 16,000 rubles from the government, and the Imperial Agricultural Society at Moscow received 14,000 rubles. "Obzor deistvii Departamenta Sel'-skago Khoziaistva," XXXI: 35.

151. Ibid., p. 33.

152. Ibid., p. 34.

153. Those outside Moscow, St. Petersburg, or the Baltic provinces were the Imperial Agricultural Society of Southern Russia (1828); the Imperial Economic Society at Kazan (1839); the Iaroslav Agricultural Society (1842); the Society for the Encouragement of Agrarian and Manufacturing Industries (in the Transcaucasus, 1833); the subsidiary branch of the Imperial Agricultural Society of Southern Russia at Ekaterinoslav (1845); the subsidiary branch of the Imperial Agricultural Society of Southern Russia at Kishnev (1845); the Lebedian Agricultural Society (in Tambov province, 1847); the Agricultural Society of Southwestern Russia (in Penza, 1848). "Obzor deistvii Departamenta Sel'skago Khoziaistva," XXXI: 33–34.

154. Ibid., p. 33.

155. Blackwell, Beginnings of Russian Industrialization, p. 348.

156. The noblemen who submitted this plan were P. Miasnov, V. Murav'ev, Count N. N. Tatishchev, M. P. Bolotov, Count V. A. Bobrinskii, I. Raevskii, Oshanin, Vorontsov-Vel'mianinov, and Kliucharev. Semevskii, Krest'ianskii vopros, II: 238–41.

157. "Kopiia predpolozhenii Venevskago Pomeshchika Statskago Sovetnika Pokhvisneva, predstavlennykh sobraniiu Tul'skago dvorianstva, na gubern-skikh vyborakh v 1846 godu," TsGIAL, fond 398, opis' 10, delo No. 3158/22.

158. Baron August Ludwig Maria von Haxthausen-Abbenberg, The Russian Empire: Its People and Resources, 2 vols., Robert Farie, trans. (London, 1856), I: 335.

159. "Kopiia predpolozhenii Venevskago Pomeshchika Pokhvisneva," TsGIAL, fond 398, opis' 10, delo No. 3158/20–21.

160. Sixty-nine nobles voted for the proposal, while 196 opposed it. Ofitsial'noe pis'mo nachal'niku Tul'skoi gubernii No. 4749—Ministra Gosudarstvennykh Imushchestv v Departament Sel'skago Khoziaistva, 7 aprelia 1847g., TsGIAL, fond 398, opis' 10, delo No. 3158/19.

161. Zablotskii-Desiatovskii, "Zapiska o roli Moskovskago i Peterburg-

skago obshchestv sel'skago khoziaistva v predstoiashchem osvobozhdenii krest'ian ot krepostnoi zavisimosti," 1856g., TsGIAL, fond 940, opis' 1, delo No. 17/9.

162. Ibid., delo No. 17/8.

163. Ibid., delo No. 17/10.

164. The following agricultural societies participated in the discussion: (1) The Iaroslav Agricultural Society, (2) The Lebedian Agricultural Society, (3) The Agricultural Society of Southwestern Russia, (4) The Imperial Economic Society at Kazan, (5) The Imperial Agricultural Society at Moscow, (6) The Kaluga Agricultural Society, (7) The Imperial Free Economic Society, (8) The Lifland Economic Society, (9) The Kurland Agricultural Society, (10) The Estland Agricultural Society, (11) The Imperial South Russian Agricultural Society. "Vypiska iz zhurnala Uchenago Komiteta Ministerstva Gosudarstvennykh Imushchestv ot 31 dekabria 1853 goda," TsGIAL, fond 398, opis' 15, delo No. 4840/303–4.

165. Ibid., delo No. 4840/303–5.

166. Zablotskii-Desiatovskii, "Zapiska o roli," TsGIAL, fond 940, opis' 1, delo No. 17/8.

167. Tsimmerman, "Vospominaniia," ORGBL, fond 325, karton 1, papka No. 2/67.

168. Pis'mo N. A. Miliutina k P. D. Kiselevu, 4 marta 1858g., ORGBL, fond 129, karton 17, papka 55.

169. Nikolai Miliutin's brother Dmitrii, at the time professor of military geography at the General Staff War Academy, was perhaps the most dramatic example of such a withdrawal from the reform debate.

170. Obolenskii, "Moi vospominaniia," CXXXVII: 505.

171. To note some of the most prominent, Shtackel'berg reached grade five in 1848, Nikolai Miliutin and Girs in 1849, Grot in 1850, Arapetov and D. N. Tolstoi in 1851, Golovnin and Veselovskii in 1852, Liuboshchinskii, Shumakher and Reitern in 1853, and Obolenskii in 1854. Zarudnyi, who did not enter the civil service until late 1842, reached grade five in 1857. See the service records of these men in TsGIAL, fondy 1349 and 1162.

172. For example, between 1848 and 1855, Zablotskii sat on six interministerial committees, Miliutin on seven, Shtackel'berg on five, Gagemeister on three, and Konstantin Grot on six before he was appointed governor of Samara province in 1853.

173. "Delo o sluzhbe A. P. Zablotskago-Desiatovskago," TsGIAL, fond 1162, opis' 6, delo No. 196.

174. Of the agencies mentioned in the preceding paragraph, N. P. Eroshkin makes passing reference only to the Department of Rural Economy in his *Istoriia gosudarstvennykh uchrezhdenii dorevoliutsionnoi Rossii* (Moscow, 1968). Such agencies fall well below the level of state administration that Professor Yaney studied in his work, *The Systematization of Russian Government.*

Chapter 5

1. Pis'mo N. A. Miliutina k D. A. Miliutinu, 10 avgusta 1839g., ORGBL, fond 169, kartonka 69, papka No. 6.

2. Shumakher, "Pozdnie vospominaniia," p. 114.

3. For some of the most prominent examples, see Chapter IV, note 172.
4. N. K. Shilder, *Imperator Nikolai Pervyi: Ego zhizn' i tsarstvovanie*, 2 vols. (St. Petersburg, 1903), II: 64–66.
5. "Velikii Kniaz' Konstantin Nikolaevich," *RBS*, Vol. kn.-kiu, p. 120.
6. Alekseev, *Fedor Petrovich Litke*, pp. 166, 173–74.
7. A. F. Koni, "Velikii Kniaz' Konstantin Nikolaevich," *Velikaia reforma*, V, p. 35.
8. Quoted in Alekseev, *Fedor Petrovich Litke*, p. 174.
9. Quoted in ibid., pp. 166–67.
10. "Velikii Kniaz' Konstantin Nikolaevich," pp. 120–21.
11. Baron M. A. Korf, "Dnevnik barona M. A. Korfa za 1848g.," TsGAOR, fond 728, opis' 1, delo No. 1818/xi/168.
12. "Dnevnik velikago kniazia Konstantina Nikolaevicha," TsGAOR, fond 722, opis' 1, delo No. 89/12.
13. A. V. Golovnin, "Materialy dlia zhizneopisaniia v. k. Konstantina Nikolaevicha," GPB, fond 208, delo No. 10/36.
14. Pis'mo v. k. Konstantina Nikolaevicha k F. P. Litke, 2 noiabria 1841g. Quoted in Alekseev, *Fedor Petrovich Litke*, p. 182.
15. Golovnin, "Materialy dlia zhizneopisaniia," GPB, fond 208, delo No. 10/25, 55–57; G. Dzhanshiev, "Spodvizhnik tsaria-osvoboditelia v. k. Konstantin Nikolaevich," in *Epokha velikikh reform*, p. 622, note 1.
16. Golovnin, "Materialy dlia zhizneopisaniia," GPB, fond 208, delo No. 10/66.
17. "Velikii Kniaz' Konstantin Nikolaevich," p. 122.
18. See, for example, Pis'mo F. P. Litke k Baronu Vrangeliu, 1 noiabria 1845g. Quoted in Alekseev, *Fedor Petrovich Litke*, pp. 200–201.
19. Golovnin, "Zapiski i primechaniia," GPB, fond 208, delo No. 1/117–18.
20. Ibid., delo No. 1/129.
21. "Dnevnik v. k. Konstantina Nikolaevicha," TsGAOR, fond 722, opis' 1, delo No. 89/57.
22. Golovnin, "Zapiski i primechaniia," GPB, fond 208, delo No. 2/148.
23. Golovnin, "Kratkii ocherk deistvii velikago kniazia Konstantina Nikolaevicha," GPB, fond 208, delo No. 2/269.
24. Ibid., delo No. 2/102, 271.
25. Lincoln, "Daily Life of St. Petersburg Officials," pp. 88–89.
26. Golovnin, "Kratkii ocherk deistvii velikago kniazia Konstantina Nikolaevicha," GPB, fond 208, delo No. 2/271.
27. Ibid., delo No. 2/277.
28. "Imperator Nikolai I i akademik Parrot," *RS*, No. 7 (July 1898), pp. 141–43.
29. Quoted in Koni, "Velikii Kniaz' Konstantin Nikolaevich," *Velikaia reforma*, V, pp. 37–38.
30. Quoted in ibid., p. 38.
31. M. S., "*Morskoi sbornik* v 1853–1863gg.," *RS*, XLV (February 1885): 412.
32. V. S. Aksakova, *Dnevnik Very Sergeevny Aksakovoi* (St. Petersburg, 1913), p. 12.
33. Demen'tev *et al.*, *Russkaia periodicheskaia pechat'*, pp. 320–21, 244; E. D. Dneprov, "*Morskoi sbornik* v obshchestvennom dvizhenii perioda pervoi revoliutsionnoi situatsii v Rossii," in M. V. Nechkina, ed., *Revoliutsionnaia situatsiia v Rossii v 1859–1861gg.* (Moscow, 1965), p. 242.

34. N. G. Chernyshevskii, *Polnoe sobranie sochinenii,* 16 vols. (Moscow, 1939), II: 580.

35. Quoted in Dzhanshiev, "Spodvizhnik tsaria-osvoboditelia," p. 622.

36. Dneprov, *"Morskoi sbornik* v obshchestvennom dvizhenii," p. 243.

37. A. V. Golovnin, "Prodolzhenie zapisok A. V. Golovnina, s dekabria 1870g. po fevral' 1871g.," TsGIAL, fond 851, opis' 1, delo No. 9/7–8.

38. Quoted in Dneprov, *"Morskoi sbornik* v obshchestvennom dvizhenii," pp. 242–43.

39. Ibid., p. 244.

40. A. F. Koni, "Velikaia kniaginia Elena Pavlovna," in S. A. Vengerov, ed., *Glavnye deiateli osvobozhdeniia krest'ian* (St. Petersburg, 1903), p. 11.

41. Quoted in S. V. Bakhrushin, "Velikaia kniaginia Elena Pavlovna," *Osvobozhdenie krest'ian: deiateli reformy* (Moscow, 1911), p. 115.

42. Koni, "Velikaia kniaginia Elena Pavlovna," in *Glavnye deiateli,* p. 11.

43. Bakhrushin, "Velikaia kniaginia Elena Pavlovna," pp. 116–17.

44. Ibid., p. 131.

45. A. F. Koni, "Velikaia kniaginia Elena Pavlovna," *Velikaia reforma,* V, pp. 15–16.

46. A. I. Skrebitskii, "Vospominaniia A. I. Skrebitskago," PD, fond 3847, delo No. xxb39/24–28.

47. Koni, "Velikaia kniaginia Elena Pavlovna," in *Glavnye deiateli,* p. 13.

48. Obolenskii, "Moi vospominaniia," CXXXVII: 517–23; Koni, "Velikaia kniaginia Elena Pavlovna," *Velikaia reforma,* V: 19.

49. K. D. Kavelin, "Velikaia Kniaginia Elena Pavlovna. Nekrolog," in *Sobranie sochinenii K. D. Kavelina,* Vol. II, col. 1227.

50. Bakhrushin, "Velikaia kniaginia Elena Pavlovna," pp. 121–22.

51. Koni, "Velikaia kniaginia Elena Pavlovna," in *Glavnye deiateli,* p. 12; Ptukha, *Ocherki po istorii statistiki,* II: 299, 362; "Delo o sluzhbe A. P. Zablotskago-Desiatovskago," TsGIAL, fond 1162, opis' 6, delo No. 196.

52. Bakhrushin, "Velikaia kniaginia Elena Pavlovna," pp. 121–23.

53. Quoted in M. M. Bogoslovskii, "O velikoi kniagine Elene Pavlovne," GIM, fond 442, delo No. 30/159.

54. Bakhrushin, "Velikaia kniaginia Elena Pavlovna," p. 125.

55. Koni, "Velikaia kniaginia Elena Pavlovna," in *Glavnye deiateli,* p. 13.

56. Quoted in Bakhrushin, "Velikaia kniaginia Elena Pavlovna," p. 125.

57. Quoted in Bogoslovskii, "O velikoi kniagine Elene Pavlovne," GIM, fond 442, delo No. 30/159.

58. Marquis de Custine, *Russia* (Cincinnati, 1856), p. 115.

59. Korf, "Dnevnik barona M. A. Korfa za 1847g.," TsGAOR, fond 728, opis' 1, delo No. 1817/x/128.

60. K. A. Bukh, "Velikaia kniaginia Elena Pavlovna," *RS,* LVII (March 1888): 808.

61. Velikaia kniaginia Elena Pavlovna, "Dnevnik za 1849g.," TsGAOR, fond 647, opis' 1, delo No. 25/2.

62. Bakhrushin, "Velikaia kniaginia Elena Pavlovna," p. 131.

63. "Delo o sluzhbe kniazia D. A. Obolenskago," TsGIAL, fond 1162, opis' 6, delo No. 375.

64. Ibid.

65. Ibid.

66. Ibid.; Golovnin, "Kratkii ocherk deistvii velikago kniazia Konstantina Nikolaevicha," GPB, fond 208, delo No. 2/271.

67. Obolenskii, "Moi vospominaniia," CXXXVII: 507.

68. Ibid., p. 508.

69. Ibid.

70. Ibid., p. 510.

71. L. A. Perovskii, "O prichinakh umnozheniia deloproizvodstva vo vnutrennem upravlenii (mart' 1851g.)," TsGIAL, fond 1287, opis' 36, delo No. 137/15.

72. L. Tengoborskii, "Extraits de Mémoire secret du Conseiller Privé Actuel Tengoborskii (janvier 1857)," TsGIAL, fond 851, opis' 1, delo No. 50/289–90.

73. Obolenskii, "Moi vospominaniia," CXXXVII: 510.

74. Koni, "Velikaia kniaginia Elena Pavlovna," Velikaia reforma, V: 124.

75. Tsimmerman, "Vospominaniia," ORGBL, fond 325, kartonka 1, papka 1/210.

76. Obolenskii, "Moi vospominaniia," CXXXVII: 510–11.

77. Kniaz' D. A. Obolenskii, Vospominaniia kniazia D. A. Obolenskago o pervoi izdanii posmertnykh sochinenii Gogolia, 1852–1855gg. (St. Petersburg, 1873), p. 11; Obolenskii, "Moi vospominaniia," CXXXVII: 514–15.

78. Bakhrushin, "Velikaia kniaginia Elena Pavlovna," pp. 135–36; Golovnin, "Kratkii ocherk deistvii Velikago kniazia Konstantina Nikolaevicha," GPB, fond 208, delo No. 2/269–287.

79. Koni, "Velikaia kniaginia Elena Pavlovna," in Glavnye deiateli, p. 13.

80. Bakhrushin, "Velikaia kniaginia Elena Pavlovna," pp. 134–35.

81. Quoted in Kniaginia O. N. Trubetskaia, Materialy dlia biografii kn. V. A. Cherkasskago, 2 vols. (Moscow, 1904), I (bk. 2): 26.

82. Obolenskii, "Moi vospominaniia," CXXXVII: 524–25.

83. Korf, "Dnevnik barona M. A. Korfa za 1849g.," TsGAOR, fond 728, opis' 1, delo No. 1817/xii/248.

84. Obolenskii, "Moi vospominaniia," CXXXVII: 524–25.

85. Ia. A. Solov'ev, "Zapiski Senatora Ia. A. Solov'eva," RS, XXXIV (1882): 129–31.

86. Obolenskii, "Moi vospominaniia," RS, CXXXVIII (April 1909): 39.

87. Bakhrushin, "Velikaia kniaginia Elena Pavlovna," p. 145.

88. August von Haxthausen, Studies on the Interior of Russia, S. F. Starr, ed. (Chicago-London, 1972), p. xxxvi.

89. For a discussion of Haxthausen's other memoranda of 1857, see ibid., pp. xxxvii–xxxix.

90. Field, The End of Serfdom, pp. 76, 391n. 77.

91. Korf, "Dnevnik barona M. A. Korfa za 1849g.," TsGAOR, fond 728, opis' 1, delo No. 1817/xii/155.

92. W. Bruce Lincoln, "The Karlovka Reform," Slavic Review, XXVIII (September 1969): 464.

93. Druzhinin, Gosudarstvennye krest'iane, I: 275–77.

94. "Polozhenie dlia barshchinnykh rabot v Karlovskom imenii," 1851g., TsGAOR, fond 647, opis', 1, delo No. 995/8. For a more extensive summary of this proposal, see Lincoln, "The Karlovka Reform," p. 464.

95. Lincoln, "The Karlovka Reform," p. 465.

96. Elena Pavlovna insisted upon larger land allotments for the peasants at Karlovka. As it emerged in its final version in 1859, her emancipation plan tripled the size of the allotments that Engelhardt had originally proposed.

"Predpolozheniia ob ustroistve Karlovskago imeniia e. i. v. v. k. Eleny Pavlovny," TsGAOR, fond 649, opis' 1, delo No. 995/64–70.

97. Bakhrushin, "Velikaia kniaginia Elena Pavlovna," pp. 139–40.

98. Koni, "Velikaia kniaginia Elena Pavlovna," *Velikaia reforma,* V: 24–25; Bakhrushin, "Velikaia kniaginia Elena Pavlovna," pp. 140–41.

99. Koni, "Velikaia kniaginia Elena Pavlovna," *Velikaia reforma,* V: 24–25.

100. Quoted in S. S. Tatishchev, *Imperator Aleksandr II: Ego zhizn' i tsarstvovanie,* 2 vols. (St. Petersburg, 1911), I: 278.

101. Koni, "Velikaia kniaginia Elena Pavlovna," in *Glavnye deiateli,* p. 19.

102. K. D. Kavelin, "Zapiska ob osvobozhdenii krest'ian v Rossii," in *Sobranie sochinenii,* Vol. II, cols. 40–50.

103. Koni, "Velikaia kniaginia Elena Pavlovna," *Velikaia reforma,* V: 26.

104. Pis'mo Imperatora Aleksandra Nikolaevicha k v. k. Elene Pavlovne, 26 oktiabria 1856g. Published in A. I. Levshin, "Dostopamiatnye minuty moei zhizni. Zapiska Alekseia Iraklievicha Levshina," *RA* (August 1885): 489.

105. Haxthausen, *Studies on the Interior of Russia,* p. xxxviii.

106. Field, *The End of Serfdom,* p. 76.

107. Quoted in P. A. Zaionchkovskii, *Otmena krepostnogo prava,* pp. 76–77.

108. Quoted in ibid., p. 76.

109. Field, *The End of Serfdom,* p. 77.

110. Ibid. p. 391n. 83.

111. See ibid., pp. 77–83; Emmons, *Russian Landed Gentry and the Emancipation of 1861,* pp. 51–62.

112. For a discussion of the details of this charter, see Lincoln, "The Karlovka Reform," pp. 466–69.

113. Solov'ev, "Zapiski," pp. 129–31; Bakhrushin, "Velikaia kniaginia Elena Pavlovna," p. 144. For Elena Pavlovna's relationship with Prince Cherkasskii at this time, see Trubetskaia, *Materialy,* I, bk. 1, where Cherkasskii's views on reforms are discussed, especially in Appendix No. 3, pp. 88–90.

114. Of those mentioned above in connection with discussions of the Karlovka reform, Miliutin, Solov'ev, Tarnovskii, Cherkasskii, and Samarin all served on the Editing Commissions. I have been unable to connect Zablotskii-Desiatovskii directly to any discussion of the Karlovka reform. Given his friendship with those enlightened bureaucrats who discussed it with the Grand Duchess, however, it would have been unusual indeed if he had not commented upon its contents in an informal manner at some point.

115. Quoted in Zablotskii-Desiatovskii, *Graf P. D. Kiselev,* II: 341.

116. P. P. Semenov-Tian-Shanskii, *Memuary,* III: 269–70; Trubetskaia, *Materialy,* I, bk. 2, pp. 127, 153, 163–65; Obolenskii, "Moi vospominaniia," CXXXVIII: 60.

117. Field, *The End of Serfdom,* p. 89.

118. Lettre de N. A. Milutine à D. A. Milutine, 11/23 décembre 1861, published in Anatole Leroy-Beaulieu, *Un homme d'état Russe (Nicolas Milutine) d'après sa correspondance inédite. Étude sur la Russie et la Pologne pendant le règne d'Alexandre II (1855–1872)* (Paris, 1884), pp. 117–18.

119. Valuev, "Duma Russkago," pp. 349–59.

120. Obolenskii, "Moi vospominaniia," CXXXVII: 505.

121. "Otchety po Inspektorskomu Departamentu Grazhdanskago Vedomstva za 1847, 1850, i 1856g.," TsGIAL, fond 1409, opis' 2, delo No. 6829.

122. Iu. N. Egorov, "Studentchestvo Sankt-Peterburgskogo Universiteta, v 30–50kh godakh XIX v. Ego sotsial'nyi sostav i raspredelenie po fakul'tetam," *Vestnik Leningradskogo Universiteta,* No. 14 (1957), pp. 6–15.

123. *Pamiatnaia knizhka litseistov* (St. Petersburg, 1907), pp. 40–42.

124. Veselovskii, "Zapiski," GPB, fond 550.IV.861/390.

125. Quoted in Wortman, *Development of a Russian Legal Consciousness*, p. 183.

126. Valuev, "Duma russkago," pp. 354–55, 357.

127. P. Dolgorukov, "O vnutrennei sostoianii Rossii," (noiabr' 1857g.), TsGAOR, fond 647, opis' 1, delo No. 50/5–40.

128. *Materialy dlia istorii uprazdneniia krepostnago sostoianiia pomeshchich'ikh krest'ian v Rossii v tsarstvovanie Imperatora Aleksandra II* (Berlin, 1860), I: 103.

129. See essays on the leading figures involved in drafting the Emancipation Acts of 1861, for example, in *Velikaia reforma*, Vol. V, as well as Leroy-Beaulieu, *Un homme d'état russe*, and A. A. Kizevetter, *Kuznets-Grazhdanin (iz epokhi 60kh godov)*, 2d. ed. (Rostov-na-Donu, 1904).

Chapter 6

1. Pis'mo K. D. Kavelina k T. N. Granovskomu, 4 marta 1855g., in Levin, "K. D. Kavelin o smerti Nikolaia I," p. 610.

2. M. P. Pogodin, "Tsarskoe vremia," in *Istoriko-politicheskie pis'ma i zapiski v prodolzhenii Krymskoi Voiny, 1853–1856 gg.* (Moscow, 1874), p. 312.

3. Borivoi Plavsic, "Seventeenth-Century Chanceries and Their Staffs," in Pintner and Rowney, eds., *Russian Officialdom*, pp. 19–45; Robert O. Crummey, "The Origins of the Noble Official: The Boyar Elite, 1613–1689," in ibid., pp. 46–75; Brenda Meehan-Waters, "Social and Career Characteristics of the Administrative Elite, 1689–1761," in ibid., pp. 76–105; Raeff, "The Well-Ordered Police State," pp. 1221–43; P. N. Miliukov, *Ocherki po istorii russkoi kul'tury*, 3 vols. (St. Petersburg, 1901), III: 313–34; A. Liutsh, "Russkii absoliutizm XVIII veka," in A. Liutsh, ed., *Itogi XVIII veka v Rossii: Vvedenie v russkuiu istoriiu XIX veka* (Moscow, 1910), pp. 8–74.

4. W. Bruce Lincoln, *The Romanovs: Autocrats of All the Russias* (New York, 1981), pp. 7–8; Miliukov, *Ocherki*, III: 31–32.

5. This argument was first advanced by A. J. Rieber, in A. J. Rieber, ed., *The Politics of Autocracy*, pp. 23–24.

6. M. Poggenpohl au Directeur de la Chancellerie de St. Petersbourg, 20 mars 1854, in Count K. V. Nesselrode, *Lettres et papiers du Chancellier Comte de Nesselrode, 1760–1850*, 11 vols. (Paris, 1905–1912), XI: 30–31.

7. P. A. Zaionchkovskii, "Dmitrii Alekseevich Miliutin: biograficheskii ocherk," in P. A. Zaionchkovskii, ed., *Dnevnik D. A. Miliutina, 1873–1875gg.* 4 vols. (Moscow, 1947) I: 17.

8. A. V. Nikitenko, *Dnevnik*, 3 vols. (Moscow, 1955), I: 421.

9. Ibid., p. 411.

10. Orlovsky, *The Limits of Reform*, p. 3.

11. *Materialy dlia istorii uprazdneniia krepostnago sostoianiia*, I, pp. 116–17.

12. Ia. A. Solov'ev, "Zapiski Senatora Ia. A. Solov'eva," *RS*, XXXIV (1882): 110–11; Semenov-Tian-Shanskii, *Memuary*, III: 25.

13. Zablotskii-Desiatovskii, "O krepostnom sostoianii v Rossii," pp. 287–327.

14. N. A. Miliutin, "Mysli o sposobakh unichtozheniia krepostnago sostoianiia v Rossii," 6 fevralia 1847g., TsGIAL, fond 869, opis' 1, delo No. 449/55.

15. See Field, *End of Serfdom*, pp. 96–101.

16. See, for example, Miliutin, "Mysli o sposobakh unichtozheniia," TsGIAL, fond 869, opis' 1, delo No. 449–55–56.

17. K. K. Grot, "Proekt osvobozhdeniia pomeshchich'ikh krest'ian v Rossii," 1857g., GPB, fond 226, delo No. 44/1–91; V. A. Tsie, "Neskol'ko slov o vliianii pomeshchikov na gosudarstvennoe upravlenie Rossii," (probably 1856), GPB, fond 833, delo No. 253/30–31; Miliutin, "Mysli o sposobakh unichtozheniia," TsGIAL, fond 869, opis' 1, delo No. 449/56–59.

18. Tsie, "Neskol'ko slov o vliianii," GPB, fond 833, delo No. 253/26–30.

19. de Custine, *Russia,* pp. vii, 499.

20. Quoted in I. I. Kostiushko, *Krest'ianskaia reforma 1864g. v Tsarstve Pol'skom* (Moscow, 1962), p. 79.

21. Raeff, "The Well-Ordered Police State," pp. 1235–43; Yaney, *Systematization,* pp. 63–68.

22. For an early statement of this view, see N. A. Miliutin, "O predpolagaemoi zheleznoi doroge mezhdu S.-Peterburgom i Moskvoiu," TsGIAL, fond 869, opis' 1, delo No. 204/181–82.

23. Valuev, "Otryvok iz zamechanii o poriadke grazhdanskoi sluzhby v Rossii," TsGIAL, fond 908, opis' 1, delo No. 24/26.

24. Pis'mo N. A. Miliutina k P. D. Kiselevu, 4 marta 1858g., ORGBL, fond 129, kartonka 17, papka 55.

25. G. A. Dzhanshiev, *A. M. Unkovskii i osvobozhdenie krest'ian* (Moscow, 1894), pp. 12–15; Semevskii, *Krest'ianskii vopros,* II: 347.

26. Emmons, *Russian Landed Gentry,* pp. 81–82.

27. Dzhanshiev, *Unkovskii,* pp. 23–25; Emmons, *Russian Landed Gentry,* pp. 84–85.

28. Emmons, *Russian Landed Gentry,* pp. 87–88.

29. "Zapiska A. A. Golovacheva i A. M. Unkovskago," (1858g.), TsGAOR, fond 109, opis' 1, delo No. 1960. The latter part of this memorandum was published in *Kolokol,* No. 39 (1 April 1959), under the title "Proekt Un'kovskago," *Kolokol. Gazeta A. I. Gertsena i N. P. Ogareva,* II, pp. 316–21. An English translation of excerpts from this memorandum can be found in Emmons, *Russian Landed Gentry,* pp. 427–43.

30. See, for example, B. N. Chicherin, "O krepostnom sostoianii," *Golosa iz Rossii* (1856), II: 127–229, especially pp. 178–99 (Soviet reprint edition), and K. D. Kavelin, "Mysli ob unichtozheniia krepostnago sostoianiia v Rossii," (1857g.), in *Sobranie sochinenii,* Vol. II, cols. 88–102.

31. "Otzyvy chlenov gubernskikh komitetov," *Prilozhenie k trudam redaktsionnykh komissii,* 9 vols. (St. Petersburg, 1859–1860), II: 661, 682–98; *Pervoe izdanie materialov redaktsionnykh kommissii dlia sostavleniia polozhenii o krest'ianakh, vykhodiashchikh iz krepostnoi zavisimosti,* Vol. XII (St. Petersburg, 1859), pp. 1–4.

32. Quoted in Emmons, *Russian Landed Gentry,* pp. 341–42.

33. Ibid., pp. 350–93.

34. Ibid., pp. 369–85.

35. Kavelin, "Dvorianstvo i osvobozhdenii krest'ian," *Sobranie sochinenii,* Vol. II, col. 140.

36. Emmons, *Russian Landed Gentry,* p. 393.

37. B. N. Chicherin, *Moskovskii universitet* (Moscow, 1929), p. 67.

38. Quoted in M. Lemke, *Ocherki osvoboditel'nago dvizheniia "shestidesiatykh godov"* (St. Petersburg, 1908), p. 449.

39. Kavelin, "Dvorianstvo i osvobozhdenie krest'ian," col. 142.

40. Zablotskii-Desiatovskii and Odoevskii, eds., *Sel'skoe chtenie*, I: 17–18, 27–28, 54, 111.

41. Pis'mo N. A. Miliutina k Ia. A. Solov'evu, 23 marta/4 aprelia 1864g., *RS*, LIV (1887), pp. 181–84.

42. Confidential report from Hugh Wyndham to Lord Russell, No. 9, July 24, 1865, Warsaw, PRO, FO 65/686.

43. "Zapiska Miliutina ot 22 maia 1864 goda," in N. A. Miliutin, ed., *Izsledovaniia v Tsarstve Pol'skom, po Vysochaishemu poveleniiu, proizvedenie pod rukovodstvom Senatora, Stats-Sekretaria Miliutina*, 6 vols. (St. Petersburg, 1863–1866), IV: 1.

44. Meehan-Waters, "Social and Career Characteristics of the Administrative Elite, 1689–1761," in Pintner and Rowney, eds., *Russian Officialdom*, pp. 77–105.

45. Miliukov, *Ocherki*, III: 90–140.

46. Lincoln, *Nicholas I*, pp. 239–52.

47. S. P. Shevyrev, "Vzgliad russkago na sovremennoe obrazovanie Evropy," *Moskvitianin*, No. 1 (1841), p. 292.

48. Quoted in Starr, *Decentralization and Self-Government*, p. 53.

49. Aleksandr Kamenskii, "Vsepoddanneishaia zapiska Kamenskago 1850 goda," *RS*, CXXII (June 1905): 629.

50. Gogol', *Polnoe sobranie sochinenii N. V. Gogolia*, VIII: 41.

51. A. V. Nikitenko, *Zapiski i dnevnik, 1826–1877*, 2 vols. (St. Petersburg, 1892), I: 553.

52. Pis'mo K. D. Kavelina k T. N. Granovskomu, 4 marta 1855g., *LN*, LXVII (1959): 610.

53. Pis'mo K. D. Kavelina k T. N. Granovskomu, 5–25 sentiabria 1848g., ibid., p. 596.

54. Pis'mo K. D. Kavelina k T. N. Granovskomu, 4 marta 1855g., ibid., p. 610.

55. A. E. Tsimmerman, "Vospominaniia," ORGBL, fond 325, kartonka 1, papka 1/42.

56. A. I. Artem'ev, "Dnevnik A. I. Artem'eva, 1 ianvaria–31 iiulia 1856g.," GPB, fond 37, delo No. 158/58.

57. Ibid., 1 ianvaria–31 maia 1857g., GPB, fond 37, delo No. 160/8.

58. Ibid., 1 ianvaria–31 iiulia 1856g., GPB, fond 37, delo No. 158/50.

59. "Pamiati A. P. Zablotskago," p. 520.

60. Theodore Taranovski, "The Aborted Counter-Reform: Muravev Commission and the Judicial Statutes of 1864," *Jahrbücher für Geschichte Osteuropas*, XXIX (1981): 164.

61. Zablotskii-Desiatovskii, "Vzgliad na istoriiu gosudarstvennykh imushchestv v Rossii," (1856g.), TsGIAL, fond 940, opis' 1, delo No. 12/66.

62. N. Bakhtin, "Dopolnenie k zapiske zakliuchaiushchei v sebe soobrazheniia ob upravlenii otdel'nym vedomstvom," 20 noiabria 1856g., TsGAOR, fond 722, opis' 1, delo No. 605/2–3.

63. Taranovski, "The Aborted Counter-Reform," pp. 162–64.

64. See especially Zarudnyi's early view, "Sergei Ivanovich Zarudnyi," *RBS*, VII: 242.

65. V. A. Tsie, "Zapiska o merakh, neobkhodimykh dlia sokrashcheniia perepiski i uproshcheniia deloproizvodstva v gosudarstvennykh uchrezhdeniiakh" (1856g.), GPB, fond 833, delo No. 292/1.

66. Ibid., delo No. 292/4.

67. Kniaz' P. A. Dolgorukov, "O vnutrennem sostoianii Rossii," noiabr', 1857g., TsGAOR, fond 647, opis' 1, delo No. 50/6.

68. Ibid., delo No. 50/27–28, 32.

69. Ibid., delo No. 50/25.

70. Quoted in Iu. I. Gerasimova, "Otnoshenie pravitel'stva k uchastii pechati v obsuzhdenii krest'ianskogo voprosa v periode revoliutsionnoi situatsii kontsa 50-kh–nachala 60-kh godov XIX v.," in M. V. Nechkina, ed., *Revoliutsionnaia situatsiia v Rossii v 1859–1861gg.*, p. 82.

71. *Kolokol,* No. 9 (15 fevralia 1859g.), in *Kolokol. Gazeta A. I. Gertsena i N. P. Ogareva,* I: 67.

72. Lettre de N. A. Milutine á D. A. Milutine, 11/23 décembre 1861. Published in Leroy-Beaulieu, *Un homme d'état russe,* pp. 118–19.

73. N. A. Miliutin, "Zapiska po voprosu o preobrazovanii zemskikh uchrezhdeniiakh," 22 maia 1862g., TsGIAL, fond 869, opis' 1, delo No. 397/28.

74. Ibid.

75. Ibid., delo No. 397/30.

76. "Zhurnal obshchago prisutstviia komissii o gubernskikh i uezdnykh uchrezhdeniiakh," zasedaniia 10–12 marta 1862g., *Materialy po zemskomu obshchestvennomu ustroistvu (Polozhenie o zemskikh uchrezhdeniiakh),* 2 vols. (St. Petersburg, 1885–1886), I: 182–185; Starr, *Decentralization and Self-Government,* 247–49; V. V. Garmiza, *Podgotovka zemskoi reformy 1864 goda* (Moscow, 1957), pp. 171–92.

77. Quoted in M. K. Lemke, *Epokha tsenzurnykh reform, 1855–1865 godov* (St. Petersburg, 1905), p. 15.

78. Nikitenko, *Dnevnik,* II: 16.

79. O. A. Przhetslavskii, "O glasnosti v russkoi zhurnal'noi literature," 20 ianvaria 1860g., TsGIAL, fond 772, opis' 1, delo No. 5129/1.

80. Ibid., delo No. 5129/3.

81. Ibid., delo No. 5129/26.

82. Ibid., delo No. 5129/4.

83. Ibid., delo No. 5129/5.

84. Ibid., delo No. 5129/27.

85. Ibid., delo No. 5129/31–33.

86. Nikitenko, *Dnevnik,* II: 17.

87. Orlovsky, *Limits of Reform,* pp. 35–37; Varadinov, *Istoriia Ministerstva Vnutrennikh Del,* III (bk. 4): 22–43.

88. Quoted in Tatishchev, *Imperator Aleksandr II,* I: 278.

89. Starr, *Decentralization and Self-Government,* p. 45.

90. These figures are taken from P. I. Liashchenko, *Istoriia narodnogo khoziaistva SSSR,* 2 vols. (Moscow, 1956), I: 473, and A. G. Troinitskii, *Krepostnoe naselenie Rossii po desiatoi narodnoi perepisi* (St. Petersburg, 1861), p. 45.

91. Bakhtin, "Dopolnenie k zapiske zakliuchaiushchei v sebe soobrazheniia ob upravlenii otdel'nym vedomstvom," 20 noiabria 1856g., TsGAOR, fond 722, opis' 1, delo No. 605/ 2–10.

92. V. A. Tsie, "Zapiska o merakh, neobkhodimykh dlia sokrashcheniia perepisi i uproshcheniia deloproizvodstva v gosudarstvennykh uchrezhdeniiakh," (1856g.), GPB, fond 833, delo No. 292/2.

93. Ibid., delo No. 292/1.

94. Ibid., delo No. 292/4.

95. Starr, *Decentralization and Self-Government,* p. 122.

96. Valuev, "Duma russkago," p. 355.

97. K. N. Lebedev, "Iz zapisok senatora K. N. Lebedeva," *RA*, bk. 1 (January 1911), p. 109.

98. Starr, *Decentralization and Self-Government*, p. 127.

99. P. A. Valuev, *Dnevnik P. A. Valueva*, I: 312.

100. Saltykov had only recently returned to the ministry's central offices from exile in Viatka. On his exile, see S. A. Makashin, *Saltykov-Shchedrin: Biografiia* (Moscow, 1951), I: 299–483.

101. Solov'ev, "Zapiski," *RS*, XXXIII (March 1882): 562–79; Starr, *Decentralization and Self-Government*, pp. 128–34, 144–47.

102. Quoted in Leroy-Beaulieu, *Un homme d'état russe*, p. 24n.

103. Solov'ev, "Zapiski," XXXIII: 562–79.

104. A. F. Koni, ed., *Viktor Antonovich Artsimovich: Vospominaniia-kharakteristika* (St. Petersburg, 1904), p. 74.

105. TsGIAL, fond 982, opis' 1, delo No. 97/25–45.

106. Ibid., delo No. 97/36.

107. Dzhanshiev, *Epokha velikikh reform*, p. 44; Starr, *Decentralization and Self-Government*, pp. 148–49; Orlovsky, "Ministerial Power and Russian Autocracy," pp. 156–57.

108. "Delo o sluzhbe kn. D. A. Obolenskago," TsGIAL, fond 1162, opis' 6, delo No. 375; D. A. Obolenskii, "Zamechaniia na proekt novago poriadka sudoproizvodstva Rossii," TsGAOR, fond 647, opis' 1, delo No. 56.

109. TsGAOR, fond 722, opis' 1, delo No. 460.

110. Obolenskii, "Zamechaniia," TsGAOR, fond 647, opis' 1, delo No. 56/7.

111. Ibid.

112. Ibid., delo No. 56/13, 5–6.

113. Ibid., delo No. 56/1.

114. "Delo o sluzhbe S. I. Zarudnago," TsGIAL, fond 1405, opis' 528, delo No. 83.

115. A. F. Koni, "Sergei Ivanovich Zarudnyi," in *Ottsy i deti sudebnoi reformy (k piatidesiatiletiiu sudebnykh ustavov)* (Moscow, 1914), pp. 80–81.

116. Obolenskii, "Zamechaniia," TsGAOR, fond 647, opis' 1, delo No. 56/5–6.

117. Kaiser, *Die russische Justizreform von 1864*, pp. 190–94; Wortman, *Development of a Russian Legal Consciousness*, pp. 247–48.

118. *Materialy po preobrazovaniiu sudebnoi chasti*, "Svod obshchikh zamechanii na proekt i na glavyne nachala sudoproizvodstva grazhdanskago priniatye soedinennymi departamentami," pp. 7–8, 19, 33, 141–43.

119. As a State Secretary in the State Council's Department of Civil and Spiritual Affairs, Zarudnyi was obliged to devote his full attention to the final stages of the emancipation debate beginning in September 1860.

120. "Delo o sluzhbe kn. D. A. Obolenskago," TsGIAL, fond 1162, opis' 6, delo No. 375; E. D. Dneprov, "Proekt ustava morskago suda i ego rol' v podgotovke sudebnoi reformy (aprel, 1860g.)," in M. V. Nechkina, ed., *Revoliutsionnaia situatsiia v Rossii v 1859–1861gg.* (Moscow, 1970), p. 59.

121. P. N. Glebov, "Morskoe sudoproizvodstvo vo Frantsii," *Morskoi sbornik*, No. 11 (November 1859), pt. 3, pp. 101–11; No. 12 (December 1859), pt. 3, pp. 344–69; No. 1 (January 1860), pt. 3, pp. 47–63; No. 4 (April 1860), pt. 3, pp. 318–52.

122. See, for example, Chechulin, ed., *Nakaz Imperatritsy Ekateriny II*, arti-

cles 98, 153, 157, pp. 39–41, and M. M. Speranskii, "O zakonakh," *SIRIO, XXX* (1880), p. 382.

123. Glebov, "Morskoe sudoproizvodstvo," No. 11 (November 1859), pp. 108–10.

124. Orlovsky, *Limits of Reform,* pp. 113–14.

125. W. Bruce Lincoln, *Petr Petrovich Semenov-Tian-Shanskii: The Life of a Russian Geographer* (Newtonville, Mass., 1980), pp. 40–42.

126. Semenov-Tian-Shanskii, *Memuary,* III: 119.

127. K. D. Kavelin, "Mnenie ob luchshem sposobe razrabotki voprosa ob osvobozhdenii krest'ian," in *Sobranie sochinenii,* Vol. II, cols. 104–5; Solov'ev, "Zapiski," *RS,* XXXVII (1883), pp. 279–81.

128. Semenov-Tian-Shanskii, *Memuary,* III: 120.

129. *Sbornik pravitel'stvennykh rasporiazhenii po ustroistvu byta krest'ian vyshedshikh iz krepostnoi zavisimosti,* 3rd. ed. (St. Petersburg, 1869), p. 42.

130. These included Miliutin, Zablotskii, Girs, I. P. Arapetov, Samarin, Iu. A. Gagemeister, A. N. Popov, S. M. Zhukovskii, E. I. Lamanskii, N. V. Kalachov, Ia. A. Solov'ev, and M. Kh. Reitern. Semenov, *Istoriia,* I: 3–4.

131. Stoianovskii and Khrushchov were not approved by their superiors for membership on the Editing Commission, and the men who took their places were less useful as advocates of an emancipation. One was Semenov's elder brother Nikolai, an honest official, but a hard-line conservative. The other was V. I. Bulygin, who served on the commission as a mouthpiece for Minister of State Domains Murav'ev and who, Semenov later remarked, "did more harm than good in the great undertaking of emancipating the peasants." Semenov-Tian-Shanskii, *Memuary,* III: 159; see also pp. 143–44, 153–54.

132. Ibid., pp. 167–69. Despite Rostovtsev's reservations, Shuvalov was appointed to the Editing Commission nonetheless.

133. Arapetov, Gagemeister, Girs, Lamanskii, Samarin, Petr Semenov, Solov'ev, and Zablotskii.

134. Samarin, P. A. Bulgakov, Cherkasskii, A. D. Zheltukhin, G. P. Galagan, and A. N. Popov. Zheltukhin was the editor of *Zhurnal zemlevladel'tsev,* the Slavophile journal devoted to the study of rural economy.

135. D. A. Miliutin, "Moi starcheskie vospominaniia," ORGBL, fond 169, kartonka 12, papka No. 4/90–92; Golovnin, "Zapiski i primechaniia," GPB, fond 208, delo No. 1/91; Panaeva, *Vospominaniia,* pp. 188–201; W. Bruce Lincoln, "The Circle of Grand Duchess Yelena Pavlovna, 1847–1861," *Slavonic and East European Review,* XLVIII (July 1970): 373–84; Obolenskii, "Moi vospominaniia," CXXXVII: 504–28; Semenov-Tian-Shanskii, *Memuary,* III: *passim.*

136. These were Petr and Nikolai Semenov, Samarin, Reitern, Kalachev, Zhukovskii, Miliutin, Popov, Gagemeister, Girs, Lamanskii, Solov'ev, Zablotskii, and Arapetov.

137. This bloc of eighteen included V. V. Tarnovskii, N. Kh. Bunge, S. M. Zhukovskii, A. K. Girs, I. P. Arapetov, N. V. Kalachov, Ia. A. Solov'ev, K. I. Domontovich, E. I. Lamanskii, Petr Semenov, Samarin, Cherkasskii, Popov, Zablotskii, Gagemeister, Reitern, N. N. Pavlov, and Miliutin. The satellite group of four sympathizers was made up of Prince S. P. Golitsyn, Liuboshchinskii, B. F. Zalesskii, and N. I. Zheleznov.

138. Lincoln, "Ministers of Nicholas I," pp. 314–15; W. Bruce Lincoln, "The Ministers of Alexander II: A Brief Survey of Their Backgrounds and Service Careers," *Cahiers du monde russe et soviétique,* XVII (October–December 1976), p. 469.

139. W. Bruce Lincoln, "The Editing Commissions of 1859–1860: Some Notes on Their Members' Backgrounds and Service Careers," *Slavonic and East European Review,* LVI (July 1978): 353–54.

140. These were Miliutin, Tarnovskii, Solov'ev, Zhukovskii, Domontovich, Arapetov, Samarin, Petr Semenov, Pavlov, and Cherkasskii.

141. These were Gechevich, Galagan, Grabianka, Prince Paskevich, Tatarinov, Shuvalov, and Iaroshchinskii.

142. Girs, Zhukovskii, Samarin, Solov'ev, and Cherkasskii.

143. Apraksin, Zheltukhin, Nikolai Semenov, Bulgakov, and Tatarinov.

144. These included Zablotskii, Domontovich, Bunge, Gagemeister, Lamanskii, Miliutin, and Reitern. They were opposed by Pozen and Kristofari.

145. "Dva pis'ma G. P. Galagana, 1859g.," *Kievskaia starina* (September 1895), p. 70. The men who supported the enlightened bureaucrats' program were Miliutin, Cherkasskii, Samarin, Popov, Petr Semenov, Kalachov, Girs, Zhukovskii, Domontovich, Tarnovskii, Solov'ev, and Liuboshchinskii. Zablotskii, as another member of this bloc, was frequently invited to the meetings of this section, although he was not formally a member.

146. Lincoln, *Petr Semenov-Tian-Shanskii,* pp. 44–45.

147. Zablotskii-Desiatovskii, "O krepostnom sostoianii v Rossii," p. 271.

148. Garmiza, *Podgotovka,* p. 132; S. Ia. Tseitlin, "Zemskaia reforma," in *Istoriia Rossii v XIX veke,* III: 197.

149. Starr, *Decentralization and Self-Government,* p. 176.

150. Robert J. Abbott, "Police Reform in Russia, 1858–1878." Unpublished Ph. D. dissertation, Princeton University, 1971, pp. 104–10.

151. Valuev, *Dnevnik,* I: 152.

152. "Zhurnal obshchago prisutstviia komissii o gubernskikh i uezdnykh uchrezhdeniiakh," zasedaniia 10–12 marta 1862g. *Materialy po zemskomu obshchestvennomu ustroistvu,* I: 182–85. See also Garmiza, *Podgotovka,* pp. 171–92; Starr, *Decentralization and Self-Government,* pp. 244–49; and Valuev, *Dnevnik,* I: 157. See Emmons, *Russian Landed Gentry,* pp. 321–94, for a discussion of the reaction of the nobility to the emancipation.

153. Lettre de N. A. Milutine à D. A. Milutine, 11/23 Decembre 1861, published in Leroy-Beaulieu, *Un homme d'état russe,* pp. 118–20.

154. N. A. Miliutin, "Zapiska po voprosu o preobrazovanii zemskikh uchrezhdeniiakh," 22 maia 1862g. TsGIAL, fond 869, opis' 1, delo No. 397/28.

155. *Materialy po zemskomu obshchestvennomu ustroistvu,* I: 211–12.

156. Starr, *Decentralization and Self-Government,* pp. 280–88. See also Baron M. A. Korf, "Vzgliad na vnutrenniia preobrazovaniia posledniago desiatiletiia," (aprel, 1866g.), TsGAOR, fond 728, opis' 1, delo No. 2863.

157. G. A. Dzhanshiev, *Stranitsa iz istorii sudebnoi reformy: D. N. Zamiatnin* (Moscow, 1883), pp. 23–27.

158. Wortman, *Development of a Russian Legal Consciousness,* pp. 252–53.

159. Vladimir Nabokov, "Raboty po sostavleniiu sudebnykh ustavov. Obshchaia kharakteristika sudebnoi reformy," in N. V. Davydov and N. N. Polianskii, eds. *Sudebnaia reforma,* 2 vols. (Moscow, 1915), I: 304.

160. These eight jurists were N. A. Butskovskii, N. I. Stoianovskii, D. A. Rovinskii, K. P. Podedonostsev, A. M. Plavskii, P. N. Danevskii, S. P. Shubin-Pozdeev, and A. P. Vilinbakhov. I. A. Blinov, "Khod sudebnoi reformy 1864 goda," *Sudebnye ustavy 20 noiabria 1864g. za piat'desiat' let,* 2 vols. (Petrograd, 1914), I: 124, 126.

161. Quoted in Dzhanshiev, *Epokha velikikh reform,* p. 400.

162. Ibid., pp. 402–5.

163. Wortman, *Development of a Russian Legal Consciousness,* pp. 259–60.

164. This biographical information is taken from *Gosudarstvennaia kantseliariia, 1810–1910; Spisok chinam Pravitel'stvuiushchago Senata i Ministerstva Iustitsii;* and *Russkii biograficheskii slovar.*

165. A detailed discussion of the provisions of these statutes can be found in Kaiser, *Die russische Justizreform von 1864,* pp. 340–406.

166. *PSZ,* sobranie 2-oe, No. 41473.

167. "Delo o sluzhbe A. P. Zablotskago-Desiatovskago," TsGIAL, fond 1162, opis' 6, delo No. 196.

168. "Delo o sluzhbe N. A. Miliutina," TsGIAL, fond 1162, opis' 6, delo No. 335.

169. "Delo o sluzhbe kn. D. A. Obolenskago," TsGIAL, fond 1162, opis' 6, delo No. 375; "Delo o sluzhbe M. N. Liuboshchinskago," TsGIAL, fond 1162, opis' 6, delo No. 305; "Delo o sluzhbe K. K. Grota," TsGIAL, fond 1162, opis' 6, delo No. 154.

170. A. V. Golovnin, "Kratkii ocherk deistvii Velikago Kniazia Konstantina Nikolaevicha," GPB, fond 208, delo No. 2/269; Golovnin, "Materialy dlia zhizneopisaniia," TsGIAL, fond 851, opis' 1, delo No. 86/39–41.

171. Golovnin, "Zapiski, A. V. Golovnina s 1861 po 1866gg.," TsGIAL, fond 851, opis' 1, delo No. 5/377, 481. Golovnin wrote his memoirs entirely in the third person.

172. Golovnin, "Raznitsa v napravlenii gosudarstvennoi deiatel'nosti v pervoi i vo vtoroi polovine nyneshnego tsarstvovaniia," (mart 1867g.), GPB, fond 208, delo No. 236/2; TsGIAL, fond 851, opis' 1, delo No. 7/3.

173. Pis'mo A. V. Golovnina k v. k. Konstantinu Nikolaevichu, 30 maia 1862g., GPB, fond 208, delo No. 44/1.

174. As had been the case with Konstantin Nikolaevich's naval reforms, and those discussions that Dmitrii Miliutin was in the process of encouraging in the Ministry of War, for example.

175. V. A. Tsie, "Zapiska o neobkhodimosti okazaniia podderzhki zhurnalam," GPB, fond 833, delo No. 72/1; "Ob otnosheniiakh Ministerstva Narodnago Prosveshcheniia k literature posle peredachi tsenzury v drugoe vedomstvo," 17 ianvaria 1863g., TsGIAL, fond 1275, opis' 1, delo No. 45/9. On the question of more direct subsidies to pro-government publications by Golovnin's ministry, see M. V. L'vova, "Kak podgotovilos' zakrytie *Sovremennika* v 1862g.," *Istoricheskie zapiski,* XLVI (1954): 309–10; E. P. Fedoseeva, "Iz istorii bor'by samoderzhaviia s izdaniami Gertsena," *LN,* LXIII (1956): 678–79; C. A. Ruud, "The Russian Empire's New Censorship Law of 1865," *Canadian Slavic Studies,* III (Summer 1969): 238–40; C. A. Ruud, "A. V. Golovnin and Liberal Russian Censorship, January–June 1862," *Slavonic and East European Review,* L (April 1972): 211–13.

176. This commission was composed of V. A. Tsie, K. S. Veselovskii, Major General Stirmer, F. F. Voronov (one of Golovnin's former associates on the Central School Directorate), and I. E. Andreevskii, a professor of law at St. Petersburg University. Lemke, *Epokha tsenzurnykh reform,* p. 133; "Delo o sluzhbe kn. D. A. Obolenskago," TsGIAL, fond 1162, opis' 6, delo No. 375; Golovnin, "Kratkii ocherk deistvii Velikago Kniazia Konstantina Nikolaevicha," GPB, fond 208, delo No. 2/271.

177. Tsie, "Zapiska o merakh, neobkhodimykh dlia sokrashcheniia perepiski," GPB, fond 833, delo No. 292/4; W. Bruce Lincoln, "Reform and Reaction

in Russia: A. V. Golovnin's Critique of the 1860s," *Cahiers du monde russe et soviétique,* XVI (April–June 1975): 169–70.

178. Later in his life, Golovnin would insist that the state ought not to interfere in the private lives of citizens except to deal with problems of security. He defined security not only as defense against foreign attack but also protection against "internal discord." A. V. Golovnin, "Prodolzhenie zapisok, 1868–1870gg.," TsGIAL, fond 851, opis' 1, delo No. 8/18–23.

179. This second Obolenskii commission included Nikitenko, V. A. Rzhevskii (a member of the editorial board of *Severniaia pochta),* and V. Ia. Fuchs as representatives of the Ministry of Internal Affairs. N. P. Giliarov-Platonov (a professor of philosophy at the Moscow Theological Seminary and a member of the Moscow Censorship Committee), I. E. Andreevskii, and E. M. Feoktistov (an official whom Golovnin had assigned to prepare press digests for the Emperor), represented the Ministry of Public Instruction. Further, there were *kollezhskii sovetnik* Pogorel'skii from the Ministry of Justice and A. F. Bychkov from the Second Section of His Majesty's Own Chancery. Nikitenko, *Dnevnik,* II: 617; Lemke, *Epokha tsenzurnykh reform,* p. 263.

180. Dzhanshiev, *Epokha velikikh reform,* pp. 355–59; Lemke, *Epokha tsenzurnykh reform,* pp. 380–89.

181. The text of the "temporary regulations" of April 6, 1865, is in *PSZ,* sobranie 2-oe, No. 41988 and No. 41990. A summary can be found in Ruud, "Russian Empire's New Censorship Law," pp. 241–44, and in Lemke, *Epokha tsenzurnykh reform,* pp. 390–97.

182. For a discussion of the imperatives that underlay these now necessary reforms, see "Vsepoddanneishii doklad Voennago Ministra, 15 ianvaria 1862g.," in D. A. Skalon, ed., *Stoletie voennago ministerstva: Prilozheniia k istoricheskomu ocherku razvitiia voennago upravleniia v Rossii, 1802–1902gg.* (St. Petersburg, 1902), I: 70–183.

183. P. A. Zaionchkovskii, *Voenny reformy 1860–1870 godov v Rossii* (Moscow, 1952), pp. 41–361, discusses these reforms in detail and with great insight. For a briefer and less probing account in English, see Forrestt A. Miller, *Dmitrii Miliutin and the Reform Era in Russia* (Nashville, 1968), pp. 67–230. On D. A. Miliutin's earlier views, see E. Willis Brooks, "D. A. Miliutin: Life and Activity to 1856." Unpublished Ph.D. dissertation, Stanford University, 1970, which is essentially a summary and uninspired critique of the first volumes of Miliutin's voluminous memoirs. By contrast, see P. A. Zaionchkovskii's brilliant synthesis of Miliutin's career and ideas in "Dmitrii Alekseevich Miliutin: biograficheskii ocherk," in P. A. Zaionchkovskii, ed., *Dnevnik D. A. Miliutina, 1873–1875gg.* Vol. I (Moscow, 1947), pp. 5–72.

184. P. A. Valuev, "O vnutrennem sostoianii Rossii," 26 iiunia 1862," in V. V. Garmiza, ed., "Predpolozheniia i proekty P. A. Valueva po voprosam vnutrennei politike (1862–1866gg.)," in *Istoricheskii arkhiv,* III (January–February, 1958): 141–43.

185. Lettre de N. A. Milutine à D. A. Milutine, 11/23 décembre 1861, published in Leroy-Beaulieu, *Un homme d'état russe,* p. 120.

186. Valuev, "O vnutrennem sostoianii Rossii," p. 143.

187. K. L. Bermanskii, "Konstitutsionnye proekty tsarstvovaniia Aleksandra II," *Vestnik prava,* XXXV (November 1905): 225–33; L. G. Zakharova, *Zemskaia kontrreforma 1890g.* (Moscow, 1968), pp. 48–49.

188. Kavelin, "Dvorianstvo i osvobozhdenie krest'ian," col. 142.

189. Bermanskii, "Konstitutsionnye proekty tsarstvovaniia Aleksandra II," pp. 271–81.

190. Golovnin, "Materialy dlia budushchikh istorikov gosudarstvennago upravleniia Rossii," TsGIAL, fond 851, opis' 1, delo No. 16/1–2; Golovnin, "Prodolzhenie zapisok (1868–1870gg.)," TsGIAL, fond 851, opis' 1, delo No. 8/24.

191. Zakharova, *Zemskaia kontrreforma*, p. 53; P. A. Zaionchkovskii, *Krizis samoderzhaviia na rubezhe 1870–1880 godov* (Moscow, 1964), pp. 128–30.

192. Zakharova, *Zemskaia kontrreforma*, p. 53.

193. Golovnin, "Prodolzhenie zapisok, 1868–1870gg.," TsGIAL, fond 851, opis' 1, delo No. 8/29.

194. *Kolokol,* No. 9 (15 fevralia 1858g.), in *Kolokol. Gazeta A. I. Gertsena i N. P. Ogareva,* I: 67.

195. Ibid., No. 102 (1 iiulia 1861g.), IV: 853, 856.

196. For a discussion of the most revolutionary statements of the year following the promulgation of the Emancipation Acts, see V. P. Koz'min, *Iz istorii revoliutsionnoi mysli v Rossii* (Moscow, 1961), pp. 122–345.

197. Th. Dan, *The Origins of Bolshevism,* J. Carmichael, trans. (New York, 1964), pp. 50–51.

198. Martin Katz, *Michael N. Katkov—A Political Biography* (The Hague, 1966), pp. 83–85.

199. N. A. Miliutin, "O poriadke vvedeniia v deistvie novykh o krest'-ianakh polozhenii," *Izsledovaniia,* I: 1–5; Shchebal'skii, "Nikolai Alekseevich Miliutin i reformy v tsarstve Pol'skom," CLXII: 349–50.

200. Quoted in Zaionchkovskii, "Dmitrii Alekseevich Miliutin: biograficheskii ocherk," p. 56.

201. Pis'mo K. D. Kavelina k grafu D. A. Miliutinu, 15 ianvaria 1882g., in D. A. Korsakov, ed., "Iz pisem K. D. Kavelina k grafu D. A. Miliutinu, 1882–1884gg.," *VE,* CCVI (January 1909): 10.

202. Golovnin, "Prodolzhenie zapisok, 1868–1870gg.," TsGIAL, fond 851, opis' 1, delo No. 8/25.

203. Ibid., delo No. 8/24.

204. Golovnin, "Zapiska o bolee sushchestvennykh prichinakh rasprostraneniia revoliutsionnoi propagandy v Rossii i o merakh dlia prekrashcheniia ee," TsGAOR, fond Lorisa-Melikova, delo No. 52. For a discussion of Golovnin's authorship of this proposal, see Zaionchkovskii, *Krizis samoderzhaviia,* p. 201.

205. Pis'mo K. D. Kavelina k kn. V. A. Cherkasskomu, 4 iiulia 1878g., ORGBL, fond Cherkasskago/II, kartonka 9, papka 2.

206. Pis'mo A. V. Golovnina k D. A. Miliutinu, 9 oktiabria i 19 noiabria 1882g., 20 marta 1884g., ORGBL, fond 169, kartonka 61, papki 32, 38, 41.

207. Golovnin, "Prodolzhenie zapisok, 1868–1870gg.," TsGIAL, fond 851, opis' 1, delo No. 8/158.

208. Zaionchkovskii, "Dmitrii Alekseevich Miliutin: biograficheskii ocherk," p. 64.

209. Zaionchkovskii, *Krizis samoderzhaviia,* pp. 376–77.

210. Theodore Taranovski, "The Politics of Counter-Reform: Autocracy and Bureaucracy in the Reign of Alexander III, 1881–1894." Unpublished Ph. D. dissertation, Harvard University, 1976, chapters 1–3, as cited in Taranovski, "The Aborted Counter-Reform," note 15. See also pp. 1–4.

211. See, for example, Pis'ma A. V. Golovnina k D. A. Miliutinu, 9 oktiabria i 19 noiabria 1882g., 28 marta 1884g., ORGBL, fond 169, kartonka 61, papki 32, 38, 41.

Selected Bibliography

This bibliography does not pretend to be an exhaustive compilation of all materials that are relevant to the study of Russia's bureaucracy in the first two thirds of the nineteenth century, nor does it provide even a comprehensive listing of all materials consulted in the research for this book. It contains mainly sources that have been cited in the notes to this study, and those additional materials that I found to be particularly useful in my research.

Archival Materials

Arkhiv Akademii Nauk S. S. S. R. (ANSSSR)
Collection 30	P. I. Keppen archive
Collection 117	K. I. Arsen'ev archive

Columbia University. Archive of Russian and East European History and Culture (CU/AREEHC)
V. P. Semenov-Tian-Shanskii family archive

Gosudarstvennaia Biblioteka S. S. S. R. imeni V. I. Lenina. Otdel Rukopisei (ORGBL)
Collection 129	Kiselev family archive
Collection 169	D. A. Miliutin archive
Collection 231	M. P. Pogodin archive
Collection 325	A. E. Tsimmerman archive
Collection 327	Prince V. A. Cherkasskii archive
Collection 334	Chicherin family archive

Gosudarstvennaia Publichnaia Biblioteka imeni M. E. Saltykova-Shchedrina. Otdel Rukopisei (GPB)
Collection 37	A. I. Artem'ev archive
Collection 163	N. I. Vtorov archive
Collection 208	A. V. Golovnin archive
Collection 380	Baron M. A. Korf archive
Collection 550	M. P. Veselovskii archive
Collection 833	V. A. Tsie archive

Gosudarstvennyi Istoricheskii Arkhiv Leningradskoi Oblasti (GIALO)
Collection 355	Imperial School of Jurisprudence materials
Collection 792	Petrograd City Duma archive
Collection 846	Committee for the Introduction of the New Statute on the Civil Administration of St. Petersburg archive

Gosudarstvennyi Istoricheskii Muzei. Otdel Rukopisei (GIM)
Collection 345	T. N. Granovskii archive
Collection 351	N. V. Stankevich archive
Collection 442	M. M. Bogoslovskii archive

Selected Bibliography

Institut Russkoi Literatury (Pushkinskii Dom) Akademii Nauk S. S. S. R. (PD)
Collection 3	Aksakov family archive
Collection 21	D. N. Bludov papers
Collection 265	Archive of the journal *Russkaia starina*
Collection 3847	A. I. Skrebitskii papers

Public Records Office. London (PRO)
Collection F065	Diplomatic correspondence from British Consuls at Warsaw. Volumes 583–584, 612, 641–644, 665, 708

Tsentral'nyi Gosudarstvennyi Arkhiv Literatury i Iskusstva S. S. S. R. (TsGALI)
Collection 264	K. D. Kavelin archive

Tsentral'nyi Gosudarstvennyi Arkhiv Oktiabr'skoi Revoliutsii (TsGAOR)
Collection 109	Archive of the Third Section of His Majesty's Own Chancery
Collection 647	Archive of the Grand Duchess Elena Pavlovna
Collection 722	Grand Duke Konstantin Nikolaevich papers (Marble Palace Archive)
Collection 728	Winter Palace archive
Collection 945	V. A. Dolgorukov archive

Tsentral'nyi Gosudarstvennyi Istoricheskii Arkhiv S. S. S. R. (TsGIAL)
Collection 91	Archive of the Imperial Free Economic Society
Collection 379	Archive of the Fifth Section of His Majesty's Own Chancery
Collection 381	Archive of the Chancery of the Minister of State Domains
Collection 382	Archive of the Agricultural Academic Committee of the Ministry of State Domains
Collection 398	Archive of the Third Department (Department of Rural Economy) of the Ministry of State Domains
Collection 673	I. P. Liprandi archive
Collection 772	Archive of the Main Censorship Directorate
Collection 775	Archive of the Central Directorate of Censorship
Collection 776	Main Directorate of Press Affairs archive
Collection 777	St. Petersburg Censorship Committee archive
Collection 851	A. V. Golovnin archive
Collection 869	N. A. Miliutin archive
Collection 908	P. A. Valuev archive

Collection 940	A. P. Zablotskii-Desiatovskii archive
Collection 950	N. V. Kalachev archive
Collection 958	P. D. Kiselev archive
Collection 982	S. S. Lanskoi archive
Collection 1021	L. A. Perovskii archive
Collection 1149	State Council. Department of Laws archive
Collection 1152	State Council. Department of Economy archive
Collection 1162	Imperial State Chancellery archive
Collection 1261	Archive of the Second Section of His Majesty's Own Chancery
Collection 1263	Archive of the Committee of Ministers
Collection 1275	Archive of the Council of Ministers
Collection 1281	Archive of the Council of the Minister of Internal Affairs
Collection 1282	Archive of the Chancery of the Minister of Internal Affairs
Collection 1284	Archive of the Department of General Affairs of the Ministry of Internal Affairs
Collection 1287	Archive of the Economic Department of the Ministry of Internal Affairs
Collection 1288	Archive of the Main Directorate of Local Economic Affairs of the Ministry of Internal Affairs
Collection 1290	Central Statistical Committee of the Ministry of Internal Affairs archive
Collection 1349	Archive of the Senate. Special Collection of Personnel Records
Collection 1405	Archive of the Ministry of Justice
Collection 1409	His Majesty's Own Chancery archive

Yale University. Sterling Memorial Library
    Osborn Collection (N. A. Miliutin papers)

Published Materials

Abbott, Robert J. "Police Reform in Russia, 1858–1878." Unpublished Ph.D. dissertation, Princeton University, 1971.

Adres'- Kalendar ili obshchii shtat rossiiskoi imperii. St. Petersburg, 1825–1882. Published annually.

Adrianov, S. A. *Ministerstvo vnutrennikh del.* 3 vols. St. Petersburg, 1901.

Selected Bibliography

Akhmatova, E. N. "Znakomstvo s A. V. Druzhininym," *Russkaia mysl'*, XII, No. 12 (December 1891): 117–47.

Akhsharumov, D. D. *Iz moikh vospominanii.* St. Petersburg, 1905.

Aksakov, I. S. *Izsledovaniia o torgovle na ukrainskikh iarmarkakh.* St. Petersburg, 1858.

Aksakova, V. S. *Dnevnik Very Sergeevny Aksakovoi.* St. Petersburg, 1913.

"Aleksandr Vasil'evich Golovnin," *RS*, LII, No. 3 (March 1887): 767–90.

Aleksandrov, M. S. *Gosudarstvo, biurokratiia, i absoliutizm v istorii Rossii.* St. Petersburg, 1910.

Alekseev, A. I. *Fedor Petrovich Litke.* Moscow, 1970.

Alexander II. "Perepiska Imperatora Aleksandra II-go s velikim kniazem Konstantinom Nikolaevichem za vremia prebyvaniia ego v dolzhnosti namestnika Tsarstva Pol'skago v 1862–1863gg.," *Dela i dni,* I (1920): 122–62; II (1921): 134–51; III (1922): 64–98.

Amburger, Erik. *Geschichte der Behördenorganisation Russlands von Peter den Grossen bis 1917.* Leiden, 1966.

Andreev, M. "Samoderzhavie i zakonnost'," *Russkoe bogatstvo,* Nos. 11–12 (November–December 1905), pp. 127–47.

Annenkov, P. V. *Literaturnye vospominaniia.* Moscow, 1960.

———. *N. V. Stankevich. Perepiska i ego biografiia.* Moscow, 1857.

Anuchin, D. G. "Monastyrskaia reforma v Tsarstve Pol'skom," *RS*, CXI, No. 9 (September 1902): 513–32; CXII, No. 10 (October 1902): 145–63; No. 12 (December 1902): 562–76; CXIII, No. 1 (January 1903): 201–10.

Anuchin, E. *Istoricheskii obzor razvitiia administrativno-politseiskikh uchrezhdenii v Rossii s uchrezhdeniia o guberniiakh do poslednego vremeni.* St. Petersburg, 1872.

Arapetov, I. P. "Istoricheskoe znachenie kapitala," *Sovremennik,* XXVII, No. 5 (May 1851) (pt. 2): 1–36.

Arkhimova, T. G. "Vysshie komitety Rossii 2-oe chetverti XIX v." Kandidatskaia dissertatsiia (Kandidat istorii Akademii Nauk), Moscow, 1970.

Armstrong, John A. *The European Administrative Elite.* Princeton, 1973.

———. "Old Regime Governors: Bureaucratic and Patrimonial Attitudes," *Comparative Studies in Society and History,* XIV (1972): 2–29.

———. "Tsarist and Soviet Elite Administrators," *Slavic Review,* XXXI, No. 1 (March 1972): 1–28.

Aronson, M., and S. Reiser. *Literaturnye kruzhki i salony.* Leningrad, 1929.

Arsen'ev, K. K. "Materialy dlia biografii M. E. Saltykova." In *Polnoe sobranie sochinenii M. E. Saltykova-Shchedrina.* 12 vols. St. Petersburg, 1905–1906, I: 35–55.

———. "Pis'mo Berr'e o sovremennom sostoianii frantsuzskoi advokatury," *RV,* XXXII (March 1861): 126–51.

———. "Vospominaniia K. K. Arsen'eva ob uchilishche pravovedeniia, 1849–1855gg," *RS*, L, No. 4 (April 1886): 199–220.

———. *Zakonodatel'stvo o pechati.* St. Petersburg, 1903.

Artem'ev, A. I. "Iz dnevnika, 1856–1857 godov." In *M. E. Saltykov-Shchedrin v vospominaniiakh sovremennikov.* Moscow, 1957, pp. 427–40.

Avinov, N. "Graf M. A. Korf i zemskaia reforma 1864 g.," *Russkaia mysl',* No. 2 (February 1904), pp. 94–111.

Avrekh, A. D."Russkii absoliutizm i ego rol' v utverzhdenii kapitalizma v Rossii," *Istoriia SSSR,* No. 2 (1968), pp. 82–104.

Baiov, A. K. *Graf Dmitrii Alekseevich Miliutin.* St. Petersburg, 1912.

Selected Bibliography

Bakhrushin, S. V. "Velikaia kniaginia Elena Pavlovna." In *Osvobozhdenie krest'ian: deiateli reformy*. Moscow, 1911.

Barshev, Ia. *Istoricheskaia zapiska o sodeistvii Vtorago Otdeleniia sobstvennoi ego i. v. kantseliarii razvitii iuridicheskikh nauk v Rossii*. St. Petersburg, 1876.

Barsukov, N. P. *Zhizn' i trudy M. P. Pogodina*. 22 vols. St. Petersburg, 1888–1906.

Bartenev, P., ed. *Deviatnadtsatyi vek: Istoricheskii sbornik*. 2 vols. Moscow, 1872.

———. "V. I. Dal'," *RA*, I (1872): 2023–31.

Bennett, Helju Aulik. "Evolution of the Meanings of *Chin*: An Introduction to the Russian Institution of Rank Ordering and Niche Assignment from the Time of Peter the Great's Table of Ranks to the Bolshevik Revolution," *California Slavic Studies*, X (1977): 1–44.

Benson, Sumner. "The Conservative Liberalism of B. N. Chicherin," *Forschungen zur osteuropäishchen Geschichte*, XXI (1975): 17–114.

Berg, L. S. *Vsesoiuznoe geograficheskoe obshchestvo za sto let*. Moscow-Leningrad, 1946.

Bermanskii, K. L. "Konstitutsionnye proekty tsarstvovaniia Aleksandra II," *Vestnik prava*, XXXV, No. 9 (November 1905): 223–91.

Beskrovnyi, L. G. *Ocherki voennoi istoriografii Rossii*. Moscow, 1962.

Binshtok, V. "Materialy po istorii russkoi tsenzury," *RS*, LXXXIX, No. 3 (March 1897): 581–97; XC, No. 4 (April 1897): 179–206; XC, No. 5 (May 1897): 341–55.

"Biurokraticheskaia voina 1839-go goda," *RS*, XXXII (1881): 890–95.

Blackwell, W. H. *The Beginnings of Russian Industrialization, 1800–1860*. Princeton, 1968.

Blinov, I. A. *Gubernatory: Istoriko-iuridicheskii ocherk*. St. Petersburg, 1905.

———. "Khod sudebnoi reformy, 1864 goda." *Sudebnye ustavy 20 noiabria 1864g. za piat'desiat' let*. 2 vols. Petrograd, 1914, I: 105–21.

Bliokh, I. S. *Finansy Rossii XIX stoletie. Istoriia-statistika*. 2 vols. St. Petersburg, 1882.

Bludov, D. N. "Dva pis'ma grafa D. N. Bludova k supruge ego," *RA*, V (1867): 1046–48.

———. *Mysli i zamechaniia*. St. Petersburg, 1866.

Bludova, A. D. "Vospominaniia gr. A. D. Bludovoi," *RA*, No. 10 (October 1872), pp. 1217–1310; No. 11 (November 1873), pp. 2049–2138.

Blum, Jerome. *Lord and Peasant in Russia from the Ninth to the Nineteenth Centuries*. Princeton, 1961.

Bobrovskii, P. "Vzgliad na grammotnost' i uchebnye komandy (ili polkovye shkoly) v nashei armii," *Voennyi sbornik*, LXXVI (1870); LXVIII–LXXIX (1871).

Bogdanovich, M., ed. *Istoricheskii ocherk deiatel'nosti voennago upravleniia v Rossii v pervoe dvadtsatipiatiletie blagopoluchnago tsarstvovaniia Gosudaria Imperatora Aleksandra Nikolaevicha (1855–1880)*. 6 vols. St. Petersburg, 1879–1881.

Borozdin, I. N. "Universitety v Rossii v pervoi polovine XIX veka." *Istoriia Rossii v XIX veke*. 9 vols. St. Petersburg, 1907, II: 349–79.

Borovkov, A. D. "Aleksandr Dmitrievich Borovkov i ego avtobiograficheskie zapiski," *RS*, No. 9 (September 1898), pp. 533–64; No. 10 (October 1898), pp. 41–63; No. 11 (November 1898), pp. 331–62; No. 12 (December 1898), pp. 591–616.

Bowman, Herbert. *Vissarion Belinskii, 1811–1848: A Study in the Origins of Social Criticism in Russia*. Cambridge, Mass., 1954.

Selected Bibliography

Bray-Steinberg, Count Otto von. "Imperator Nikolai I i ego spodvizhniki," *RS,* CIX, No. 1 (January 1902): 115–39.

Brodskii, N. L., ed. *Literaturnye salony i kruzhki. Pervaia polovina XIX veka.* Moscow-Leningrad, 1930.

———, ed. *V. P. Botkin i I. S. Turgenev. Neizdannaia perepiska, 1851–1869gg.* Moscow-Leningrad, 1930.

Brooks, E. Willis. "D. A. Miliutin: Life and Activity to 1856." Unpublished Ph.D. dissertation, Stanford University, 1970.

Brower, Daniel. *Training the Nihilists: Education and Radicalism in Tsarist Russia.* Ithaca, 1975.

Brown, E. *Stankevich and His Moscow Circle, 1830–1840.* Stanford, 1961.

Bukh, K. A. "Velikaia kniaginia Elena Pavlovna." *RS,* LVII, No. 3 (March 1888): 803–10.

Bykova, V. P. *Zapiski staroi smolianki.* St. Petersburg, 1898.

Byrnes, R. F. *Pobedonostsev: His Life and Thought.* Bloomington, Ind., 1968.

Chechulin, N. D., ed. *Nakaz Imperatritsy Ekateriny II, dannyi kommissii o sochinenii proekta novago ulozheniia.* St. Petersburg, 1907.

———. *Ocherki po istorii russkikh finansov v tsarstovovanie Ekateriny II.* St. Petersburg, 1906.

Chernukha, V. G. "Problema politicheskoi reformy v pravitel'stvennykh krugakh Rossii v nachale 70-kh godov XIX v." In Akademiia Nauk SSSR, Institut istorii SSSR, Leningradskoe otdelenie. *Problemy krest'ianskogo zemlevladeniia i vnutrennei politiki Rossii: dooktiabr'skii period.* Leningrad, 1972, pp. 138–91.

———. "Sovet Ministrov v 1857–1861gg." In Akademiia Nauk SSSR, otdelenie istorii, Arkhiograficheskaia komissiia, Leningradskoe otdelenie. *Vspomogatel'nye istoricheskie ditsipliny.* Leningrad, 1973. Vol. V, pp. 120–36.

Chernyshevskii, N. G. *Polnoe sobranie sochinenii.* 16 vols. Moscow, 1939–1955.

Chicherin, B. N. *Moskovskii universitet.* Moscow, 1929.

———. *Moskva sorokovykh godov.* Moscow, 1929.

———. *Zemstvo i moskovskaia duma.* Moscow, 1934.

Chistozvonov, A. N. "Nekotorye aspekty problemy genezisa absoliutizma," *Voprosy istorii,* No. 5 (1968), pp. 46–62.

Chizhevskii, D. I. *Gegel' v Rossii.* Paris, 1939.

Christoff, P. K. *An Introduction to Nineteenth-Century Russian Slavophilism.* 2 vols. Paris, The Hague, 1961, 1972.

Chubinskii, M. "Pamiati D. A. Miliutina," *VE,* No. 9 (September 1912), pp. 316–38.

Chumikov, A. A. "Studencheskie korporatsii v Sanktpeterburgskom universitete, 1830–1840gg," *RS,* XXX, No. 2 (February 1881): 367–80.

Confino, Michael. *Systèmes agraires et progrès agricole. L'assolement triennal en Russie aux XVIII-XIX siècles. Étude d'économie et de sociologie rurales.* Paris, The Hague, 1969.

Crozier, Michel. *The Bureaucratic Phenomenon.* Chicago, 1967.

Curtiss, J. S. *The Russian Army under Nicholas I, 1825–1855.* Durham, N.C., 1965.

de Custine, Marquis A. *La Russie en 1839.* 8 vols. Brussels, 1845.

———. *Russia.* Cincinnati, 1856.

Czap, P. "P. A. Valuev's Proposal for a *Vyt'* Administration, 1864," *Slavonic and East European Review,* XLV, No. 105 (July 1967): 391–410.

Selected Bibliography

Czartoryski, Prince Adam. *Memuary kniazia Adama Chartorizhskago.* 2 vols. Moscow, 1912.

Dal', V. I. "Materialy dlia istorii khlystovskoi i skopcheskoi eresei," *Chtenie obshchestva istorii i drevnostei rossiiskikh,* IV (1872).

Dan, Th. *The Origins of Bolshevism.* Translated by J. Carmichael. New York, 1964.

Davidovich, A. M., and S. A. Pokrovskii. "O klassovoi sushchnosti i etapakh razvitiia russkogo absoliutizma," *Istoriia SSSR,* No. 1 (1969), pp. 58–78.

Davydov, I. I. "O naznachenii russkikh universitetov i uchastie ikh v obshchestvennom obrazovanii," *Sovremennik,* No. 3 (March 1849), pp. 37–46.

Davydov, N. V. *Iz proshlago.* Moscow, 1913.

———, and N. N. Polianskii. *Sudebnaia reforma.* 2 vols. Moscow, 1915.

Dement'ev, A. G. *Ocherki po istorii russkoi zhurnalistiki, 1840–1850gg.* Moscow-Leningrad, 1951.

———, A. V. Zapadov, and M. S. Cherepakhov, eds. *Russkaia periodicheskaia pechat' (1702–1894).* Moscow, 1959.

Demidova, N. F. "Biurokratizatsiia gosudarstvennogo apparata absoliutizma v XVII–XVIIIvv." In *Absoliutizm v Rossii XVII–XVIIIvv. Sbornik statei.* Moscow, 1964, pp. 206–42.

Derzhavin, G. R. *Zapiski Gavriila Romanovicha Derzhavina, 1743–1812.* Moscow, 1860.

"Deviatnadtsatoe fevralia. Chestvovanie etogo dnia litsami, prinimavshimi uchastie v sozdanii Polozhenii 19-go fevralia 1861g. i byvshimi neposredstvennymi ego primeniteliami," *RS,* XLI, No. 3 (March 1884): 669–732.

Diatlova, N. P. "Otchety gubernatorov kak istoricheskii istochnik." In Glavnoe arkhivnoe upravlenie. *Problemy arkhivovedeniia i istochnikovedeniia.* Leningrad, 1964, pp. 227–46.

Ditiatin, I. I. *Stat'i po istorii russkago prava.* St. Petersburg, 1895.

———. *Stoletie S.-Peterburgskago gorodskago obshchestva.* St. Petersburg, 1885.

———. *Ustroistvo i upravlenie gorodov v Rossii.* 2 vols. Iaroslavl', 1877.

Dmitriev, S. S. "Arkhiv redaktsii Sel'skogo blagoustroistva, 1858–1859gg.," *Zapiski otdela rukopisei Gosudarstvennoi biblioteki SSSR im. V. I. Lenina.* X (1941): 33–43.

Dneprov, E. D. "*Morskoi sbornik* v obshchestvennom dvizhenii perioda pervoi revoliutsionnoi situatsii v Rossii." In *Revoliutsionnaia situatsiia v Rossii v 1859–1861gg.* Edited by M. V. Nechkina. Moscow, 1965.

———. "Proekt ustava morskogo suda i ego rol' v podgotovke sudebnoi reformy (aprel' 1860g.)." In *Revoliutsionnaia situatsiia v Rossii v 1859–1861gg.* Edited by M. V. Nechkina. Moscow, 1970.

Dobroliubov, N. A. *Sobranie sochinenii.* 9 vols. Moscow-Leningrad, 1961–1964.

Dolgorukov, P. V. *Peterburgskie ocherki.* Moscow, 1934.

Dostoevskii, F. M. *Polnoe sobranie sochinenii.* 22 vols. Leningrad, 1972–.

Druzhinin, N. M., ed. *Absoliutizm v Rossii XVII–XVIII vv. Sbornik statei.* Moscow, 1964.

———. *Gosudarstvennye krest'iane i reformy P. D. Kiseleva.* 2 vols. Moscow, 1946, 1958.

———. "Senatorskie revizii 1860–1870kh godov (k voprosu o realizatsii reformy 1861g.)," *Istoricheskie zapiski.* LXXIX (1966): 139–75.

———. "Zhurnal zemlevladel'tsev, 1858–1860gg.," *Trudy instituta istorii RANIION.* I (1926): 463–507; *Institut istorii (RANIION). Uchenye zapiski.* II (1927): 251–310.

Selected Bibliography

Dubrovin, N. F., ed. *Materialy i cherty k biografii Imperatora Nikolaia I i k istorii ego tsarstovovanie.* St. Petersburg, 1896.

"Dvadtsat' sed'maia godovshchina dnia osvobozhdeniia krest'ian," *RS,* LVII, No. 3 (March 1888): 818–30.

Dzhanshiev, G. A. *A. M. Unkovskii i osvobozhdenie krest'ian.* Moscow, 1894.

———. *Epokha velikikh reform.* St. Petersburg, 1905.

———. *Osnovy sudebnoi reformy.* Moscow, 1891.

———. *Sbornik statei.* Moscow, 1914.

———. *S. I. Zarudnyi i sudebnaia reforma. Istoriko-biograficheskii eskiz.* Moscow, 1889.

———. *Stranitsa iz istorii sudebnoi reformy: D. N. Zamiatnin.* Moscow, 1883.

Dzhivelegov, A. K. "Graf V. N. Panin," *Velikaia reforma,* Vol. V. Moscow, 1911, pp. 68–87.

———, S. P. Melgunov, and V. I. Picheta, eds. *Velikaia reforma. Russkoe obshchestvo i krest'ianskii vopros v proshlom i nastoiashchem.* 6 vols. Moscow, 1911.

Edeen, Alf. "The Civil Service: Its Composition and Status." In *The Transformation of Russian Society: Aspects of Social Change since 1861.* Edited by C. E. Black. Cambridge, Mass., 1960, pp. 274–92.

Egorov, Iu. N. "Reaktsionnaia politika tsarizma v voprosakh universitetskogo obrazovaniia v 30kh–50kh gg. XIX v.," *Nauchnye doklady vysshei shkoly: Istoricheskie nauki.* No. 3 (1960), pp. 60–75.

———. "Studenchestvo Sankt-Peterburgskogo Universiteta v 30–50kh godakh XIX v. Ego sotsial'nyi sostav i raspredelenie po fakul'tetam," *Vestnik Leningradskogo Universiteta,* No. 14 (1957), pp. 5–19.

Ehrhard, Marcelle, *V. A. Joukovskii et le préromantisme russe.* Paris, 1938.

Ekonomicheskoe sostoianie gorodskikh poselenii Evropeiskoi Rossii v 1861–1862gg. 2 vols. St. Petersburg, 1863.

Emel'ianova, I. A. *Vysshie organy gosudarstvennoi vlasti i upravleniia Rossii v doreformennyi period.* Kazan, 1962.

Emmons, Terence. *The Russian Landed Gentry and the Peasant Emancipation of 1861.* Cambridge, 1968.

Engel'gardt, N. "Samoderzhavie i biurokratiia v tsarstvovanie imperatora Nikolaia Pavlovicha," *RV,* No. 12 (December 1902), pp. 465–75.

Engelman, I. *Istoriia krepostnago prava v Rossii.* Translated by V. Shcherb. Moscow, 1906.

Eroshkin, N. P. *Istoriia gosudarstvennykh uchrezhdenii dorevoliutsionnoi Rossii.* Moscow, 1968.

———. "Samoderzhavie pervoi poloviny XIX veka i ego politicheskie instituty (k voprosu o klassovoi sushchnosti absoliutizma)," *Istoriia SSSR.* No. 1 (January–February 1975), pp. 37–59.

Evgenev-Maksimov, I. *"Sovremennik" pri Chernyshevskom i Dobroliubove.* Leningrad, 1936.

———. *Zhizn' i deiatel'nost' N. A. Nekrasova.* 2 vols. Leningrad, 1947–1950.

Evreinov, V. A. *Grazhdanskoe chinoproizvodstvo v Rossii.* St. Petersburg, 1887.

Fedorov, A. V. *Obshchestvenno-politicheskoe dvizhenie v russkoi armii, 40–70gg. XIX v.* Moscow, 1958.

———. *Russkaia armiia v 50–70gg. XIX v. Ocherki.* Leningrad, 1959.

Fedoseeva, E. P. "Iz istorii bor'by samoderzhaviia s izdaniami Gertsena," *LN,* LXIII (1956): 677–94.

Fedosov, I. A. "Sotsial'naia sushchnost' i evoliutsiia rossiiskogo absoliutizma," *Voprosy istorii,* No. 7 (1971), pp. 46–65.

Feoktistov, E. M. *Vospominaniia za kulisami politiki i literatury, 1848–1896gg.* Leningrad, 1929.

Ferguson, A., and A. Levin, eds. *Essays in Russian History. A Collection Dedicated to George Vernadsky.* Hamden, Conn., 1964.

Fet, A. *Moi vospominaniia (1848–1889).* Moscow, 1890.

Field, Daniel. *The End of Serfdom: Nobility and Bureaucracy in Russia, 1855–1861.* Cambridge, Mass., 1976.

————. "Kavelin and Russian Liberalism," *Slavic Review.* XXXII, No. 1 (March 1973): 59–78.

Filippov, A. N. "Istoricheskii ocherk obrazovaniia Ministerstv v Rossii," *ZhMIu,* No. 9 (November 1902), pp. 39–73; No. 10 (December 1902), pp. 1–26.

Fischer, G. *Russian Liberalism. From Gentry to Intelligentsia.* Cambridge, Mass., 1958.

Florinsky, Michael T. *Russia: A History and an Interpretation.* 2 vols. New York, 1968.

Florovskii, Prot. Georgii. *Puti russkago bogosloviia.* Paris, 1937.

Flynn, James. "The Universities, the Gentry, and the Russian Imperial Services, 1815–1825," *Canadian Slavic Studies,* II (Winter 1968): 486–503.

Galagan, G. P. "Dva pis'ma G. P. Galagana, 1859g.," *Kievskaia starina* (September 1895), pp. 68–70.

Galakhov, A. D. "Literaturnye kofeiniia v Moskve v 1830–1840gg.," *RS,* L, No. 4 (April 1886), pp. 181–98; No. 6 (June 1886), pp. 691–706.

Garmiza, V. V. *Podgotovka zemskoi reformy 1864 goda.* Moscow, 1957.

————, ed. "Predpolozheniia i proekty P. A. Valueva po voprosam vnutrennei politike (1862–1866gg.)," *Istoricheskii arkhiv,* III (January–February 1958): 138–53.

Gerasimova, Iu. I. "Krizis pravitel'stvennoi politiki v gody revoliutsionnoi situatsii i Aleksandr II." In *Revoliutsionnaia situatsiia v Rossii v 1859–1861gg.* Edited by M. V. Nechkina. Moscow, 1962.

————. "Onoshenie pravitel'stva k uchastii pechati v obsuzhdenii krest'ianskogo voprosa v period revoliutsionnoi situatsii kontsa 50kh–nachala 60kh godov XIX v." In *Revoliutsionnaia situatsiia v Rossii v 1859–1861gg.* Edited by M. V. Nechkina. Moscow, 1974.

German, K. F. *Istoricheskoe obozrenie literatury statistiki, v osobennosti rossiiskago gosudarstva.* St. Petersburg, 1817.

————. "Vzgliad na nyneshnee sostoianie statistiki v prosveshchennykh gosudarstvakh Evropy," *ZhMVD,* I (1829).

Gerschenkron, A. *Continuity in History and Other Essays.* Cambridge, Mass., 1968.

Gershenzon, M. O., ed. *Epokha Nikolaia I.* Moscow, 1910.

Gertsen, A. I. *Polnoe sobranie sochinenii i pisem Aleksandra Ivanovicha Gertsena.* 22 vols. Petrograd, 1918–1920.

Gessen, I. V. *Istoriia russkoi advokatury.* Moscow, 1914.

————. *Sudebnaia reforma.* St. Petersburg, 1905.

Glebov, P. N. "Morskoe sudoproizvodstvo vo Frantsii," *Morskoi sbornik,* No. 11 (1859), pp. 101–11; No. 12 (1859), pp. 344–69; No. 1 (1860), pp. 47–63; No. 4 (1860), pp. 318–52.

————. "Vvedenie ili ob" iasnitel'naia zapiska k proektu ustava morskago sudoustroistva i sudoproizvodstva," *Morskoi sbornik,* No. 5 (1860), pp. 1–54.

Gogol', N. V. *Polnoe sobranie sochinenii N. V. Gogolia.* 8 vols. Moscow, 1913.

Selected Bibliography

————. *Sobranie sochinenii N. V. Gogolia.* 6 vols. Moscow, 1959.

Golosa iz Rossii. Edited by A. I. Gertsen and N. P. Ogarev. 10 vols. London, 1856–1860. Reprinted, Moscow, 1974.

Golovachev, A. A. *Desiat' let reform, 1861–1871.* St. Petersburg, 1872.

Golovine, Ivan. *Russia under the Autocrat Nicholas I.* 2 vols. London, 1845.

Golovnin, A. V. "Obshchie zametki o poezdke po nekotorym guberniiam v 1860 godu," *Zapiski nauchnago obshchestva marksistov,* No. 7 (1927).

Gol'sten, A. "Dmitrii Ivanovich Meier: Ego zhizn' i deiatel'nost'." In D. I. Meier, *Russkoe grazhdanskoe pravo.* St. Petersburg, 1897, pp. i–xvi.

Goncharov, I. A. "Iz universitetskikh vospominanii," *VE,* CXXVII, No. 4 (April 1887): 489–517.

————. *Obyknovennaia istoriia.* Moscow, 1960.

Gorfein, G. M. "Osnovnye istochniki po istorii vysshikh i tsentral'nykh uchrezhdenii XIX–nachala XX vv." In Glavnoe arkhivnoe upravlenie SSSR. *Nekotorye voprosy izucheniia istoricheskikh dokumentov XIX–nachala XX vv.: Sbornik statei.* Leningrad, 1967, pp. 73–110.

Gorodskie poseleniia v rossiiskoi imperii. 7 vols. St. Petersburg, 1860–1865.

Gosudarstvennaia kantseliariia, 1810–1910. St. Petersburg, 1910.

Gosudarstvennyi Sovet, 1801–1901. St. Petersburg, 1901.

Got'e, Iu. V. *Istoriia oblastnago upravleniia v Rossii ot Petra I do Ekateriny II.* 2 vols. Moscow, 1913, 1941.

Gradovskii, A. D. *Istoricheskii ocherk uchrezhdeniia general-gubernatorstva v Rossii.* St. Petersburg, 1869.

————. *Sobranie sochinenii A. D. Gradovskago.* 9 vols. St. Petersburg, 1898–1908.

Grigor'ev, V. V. *Imperatorskii S.-Peterburgskii Universitet v techenii pervykh piatidesiati let ego sushchestvovaniia.* St. Petersburg, 1870.

Grigorovich, D. V. *Literaturnye vospominaniia.* Moscow, 1961.

Grimstead, Patricia Kennedy. *The Foreign Ministers of Alexander I.* Berkeley, 1969.

"Graf Aleksei Kirillovich Razumovskii," *Sovetskaia Istoricheskaia Entsiklopediia.* Vol. XI, col. 857.

Grosul, V. Ia. *Reformy v Dunaiskikh kniazhestvakh i Rossiia.* Moscow, 1966.

Grot, Ia. K. *Pushkin, ego litseiskie tovarishchi i nastavniki.* St. Petersburg, 1899.

————. "Vospominaniia o Grafe M. A. Korfe," *RS,* XV, No. 1 (January 1876): 422–25.

Haywood, R. M. *The Beginnings of Railroad Development in Russia in the Reign of Nicholas I, 1825–1842.* Durham, N.C., 1969.

Haxthausen-Abbenberg, Baron August Ludwig Maria von. *The Russian Empire: Its People and Resources.* Translated by Robert Farie. 2 vols. London, 1856.

————. *Studies on the Interior of Russia.* Edited by S. Frederick Starr. Translated by Eleanore L. M. Schmidt. Chicago and London, 1972.

Huntington, Samuel. "Political Development and Decay," *World Politics,* XVII, No. 3 (April 1965): 386–430.

Hutton, Lester T. "The Reform of City Government in Russia, 1860–1870." Unpublished Ph.D. dissertation, University of Illinois, 1972.

Iakhontov, A. N. "Vospominaniia tsarskosel'skago litseista 1832–1838gg.," *RS,* LX, No. 10 (October 1888).

"Iakov Karlovich Grot: Akademik, professor, i pisatel'. Piatidesiatiletniaia godovshchina ego deiatel'nosti, 1832–1882gg.," *RS,* XXXVII, No. 1 (January 1883): 213–50.

Iakushkin, V. E. "N. A. Miliutin i redaktsionnye komissii," *RS,* XCII (1897).

Selected Bibliography

Iampol'skii, I. "Literaturnye deiatel'nosti I. I. Panaeva." In I. I. Panaev, *Literaturnye vospominaniia* (Moscow, 1950), pp. iv–xvi.
Ignatovich, I. I. *Pomeshchich'i krest'iane nakanune osvobozhdeniia.* Moscow, 1910.
Ikonnikov, V. "Russkie universitety v sviazi s khodom obshchestvennago obrazovaniia," *VE*, No. 9 (September 1876), pp. 161–206.
"Imperator Nikolai i akademik Parrot," *RS*, No. 7 (July 1898), pp. 139–52.
Insarskii, V. A. *Zapiski V. A. Insarskago.* 2 vols. St. Petersburg, 1898.
Iordanskii, N. I. *Konstitutsionnoe dvizhenie 60kh godov.* St. Petersburg, 1906.
Istoricheskoe obozrenie piatidesiatiletnei deiatel'nosti Ministerstva Gosudarstvennykh Imushchestv, 1837–1887gg. 5 vols. St. Petersburg, 1888.
Istoriia Ministerstva Finansov, 1802–1902. 2 vols. St. Petersburg, 1902.
Istoriia pravitel'stvuiushchago senata za dvesti let. 5 vols. St. Petersburg, 1911.
Istoriia Rossii v XIX veke. 9 vols. St. Petersburg, 1907–1911.
Istoriia udelov za stoletie ikh sushchestvovaniia, 1797–1897gg. 2 vols. St. Petersburg, 1902.
Ivaniukov, I. *Padenie krepostnago prava v Rossii.* St. Petersburg, 1903.
Ivanov, P. *Opyt biografii general-prokurorov i ministrov iustitsii.* St. Petersburg, 1863.
Ivanov-Razumnik, R. V., ed. *Sobranie sochinenii V. G. Belinskago.* 3 vols. St. Petersburg, 1919.
Ivanovskii, V. V. "Biurokratiia kak samostoiatel'nyi obshchestvennyi klass," *Russkaia mysl'*, No. 8 (August 1903), pp. 1–23.
———. *Istoricheskie osnovy zemskago upravleniia v Rossii.* St. Petersburg, 1892.
———. "Kollegial'noe nachalo v ministerskoi organizatsii," *Zhurnal iuridicheskago obshchestva pri Imperatorskom Sankt-Peterburgskom universitete*, No. 7 (1895), pp. 1–28.
"Izsledovaniia o gorodakh russkikh," *ZhMVD*, VI–VII, Nos. 4–6 (1844).
Jelavich, Charles and Barbara, eds. *The Education of a Russian Statesman: The Memoirs of Nicholas Karlovich Giers.* Berkeley and Los Angeles, 1962.
Kabuzan, V. M. *Izmeneniia v razmeshchenii naseleniia Rossii v XVII–pervoi polovine XIX v.* Moscow, 1971.
Kaiser, Friedhelm Berthold. *Die russische Justizreform von 1864: Zur Geschichte der russischen Justiz von Katherina II bis 1917.* Leiden, 1972.
Kamenskii, Aleksandr. "Vsepoddanneishaia zapiska Kamenskago 1850 goda," *RS*, CXXII (June 1905): 629–57.
Karamzin, N. M. *Karamzin's Memoir on Ancient and Modern Russia.* Edited and translated by Richard Pipes. Cambridge, Mass., 1959.
Karnovich, E. *Russkoe chinovnichestvo v byloe i nastoiashchee vremia.* St. Petersburg, 1897.
Kartsov, P. P. "Graf F. F. Berg, namestnik v Tsarstve Pol'skom. Ocherk iz vospominanii," *RS*, XXXVII, No. 2 (February 1883): 305–22.
Kataev, I. M. *Doreformennaia biurokratiia.* St. Petersburg, 1914.
Katz, Martin. *Michael N. Katkov—A Political Biography.* Paris, The Hague, 1966.
Kavelin, K. D. *Sobranie sochinenii K. D. Kavelina.* 4 vols. St. Petersburg, 1898–1899.
Kaznacheev, A. "Mezhdu strokami odnago formuliarnago spiska," *RS*, XXXII, No. 12 (December 1881): 817–80.
Keep, John. "Light and Shade in the History of the Russian Administration," *Canadian-American Slavic Studies*, VI, No. 1 (Spring 1972): 1–9.
———. "Programming the Past: Imperial Russian Bureaucracy and Society under the Scrutiny of Mr. George Yaney," *Canadian-American Slavic Studies*, VIII, No. 2 (Winter 1974): 569–90.

Selected Bibliography

Kharytonov, A. A. "Iz vospominanii A. A. Kharytonova," *RS,* LXXXI, No. 1 (January 1894): 101–32.

Khodnev, A. I. *Istoriia Imperatorskago Vol'nago Ekonomicheskago Obshchestva, s 1765 do 1865 goda.* St. Petersburg, 1865.

Kiniapina, N. S. *Politika russkogo samoderzhaviia v oblasti promyshlennosti (20–50kh gody XIX v.).* Moscow, 1968.

Kipp, Jacob W. "Consequences of Defeat: Modernizing the Russian Navy, 1856–1863," *Jahrbücher für Geschichte Osteuropas,* XX (1972): 210–25.

———. "M. Kh. Reutern on the Russian State and Economy: A Liberal Bureaucrat during the Crimean Era, 1854–1860," *Journal of Modern History,* XLVII (September 1975): 437–59.

Kizevetter, A. A. *Istoricheskie otkliki.* Moscow, 1915.

———. *Kuznets-Grazhdanin (iz epokhi 60kh godov).* 2d ed. Rostov-on-the-Don, 1904.

———. "Posadskaia obshchina v Rossii XVIII stoletiia." *Istoricheskie ocherki.* Moscow, 1912.

———. "Vnutrenniaia politika Imperatora Nikolaia Pavlovicha." *Istoricheskie ocherki.* Moscow, 1912.

Klochkov, M. V. *General-Prokurory pri Pavle I.* St. Petersburg, 1912.

———. *Ocherk pravitel'stvennoi deiatel'nosti vremeni Pavla I.* Petrograd, 1916.

Knirim, A. "O Gannoverskom grazhdanskom sudoproizvodstve," *ZhMIu,* No. 3 (March 1862), pt. 2, pp. 545–608.

Kobeko, D. F. *Imperatorskii tsarskosel'skii litsei, 1811–1843gg.* St. Petersburg, 1911.

Koberdowa, I. *Wielki książe Konstanty w Warszawie, 1862–1863.* Warsaw, 1963.

Kolmakov, N. M. "Ocherki i vospominaniia N. M. Kolmakova," *RS,* LXX, No. 4 (April 1891), pp. 23–43; No. 5 (May 1891), pp. 449–69; No. 6 (June 1891), pp. 657–79; LXXI, No. 7 (July 1891), pp. 119–148.

———. "Staryi sud," *RS,* LII, No. 12 (December 1886): 511–44.

Kolokol. Gazeta A. I. Gertsena i N. P. Ogareva. 11 vols. Moscow, 1961–1965.

Koni, A. F. *Ottsy i deti sudebnoi reformy (k piatidesiatiletiiu Sudebnykh ustavov).* Moscow, 1914.

———. *Sobranie sochinenii A. F. Koni.* 8 vols. Moscow, 1966–1969.

———. "Velikaia kniaginia Elena Pavlovna." In *Glavnye deiateli osvobozhdeniia krest'ian.* Edited by S. A. Vengerov. St. Petersburg, 1903.

———. "Velikaia kniaginia Elena Pavlovna." *Velikaia reforma.* V: 14–33.

———. "Velikii kniaz' Konstantin Nikolaevich," *Velikaia reforma.* V: 34–51.

———, ed. *Viktor Antonovich Artsimovich: Vospominaniia-kharakteristika.* St. Petersburg, 1904.

Konstantin Nikolaevich, velikii kniaz'. "Iz dnevnika v. k. Konstantina Nikolaevicha," *Krasnyi arkhiv,* X (1925): 217–60.

Kopanev, A. I. *Naselenie Peterburga v pervoi polovine XIX veka.* Moscow-Leningrad, 1957.

Korf, Baron M. A. "Iz zapisok barona M. A. Korfa," *RS,* XCVIII, No. 5 (May 1899), pp. 371–95; No. 6 (June 1899), pp. 511–42; XCIX, No. 7 (July 1899), pp. 3–30; No. 8 (August 1899), pp. 271–95; No. 9 (September 1899), pp. 480–515; C, No. 10 (October 1899), pp. 238–58; No. 11 (November 1899), pp. 267–99; CI, No. 1 (January 1900), pp. 25–56; No. 2 (February 1900), pp. 317–54; No. 3 (March 1900), pp. 545–88; CII, No. 4 (April 1900), pp. 27–50;

Selected Bibliography

No. 5 (May 1900), pp. 261–92; No. 6 (June 1900), pp. 505–27; CIII, No. 7 (July 1900), pp. 33–55.

———. "Materialy i cherty k biografii Imperatora Nikolaia I i k istorii ego tsarstvovanie. Rozhdenie i pervye dvadtsat' let zhizni (1796–1817gg.). In *Materialy i cherty k biografii Imperatora Nikolaia I i k istorii ego tsarstvovaniia*. Edited by N. F. Dubrovin. St. Petersburg, 1896.

———. "Zapiska M. Korfa nasledniku 24 fevralia 1848g.," *Golos minuvshego*, No. 3 (1913), pp. 217–29.

———. *Zhizn' grafa Speranskago*. 2 vols. St. Petersburg, 1861.

Korf, Baron S. A. *Administrativnaia iustitsiia v Rossii*. 2 vols. St. Petersburg, 1910.

———. *Dvorianstvo i ego soslovnoe upravlenie za stoletie 1762–1861*. St. Petersburg, 1906.

Korkunov, N. M. *Russkoe gosudarstvennoe pravo*. 2 vols. St. Petersburg, 1903.

Kornilov, A. A. *Krest'ianskaia reforma*. St. Petersburg, 1905.

———. *Kurs istorii Rossii XIX veka*. 3 vols. Moscow, 1918.

———. *Obshchestvennoe dvizhenie pri Aleksandre II (1855–1881). Istoricheskie ocherki*. Moscow, 1909.

———. *Ocherki po istorii obshchestvennago dvizheniia i krest'ianskago dela v Rossii*. St. Petersburg, 1905.

———. *Russkaia politika v Pol'she so vremeni razdelov do nachala XX veka*. Petrograd, 1915.

Korsakov, D. A., ed. "Iz pisem K. D. Kavelina k grafu D. A. Miliutinu, 1882–1884gg.," *VE*, CCVI, No. 1 (January 1909): 5–41.

———. "K. D. Kavelin, " *RS*, LIII, No. 2 (February 1887): 431–50.

———, ed. "Pis'ma K. D. Kavelina k K. K. Grotu (1862–1883g.)," *RS*, XCVII, No. 1 (January 1899), pp. 135–57; No. 2 (February 1899), pp. 377–99.

Kosachevskaia, M. E. *M. A. Balug'ianskii i Peterburgskii universitet*. Leningrad, 1971.

Koshelev, A. I. *Konstitutsiia, samoderzhavie, i zemskaia duma*. Leipzig, 1862.

———. *Zapiski A. I. Kosheleva, 1812–1883gg.* 2 vols. Berlin, 1884.

Kostiushko, I. I. *Krest'ianskaia reforma 1864g. v Tsarstve Pol'skom*. Moscow, 1962.

Kotliarevskii, N. *Kanun osvobozhdeniia, 1855–1861. Iz zhizni idei i nastroenii v radikal'nykh krugakh togo vremeni*. Petrograd, 1916.

Kovalevskii, E. P. *Graf Bludov i ego vremia*. St. Petersburg, 1871.

Kovnatov, R. A., ed. *Moskovskii Universitet v vospominaniiakh sovremennikov*. Moscow, 1956.

Koz'min, V. P. *Iz istorii revoliutsionnoi mysli v Rossii*. Moscow, 1961.

Kratkii istoricheskii ocherk razvitiia i deiatel'nosti vedomstva putei soobshcheniia za sto let ego sushchestvovaniia (1798–1898). St. Petersburg, 1898.

Krest'ianskaia reforma v Rossii v 1861 goda. Sbornik zakonodatel'skikh aktov. Moscow, 1954.

Krylov, N. A. "Kadety 40-kh godov. Lichnye vospominaniia," *IV*, LXXXV, No. 9 (September 1901): 943–67.

Kucherov, Samuel. *Courts, Lawyers, and Trials under the Last Three Tsars*. New York, 1953.

Kulomzin, A. N. "Dmitrii Nikolaevich Zamiatnin," *ZhMIu*, No. 9 (November 1914), pp. 233–322.

Kulomzin, A. V. "Vospominaniia mirovogo posrednika." *Zapiski otdela rukopisei Vsesoiuznoi biblioteki im. V. I. Lenina* (Moscow, 1941), Vol. X, pp. 5–32.

Selected Bibliography

Kutuzov, N. "Sostoianie gosudarstva v 1841g.," *RS,* No. 9 (September 1898), pp. 517–31.

Kuzmin, P. A. "Iz zapisok generala-leitenanta Pavla Alekseevicha Kuzmina," *RS,* No. 2 (February 1895), pp. 154–73; No. 3 (March 1895), pp. 76–91; No. 4 (April 1895), pp. 71–86.

La société russe par un russe. Traduit par M. M. Ernest Figurey et Désiré Corbier, avec une introduction de M. Antonin Proust. Paris, 1877.

Lamanskii, E. I. "Iz vospominanii Evgenii Ivanovicha Lamanskago," *RS,* CLXI, No. 1 (January 1915), pp. 73–87; No. 2 (February 1915), pp. 367–75; No. 3 (March 1915), pp. 576–89.

LaPalombara, Joseph, ed. *Bureaucracy and Political Development.* Princeton, 1963.

Lebedev, K. N. "Iz zapisok Senatora K. N. Lebedeva," *RA,* bk. 1 (January 1888), pp. 481–88, 617–28; bk. 2 (1888), pp. 0133–0144, 0232–0243, 0345–0356; bk. 3 (1888), pp. 249–70, 455–67; bk 1 (1893), pp. 284–97, 337–99; bk. 2 (1897), pp. 633–55; bk. 3 (1900), pp. 55–70, 244–80; bk. 2 (1910), pp. 333–408, 465–524; bk. 3 (1910), pp. 183–253, 353–76; bk. 1 (1911), pp. 87–128; 216–34, 375–422, 534–66; bk. 2 (1911), pp. 132–60, 224–60, 343–94, 465–511; bk. 3 (1911), pp. 53–107, 191–216, 321–52.

LeDonne, John. "Criminal Investigations before the Great Reforms" *Russian History,* I, No. 2 (1974): 101–18.

Leikina-Svirskaia, V. R. *Intelligentsiia v Rossii vo vtoroi polovine XIX veka.* Moscow, 1971.

Lemke, M. K. *Epokha tsenzurnykh reform, 1855–1865 godov.* St. Petersburg, 1905.

———. *Ocherki osvoboditel'nago dvizheniia "shestidesiatykh godov."* St. Petersburg, 1908.

———. *Ocherki po istorii russkoi tsenzury i zhurnalistiki XIX stoletiia.* St. Petersburg, 1904.

———, ed. *M. M. Stasiulevich i ego sovremenniki v ikh perepiske.* 5 vols. St. Petersburg, 1912.

Leroy-Beaulieu, Anatole. *The Empire of the Tsars and the Russians.* Translated by Z. Ragozin. 3 vols. New York, 1898.

———. *Un homme d'état russe (Nicolas Milutine) d'après sa correspondance inédite. Étude sur la Russie et la Pologne pendant le règne d'Alexandre II (1855–1872).* Paris, 1884.

Leslie, R. *Reform and Insurrection in Poland, 1856–1865.* London, 1963.

———. *Polish Politics and the Revolution of November 1830.* London, 1956.

Levin, Sh. M. *Obshchestvennoe dvizhenie v Rossii v 60–70e gody XIX veka.* Moscow, 1958.

———, ed. "K. D. Kavelin o smerti Nikolaia I: Pis'ma k T. N. Granovskomu, *LN,* LXVII (1959): 596–612.

Levshin, A. I. "Dostopamiatnye minuty moei zhizni. Zapiska Alekseia Iraklievicha Levshina," *RA,* No. 8 (August 1885): 475–558.

Liashchenko, P. I. *Istoriia narodnago khoziaistva SSSR.* 2 vols. Moscow, 1956.

———. *Poslednyi sekretnyi komitet po krest'ianskomu delu. 3 ianvaria 1857g.–16 fevralia 1858g. (po materialam Arkhiva Gosudarstvennago Soveta).* St. Petersburg, 1911.

Liatskii, E. A. "N. G. Chernyshevskii i I. I. Vvedenskii," *Sovremennyi mir,* No. 6 (June 1910), pp. 147–64.

Lincoln, W. Bruce. "The Circle of Grand Duchess Yelena Pavlovna, 1847–1861," *Slavonic and East European Review,* XLVIII, No. 112 (July 1970): 373–87.

———. "The Circle of M. V. Butashevich-Petrashevskii: Some Comments about the Social and Intellectual Climate of St. Petersburg in the 1840s,"

Selected Bibliography

The Australian Journal of Politics and History, XIX, No. 3 (December 1973): 366–73.

———. "The Composition of the Imperial Russian State Council under Nicholas I," *Canadian-American Slavic Studies,* X, No. 3 (Fall 1976): 369–81.

———. "Count P. D. Kiselev: A Reformer in Imperial Russia," *The Australian Journal of Politics and History,* XVI, No. 2 (August 1970): 177–88.

———. "The Daily Life of St. Petersburg Officials in the Mid-Nineteenth Century," *Oxford Slavonic Papers,* VIII (1975): 82–100.

———. "The Editing Commissions of 1859–1860: Some Notes on Their Members' Backgrounds and Service Careers," *Slavonic and East European Review,* LVI, No. 3 (July 1978): 346–59.

———. "The Genesis of an 'Enlightened' Bureaucracy in Russia," *Jahrbücher für Geschichte Osteuropas,* XX, No. 3 (September 1972): 321–30.

———. "The Karlovka Reform," *Slavic Review,* XXVIII, No. 3 (September 1969): 463–71.

———. "The Last Years of the Nicholas System," *Oxford Slavonic Papers,* VI (1973): 12–27.

———. "The Ministers of Alexander II: A Brief Survey of Their Backgrounds and Service Careers," *Cahiers du monde russe et soviétique,* XVII, No. 4 (October–December 1976): 467–83.

———. "The Ministers of Nicholas I: A Brief Inquiry into Their Backgrounds and Service Careers," *The Russian Review,* XXXIV, No. 3 (July 1975): 308–23.

———. "N. A. Miliutin and the St. Petersburg Municipal Act of 1846: A Study in Reform under Nicholas I," *Slavic Review,* XXXIII, No. 1 (March 1974): 55–68.

———. *Nicholas I: Emperor and Autocrat of All the Russias.* Bloomington, Ind., 1978.

———. *Nikolai Miliutin: An Enlightened Russian Bureaucrat of the Nineteenth Century.* Newtonville, Mass., 1977.

———. *Petr Petrovich Semenov-Tian-Shanskii: The Life of a Russian Geographer.* Newtonville, Mass., 1980.

———. "A Profile of the Russian Bureaucracy on the Eve of the Great Reforms," *Jahrbücher für Geschichte Osteuropas,* XXVII, No. 2 (1979): 181–96.

———. "Reform and Reaction in Russia: A. V. Golovnin's Critique of the 1860s," *Cahiers du monde russe et soviétique,* XVI, No. 2 (April–June 1975): 167–79.

———. "Reform in Action: The Implementation of the Municipal Reform Act of 1846 in St. Petersburg," *Slavonic and East European Review,* LIII, No. 131 (April 1975): 202–9.

———. *The Romanovs: Autocrats of All the Russias.* New York, 1981.

———. "Russia on the Eve of Reform: A *Chinovnik's* View," *The Slavonic and East European Review,* LIX, No. 2 (April 1981): 264–71.

———. "The Russian State and Its Cities: A Search for Effective Municipal Government, 1786–1842," *Jahrbücher für Geschichte Osteuropas,* XVII, No. 4 (December 1969): 531–41.

———. "Russia's Enlightened Bureaucrats and Problems of State Reform, 1848–1856," *Cahiers du monde russe et soviétique,* XII, No. 4 (October–December 1971): 410–21.

———, with Jacob Kipp. "Autocracy and Reform: Bureaucratic Absolutism and Political Modernization in Nineteenth-Century Russia," *Russian History,* VI, No. 1 (1979): 1–21.

Selected Bibliography

Liprandi, I. P. "Zapiski," *RS,* VI (1872): 70–86.

Lisicki, H. *Aleksander Wielopolski, 1803–1877.* 2 vols. Kraków, 1878.

Liutsh, A. "Russkii absoliutizm XVIII veka." In *Itogi XVIII veka v Rossii: Vvedenie v russkuiu istoriiu XIX veka,* Edited by A. Liutsh. Moscow, 1910, pp. 1–256.

Longinov, M. N. "Vmesto predisloviia (listok iz vospominanii)," *Sobranie sochinenii A. V. Druzhinina.* 8 vols. St. Petersburg, 1867, VIII, pp. v–xiv.

Luig, Lucie. *Zur Geschichte des russischen Innenministerismus unter Nikolaus I.* Weisbaden, 1968.

Lutskii, V. K. "Iz zapisok V. K. Lutskago," *RS,* CXVII, No. 2 (February 1904), pp. 303–23; No. 3 (March 1904), pp. 557–75; CXVIII, No. 4 (April 1904) pp. 137–50; No. 5 (May 1904), pp. 321–36.

L'vova, M. V. "Kak podgotovilos' zakrytie Sovremennika v 1862g.," *Istoricheskie zapiski,* XLVI (1954): 305–21.

McFarlin, Harold A. "The Extension of the Imperial Russian Civil Service to the Lowest Office Workers: The Creation of the Chancery Clerkship, 1827–1833," *Russian History,* I, No. 1 (1974): 1–17.

——. "Recruitment Norms for the Russian Civil Service in 1833: The Chancery Clerkship," *Societas: A Review of Social History* (Summer 1973), pp. 61–73.

MacMaster, R. E. *Danilevsky: A Russian Totalitarian Philosopher.* Cambridge, Mass., 1967.

Maikov, P. M. "Graf Lev Alekseevich Perovskii," *RBS,* Vol. Pav-Pet, pp. 540–551.

——. "Speranskii i studenty zakonovedeniia," *RV,* CCLXII, No. 8 (August 1899), pp. 609–26; CCLXIII, No. 9 (September 1899), pp. 239–56; CCLXIV, No. 10 (October 1899), pp. 673–82.

——. *Vtoroe otdelenie sobstvennoi e. i. v. kantseliarii, 1826–1882: Istoricheskii ocherk.* St. Petersburg, 1906.

Maikov, V. N. *Kriticheskie opyty.* St. Petersburg, 1891.

Makashin, S. A. *Saltykov-Shchedrin na rubezhe 1850–1860 godov. Biografiia.* Moscow, 1972.

——. *Saltykov-Shchedrin. Biografiia.* Moscow, 1951.

Makeev, N. *N. G. Chernyshevskii—redaktor "Voennago sbornika."* Moscow, 1950.

Malia, Martin. *Alexander Herzen and the Birth of Russian Socialism, 1812–1855.* Cambridge, Mass., 1961.

Malkova, Z. I., and M. A. Pliukhina. "Dokumenty vysshikh i tsentral'nykh uchrezhdenii XIX-nachala XX v. kak istochnik biograficheskikh svedenii." In Glavnoe arkhivnoe upravlenie SSSR. *Nekotorye voprosy izucheniia istoricheskikh dokumentov XIX—nachala XXv.: Sbornik statei.* Leningrad, 1967, pp. 204–28.

Mardarev, M. "Pis'ma i zapiski Georga-Fridrikha Parrota k Imperatoram Aleksandru I i Nikolaiu I," *RS,* LXXXII, No. 4 (April 1895): 191–219.

Materialy dlia istorii uprazdneniia krepostnago sostoianiia pomeshchich'ikh krest'ian v Rossii v tsarstvovanie Imperatora Aleksandra II. 3 vols. Berlin, 1860–1862.

Materialy dlia statistiki Rossiiskoi imperii, izdavaemye s Vysochaishego soizvoleniia, pri statisticheskom otdelenii Soveta Ministerstva Vnutrennikh Del. 2 vols. St. Petersburg, 1839, 1841.

Materialy otnosiashchiesia do novago obshchestvennago ustroistva v gorodakh imperii. 6 vols. St. Petersburg, 1877–1883.

Materialy po zemskomu obshchestvennomu ustroistvu (Polozhenie o zemskikh uchrezhdeniiakh). 2 vols. St. Petersburg, 1885–1886.

Selected Bibliography

Materialy sobrannye dlia Vysochaishei uchrezhdennoi komissii o preobrazovanii gu-bernskikh i uezdnykh uchrezhdenii. St. Petersburg, 1870.

Materialy sobrannye osoboiu komissieiu, vysochaishe uchrezhdennoiu 2-go noiabria 1869 goda, dlia peresmotra deistvuiushchikh postanovlenii o tsenzure i pechati. St. Petersburg, 1870, pt. I.

Matskina, R. Iu. "Ministerskie otchety i ikh osobennosti kak istoricheskii isto-chinik." In Glavnoe arkhivnoe upravlenie. *Problemy arkhivovedeniia i istoch-nikovedeniia.* Leningrad, 1964, pp. 209–26.

Meier, D. I. *O znachenii praktiki v sisteme sovremennago iuridicheskago obrazovaniia.* Kazan, 1855.

———. *Russkoe grazhdanskoe pravo.* St. Petersburg, 1897.

Mel'nikov-Pecherskii. "Vladimir Ivanovich Dal': Kritiko-biograficheskii ocherk." In *Polnoe sobranie sochinenii Vladimira Ivanovicha Dalia.* St. Peters-burg, 1876, Vol. I, pp. i–xc.

———. "Vospominaniia o V. I. Dale," *RV,* CIV (1873).

Merton, Robert K., ed. *Reader in Bureaucracy.* New York, 1952.

Meshcherskii, kniaz' V. P. *Moi vospominaniia.* 2 vols. St. Petersburg, 1897.

Mikhailov, I. I. "Kazanskaia starina (iz vospominanii Iv. Iv. Mikhailova)," *RS,* C, No. 10 (October 1899), pp. 99–113; No. 11 (November 1899), pp. 399–419.

Miklashevskii, I. "Statistika," *Entsiklopedicheskii slovar' Brokgauza-Eifrona.* St. Petersburg, 1901, Vol. XXXI, pp. 476–505.

Miliukov, A. P. "Irinarkh Ivanovich Vvedenskii (iz moikh vospominanii), *IV,* XXXIII, No. 9 (September 1888): 576–83.

———. *Literaturnye vstrechi i znakomstva.* St. Petersburg, 1890.

———. "Otryvok iz vospominanii," *IV,* XV, No. 1 (January 1884): 88–96.

Miliukov, P. N. *Iz istorii russkoi intelligentsii: sbornik statei i etiudov.* St. Peters-burg, 1903.

———. *Ocherki po istorii russkoi kul'tury.* 3 vols. St. Petersburg, 1901.

Miliutin, D. A. *Dnevnik D. A. Miliutina.* Edited by P. A. Zaionchkovskii. 4 vols. Moscow, 1947–1950.

———. *Pervoe opyty voennoi statistiki.* 2 vols. St. Petersburg, 1847–1848.

———. "Suvorov kak polkovodets," *OZ,* III (April–May 1839): 71–94.

———. "Voennye reformy Imperatora Aleksandra II," *VE,* XCIII, No. 1 (Janu-ary 1882): 1–35.

———. *Vospominaniia Generala Fel'dmarshala Grafa Dmitriia Alekseevicha Miliu-tina.* Tomsk, 1919.

Miliutin, N. A. "Chislo gorodskikh i zemledel'cheskikh poselenii v Rossii," *Sbornik statisticheskikh svedenii o Rossii.* St. Petersburg, 1851, pp. 228–76.

———, ed. *Izsledovaniia v Tsarstve Pol'skom po Vysochaishemu poveleniiu, pod ruko-vodstvom Senatora Stats-Sekretaria Miliutina.* 6 vols. St. Petersburg, 1863–1866.

———. "Kratkoe obozrenie goroda Khar'kova," *ZhMVD,* XXVIII, Nos. 4–6 (1838).

———. *Obshchestvennoe ustroistvo i khoziaistvo gorodov.* 2 vols. St. Petersburg, 1859.

———. "Pis'ma k Vasiliiu Alekseevichu Longinovu, 1844–1845gg.," *RS,* XXXI (1881): 241–46.

———. "Pis'ma k zhene i Ministru vnutrennikh del S. S. Lanskomu v 1857g.," *RS,* XXXI (1881): 401–10.

Miliutin, V. A. *V. A. Miliutin: Izbrannye proizvedeniia.* Moscow, 1946.

Selected Bibliography

Miliutina, M. A. "Iz zapisok Marii Ageevny Miliutinoi," *RS,* XCVII, No. 1 (January 1899), pp. 39–65; No. 2 (February 1899), pp. 265–88; No. 3 (March 1899), pp. 575–601; XCVIII, No. 4 (April 1899), pp. 105–7.

Miller, Forrestt A. *Dmitrii Miliutin and the Reform Era in Russia.* Nashville, 1968.

Ministerstvo iustitsii za sto let, 1802–1902. St. Petersburg, 1902.

Ministerstvo vnutrennikh del. Istoricheskii ocherk. 3 vols. St. Petersburg, 1902.

Mintslov, S. P. *Obzor dnevnikov, zapisok, vospominanii, pisem, i t. d.* 5 vols. Novgorod, 1911–1912.

Molchanov, M. M. "Aleksandr Nikolaevich Serov v vospominaniiakh starago pravoveda," *RS,* No. 8 (August 1883), pp. 331–60.

———. *Pol-veka nazad: Pervye gody uchilishcha pravovedeniia v Peterburge.* St. Petersburg, 1892.

Monas, Sidney. "Bureaucracy in Russia under Nicholas I." In *The Structure of Russian History: Interpretive Essays.* Edited by Michael Cherniavsky. New York, 1970, pp. 269–81.

———. *The Third Section: Police and Society in Russia under Nicholas I.* Cambridge, Mass., 1961.

Mordovtsev, D. L. "Istoricheskie pominki po N. I. Kostomarove," *RS,* LXVI, No. 6 (June 1855): 617–25.

Morrison, Kerry, "Catherine II's Legislative Commission: An Administrative Interpretation," *Canadian Slavic Studies,* IV, No. 3 (Fall 1970): 467–71.

Mosse, W. E. *Alexander II and the Modernization of Russia.* New York, 1962.

———. *The Rise and Fall of the Crimean System, 1855–1871.* London, 1973.

Mozdalevskii, B. L., and A. A. Sivers, eds. *Vosstanie dekabristov. Materialy.* Vol. 8. Leningrad, 1925.

Mullov, P. A. *Istoricheskoe obozrenie pravitel'stvennykh mer po ustroistvu gorodskago obshchestvennago upravleniia.* St. Petersburg, 1864.

Murav'ev, M. V. *Prokurorskii nadzor v ego ustroistve i deiatel'nosti.* Moscow, 1889.

Na konchinu Nikolaia Alekseevicha Miliutina. Sbornik nekrologicheskikh statei. Moscow, 1872.

"Naselenie S.-Peterburgskoi stolitsy v 1843 godu," *ZhMVD,* V (1844).

Nebolsin, P. I. "Biudzhety Peterburgskikh chinovnikov," *Ekonomicheskii ukazatel',* No. 11 (16 March 1857), pp. 241–50.

Nechkina, M. V., ed. *Revoliutsionnaia situatsiia v Rossii v 1859–1861gg.* 8 vols. Moscow, 1960–1979.

———, ed. *Revoliutsionnaia situatsiia v Rossii v seredine XIX veka.* Moscow, 1978.

Nelidov, N. K. *Iuridicheskoe i politicheskoe osnovanie gosudarstvennoi sluzhby.* Iaroslavl', 1874.

Nesselrode, Count K. V. *Lettres et papiers du Chancellier Comte de Nesselrode, 1760–1850.* 11 vols. Paris, 1905–1912.

Netting, Anthony. "Russian Liberalism: The Years of Promise, 1842–1855." Unpublished Ph.D. dissertation, Columbia University, 1967.

Nevedenskii, S. *Katkov i ego vremia.* St. Petersburg, 1888.

Nicholas I, Emperor. "Zapiski Nikolaia I o vstuplenii na prestol'." In *Mezhdutsarstvie 1825 goda i vosstanie dekabristov v perepiske i memuarakh chlenov tsarskoi sem'i.* Edited by B. E. Syroechkovskii. Moscow-Leningrad, 1926.

Nifontov, A. S. *Rossia v 1848 godu.* Moscow, 1949.

Nikitenko, A. V. *Dnevnik.* 3 vols. Moscow, 1955.

———. *Zapiski i dnevnik, 1826–1877.* 2 vols. St. Petersburg, 1892.

"Nikolai Alekseevich Miliutin." *Drevniaia i novaia Rossiia,* XIX (1881).

Nikolai Mikhailovich, velikii kniaz'. *Graf P. A. Stroganov (1774–1817): Istoricheskoe izsledovanie epokhi Imperatora Aleksandra I.* 3 vols. St. Petersburg, 1903.

Nol'de, A. E. K. P. *Pobedonostsev i sudebnaia reforma.* Petrograd, 1915.

Nol'de, B. E. *Iurii Samarin i ego vremia.* Paris, 1926.

Nosov, N. E. *et al.*, eds. *Vnutrenniaia politika tsarizma.* Leningrad, 1967.

Obolenskii, kniaz' D. A. "Moi vospominaniia o velikoi kniagine Elene Pavlovne," *RS,* CXXXVII, No. 3 (March 1909): 504–28; CXXXVIII, No. 4 (April 1909): 37–62.

———. *Vospominaniia kniazia D. A. Obolenskago o pervoi izdanii posmertnykh sochinenii Gogolia, 1852–1855gg.* St. Petersburg, 1873.

Obukhov, B. *Russkii administrator noveishei shkoly: zapiska pskovskago gubernatora i otvet na nee.* Berlin, 1868.

"Obzor deistvii Departamenta Sel'skago Khoziaistva v techenii piati let, s 1844 po 1849 goda," *ZhMGI,* XXXI–XXXIII (1849).

Ocherk piatidesiatiletnei deiatel'nosti Ministerstva Gosudarstvennykh Imushchestv, 1837–1887gg. St. Petersburg, 1887.

Ogareva-Tuchkova, N. A. *Vospominaniia, 1848–1870gg.* Moscow, 1903.

Ogorodnikov, S. F. *Istoricheskii obzor razvitiia i deiatel'nosti Morskago Ministerstva za sto let ego sushchestvovaniia (1802–1902).* St. Petersburg, 1902.

Ol'minskii, M. S. *Gosudarstvo, biurokratiia, i absoliutizm v istorii Rossii.* Moscow, 1925.

Opis' del arkhiva Gosudarstvennago Soveta. 21 vols. St. Petersburg, 1908–1914.

Orlov, A. "O sovremennom iuridicheskom obrazovanii v Rossii," *Sovremennik,* XXI, No. 5 (May 1850): 87–96.

Orlovsky, Daniel T. *The Limits of Reform: The Ministry of Internal Affairs in Imperial Russia, 1802–1881.* Cambridge, Mass., 1981.

———. "Ministerial Power and Russian Autocracy: The Ministry of Internal Affairs, 1802–1881." Unpublished Ph.D. dissertation, Harvard University, 1976.

Orzhekovskii, I. V. *Administratsiia i pechat' mezhdu dvumia revoliutsionnymi situatsiiami (1866–1878).* Gor'kii, 1973.

Ozvobozhdenie krest'ian: deiateli reformy. Moscow, 1911.

Otchet Ministerstva Iustitsii za 1844g. St. Petersburg, 1845.

Ovsianniko-Kulikovskii, D. A., ed. *Istoriia russkoi literatury XIX veka.* 5 vols. Moscow, 1911.

"Pamiati A. P. Zablotskago," *RS,* XXXIII, No. 2 (February 1882): 531–60.

Pamiatnaia knizhka kaluzhskoi gubernii za 1861g. Kaluga, 1861.

Pamiatnaia knizhka litseistov. St. Petersburg, 1907.

Panaeva, A. Ia. *Vospominaniia.* Moscow, 1956.

Panaev, I. I. *Literaturnye vospominaniia.* Moscow, 1928.

———. *Literaturnye vospominaniia.* Moscow, 1950.

Paul I, Emperor. "Zapiska Imperatora Pavla I ob ustroistve raznykh chastei gosudarstvennago upravleniia," *SIRIO,* XC (1894): 1–4.

Pazhitnikov, K. *Gorodskoe i zemskoe samoupravlenie.* St. Petersburg, 1913.

Pekarskii, P. P. "Studencheskaia vospominaniia o Dmitrie Ivanoviche Meiere." *Bratchina.* St. Petersburg, 1959, pp. 209–42.

Peretts, E. A. *Dnevnik E. A. Perettsa, gosudarstvennogo sekretaria (1880–1883).* Moscow-Leningrad, 1927.

Pervoe izdanie materialov redaktsionnykh komissii dlia sostavleniia polozhenii o krest-

ianakh vykhodiashchikh iz krepostnoi zavisimosti. 18 vols. St. Petersburg, 1859–1860.

Pintner, W. M. "The Russian Higher Civil Service on the Eve of the 'Great Reforms,'" *Journal of Social History* (Spring 1975), pp. 55–69.

———. "The Social Characteristics of the Early Nineteenth-Century Russian Bureaucracy," *Slavic Review,* XXIX, No. 3 (September 1970): 429–43.

———. *Russian Economic Policy under Nicholas I.* Ithaca, 1967.

———, and Don Karl Rowney, eds. *Russian Officialdom: The Bureaucratization of Russian Society from the Seventeenth to the Twentieth Century.* Chapel Hill, 1980.

Pipes, Richard. *Russia under the Old Regime.* New York, 1974.

Pobedonostsev, K. P. *Dlia nemnogikh: otryvk iz shkol'nago dnevnika.* St. Petersburg, 1885.

———. "Graf V. N. Panin," *Golosa iz Rossii,* No. 7 (1859). Reprinted, Moscow, 1975, pp. 3–142.

———. "O reformakh v grazhdanskom sudoproizvodstve," *RV,* XXI (1859): 541–80; XXII (1959): 5–34, 153–90.

———. "Vospominaniia o V. P. Zubkove," *RA,* bk. 1 (1904): 301–5.

———. *Istoriko-politicheskie pis'ma i zapiski v prodolzhenii Krymskoi Voiny, 1853–1856gg.* Moscow, 1874.

———. "Vospominaniia o N. A. Miliutina," *Golos,* No. 30 (1872).

Pokrovskii, M. N. "Krest'ianskaia reforma." *Istoriia Rossii v XIX veke.* 9 vols. III: 68–179.

Pokrovskii, S. P. *Ministerskaia vlast' v Rossii. Istoriko-iuridicheskoe izsledovanie.* Iaroslavl', 1906.

Polievktov, N. *Nikolai I. Biografiia i obzor tsarstvovaniia.* Moscow, 1918.

Polnoe sobranie zakonov rossiiskoi imperii s 1649 g. Sobranoe 1-oe. 45 vols. St. Petersburg, 1830.

Polnoe sobranie zakonov rossiiskoi imperii. Sobranie 2-oe. 55 vols. St. Petersburg, 1830–1882.

Polovtsov, A. A. *Dnevnik gosudarstvennogo sekretaria A. A. Polovtsova v dvukh tomakh.* Edited by P. A. Zaionchkovskii. Moscow, 1966.

Popel'nitskii, A. "Delo osvobozhdeniia krest'ian v Gosudarstvennom Sovete, 28 ianvaria-17 fevralia 1861g.," *Russkaia mysl',* No. 2 (February 1911), pp. 126–60.

Popov, P. S., ed. *Pis'ma k A. V. Druzhininu, 1850–1863gg.* Moscow, 1948.

Popova, E. I. *Dnevnik E. I. Popovoi, 1847–1852.* St. Petersburg, 1911.

Portal, Roger, ed. *Le statut des paysans libérés du servage.* Paris, The Hague, 1963.

"Prazdnovanie XXXVII godovshchinu osvobozhdeniia krest'ian," *RS,* XCIV (1898).

Predtechenskii, A. V. *Ocherki obshchestvenno-politicheskoi istorii Rossii v pervoi chetverty XIX veka.* Moscow-Leningrad, 1957.

Presniakov, A. E. *Apogei samoderzhaviia: Nikolai I.* Leningrad, 1925.

———. "Samoderzhavie Aleksandra II," *Russkoe proshloe,* I, No. 4 (1923): 3–20.

Prilozheniia k trudam Redaktsionnykh komissii dlia sostavleniia polozhenii o krest'ianakh vykhodiashchikh iz krepostnoi zavisimosti. 9 vols. St. Petersburg, 1859–1860.

Ptukha, M. V. *Ocherki po istorii statistiki v SSSR.* 2 vols. Moscow, 1959.

———. "Statistika v Rossii v nachale XIX veka." In *Ocherki po istorii statistiki SSSR. Sbornik statei.* Moscow, 1955.

Pule, M. F. de "Kul'turnyi ocherk i vospominaniia 1840-kh godov," *VE,* XLV, No. 1 (January 1874): 75–115.

———. "Nikolai Ivanovich Vtorov," *RA,* Nos. 5–8 (1887).

Pypin, A. N. *Istoriia russkoi literatury.* 4 vols. St. Petersburg, 1913.

———. *Kharakteristiki literaturnykh mnenii ot dvadtsatykh do piatidesiatykh godov.* 2d ed. St. Petersburg, 1890.

———. *Moi zametki.* Moscow, 1910.

———. "U A. A. Kraevskago." In *Literaturnye saloni i kruzhki: pervaia polovina XIX veka.* Edited by N. L. Brodskii. Moscow-Leningrad, 1930.

Raeff, Marc. "L'état, le gouvernement, et la tradition politique en russie imperiale avant 1861," *Revue d'histoire moderne et contemporaine,* IX (October–December, 1962): pp. 295–307.

———. *Michael Speransky: Statesman of Imperial Russia, 1772–1839.* 2d. ed. Paris, The Hague, 1969.

———. *The Origins of the Russian Intelligentsia: The Eighteenth-Century Nobility.* New York, 1966.

———, ed. *Plans for Political Reform in Imperial Russia, 1730–1905.* Englewood Cliffs, N. J., 1966.

———. "The Russian Autocracy and Its Officials," *Harvard Slavic Studies,* IV (1957): 77–91.

———. "The Well-Ordered Police State and the Development of Modernity in Seventeenth- and Eighteenth-Century Europe: An Attempt at a Comparative Approach," *The American Historical Review,* LXXX, No. 5 (December 1975): 1221–43.

Ramotowska, F. *Rząd carski wobec manifestacji patriotycznych w Królestwie Polskim w latach 1860–1862.* Warsaw, 1971.

Ransel, David. *The Politics of Catherinian Russia: The Panin Party.* New Haven and London, 1975.

Rashin, A. G. *Naselenie Rossii za 100 let (1811–1913): Statisticheskie ocherki.* Moscow, 1956.

Riasanovsky, N. V. *A Parting of Ways: Government and the Educated Public in Russia, 1801–1855.* Oxford, 1976.

———. *Nicholas I and Official Nationality in Russia, 1825–1855.* Berkeley and Los Angeles, 1959.

———. *Russia and the West in the Teachings of the Slavophiles. A Study of Romantic Ideology.* Cambridge, Mass., 1952.

Rieber, A. J. "Alexander II: A Revisionist View," *Journal of Modern History,* XLIII, No. 1 (March 1971): 42–58.

———, ed. *The Politics of Autocracy: The Letters of Alexander II to Prince A. I. Bariatinskii, 1857–1864.* Paris, The Hague, 1966.

Riggs, Fred W. *Administration in Developing Countries: The Theory of Prismatic Society.* Boston, 1964.

Rosenberg, Hans. *Bureaucracy, Aristocracy, and Autocracy: The Prussian Experience, 1660–1815.* Cambridge, Mass., 1958.

Roseveare, I. M. "From Reform to Rebellion: A. Wielopolski and the Polish Question, 1861–1863," *Canadian Slavic Studies,* II, No. 2 (Summer 1969): 263–85.

Roskovshenko, I. V. "Peterburg v 1831–1822gg.," *RS,* CI, No. 2 (February 1900): 477–90.

Rostovtsev, Ia. I. "Pis'mo k kniaziu E. P. Obolenskomu i pis'mo Obolenskago k Rostovtsovu, 1858–1859gg.," *RS,* LXIII, No. 9 (September 1889): 617–39.

Rozental', V. N. "Ideinye tsentry liberal'nogo dvizheniia v Rossii nakanune revoliutsionnoi situatsii." In *Revoliutsionnaia situatsiia v Rossii v 1857–1861gg.* Edited by M. V. Nechkina. Moscow, 1963, pp. 372–98.

——. "Obshchestvenno-politicheskaia programma russkago liberalizma v srediny 50-kh godov XIX v.," *Istoricheskie zapiski Akademii Nauk SSSR,* LXX (1961): 197–222.

Rozhdestvenskii, S. V. *Istoricheskii obzor deiatel'nosti Ministerstva Narodnago Prosveshcheniia, 1802–1902.* St. Petersburg, 1902.

——. "Posledniaia stranitsa iz istorii politiki narodnago prosveshcheniia Imperatora Nikolaia I," *Russkii istoricheskii zhurnal,* Nos. 3–4 (1917): 37–59.

Rubinshtein, A. G. "Vospominaniia A. G. Rubinshteina," *RS,* LXIV, No. 11 (November 1889): 517–600.

Russkii biograficheskii slovar'. 25 vols. St. Petersburg, 1896–1913.

Russkii erot. Ne dlia dam. Geneva, 1879.

Ruud, Charles A. "A. V. Golovnin and Liberal Russian Censorship, January–June 1862," *Slavonic and East European Review,* L, No. 119 (April 1972): 191–219.

——. "The Russian Empire's New Censorship Law of 1865," *Canadian Slavic Studies,* III, No. 2 (Summer 1969): 235–45.

Ryndziunskii, P. G. *Gorodskoe grazhdanstvo doreformennoi Rossii.* Moscow, 1958.

Rzhevskii, V. "Vzgliad na teoriiu biurokraticheskoi administratsii," *RV,* XXIX, No. 10 (October 1860): 756–810.

S., M. "Morskoi sbornik v 1853–1856gg.," *RS,* XLV, No. 2 (February 1885): 411–18.

Saltykov-Shchedrin, M. E., "M. E. Saltykov-Shchedrin: Pis'ma, 1845–1889." *Trudy Pushkinskogo Doma pri Rossiiskoi Akademii Nauk.* Leningrad, 1925.

——. *Sobranie sochinenii.* 20 vols. Moscow, 1965–1977.

Samarin, Iu. F. "Iurii Fedorovich Samarin i N. A. Miliutin v ianvare 1859g.," *RS,* XLV, No. 2 (February 1885): 431–32.

——. *Sochineniia Iu. F. Samarina.* 8 vols. St. Petersburg, 1877–1911.

Sbornik postanovlenii i rasporiazhenii po tsenzure s 1720 po 1862 goda. St. Petersburg, 1862.

Sbornik pravitel'stvennykh rasporiazhenii po Uchreditel'nomu Komitetu Tsarstva Pol'skago. 22 vols. Warsaw, 1864–1867.

Sbornik pravitel'stvennykh rasporiazhenii po ustroistvu byta krest'ian vyshedshikh iz krepostnoi zavisimosti. 3rd ed. St. Petersburg, 1869.

Sbornik tsirkuliarov i instruktsii Ministerstva vnutrennikh del za 1858–1879gg. 11 vols. St. Petersburg, 1873–1880.

Schedo-Ferroti, D. K. (Baron Firks). *Études sur l'avenir de la Russie.* 2 vols. Berlin, 1857–1858.

Scheibert, P. "Marginalien zur einer neuen Speranskij-Biografie," *Jahrbücher für Geschichte Osteuropas,* VI, No. 4 (1958): 449–67.

Schiemann, Th. *Geschichte Russlands unter Kaiser Nikolaus I.* 4 vols. Berlin, 1904–1919.

Seleznev, I. Ia. *Istoricheskii ocherk Imperatorskago, byvshego tsarskosel'skago, nyne Aleksandrovskago, litseia.* St. Petersburg, 1861.

Semenov, N. P. "Deiatel'nost' Ia. I. Rostovtsova v redaktsionnykh komissiiakh po krest'ianskomu delu," *RV,* Nos. 10–12 (1864).

——. "Graf Viktor Nikitich Panin," *RA,* bk. 3 (1887): 537–66.

——. *Osvobozhdenie krest'ian v tsarstvovanie Imperatora Aleksandra II. Khronika deiatel'nosti komissii po krest'ianskomu delu.* 3 vols. in 5 parts. St. Petersburg, 1889–1891.

Selected Bibliography

Semenov (-Tian-Shanskii), P. P. *Geografichesko-statisticheskii slovar' rossiiskoi imperii.* 5 vols. St. Petersburg, 1863–1885.

——. *Istoriia poluvekovoi deiatel'nosti imperatorskago russkago geograficheskago obshchestva, 1845–1895gg.* 3 vols. St. Petersburg, 1896.

——. *Memuary.* 3 vols. Petrograd, 1915–1917.

Semevskii, M. "K. I. Domontovich: Ocherk k ego biografii," *RS,* LXII. No. 6 (June 1889): 755–72.

Semevskii, V. I. *Krest'ianskii vopros v Rossii v XVIII i pervoi polovine XIX stoletiia.* 2 vols. St. Petersburg, 1888.

——. *M. V. Butashevich-Petrashevskii i Petrashevtsy.* Moscow, 1922.

Seredonin, S. M. *Istoricheskii obzor deiatel'nosti komiteta ministrov.* 3 vols in 5 parts. St. Petersburg, 1902.

Shchebal'skii, P. K. "Nikolai Alekseevich Miliutin i reformy v Tsarstve Pol'skom," *RV,* CLXI (October 1882): 548–81; CLXII (November 1882): 313–68; (December 1882): pp. 774–805.

——. *Istoricheskie svedeniia o tsenzure v Rossii.* St. Petersburg, 1862.

Shchegolov, V. G. *Gosudarstvennyi Sovet v Rossii.* Iaroslavl', 1903.

Shchepetov, K. N. *Krepostnoe pravo v votchinakh Sheremet'evykh (1708–1885).* Moscow, 1947.

Shevyrev, S. P. "Vzgliad russkago na sovremennoe obrazovanie Evropy," *Moskvitianin,* No. 1 (1841), pp. 219–96.

Shilder, N. K. *Imperator Nikolai Pervyi: Ego zhizn' i tsarstvovanie.* 2 vols. St. Petersburg, 1903.

"Shkola gvardeiskikh podpraporshchikov i iunkerov v vospominaniiakh odnago iz eia vospitannikov, 1845–1849gg.," *RS,* XLI, No. 1 (January 1884), pp. 203–16; No. 2 (February 1884), pp. 441–54.

Shtakel'berg, N. "Zagadka smerti Nikolaia I," *Russkoe proshloe,* I (1923): 60–71.

Shubin-Pozdeev, D. "K kharakteristike lichnosti i sluzhebnoi deiatel'nosti S. I. Zarudnago," *RS,* LVII, No. 2 (February 1888): 477–84.

Shumakher, A. D. "Neskol'ko slov o g.-a Timasheva i otnoshenii ego k obshchestvennym uchrezhdeniiam," *VE,* VI, No. 12 (1893): 846–57.

——. "Pozdnie vospominaniia o davno minuvshikh vremenakh. Dlia moikh detei i vnuchat," *VE,* CXCVI, No. 3 (March 1899), pp. 89–128; No. 4 (April 1899), pp. 694–728.

Simmons, E. J., ed. *Continuity and Change in Russian and Soviet Thought.* Cambridge, Mass., 1955.

Simon, Herbert A. *Administrative Behavior.* New York, 1957.

Sinel, Allen. *The Classroom and the Chancellery: State Educational Reform in Russia under Count Dmitrii Tolstoi.* Cambridge, Mass., 1973.

Siuzor, Georgii. *Ko dniu LXXV iubileia imperatorskago uchilishcha pravovedeniia, 1835–1910.* St. Petersburg, 1910.

Skabichevskii, A. M. *Literaturnye vospominaniia.* Moscow, 1928.

——. *Ocherki istorii russkoi tsenzury (1700–1863).* St. Petersburg, 1893.

Skal'kovskii, K. A. *Vospominaniia molodosti, 1843–1861.* St. Petersburg, 1906.

Skalon, D. A., ed. *Stoletie voennago ministerstva, 1802–1902.* 13 vols. St. Petersburg, 1902–1914.

Skrebitskii, A. I. *Krest'ianskoe delo v tsarstvovanie Imperatora Aleksandra II.* 5 vols. Bonn, 1862–1868.

Sladkevich, N. G. *Ocherki istorii obshchestvennoi mysli v Rossii v kontse 50-kh godov–nachale 60-kh godov XIX-go veka.* Leningrad, 1962.

Sliosberg, G. B. *Dorevoliutsionnyi stroi Rossii.* Paris, 1933.

Sliwowska, Wiktoria. *Mikołaj I i jego czasy (1825–1855).* Warsaw, 1965.

Selected Bibliography

Smirnova, A. O. *Zapiski (1824–1845).* St. Petersburg, 1895.

Solov'ev, Ia. A. "Pamiatniki i predanii Vladimirskoi gubernii," *OZ,* CXII (1857): 521–68.

——. *Sel'sko-khoziaistvennaia statistika smolenskoi gubernii.* Moscow, 1855.

——. "Zapiski senatora Ia. A. Solov'eva," *RS* (February 1881–March 1884), XXX, pp. 213–46, 721–56; XXXI, pp. 1–32; XXXIII, pp. 227–58, 561–96; XXXIV, pp. 105–54, 389–426; XXXVI, pp. 131–54, 389–426; XXXVIII, pp. 259–90, 579–614; XLI, pp. 241–76, 575–608.

Solov'ev, Iu. B. *Samoderzhavie i dvorianstvo v kontse XIX veka.* Leningrad, 1973.

Solov'ev, S. M. *Istoriia Rossii s dreveneishikh vremen.* 15 vols. Moscow, 1963.

Sovetskaia istoricheskaia ektsiklopediia. 16 vols. Moscow, 1961–1976.

Spasovich, V. D. *Zhizn' i politika Markiza Velopol'skago.* 2 vols. St. Petersburg, 1882.

Speranskii, M. M. "O zakonakh. Besedy grafa M. M. Speranskago s Ego Imperatorskim Vysochaishestvom Gosudarem Naslednikom Tsesarevichem Velikim Kniazem Aleksandrom Nikolaevichem, s 12 oktiabria 1835g. po 10 aprelia 1837 goda," *SIRIO,* XXX, St. Petersburg, 1880.

——. "Imperatorskoe Uchilishche Pravovedeniia," *RS,* XLVIII, No. 12 (December 1885), pp. i–iv.

Spisok grazhdanskim chinam pervykh chetyrekh klassov. St. Petersburg, 1842–1882. (Published annually).

Spisok grazhadanskim chinam pervykh trekh klassov. St. Petersburg, 1855–1882. (Published annually).

Spisok naselennykh mest iaroslavskoi gubernii. St. Petersburg, 1865.

Spisok vysshym chinam gosudarstvennago, gubernskago, i eparkhial'nago upravleniia. St. Petersburg, 1834–1882. (Published annually).

Squire, P. S. *The Third Department. The Establishment and Practice of the Political Police in the Russia of Nicholas I.* Cambridge, 1968.

Stankevich, A. V. *Granovskii i ego perepiska,* 2 vols. Moscow, 1891.

Starchevskii, A. V. "Odin iz zabytnykh zhurnalistov (iz vospominanii starago literatora)," *IV,* XXIII (1886).

——. "Vospominaniia starago literatora," *IV,* XLV, No. 9 (September 1891): 559–92.

Starr, S. Frederick. *Decentralization and Self-Government in Russia, 1830–1870.* Princeton, 1972.

Stasov, V. V. "Graf Modest Andreevich Korf. Biograficheskii ocherk, 1800–1876," *RS,* XV, No. 1 (January 1886): 402–21.

——. "Uchilishche pravovedeniia sorok let tomu nazad, v 1836–1842gg.," *RS,* XXIX, No. 12 (December 1880), pp. 1015–42; XXX, No. 2 (February 1881), pp. 393–422; No. 3 (March 1881), pp. 573–602; XXXI, No. 6 (June 1881), pp. 247–306.

——. *Vospominaniia tovarishcha o D. A. Rovinskom.* St. Petersburg, 1896.

Steel [Miliutina], M. A. "N. A. Miliutin v ego zabotakh o krest'ianskom i sudebnom dele v Tsarstve Pol'skom," *RS,* XLII (1884).

Stein, H. P. "Der Offizier des russischen Heeres im Zeitabschnitt zwischen Reform und Revolution 1861–1905," *Forschungen zur osteuropäischen Geschichte,* XIII (1967).

Stoianovskii, N. I. *Kratkii ocherk ob osnovanii i razvitii imperatorskago uchilishcha pravovedeniia.* St. Petersburg, 1885.

——. *Vospominaniia o 5-om i 7-om dekabria 1860 goda.* St. Petersburg, 1860.

Stoiunin, V. Ia. "Konservatory sorokovykh godakh," *IV,* XXXIX, No. 1 (January 1882): 5–28.

Stremoukhov, P. D. "Iz vospominanii o grafe P. A. Valueve," *RS,* CXVI, No. 11 (November 1903): 273–93.

Stroev, V. N. *Stoletie sobstvennoi e. i. v. kantseliarii.* St. Petersburg, 1912.

Sudebnye ustavy 20 noiabria 1864 g. za piat'desiat' let. 2 vols., plus appendices. St. Petersburg, 1914.

Svod soobrazhenii mestnykh komissii ob uluchshenii gorodskago obshchestvennago upravleniia. St. Petersburg, 1864.

Svod zakonov rossiiskoi imperii, izdaniia 1857g. St. Petersburg, 1857.

Svod zakonov rossiiskoi imperii. St. Petersburg, 1897.

Taranovski, Theodore. "The Aborted Counter-Reform: Murav'ev Commission and the Judicial Statutes of 1864," *Jahrbücher für Geschichte Osteuropas,* XXIX, No. 2 (1981): 161–84.

————. "The Politics of Counter-Reform: Autocracy and Bureaucracy in the Reign of Alexander III, 1881–1894." Unpublished Ph.D. dissertation, Harvard University, 1976.

Tatishchev, S. S. *Imperator Aleksandr II. Ego zhizn' i tsarstvovanie.* 2 vols. St. Petersburg, 1911.

Tęgoborski, L. *Commentaries on the Productive Forces of Russia.* 3 vols. London, 1855.

Tel'berg, Georgii. *Pravitel'stvuiushchii Senat i samoderzhavnaia vlast' v nachale XIX veka.* Moscow, 1914.

Terner, F. G. *Vospominaniia zhizni F. G. Ternera.* 2 vols. St. Petersburg, 1910–1911.

Tikhonov, V. V. "Ofitsial'nye zhurnaly vtoroi poloviny 20-50kh godov XIX v.," *Problemy istochnikovedeniia,* VIII (1959): 150–203.

Timiriazev, F. "Deviatnadtsatoe fevralia 1872 goda. Posviashchaetsia pamiati N. A. Miliutina," *RA,* Nos. 3–4 (1872): 0866–0872.

Tiutchev, I. A. "V uchilishche pravovedeniia v 1847–1852gg.," *RS,* XLVIII, No. 11 (November 1885), pp. 436–52; No. 12 (December 1885), pp. 663–78; XLIX, No. 1 (January 1886), pp. 361–76.

Tiutcheva, A. F. *Pri dvore dvukh imperatorov. Vospominaniia, dnevnik, 1855–1882.* 2 vols. Moscow, 1928.

Tolstoi, D. N. "Zapiska grafa Dmitriia Nikolaevicha Tolstago," *RA,* XXIII, bk. 2, Nos. 5–8 (1885), pp. 5–70

Torke, H.-J. "Continuity and Change in the Relations between Bureaucracy and Society in Russia, 1613–1861," *Canadian Slavic Studies,* V, No. 4 (Winter, 1971): 457–76.

————. "Das russische Beamtentum in der ersten Hälfte des 19. Jahrhunderts," *Forschungen zur osteuropäischen Geschichte,* XIII, (1967): 7–345.

————. "Die neuere Sowjethistoriographie zum Problem der russischen Absolutismus," *Forschungen zur osteuropäischen Geschichte,* XX (1973): 113–33.

————. "Die Entwicklung des Absolutismus—Problems in der sowjetischen Historiographie seit 1917," *Jahrbücher für Geschichte Osteuropas,* XXI, No. 4 (December 1973): 493–508.

Troinitskii, A. G. *Krepostnoe naselenie Rossii do desiatoi narodnoi perepisi.* St. Petersburg, 1861.

Troinitskii, G. A., ed. "P. A. Valuev i A. G. Troinitskii," *RS,* XCIX, No. 8 (August 1899), pp. 467–80; No. 9 (September 1899), pp. 697–706; C, No. 10 (October 1899), pp. 231–39.

Selected Bibliography

Troitskii, S. M. *Russkii absoliutizm i dvorianstvo v XVIII v. Formirovanie biurokratii.* Moscow, 1974.

———. *Finansovaia politika russkogo absoliutizma v XVIII veke.* Moscow, 1966.

———. "O nekotorykh spornykh voprosakh istorii absoliutizma v Rossii," *Istoriia SSSR,* No. 3 (1969), pp. 130–49.

Troshchinskii, D. P. "Zapiska Dmitriia Prokof'evicha Troshchinskago o Ministerstvakh," *SIRIO,* III (1868): 1–162.

Trubetskaia, Kniaginia O. N. *Materialy dlia biografi kn. V. A. Cherkasskago.* 2 vols. Moscow, 1901, 1904.

Trudy komissii o gubernskikh i uezdnykh uchrezhdeniiakh. 6 vols. St. Petersburg, 1860–1863.

Tsagolov, N. A. *Ocherki russkoi ekonomicheskoi mysli perioda padeniia krepostnogo prava.* Moscow, 1956.

Tseitlin. S. Ia. "Zemskaia reforma." In *Istoriia Rossii v XIX veke.* 9 vols. III: 179–231.

Turgenev i krug "Sovremennika." Neizdannye materialy, 1847–1861gg. Moscow-Leningrad, 1930.

Turgenev, I. S. "Ivan Sergeevich Turgenev v zapiskakh i pis'makh k M. A. i N. A. Miliutinym, 1867–1875gg.," *RS,* XLI, No. 1 (January 1884): 175–94.

———. *Sobranie sochinenii.* 10 vols. Moscow, 1961–1962.

Turgenev (Tourgueneff), Nicolas. *La Russie et les Russes.* 3 vols. Paris, 1847.

Ustrialov, N. F. "Vospominaniia o St. Peterburgskom universitete v 1852–1856gg.," *IV,* XVI, No. 6 (June 1884), pp. 578–604; No. 7 (July 1884), pp. 112–34; No. 8 (August 1884), pp. 287–312.

Utin, B. Y. "Ocherk istorii obrazovaniia suda prisiazhnykh v Anglii," *RV,* XXVI, No. 3 (March 1860): 207–56.

"V Pribaltiiskom krae: iz zapisok russkago chinovnika, 1856–1866," *RS,* XXXV, No. 10 (October 1882): 59–90; XL, No. 12 (December 1883): 553–72.

Valk, S. N., ed. *M. M. Speranskii: Proekty i zapiski.* Moscow-Leningrad, 1961.

Valuev, P. A. *Dnevnik P. A. Valueva, Ministra vnutrennikh del.* 2 vols. Moscow, 1961.

———. "Dnevnik grafa P. A. Valueva," *RS,* LXX, No. 4 (April 1891), pp. 167–82; No. 5 (May 1891), pp. 339–49; No. 6 (June 1891), pp. 603–16; LXXI, No. 7 (July 1891), pp. 71–82; No. 8 (August 1891), pp. 265–78; No. 9 (September 1891), pp. 547–602; LXXII, No. 10 (October 1891), pp. 139–54; No. 11 (November 1891), pp. 393–459.

———. "Duma russkago vo vtoroi polovine 1855g.," *RS,* LXX, No. 5 (May 1891): 348–59.

———. "Zapiska Aleksandru II o polozhenii krest'ianskogo dela v nachale sentiabria 1861 goda," *Istoricheskii arkhiv,* No. 1 (January–February 1961), pp. 65–81.

Varadinov, N. V. *Deloproizvodstvo ili teoreticheskoe i prakticheskoe rukovodstvo k grazhdanskomu i ugolovnomu, kollegial'nomu i odnolichnomu pis'movodstvu, k sostavleniiu vsekh pravitel'stvennykh i chastnykh delovykh bumag i k vedeniiu samykh del, s prilozheniem k onym obraztsov i form.* 2 vols. St. Petersburg, 1857.

———. *Istoriia Ministerstva Vnutrennikh del.* 8 bks. St. Petersburg, 1858–1863.

"Velikaia kniaginia Elena Pavlovna: ocherk k eiu zhizneopisaniiu," *RS,* XXXIII, No. 3 (March 1882): 781–802.

Venturi, Franco. *Roots of Revolution.* New York, 1961.

Veselovskii, A. V. *V. A. Zhukovskii: poeziia chuvstva i "serdechnago voobrazhenniia."* Petrograd, 1918.

Selected Bibliography

Veselovskii, B. B. *Istoriia zemstva za sorok let.* 4 vols. St. Petersburg, 1911.

Veselovskii, K. S. "Otgoloski staroi pamiati," *RS,* C, No. 10 (October 1899): 5–23.

――――. "Vospominaniia," *RS,* CVIII, No. 12 (December 1901): 495–528; CXVI, No. 10 (October 1903): 5–42.

――――. "Vospominaniia o tsarskosel'skom litsee, 1832–1838," *RS,* CIV, No. 10 (October 1900): 3–29.

Vestnik imperatorskago russkago geograficheskago obshchestva. St. Petersburg, 1851–1860.

Vetrinskii, Ch. "Umstvennoe i obshchestvennoe dvizhenie sorokovykh godov." In *Istoriia russkoi literatury.* 5 vols. Edited by D. N. Ovsianniko-Kulikovskii. Moscow, 1909, II: 66–130.

Viazemskii, kniaz' P. A. *Zapisnye knizhki.* Moscow, 1963.

Vigel', F. F. *Zapiski.* Edited by S. Ia. Shtraikh. 2 vols. Moscow, 1928.

Vilenskii, B. V. *Sudebnaia reforma i kontrreforma v Rossii.* Saratov, 1969.

Vinogradova, L. V. "Osnovnye vidy dokumentov Senata i organizatsiia ego deloproizvodstva." In Glavnoe arkhivnoe upravlenie. *Nekotorye voprosy izucheniia istoricheskikh dokumentov XIX–nachala XX veka.* Leningrad, 1967, pp. 111–32.

Virginskii, V. S. *Vozniknovenie zheleznykh dorog v Rossii do nachala 40-kh godov XIX v.* Moscow, 1949.

Volodarskii, I. B., and G. A. Kaikova, eds. *N. A. Serno-Solov'evich: publitsistika, pis'ma.* Moscow, 1963.

Vtorov, N. I. *Sravnitel'noe obozrenie munitsipal'nykh uchrezhdenii Frantsii, Bel'gii, Italii, Avstrii, i Prussii, s prisovokupleniem ocherka mestnago samoupravleniia v Anglii.* St. Petersburg, 1864.

Vucinich, A. S. *Science and Russian Culture: A History to 1860.* Stanford, 1960.

Wahlde, P. von. "Dmitrii Miliutin: Appraisals," *Canadian Slavic Studies,* III, No. 2 (1969): 400–414.

Weber, Max. *The Theory of Social and Economic Organization.* Translated by Talcott Parsons. New York, 1947.

Wittram, Reinhard. *Peter I: Czar und Kaiser.* 2 vols. Göttingen, 1964.

Woehrlin, William. *Chernyshevskii: The Man and the Journalist.* Cambridge, Mass., 1971.

Wortman, Richard. *The Development of a Russian Legal Consciousness.* Chicago, 1976.

Yaney, George. *The Systematization of Russian Government: Social Evolution in the Domestic Administration of Imperial Russia, 1711–1905.* Urbana, 1973.

Zablotskii-Desiatovskii, A. P. *Graf P. D. Kiselev i ego vremia,* 4 vols. St. Petersburg, 1882.

――――. "Khoziaistvennye aforizmy," *OZ,* LXII, No. 1 (January 1849), sect 4, pp. 1–16; LXIII, No. 4 (April 1849), sect. 4, pp. 1–14.

――――. "Materialy dlia khoziaistvennoi statistiki Rossii," *ZhMGI* (1851), sect. 1, pp. 209–22, 323–36.

――――. "Ob ulozhenii sel'skikh postroek," *OZ,* LXI, No. 12 (December 1848): 1–22.

――――. "O krepostnom sostoianii v Rossii." In A. P. Zablotskii-Desiatovskii, *Graf P. D. Kiselev i ego vremia.* St. Petersburg, 1881, IV, pp. 271–345.

――――. "Opyt prostonarodnago nastavleniia v sel'skom khoziaistve," *ZhMGI,* XXVII (1848), sect. 2, pp. 216–66, 321–26; XXXIII (1849), sect. 2, pp. 119–31.

――――. "Prichiny kolebaniia tsen na khleb v Rossii," *OZ,* LII, No. 5 (May 1847): 1–30.

Selected Bibliography

————. "Vospominaniia ob Anglii," *OZ*, LXII, No. 1 (January 1848), pp. 1–16; No. 2 (February 1848), pp. 193–215.

————, and kn. V. F. Odoevskii, eds. *Sel'skoe chtenie.* 4 vols. St. Petersburg, 1843–1848.

Zaionchkovskii, P. A. "Dmitrii Alekseevich Miliutin: biograficheskii ocherk." In *Dnevnik D. A. Miliutina, 1873–1875gg.* Edited by P. A. Zaionchkovskii. Moscow, 1947, I: 5–72.

————. "Arkhiv D. A. Miliutina," *Voprosy istorii,* Nos. 5–6 (1946), pp. 96–104.

————. "Gubernskaia administratsiia nakanune Krymskoi voiny," *Voprosy istorii,* No. 9 (September 1975), pp. 33–51.

————. *Krizis samoderzhaviia na rubezhe 1870–1880 godov.* Moscow, 1964.

————. *Otmena krepostnago prava v Rossii.* 3rd ed. Moscow, 1968.

————. "Perevooruzhenie russkoi armii v 60–70kh godakh XIX v.," *Istoricheskie zapiski,* XXXVI (1951): 64–100.

————. "Podgotovka voennoi reformy 1874g.," *Istoricheskie zapiski,* XXVI (1948): 170–201.

————. *Pravitel'stvennyi apparat samoderzhavnoi Rossii v XIX v.* Moscow, 1978.

————. *Provedenie v zhizn' krest'ianskoi reformy 1861g.* Moscow, 1958.

————. *Samoderzhaviia i russkaia armiia na rubezhe XIX–XX stoletii.* Moscow, 1973.

————. *Voennye reformy 1860–1870 godov v Rossii.* Moscow, 1952.

————. "Voennye reformy D. A. Miliutina," *Voprosy istorii,* No. 2 (1945), pp. 3–26.

————. "Vysshaia biurokratiia nakanune Krymskoi voiny," *Istoriia SSSR,* No. 4 (1974), pp. 154–64.

————, ed. *Istoriia dorevoliutsionnoi Rossii v dnevnikakh i vospominaniiakh. Annotirovannyi ukazatel' knig i publikatsii v zhurnalakh.* 3 vols. in 5 parts. Moscow, 1976–1978. (Additional volumes forthcoming).

————, ed. *Spravochnik po istorii dorevoliutsionnoi Rossii: bibliografiia.* Moscow, 1971.

Zakharova, L. G. *Zemskaia kontrreforma 1890g.* Moscow, 1968.

Zapiski imperatorskago russkago geograficheskago obshchestva. St. Petersburg, 1846–1859gg.

Zarudnyi, S. I. "O reformakh sudoproizvodstva v Italii," *ZhMIu* (December 1852), pp. 529–46.

————. "O spetsial'nykh prisiazhnykh dlia osobago roda del v Anglii, Frantsii, i Italii," *ZhMIu* (November 1862), pp. 267–83.

————. "Pis'mo opytnago chinovnika sorokovykh godov mladshemu ego sobratu, postupaiushchemu na sluzhbu." Edited by A. S. Zarudnyi, *RS,* C, No. 12 (December 1899): 543–46.

————. "Zapiski S. I. Zarudnago," *RS,* LIX, No. 9 (September 1888): 611–16.

Zelnik, Reginald. *Labor and Society in Tsarist Russia: The Factory Workers of St. Petersburg, 1855–1870.* Stanford, 1971.

Zhemchuzhnikov, L. M. "Moi vospominaniia iz proshlago, 1830–1850gg.," *VE,* CCVI, No. 11 (November 1900), pp. 41–87; No. 12 (December 1900), pp. 477–525.

Zhukovskii, V. A. "Pis'ma V. A. Zhukovskago k grafu F. P. Litke," *RA,* Nos. 5–8 (1887): 327–40.

Zhurnala i memorii obshchago sobraniia Gosudarstvennago Soveta po krest'ianskomu delu, s 28 ianvaria po 14 marta 1861 goda. Petrograd, 1915.

Selected Bibliography

"Zhurnaly komiteta uchrezhdennago Vysochaishim reskriptom 6 dekabria 1826 goda," *SIRIO,* LXXIV (1891).

Zhurnaly sekretnago i glavnago komitetov po krest'ianskomu delu s 10 oktiabria 1860 goda po 13 fevralia 1861 goda. Petrograd, 1915.

Znamenskii, D. N. "Iz dnevnika russkago chinovnika (Pribaltiiskii krai v 1845–1846gg.)," *RA,* bk. 3 (1881): 85–112.

Zotov, V. R. "Peterburg v sorokovykh godakh," *IV,* XXXIX (January 1890): 29–53, 324–43, 553–72; XL (1890): 93–115, 290–319.

Zyzniewski, S. J. "Miliutin and the Polish Question," *Harvard Slavic Studies,* IV (1957).

Index

Page numbers in boldface refer to illustrations.

Index

autocracy, 182; on *glasnost'*, 185; and emancipation, 208
Herzen circle, 80
Hess, Hermann Heinrich, 92
History of the Russian State (Karamzin), 94, 149
Hugo, Victor, 70
Humboldt, Alexander von, 92, 97

Iakhontov, Aleksei, 72
Iazykov, N., 86
Illichevskii, P. D., 66
Imperial Agricultural Society, 130
Imperial Naval Ministry, 140, 165; and judicial reform, 193
Imperial Russian Geographical Society, 85, 91–100; use of, by enlightened bureaucrats, 99–100; and Great Reform legislation, 100; and rural life, 124; and Konstantin Nikolaevich, 143, 145
Imperial School of Jurisprudence, 72, 73–74, 164
Insarskii, V. A., 46
Intellectuals: and Perovskii, 69; and obligation to pursue knowledge for benefit of society, 77; and change, 78; circles in St. Petersburg, 80–91; and Nicholas I, 91–92; radical and enlightened bureaucrats, 207
Ivanov, Aleksandr, 149

Jacobi, Moritz, 92, 146
Journal des Débats, 82
The Journal of the Ministry of Internal Affairs, 82, 86, 113, 117–18
The Journal of the Ministry of Justice, 200
Journals, official: and civil servants, 20
Judicial reform, 192–94, 199–201
Judicial Reform Statute of 1864, 15, 92, 100

Kalachov, Nikolai, 197, 198
Kankrin, Count E. F., Minister of

Finance, 33, 89, 171
Kant, Immanuel, 86
Karamzin, Nikolai, 94; and Alexander I, 7–8; on education of civil servants, 11–12; and Kiselev, 31; *History of the Russian State*, 149
Karlovka reform, 157–59, 161, 162
Karneev, V. I., 45, 46, 55
Karniolin-Pinskii, M. M., 66
Katkov, Mikhail, 208
Kavelin, Konstantin, 85, 86; and Perovskii, 69; and serfdom, 70–71, 115; and Miliutin circle, 84–85; and Belinskii, 90; and Panaev circle, 90; and autocracy, 91; and Geographical Society, 99; and state's welfare, 108; and Municipal Section, 113, 134–35; on first months of Alexander II's reign, 138; and Provisional Section, 112; and Wildbad Conference, 157; and serfs and Elena Pavlovna, 159, 160; and Karlovka reform, 161; and bureaucracy, 164; on Nicholas I, 168, 182; and Unkovskii, 178; and politics, 179–80; and emancipation, 192; on loss of influence, 209; in 1870s, 210
Keppen, Petr, 80, 82; and study of peasants, 48; and Geographical Society, 93, 97, 99; and serfs, 108; and statistics, 119; and Department of Rural Economy, 122; and agricultural education, 127
Khanykov, Aleksandr, 85, 94
Khanykov, Iakov, 85, 94, 97
Khanykov, Nikolai, 85, 94
Kheraskov, Mikhail, 94
Khrushchov, Dmitrii, 156, 195
Kireevskii, Ivan, 86
Kiselev, Count P. D., 30, **35**, 41, 42, 43, 55, 61, 65, 67, 94, 100, 136, 166; and peasant affairs, xiii, 44; as Chief of Staff for Peasant Affairs, 7, 32–33; as reformer, 31–32; background and career of, 31–33; and Speranskii, 33; as administrator, 39; and laws, 48;

289

Index